THE CLAY SANSKRIT LIBRARY

FOUNDED BY JOHN & JENNIFER CLAY

WWW.CLAYSANSKRITLIBRARY.COM

WWW.NYUPRESS.ORG

First Edition 2005

ISBN 0-8147-5207-1 (cloth : alk. paper)

The Clay Sanskrit Library is co-published by
New York University Press
and the JJC Foundation.

Further information about this volume
and the rest of the Clay Sanskrit Library
is available on the following websites:
www.claysanskritlibrary.com
www.nyupress.org

Artwork by Robert Beer.
Typeset in Adobe Garamond at 10.25 : 12.3+ pt.
Printed in Great Britain by St Edmundsbury Press Ltd,
Bury St Edmunds, Suffolk, on acid-free paper.
Bound by Hunter & Foulis, Edinburgh, Scotland.

RĀMĀYAṆA
BOOK FOUR
KIṢKINDHĀ

BY VĀLMĪKI

TRANSLATED BY
ROSALIND LEFEBER

NEW YORK UNIVERSITY PRESS
JJC FOUNDATION
2005

Library of Congress Cataloging-in-Publication Data
Vālmīki
[Rāmāyaṇa. Kiṣkindhākāṇḍa. English & Sanskrit]
Ramayana. Book four, Kiskindha / by Valmiki ;
translated by Rosalind Lefeber.
p. cm. – (The Clay Sanskrit library)
In English and Sanskrit on facing pages; translated from Sanskrit.
Includes bibliographical references and index.
ISBN-13: 978-0-8147-5207-4 (cloth : alk. paper)
ISBN-10: 0-8147-5207-1 (cloth : alk. paper)
1. Epic literature, Sanskrit. I. Lefeber, Rosalind.
II. Title. III. Series.
BL1139.242.K57E5 2005
294.5'92204521–dc22 2005010435

CONTENTS

A *sandhi* grid is printed on the inside of the back cover

CSL CONVENTIONS

SANSKRIT ALPHABETICAL ORDER

Vowels:	*a ā i ī u ū ṛ ṝ ḷ ḹ e ai o au ṃ ḥ*
Gutturals:	*k kh g gh ṅ*
Palatals:	*c ch j jh ñ*
Retroflex:	*ṭ ṭh ḍ ḍh ṇ*
Labials:	*p ph b bh m*
Semivowels:	*y r l v*
Spirants:	*ś ṣ s h*

GUIDE TO SANSKRIT PRONUNCIATION

a	b*u*t
ā, â	r*a*ther
i	s*i*t
ī, î	f*ee*
u	p*u*t
ū, û	b*oo*
ṛ	vocalic *r*, American p*ur*dy or English p*re*tty
ṝ	lengthened *ṛ*
ḷ	vocalic *l*, ab*le*
e, ê, ē	m*a*de, esp. in Welsh pronunciation
ai	b*i*te
o, ô, ō	r*o*pe, esp. Welsh pronunciation; Italian s*o*lo
au	s*ou*nd
ṃ	*anusvāra* nasalizes the preceding vowel
ḥ	*visarga*, a voiceless aspiration (resembling English *h*), or like Scottish lo*ch*, or an aspiration with a faint echoing of the preceding vowel so that *taiḥ* is pronounced *taih*^{i}
k	lu*ck*
kh	blo*ckh*ead
g	*g*o
gh	bi*gh*ead
ṅ	a*n*ger
c	*ch*ill
ch	mat*chh*ead
j	*j*og
jh	aspirated *j*, he*dgeh*og
ñ	ca*ny*on
ṭ	retroflex *t*, *t*ry (with the tip of tongue turned up to touch the hard palate)
ṭh	same as the preceding but aspirated
ḍ	retroflex *d* (with the tip of tongue turned up to touch the hard palate)
ḍh	same as the preceding but aspirated
ṇ	retroflex *n* (with the tip of tongue turned up to touch the hard palate)

t	French *t*out
th	ten*t h*ook
d	*d*inner
dh	guil*dh*all
n	*n*ow
p	*p*ill
ph	u*ph*eaval
b	*b*efore
bh	a*bh*orrent
m	*m*ind
y	*y*es
r	trilled, resembling the Italian pronunciation of *r*
l	*l*inger
v	*w*ord
ś	*sh*ore
ṣ	retroflex *sh* (with the tip of the tongue turned up to touch the hard palate)
s	hi*ss*
h	*h*ood

CSL PUNCTUATION OF ENGLISH

The acute accent on Sanskrit words when they occur outside of the Sanskrit text itself, marks stress, e.g. Ramáyana. It is not part of traditional Sanskrit orthography, transliteration or transcription, but we supply it here to guide readers in the pronunciation of these unfamiliar words. Since no Sanskrit word is accented on the last syllable it is not necessary to accent disyllables, e.g. Rama.

The second CSL innovation designed to assist the reader in the pronunciation of lengthy unfamiliar words is to insert an unobtrusive middle dot between semantic word breaks in compound names (provided the word break does not fall on a vowel resulting from the fusion of two vowels), e.g. Maha·bhárata, but Ramáyana (not Rama·áyana). Our dot echoes the punctuating middle dot (·) found in the oldest surviving forms of written Sanskrit, the Ashokan inscriptions of the third century BCE.

The deep layering of Sanskrit narrative has also dictated that we use quotation marks only to announce the beginning and end of every direct speech, and not at the beginning of every paragraph.

CSL PUNCTUATION OF SANSKRIT

The Sanskrit text is also punctuated, in accordance with the punctuation of the English translation. In mid-verse, the punctuation will not alter the *sandhi* or the scansion. Proper names are capitalized. Most

Sanskrit metres have four "feet" *(pāda):* where possible we print the common *śloka* metre on two lines. In the Sanskrit text, we use French *Guillemets* (e.g. *«kva saṃcicīrṣuḥ?»*) instead of English quotation marks (e.g. "Where are you off to?") to avoid confusion with the apostrophes used for vowel elision in *sandhi.*

Sanskrit presents the learner with a challenge: *sandhi* ("euphonic combination"). *Sandhi* means that when two words are joined in connected speech or writing (which in Sanskrit reflects speech), the last letter (or even letters) of the first word often changes; compare the way we pronounce "the" in "the beginning" and "the end."

In Sanskrit the first letter of the second word may also change; and if both the last letter of the first word and the first letter of the second are vowels, they may fuse. This has a parallel in English: a nasal consonant is inserted between two vowels that would otherwise coalesce: "a pear" and "an apple." Sanskrit vowel fusion may produce ambiguity. The chart at the back of each book gives the full *sandhi* system.

Fortunately it is not necessary to know these changes in order to start reading Sanskrit. For that, what is important is to know the form of the second word without *sandhi* (pre-*sandhi*), so that it can be recognized or looked up in a dictionary. Therefore we are printing Sanskrit with a system of punctuation that will indicate, unambiguously, the original form of the second word, i.e., the form without *sandhi*. Such *sandhi* mostly concerns the fusion of two vowels.

In Sanskrit, vowels may be short or long and are written differently accordingly. We follow the general convention that a vowel with no mark above it is short. Other books mark a long vowel either with a bar called a macron (*ā*) or with a circumflex (*â*). Our system uses the macron, except that for initial vowels in *sandhi* we use a circumflex to indicate that originally the vowel was short, or the shorter of two possibilities (*e* rather than *ai*, *o* rather than *au*).

When we print initial	before *sandhi* that vowel was
â,	*a*
î or *ê*,	*i*
û or *ô*,	*u*
âi,	*e*
âu,	*o*
ā,	*ā* (i.e., the same)

ī,	*ī* (i.e., the same)
ū,	*ū* (i.e., the same)
ē,	*ī*
ō,	*ū*
āi,	*ai*
āu,	*au*
', before *sandhi* there was a vowel *a*	

FURTHER HELP WITH VOWEL SANDHI

When a final short vowel (*a*, *i* or *u*) has merged into a following vowel, we print *'* at the end of the word, and when a final long vowel (*ā*, *ī* or *ū*) has merged into a following vowel we print *"* at the end of the word. The vast majority of these cases will concern a final *a* or *ā*.

Examples:

What before *sandhi* was *atra asti* is represented as *atr' âsti*

atra āste	*atr' āste*
kanyā asti	*kany" âsti*
kanyā āste	*kany" āste*
atra iti	*atr' êti*
kanyā iti	*kany" êti*
kanyā īpsitā	*kany" ēpsitā*

Finally, three other points concerning the initial letter of the second word:

(1) A word that before *sandhi* begins with *ṛ* (vowel), after *sandhi* begins with *r* followed by a consonant: *yatha" rtu* represents pre-*sandhi* *yathā ṛtu*.

(2) When before *sandhi* the previous word ends in *t* and the following word begins with *ś*, after *sandhi* the last letter of the previous word is *c* and the following word begins with *ch*: *syāc chāstravit* represents pre-*sandhi syāt śāstravit*.

(3) Where a word begins with *h* and the previous word ends with a double consonant, this is our simplified spelling to show the pre-*sandhi* form: *tad hasati* is commonly written as *tad dhasati*, but we write *tadd hasati* so that the original initial letter is obvious.

COMPOUNDS

We also punctuate the division of compounds (*samāsa*), simply by inserting a thin vertical line between words. There are words where the decision whether to regard them as compounds is arbitrary. Our principle has been to try to guide readers to the correct dictionary entries.

EXAMPLE

Where the Deva·nágari script reads:

कुम्भस्थली रक्षतु वो विकीर्णसिन्दूररेणुर्द्विरदाननस्य ।
प्रशान्तये विघ्नतमश्छटानां निष्ठ्यूतबालातपपल्लवेव ॥

Others would print:

kumbhasthalī rakṣatu vo vikīrṇasindūrareṇur dviradānanasya /
praśāntaye vighnatamaśchaṭānāṃ niṣṭhyūtabālātapapallaveva //

We print:

Kumbha|sthalī rakṣatu vo vikīrṇa|sindūra|reṇur dvirad'|ānanasya
praśāntaye vighna|tamaś|chaṭānāṃ niṣṭhyūta|bāl'|ātapa|pallav" êva.

And in English:

"May Ganésha's domed forehead protect you! Streaked with vermilion dust, it seems to be emitting the spreading rays of the rising sun to pacify the teeming darkness of obstructions."

"Nava·sáhasanka and the Serpent Princess" I.3 by Padma·gupta

INTRODUCTION

"All the monkeys on earth are coming at your command."
"Kishkíndha" 36.36

NAMED FOR THE CAPITAL city of the monkey kingdom, "Kishkíndha" *(Kiṣkindhā/kāṇḍa)* is the fourth book of Valmíki's "Ramáyana." In spite of the title, very little of the action takes place in Kishkíndha itself. Instead, the setting is still largely that introduced in the "The Forest" ("Ramáyana" Book Three): the forest world full of beauty and menace, a place outside human society where extraordinary events can seem commonplace.

What the title does announce is the extension of Rama's story to include another dynastic struggle, this time between two monkeys, the brothers Valin and Sugríva. Though their battle for control of the monkey kingdom intersects with Rama's search for his abducted wife, it is the monkeys' deeds that come to dominate the book. As their story progresses, Rama himself gradually recedes from the foreground, making way ultimately for the monkey superhero Hánuman, whose adventures will then occupy the whole of the following book, "Súndara."

Synopsis

In the first three books of the "Ramáyana," we were told how Rama, eldest son of King Dasha·ratha of Ayódhya, was prevented from being installed as heir apparent and was instead exiled for fourteen years. He passed this time in the forest with his wife, Sita, daughter of King Jánaka, and with one of his brothers, Lákshmana. As they neared the end of their stay in a part of the Dándaka forest called

Jana·sthana, a powerful *rākṣasa*, or demon, named Rávana abducted Sita by a ruse, killed the vulture-king Jatáyus, who tried to save her and took her to his island kingdom, Lanka, in the south. Searching vainly for his wife, Rama was advised by another demon, Kabándha, to seek an alliance with the monkey Sugríva, who would help him to find Sita.

In "Kishkíndha," Rama and Lákshmana first meet the monkey Hánuman. He then takes them to meet his leader Sugríva, who is living in exile because of a dispute with his elder brother Valin, king of the monkeys (cantos 1–4). Rama and Sugríva form an alliance, with the solemn understanding that Rama will help Sugríva become king, while the latter will in turn mobilize all the monkeys to discover where Rávana is keeping Sita (cantos 5–8).

Sugríva explains the genesis of the hostility between himself and Valin: While Valin was in a cave battling a demon, Sugríva, mistakenly believing him to be dead, shut him inside by rolling a rock across the opening. When Valin finally escaped from the cave and found Sugríva in possession of his wife and consecrated as king in his stead, he banished him from the kingdom (cantos 9–10).

Uncertain that Rama is a match for Valin, Sugríva describes his brother's prowess and demands reassurance from Rama. Rama satisfies him by shooting a single arrow through seven *sāla* trees. Promising his help, Rama instructs Sugríva to challenge Valin to single combat. But Rama is unable to distinguish the two brothers as they fight and refrains from shooting Valin. Sugríva flees but is persuaded by Rama to return to combat wearing a flower garland that will identify him (cantos 11–13). Encouraged yet again by Rama, Sugríva repeats his challenge to his brother. Though Valin's wife Tará tries to dissuade him, Valin goes out to fight again and is killed by Rama, who is in ambush. As Valin lies dying, he reproaches Rama, who then justifies his action (cantos 14–18).

After Valin's widow mourns the death of her husband, he is cremated. Sugríva is consecrated king, and Valin's son Ángada is made heir apparent (cantos 19–25). It is agreed that when the rainy season has ended, Sugríva will summon all the monkeys in his kingdom to begin the search for Sita. But autumn comes with no sign that Sugríva has begun any preparations, so Rama sends Lákshmana into Kishkínda to demand immediate action (cantos 26–33). Lákshmana is reassured that Sugríva has not forgotten his promise to Rama. After all the monkey troops are summoned, Lákshmana and Sugríva rejoin Rama, who is gratified to see the countless monkeys beginning to arrive (cantos 34–38).

Sugríva dispatches the monkey searchers in the four directions, with orders to return within a month (cantos 39–42). Rama notices Sugríva's special confidence in the monkeys who are to go south under Ángada's leadership. In this group is heroic Hánuman, to whom Rama gives a ring to be shown to Sita as a token of recognition. At the end of the month, the search parties from east, west and north return unsuccessful (cantos 43–46). After a month of fruitless efforts, the monkeys searching the south enter a magical cave, from which they are delivered by an ascetic woman named Svayam·prabha, who leaves them near the ocean (cantos 47–52). Dejected because they have overstayed Sugríva's time limit without finding Sita, they decide to fast to death (cantos 53–54). A vulture called Sampáti, older brother of the vulture who had earlier tried to rescue Sita, observes the fasting monkeys. After hearing their story, he explains how his wings were burned as he once protected his brother from the sun. He also tells them that he saw Rávana carrying Sita away and that she is being kept in Lanka (cantos 55–57).

Questioned again by the monkey Jámbavan, Sampáti tells how his son saw Rávana carrying Sita away. He also repeats the story of his own misadventure protecting his brother and explains that he was instructed by a sage to remain waiting for Rama's monkey helpers to arrive. Having delivered his own message to them, he sprouts new wings and flies away (cantos 58–62). Daunted by the sight of the vast ocean lying between them and Lanka, the monkeys debate which of them can make the great leap. Jámbavan discourages Ángada from making the attempt, and instead reminds Hánuman of his birth as son of the wind god and his amazing childhood and endowments (cantos 63–65). As "Kishkíndha" ends, Hánuman is preparing to jump across the ocean to Lanka to find Sita (canto 66).

The Monkeys

Central to the narrative in "Kishkíndha" is Rama's agreement to kill Valin and thereby regain Sugríva's kingship, in exchange for help in finding Sita. Sugríva says he will provide an army of his fellow *vānaras* for the search. The term *vānara* commonly denotes a monkey, and for many centuries there appears to have been nothing troublesome about that meaning. But in more recent times a number of scholars have objected, insisting that the *vānaras* were tribal people of some kind, perhaps with a monkey banner.

What matters for the advancement of Rama's interest and the plot, however, is not whether these are monkeys who are like men or men who are like monkeys. What matters is that they are energetic and swift and exist in great numbers. Rama needs millions of searchers to find Sita and then an equally large army to help defeat Rávana and his forces. The question arises as to why, under the circumstances, Rama did not save himself a good deal of trouble and avoid the risk to his life (and his honor as a warrior) simply by making an alliance with the superhero Valin instead of killing him. There are passages in the epic that suggest destiny is the reason, but ultimately it is the similarity in their circumstances that makes Rama and Sugríva natural allies: each is an exile, each has lost his wife, each has been deprived of a kingship that has gone to his brother.

What is totally different about Rama and Sugríva is the manner in which they and their respective brothers and wives behave, and therein lies the chief dramatic utility of the *vānaras*. The stark contrast between the men and the monkeys is rarely commented on yet is constantly felt, thereby enriching both the characterizations and the dramatic tension. For much of "Kishkíndha," Sugríva gives vent to his resentment, his ambition and his open hostility to his brother, who of course reciprocates the ill feeling. Their undisguised enmity and the erotic overtones of their rivalry for the kingship serve as an effective foil for Rama's absolute virtuousness in his dealings with his own brothers and his pure relationship with his wife.

Furthermore, men or monkeys, the *vānaras* are outside the society to which Rama properly belongs and in a sense scarcely worthy to be his allies. The picture of the noble prince forced to seek help from forest-dwellers shows us to what dire straits he has been reduced by his unjust exile. The lowly nature of Rama's allies lends irony to Rávana's ultimate defeat and death. The mightiest of *rākṣasas*, incapable of being killed by gods or demigods, will be destroyed through the combined efforts of two men and an army of monkeys, the only kind of adversaries he was too arrogant to fear.

The Killing of Valin

From the point of view of the main plot, the most important event in "Kishkíndha" is the creation of the alliance between Rama and Sugríva. But the concentration of both literary *kāvya* and didactic verses around Valin's death reveals that this has long been felt to be not only the most dramatic event in the book but also the dominant moral issue. Since Rama's behavior is elsewhere exemplary, and he is in fact the very model of virtuous conduct, it has been a source of considerable discomfort for most traditional readers of the "Ramáyana" that the ideal hero concealed himself and without warning or challenge shot Valin while he was engaged in hand-to-hand combat with Sugríva. Most of the commentators focus on the righteousness of the kshatriya Rama's administering punishment, no matter how he does so, to adulterous Valin and in spite of Valin's own nominal status as king. If, however, one examines the Valin episode strictly as it appears in the critical text of "Kishkíndha," it is possible to entertain a more direct explanation: Rama killed

Valin treacherously because, as a human hero (not a god), that was the only way he could be sure of killing him at once, as promised. Rama is presented in the critical text as a mighty warrior, but one not necessarily capable of successfully challenging a superhuman creature like Valin, whose strength and speed are described at length by awestruck Sugríva.

However one explains Rama's manner of killing Valin, one must conclude from it that this episode was part of the Rama story at a very early stage. As a repository of traditional values, the book of "Kishkíndha" presumably added much of its morally uplifting material over the centuries – maxims (*su/bhāṣitas*), the perorations by Hánuman, and the like. But no obvious purpose would have been served by adding anything that creates discomfort about Rama's behavior, especially since he was always in later times an object not only of veneration but of emulation as well.

Furthermore, the debate between Valin and Rama in cantos 17 and 18 presumably has a didactic function. The application of the *dharma* is not simple or straightforward, and in a narrative poem, just as in life, when basic values conflict, one view must at last prevail. Not unreasonably, then, Rama, as spokesman for the dominant human clan, has the final word. For no matter how the focus shifts in the course of the narrative between *vānaras* as true monkeys and as warriors indistinguishable from men, in the end they are viewed as Rama's inferiors. It is the success of the "descendants of Ragu" (*Rāghavas*) that must engage the deepest concern of the listener/reader.

The preceding is a highly condensed version of ROSALIND LEFEBER's original introduction to her Princeton translation of "Kishkíndha," (pp. 3–52) to which the interested reader is referred for a more detailed discussion of the text. To read LEFEBER's full introduction, extensive annotation and bibliography of works consulted, as well as the full introductions to the other volumes of the Princeton "Ramáyana" translations, please visit the CSL website. There, a general introduction to the whole "Ramáyana" can be found in ROBERT GOLDMAN's introduction to his Princeton translation of "Boyhood," the first of the epic's seven books.

TRANSLATION ORIGINALLY PUBLISHED AS:

The Rāmāyaṇa of Vālmīki: an epic of ancient India, Volume IV: Kiṣkindhākāṇḍa. Introduction, translation and annotation by ROSALIND LEFEBER; edited by ROBERT P. GOLDMAN. Princeton. 1994.

1–4
MEETING THE MONKEYS

1.1 SA TĀṂ PUṢKARIṆĪṂ gatvā padm'|ôtpala|jhaṣ'|ākulām
Rāmaḥ Saumitri|sahito vilalāp' ākul'|êndriyaḥ.
tasya dṛṣṭv" âiva tāṃ harṣād indriyāṇi cakampire.
sa kāma|vaśam āpannaḥ Saumitrim idam abravīt:
«Saumitre, paśya Pampāyāḥ kānanaṃ śubha|darśanam
yatra rājanti śail'|ābhā drumāḥ sa|śikharā iva!
māṃ tu śok'|âbhisaṃtaptam ādhayaḥ pīḍayanti vai
Bharatasya ca duḥkhena Vaidehyā haraṇena ca.
1.5 adhikaṃ pravibhāty etan nīla|pītaṃ tu śādvalam
drumāṇāṃ vividhaiḥ puṣpaiḥ paristomair iv' ârpitam.
sukh'|ânilo 'yaṃ, Saumitre, kālaḥ pracura|manmathaḥ
gandhavān surabhir māso jāta|puṣpa|phala|drumaḥ.
paśya rūpāṇi, Saumitre, vanānāṃ puṣpa|śālinām
sṛjatāṃ puṣpa|varṣāṇi varṣaṃ toyamucām iva.
prastareṣu ca ramyeṣu vividhāḥ kānana|drumāḥ
vāyu|vega|pracalitāḥ puṣpair avakiranti gām.
mārutaḥ sukha|saṃsparśo vāti candana|śītalaḥ
ṣaṭpadair anukūjadbhir vaneṣu madhu|gandhiṣu.
1.10 giri|prastheṣu ramyeṣu puṣpavadbhir mano|ramaiḥ
saṃsakta|śikharā śailā virājanti mahā|drumaiḥ.
puṣpit'|âgrāṃś ca paśy' êmān karṇikārān samantataḥ:
hāṭaka|pratisaṃchannān narān pīt'|âmbarān iva.
ayaṃ vasantaḥ, Saumitre, nānā|vihaga|nāditaḥ
Sītayā viprahīṇasya śoka|saṃdīpano mama.
māṃ hi śoka|samākrāntaṃ saṃtāpayati manmathaḥ
hṛṣṭaḥ pravadamānaś ca samāhvayati kokilaḥ.
eṣa dātyūhako hṛṣṭo ramye māṃ vana|nirjhare

When Rama arrived with Saumítri at that lake over- 1.1
flowing with lotuses, water lilies and fish, his passions overflowed, and he lamented. As soon as he saw it,
he trembled with rapture. Yielding to the power of love, he
said to Saumítri:

"Saumítri, see how lovely the forest is around Lake Pampa. Its crested trees are as splendid as mountains. But anguish still torments me, as I grieve over Bharata's sorrow
and the abduction of Vaidéhi.

And yet this grassy plot, deep green and yellow, glis- 1.5
tens brightly, carpeted with many-colored blossoms from
the trees. With gentle breezes and with blossoms and fruit
growing on the trees, this fragrant spring month is a time
of heightened passion, Saumítri. And look, Saumítri, beautiful flowering thickets are pouring down showers of blossoms, like clouds releasing showers of rain. Forest trees of
every kind, shaken by the force of the wind, are scattering
blossoms on the ground among the lovely stones. In glades
fragrant with honey, where bees hum, a gentle breeze is
blowing, cooled by sandalwood trees. The mountains, with 1.10
beautiful tall trees blossoming near their lovely crests, look
as if their peaks were touching. And look at these *karni·kara*
trees everywhere in full flower: They are like yellow-robed
men covered with gold ornaments.

This springtime, resounding with birdsong of every kind,
only inflames my pain, Saumítri, for I am without Sita.
Overcome by grief, I am tormented by love, while the joyous
cuckoo, raising its voice, calls out to me. This water-cock
crying joyously by the lovely forest cataract makes me grieve,
Lákshmana, for I am possessed by love. Birds united with 1.15

praṇadan manmath'|āviṣṭaṃ śocayiṣyati, Lakṣmaṇa.
1.15 vimiśrā vihagāḥ pumbhir ātma|vyūh'|âbhinanditāḥ
bhṛṅga|rāja|pramuditāḥ, Saumitre, madhura|svarāḥ.
māṃ hi sā mṛga|śāv'|âkṣī cintā|śoka|balāt|kṛtam
saṃtāpayati, Saumitre, krūraś caitra|van'|ânilaḥ.
śikhinībhiḥ parivṛtā mayūrā giri|sānuṣu
manmath'|âbhiparītasya mama manmatha|vardhanāḥ.
paśya, Lakṣmaṇa, nṛtyantaṃ mayūram upanṛtyati
śikhinī manmath'|ārt" âiṣā bhartāraṃ giri|sānuṣu.
mayūrasya vane nūnaṃ rakṣasā na hṛtā priyā.
mama tv ayaṃ vinā|vāsaḥ puṣpa|māse su|duḥsahaḥ.
1.20 paśya, Lakṣmaṇa, puṣpāṇi niṣphalāni bhavanti me
puṣpa|bhāra|samṛddhānāṃ vanānāṃ śiśir'|âtyaye.
vadanti rāvaṃ muditāḥ śakunāḥ saṃghaśaḥ kalam
āhvayanta iv' ânyonyaṃ kām'|ônmāda|karā mama.
nūnaṃ para|vaśā Sītā s" âpi śocaty ahaṃ yathā
śyāmā padma|palāś'|âkṣī mṛdu|bhāṣā ca me priyā.
eṣa puṣpa|vaho vāyuḥ sukha|sparśo him'|āvahaḥ
tāṃ vicintayataḥ kāntāṃ pāvaka|pratimo mama.
tāṃ vin" âtha vihaṃgo 'sau pakṣī praṇaditas tadā
vāyasaḥ pādapa|gataḥ prahṛṣṭam abhinardati.
1.25 eṣa vai tatra Vaidehyā vihagaḥ pratihārakaḥ
pakṣī māṃ tu viśāl'|âkṣyāḥ samīpam upaneṣyati.
paśya, Lakṣmaṇa, saṃnādaṃ vane mada|vivardhanam
puṣpit'|âgreṣu vṛkṣeṣu dvijānām upakūjatām.

their mates rejoice in flocks of their own kind, Saumítri. Delighted by the hum of bumblebees, they make a sweet sound.

Overpowered by care and grief, Saumítri, I am tormented by that fawn-eyed woman and by the cruel breeze from the spring forest. The peacocks circled by peahens on the mountain ridges heighten my desire, though I am already filled with desire. See, Lákshmana, how this peahen sick with love dances before her dancing peacock mate on the mountain ridges. Surely the peacock's beloved was not carried off by a *rákshasa* in the forest. But, for me, living without Sita in this month of flowers is unbearable.

Consider, Lákshmana, in these forests rich with the bur- 1.20
den of their blossoms now that the cool season has passed, how unfruitful the blossoms will be for me. As if to challenge one another, the joyful birds in flocks utter sweet cries, maddening me with desire. In the power of another, Sita, my sweet-speaking, dark beloved with eyes like lotus petals, must surely grieve as I do. This gentle, cooling breeze, fragrant with flowers, feels like fire to me as I think of my dear wife. She is gone; but now the crow, that bird who once cried out while flying through the sky, is singing joyfully in a tree. The very bird who, flying through the sky, 1.25
once foretold Vaidéhi's abduction will now lead me to my large-eyed wife.

Listen, Lákshmana! Here in the forest the sound of birds warbling in the blossoming treetops increases my desire.

Saumitre, paśya Pampāyāś citrāsu vana|rājiṣu
nalināni prakāśante jale taruṇa|sūryavat.
eṣā prasanna|salilā padma|nīl'|ôtpal'|āyatā
haṃsa|kāraṇḍav'|ākīrṇā Pampā saugandhik'|āyutā.
cakravāka|yutā nityaṃ citra|prastha|van'|ântarā
mātaṅga|mṛga|yūthaiś ca śobhate salil'|ârthibhiḥ.
1.30 padma|kośa|palāśāni draṣṭuṃ dṛṣṭir hi manyate
Sītāyā netra|kośābhyāṃ sadṛśān' îti, Lakṣmaṇa.
padma|kesara|saṃsṛṣṭo vṛkṣ'|ântara|viniḥsṛtaḥ
niḥśvāsa iva Sītāyā vāti vāyur mano|haraḥ.
Saumitre, paśya Pampāyā dakṣiṇe giri|sānuni
puṣpitāṃ karṇikārasya yaṣṭiṃ parama|śobhanām.
adhikaṃ śaila|rājo 'yaṃ dhātubhis tu vibhūṣitaḥ
vicitraṃ sṛjate reṇuṃ vāyu|vega|vighaṭṭitam.
giri|prasthās tu, Saumitre, sarvataḥ saṃprapuṣpitaiḥ
niṣpatraiḥ sarvato ramyaiḥ pradīpā iva kiṃśukaiḥ.
1.35 Pampā|tīra|ruhāś c' ême saṃsaktā madhu|gandhinaḥ
mālatī|mallikā|ṣaṇḍāḥ karavīrāś ca puṣpitāḥ
ketakyaḥ sinduvārāś ca vāsantyaś ca supuṣpitāḥ
mādhavyo gandha|pūrṇāś ca kunda|gulmāś ca sarvaśaḥ
ciribilvā madhūkāś ca vañjulā bakulās tathā
campakās tilakāś c' âiva nāga|vṛkṣāś ca puṣpitāḥ
nīpāś ca varaṇāś c' âiva kharjūrāś ca supuṣpitāḥ.
aṅkolāś ca kuraṇṭāś ca cūrṇakāḥ pāribhadrakāḥ
cūtāḥ pāṭalayaś c' âiva kovidārāś ca puṣpitāḥ
mucukund'|ârjunāś c' âiva dṛśyante giri|sānuṣu

And look, Saumítri, among Pampa's brightly colored rows of trees, red lotuses shine in the water like the newly risen sun. With its clear waters, filled with red and blue lotuses and fragrant water lilies, Lake Pampa is crowded with geese and ducks. Always full of *chakra·vaka* birds, its forests enclosing bright glades, Pampa is resplendent with herds of elephants and deer seeking its waters.

My eyes long to see the petals of the lotus buds, Láksh- 1.30
mana, for they are like Sita's eyelids. Like Sita's sighs, the captivating wind blows, passing through the trees after mingling with lotus filaments.

Look, Saumítri, there on the southern slope of Pampa's mountain stands the splendid flowering column of the *karni·kara* tree. This king of mountains, richly adorned with veins of minerals, releases dust of many colors scattered by the force of the wind. And the mountaintops, Saumítri, seem to be all aflame with lovely *kin·shuka* trees, leafless and in full bloom.

Here, growing on the banks of the Pampa, are dense and 1.35
honey-fragrant masses of *málati* and *mállika*, and blossoming *karavíra*; and *kétakas* and *sinduváras* and *vasánti* creepers in full bloom, and *mádhavis* full of fragrance and *kunda* bushes everywhere; and *chiri·bilvas* and *madhúkas*, *váñjulas* and *bákulas*, and *chámpakas* and also *tílakas*, and *naga* trees flowering; and *nipas* and *váranas* as well, and *kharjúras* in full bloom. And *ankólas* and *kurántas* and *chúrnakas* and *paribhádrakas*, *chutas* and *pátalis* also, and flowering *kovidáras* and *muchukúndas* and *árjunas* are seen on the
mountain peaks; and *kétakas* and *uddálakas*, too, *shiríshas*, 1.40
shínshapas, and *dhavas*, *shálmalis*, and *kínshukas*, and red

1.40 ketak'|ôddālakāś c' âiva śirīṣāḥ śiṃśapā dhavāḥ
śālmalyaḥ kiṃśukāś c' âiva raktāḥ kurabakās tathā
tiniśā|nakta|mālāś ca candanāḥ syandanās tathā.
vividhā vividhaiḥ puṣpais tair eva naga|sānuṣu
vikīrṇaiḥ pīta|rakt'|ābhāḥ, Saumitre, prastarāḥ kṛtāḥ.
him'|ânte paśya, Saumitre, vṛkṣāṇāṃ puṣpa|saṃbhavam
puṣpa|māse hi taravaḥ saṃgharṣād iva puṣpitāḥ.
paśya śīta|jalāṃ c' êmāṃ, Saumitre, puṣkar'|āyutām
cakravāk'|ânucaritāṃ kāraṇḍava|niṣevitām
plavaiḥ krauñcaiś ca saṃpūrṇāṃ varāha|mṛga|sevitām.
adhikaṃ śobhate Pampā vikūjadbhir vihaṃ|gamaiḥ.
1.45 dīpayant' îva me kāmaṃ
vividhā muditā dvijāḥ
śyāmāṃ candra|mukhīṃ smṛtvā
priyāṃ padma|nibh'|ēkṣaṇām.
paśya sānuṣu citreṣu mṛgībhiḥ sahitān mṛgān
māṃ punar mṛga|śāv'|âkṣyā Vaidehyā virahī|kṛtam.»
evaṃ sa vilapaṃs tatra śok'|ôpahata|cetanaḥ
avekṣata śivāṃ Pampāṃ ramya|vāri|vahāṃ śubhām.
nirīkṣamāṇaḥ sahasā mah"|ātmā
sarvaṃ vanaṃ nirjhara|kandaraṃ ca.
udvigna|cetāḥ saha Lakṣmaṇena
vicārya duḥkh'|ôpahataḥ pratasthe.
tāv Ṛśyamūkaṃ sahitau prayātau
Sugrīva|śākhā|mṛga|sevitaṃ tam.
trastās tu dṛṣṭvā harayo babhūvur
mah"|âujasau Rāghava|Lakṣmaṇau tau.

2.1 TAU tu dṛṣṭvā mah"|ātmānau bhrātarau Rāma|Lakṣmaṇau
var'|āyudha|dharau vīrau Sugrīvaḥ śaṅkito 'bhavat.
udvigna|hṛdayaḥ sarvā diśaḥ samavalokayan

kurábakas, too, *tínishas* and *nakta·malas*, *chándanas*, and *syándanas*.

Many beds of red and yellow have formed from the countless blossoms scattered on the mountainsides, Saumítri. Look, Saumítri, blossoms are bursting forth on the trees, now that the cold has ended; for in spring, trees blossom as if to rival one another.

And see, Saumítri, how Lake Pampa with its cool waters abounding in blue lotuses is sought after by *chakra·vaka* birds, frequented by *karándava* birds, filled with *plava* and *krauñcha* birds, and visited by boars and deer. Pampa looks
even lovelier with its warbling birds. Joyful birds of every 1.45
kind seem to inflame my love as I think of my dark, lotus-eyed beloved whose face is like the moon. And look, there on the brightly colored mountainsides the deer are with their does, while I am parted from my fawn-eyed Vaidéhi."

Lamenting in this way, his mind assailed by grief, he gazed at the lovely flowing waters of beautiful, auspicious Pampa. Anxious and assailed by sorrow, great Rama intently examined the entire forest with its waterfalls and caves. Then, after deliberating with Lákshmana, he set forth. Those two set out together for the mountain Rishya·muka, where Sugríva and his monkeys dwelled. But the monkeys were terrified when they saw powerful Rághava and Lákshmana.

Now, WHEN Sugríva saw the brothers Rama and Láksh- 2.1
mana, those two great warriors bearing the finest weapons, he became alarmed. That bull among monkeys looked anx-

na vyatiṣṭhata kasmiṃś cid deśe vānara|puṃgavaḥ.
n' âiva cakre manaḥ sthāne vīkṣamāṇo mahā|balau
kapeḥ parama|bhītasya cittaṃ vyavasasāda ha.
cintayitvā sa dharm'|ātmā vimṛśya guru|lāghavam
Sugrīvaḥ param'|ôdvignaḥ sarvair anucaraiḥ saha.
2.5 tataḥ sa sacivebhyas tu Sugrīvaḥ plavag'|âdhipaḥ
śaśaṃsa param'|ôdvignaḥ paśyaṃs tau Rāma|Lakṣmaṇau:

«etau vanam idaṃ durgaṃ Vāli|praṇihitau dhruvam.
chadmanā cīra|vasanau pracarantāv ih' āgatau.»

tataḥ Sugrīva|sacivā dṛṣṭvā parama|dhanvinau
jagmur giri|taṭāt tasmād anyac chikharam uttamam.

te kṣipram abhigamy' âtha yūthapā yūthapa'|rṣabham
harayo vānara|śreṣṭhaṃ parivāry' ôpatasthire.
ekam ek'|âyana|gatāḥ plavamānā girer girim
prakampayanto vegena girīṇāṃ śikharāṇi ca.
2.10 tataḥ śākhā|mṛgāḥ sarve plavamānā mahā|balāḥ
babhañjuś ca nagāṃs tatra puṣpitān durga|saṃśritān.
āplavanto hari|varāḥ sarvatas taṃ mahā|girim
mṛga|mārjāra|śārdūlāṃs trāsayanto yayus tadā.
tataḥ Sugrīva|sacivāḥ parvat'|êndraṃ samāśritāḥ
saṃgamya kapi|mukhyena sarve prāñjalayaḥ sthitāḥ.
tatas taṃ bhaya|saṃtrastaṃ Vāli|kilbiṣa|śaṅkitam
uvāca Hanumān vākyaṃ Sugrīvaṃ vākya|kovidaḥ:

iously in all directions and could not settle down anyplace.
Beholding those two powerful men, the terrified monkey
could not steady his mind, and his heart sank. Righteous
Sugríva was deeply distressed as he reflected and weighed
the alternatives with all his followers. As he watched Ra- 2.5
ma and Lákshmana with great anxiety, the lord of monkeys
Sugríva said to his companions:

"Surely Valin has sent those two to this inaccessible forest as spies. Disguised in bark garments, they have come
prowling about here."

Then, when Sugríva's companions had seen those two
excellent bowmen, they went from that mountain slope to
another very high peak.

Those leaders of the troops of monkeys then swiftly approached and stood surrounding that bull among troop
leaders, best of monkeys. Leaping from mountain to mountain and making the mountain peaks tremble with their
force, they reached a meeting place. And then all those pow- 2.10
erful, leaping monkeys shattered the flowering trees that
stood there on the mountain pass. Those great monkeys
went leaping everywhere on that big mountain, terrifying
the deer, wildcats and tigers. Assembling on that lord of
mountains with their monkey chief, the companions of
Sugríva stood before him with their palms cupped in reverence. Then Hánuman, skilled in speech, spoke to Sugríva,
who was trembling with alarm, fearing some harm from his
brother Valin:

«yasmād udvigna|cetās tvaṃ pradruto, hari|puṃgava,
taṃ krūra|darśanaṃ krūraṃ n' êha paśyāmi Vālinam.
2.15 yasmāt tava bhayaṃ, saumya, pūrvajāt pāpa|karmaṇaḥ
sa n' êha Vālī duṣṭ'|ātmā, na te paśyāmy ahaṃ bhayam.
aho śākhā|mṛgatvaṃ te vyaktam eva, plavaṃ|gama:
laghu|cittatay" ātmānaṃ na sthāpayasi yo matau.
buddhi|vijñāna|saṃpanna iṅgitaiḥ sarvam ācara.
na hy abuddhiṃ gato rājā sarva|bhūtāni śāsti hi.»

Sugrīvas tu śubhaṃ vākyaṃ śrutvā sarvaṃ Hanūmataḥ
tataḥ śubhataraṃ vākyaṃ Hanūmantam uvāca ha:

«dīrgha|bāhū viśāl'|âkṣau śara|cāp'|âsi|dhāriṇau
kasya na syād bhayaṃ dṛṣṭvā etau sura|sut'|ôpamau?
2.20 Vāli|praṇihitāv etau śaṅke 'haṃ puruṣ'|ôttamau
rājāno bahu|mitrāś ca viśvāso n' âtra hi kṣamaḥ.
arayaś ca manuṣyeṇa vijñeyāś channa|cāriṇaḥ
viśvastānām aviśvastāś chidreṣu praharanti hi.
kṛtyeṣu Vālī medhāvī. rājāno bahu|darśanāḥ
bhavanti para|hantāras te jñeyāḥ prākṛtair naraiḥ.
tau tvayā prākṛten' âiva gatvā jñeyau, plavaṃ|gama,
śaṅkitānāṃ prakāraiś ca rūpa|vyābhāṣaṇena ca.
lakṣayasva tayor bhāvaṃ. prahṛṣṭa|manasau yadi
viśvāsayan praśaṃsābhir iṅgitaiś ca punaḥ punaḥ.
2.25 mam' âiv' âbhimukhaṃ sthitvā pṛccha tvaṃ, hari|puṃgava,
prayojanaṃ praveśasya vanasy' âsya dhanur|dharau.
śuddh'|ātmānau yadi tv etau jānīhi tvaṃ, plavaṃ|gama,
vyābhāṣitair vā rūpair vā vijñeyā duṣṭat" ânayoḥ.»

"Bull among monkeys, I do not see here fierce Valin,
whose cruel looks you fled with an anxious heart. My friend, 2.15
I see no danger to you. Evil-minded Valin, your wicked elder brother whom you fear, is not here. Ah, monkey, it is all too clear that you are a monkey: You are too capricious to reach any firm decision. You have both intelligence and knowledge, so judge people's true intentions before you do anything. For a king who lapses into folly cannot govern others."

When Sugríva heard this entire fine speech of Hánuman's, he addressed to him one finer still:

"Who would not be afraid upon seeing those two who are like sons of the gods, long-armed and large-eyed, bearing
bows, arrows and swords? I suspect that those two excel- 2.20
lent men have been sent as spies by Valin; for kings have many friends, and one cannot trust them. And a man must recognize enemies who go around disguised; for untrustworthy people strike at the weak points of those who are trusting. Valin is shrewd about his objectives. Kings have many stratagems to destroy their enemies, and their schemes must be uncovered by ordinary-looking men. You must go as an ordinary person, monkey, and find out about those two from their various gestures, their appearance, and their manner of speaking. Observe their state of mind. If they seem well meaning, reassure them again and again by flattery and suitable gestures, making them well disposed to
me. Then ask those two bowmen their purpose in entering 2.25
this forest, best of monkeys. Find out, monkey, if those two are pure in heart. Their innocence can be discovered by their speech or by their appearance."

ity evaṃ kapi|rājena saṃdiṣṭo Mārut'|ātmajaḥ
cakāra gamane buddhiṃ yatra tau Rāma|Lakṣmaṇau.
«Tath" êti» saṃpūjya vacas tu tasya
kapeḥ subhītasya durāsadasya
mah"|ânubhāvo Hanumān yayau tadā
sa yatra Rāmo 'tibalaś ca Lakṣmaṇaḥ.

3.1 VACO VIJÑĀYA Hanumān Sugrīvasya mah"|ātmanaḥ
parvatād Ṛśyamūkāt tu pupluve yatra Rāghavau.
sa tatra gatvā Hanumān balavān vānar'|ôttamaḥ
upacakrāma tau vāgbhir mṛdvībhiḥ satya|vikramaḥ.
svakaṃ rūpaṃ parityajya bhikṣu|rūpeṇa vānaraḥ
ābabhāṣe ca tau vīrau yathāvat praśaśaṃsa ca:
«rājarṣi|deva|pratimau tāpasau saṃśita|vratau
deśaṃ katham imaṃ prāptau bhavantau vara|varṇinau?
3.5 trāsayantau mṛga|gaṇān anyāṃś ca vana|cāriṇaḥ
Pampā|tīra|ruhān vṛkṣān vīkṣamāṇau samantataḥ?
imāṃ nadīṃ śubha|jalāṃ śobhayantau tarasvinau
dhairyavantau suvarṇ'|ābhau kau yuvāṃ cīra|vāsasau
siṃha|viprekṣitau vīrau siṃh'|âtibala|vikramau
Śakra|cāpa|nibhe cāpe pragṛhya vipulair bhujaiḥ
śrīmantau rūpa|saṃpannau vṛṣabha|śreṣṭha|vikramau
hasti|hast'|ôpama|bhujau dyutimantau nara'|rṣabhau?
prabhayā parvat'|êndro 'yaṃ yuvayor avabhāsitaḥ.
rājy'|ârhāv amara|prakhyau kathaṃ deśam ih' āgatau?
3.10 padma|patr'|ēkṣaṇau vīrau jaṭā|maṇḍala|dhāriṇau
anyonya|sadṛśau vīrau deva|lokād iv' āgatau.
yadṛcchay" êva saṃprāptau candra|sūryau vasuṃ|dharām
viśāla|vakṣasau vīrau mānuṣau deva|rūpiṇau

Ordered in this way by the monkey-king, the wind god's son resolved to go where Rama and Lákshmana were. Saying, "So be it!" powerful Hánuman honored the words of the unassailable monkey who was so frightened. Then he went where mighty Rama and Lákshmana were.

UNDERSTANDING great Sugríva's words, Hánuman then 3.1
leaped from the mountain Rishya·muka to where the Rághavas were. When he arrived there, powerful Hánuman, that truly valiant best of monkeys, approached those two with gentle words. Giving up his own form for that of a mendicant, the monkey addressed them and duly praised them:

"With your fair complexions, you ascetics strict in your
vows resemble gods or royal sages. Why have you come to 3.5
this place, frightening the herds of deer and other forest-dwellers, and examining on all sides the trees growing on the banks of the Pampa? Who are you in these bark garments, best of men, strong, steadfast, bright as gold, enhancing the beauty of this river of auspicious waters, you splendid warriors with the gaze of lions, courageous and strong as lions, majestic, handsome, with the gait of fine bulls, with arms like elephants' trunks, great arms holding bows like Shakra's?

Your radiance makes this majestic mountain shine. You
look like gods and are worthy of royal sovereignty. With 3.10
eyes like lotus leaves, you seem to be warriors, yet you wear coils of matted locks. Resembling one another, you are like warriors come from the world of the gods, or like the moon and the sun come to earth by chance. You are broad-chested warriors, men with the look of gods, lion-shouldered and

siṃha|skandhau mahā|sattvau samadāv iva go|vṛṣau
āyatāś ca suvṛttāś ca bāhavaḥ parigh'|ôttamāḥ
sarva|bhūṣaṇa|bhūṣ"|ârhāḥ kim arthaṃ na vibhūṣitāḥ?

ubhau yogyāv ahaṃ manye rakṣituṃ pṛthivīm imām
sa|sāgara|vanāṃ kṛtsnāṃ Vindhya|Meru|vibhūṣitām.

ime ca dhanuṣī citre ślakṣṇe citr'|ânulepane
prakāśete yath" Êndrasya vajre hema|vibhūṣite.

3.15 saṃpūrṇā niśitair bāṇair tūṇāś ca śubha|darśanāḥ
jīvit'|ânta|karair ghorair jvaladbhir iva pannagaiḥ.
mahā|pramāṇau vipulau tapta|hāṭaka|bhūṣitau.
khaḍgāv etau virājete nirmukta|bhujagāv iva.
evaṃ māṃ paribhāṣantaṃ kasmād vai n' âbhibhāṣathaḥ?

Sugrīvo nāma dharm'|ātmā kaś cid vānara|yūthapaḥ.
vīro vinikṛto bhrātrā jagad bhramati duḥkhitaḥ.
prāpto 'haṃ preṣitas tena Sugrīveṇa mah"|ātmanā
rājñā vānara|mukhyānāṃ Hanumān nāma vānaraḥ.

3.20 yuvābhyāṃ saha dharm'|ātmā Sugrīvaḥ sakhyam icchati.
tasya māṃ sacivaṃ vittaṃ vānaraṃ Pavan'|ātmajam.
bhikṣu|rūpa|praticchannaṃ Sugrīva|priya|kāmyayā
Ṛśyamūkād iha prāptaṃ kāmagaṃ kāma|rūpiṇam.»

evam uktvā tu Hanumāṃs tau vīrau Rāma|Lakṣmaṇau
vākyajñau vākya|kuśalaḥ punar n' ôvāca kiṃ cana.

etac chrutvā vacas tasya Rāmo Lakṣmaṇam abravīt
prahṛṣṭa|vadanaḥ śrīmān bhrātaraṃ pārśvataḥ sthitam:
«sacivo 'yaṃ kap'|îndrasya Sugrīvasya mah"|ātmanaḥ.
tam eva kāṅkṣamāṇasya mam' ântikam upāgataḥ.

powerful, like furious bulls. Why have you come to this place? Your arms are like iron clubs, long and well-rounded, worthy of every adornment. Why are they unadorned?

I believe you are both capable of protecting this whole earth, complete with its oceans and forests and adorned with the Vindhya and Meru mountains.

These two bright-colored bows, polished and brightly painted, adorned with gold, gleam like Indra's thunderbolts.
Your beautiful quivers are full of sharp, glittering arrows like 3.15
terrible, death-dealing snakes. Your two broad swords are very long and adorned with refined gold. They shine like snakes that have just shed their skins. Why do you not speak to me when I address you this way?

There is a righteous leader of the monkey troops named Sugríva. Mistreated by his brother, this hero wanders the world in distress. Sent by that illustrious Sugríva, king of monkey chiefs, I have come to you. I am a monkey named
Hánuman. Righteous Sugríva desires friendship with you. 3.20
Know that I am his companion, the monkey-son of the wind god. Wishing to help Sugríva, I have come here from Rishya·muka disguised as a mendicant. I can go wherever I wish in whatever form I choose."

After Hánuman, that skillful speaker, had spoken this way to Rama and Lákshmana, warriors skilled in speech, he said nothing further.

Now, when he heard those words of his, majestic Rama, his face showing delight, spoke to his brother Lákshmana, who stood by his side: "This is the companion of mighty Sugríva, lord of monkeys. Just when I was wishing for him,

3.25 tam abhyabhāṣa, Saumitre, Sugrīva|sacivaṃ kapim
vākyajñaṃ madhurair vākyaiḥ sneha|yuktam ariṃ|damam!»

4.1 Tataḥ prahṛṣṭo Hanumān kṛtyavān iti tad vacaḥ
śrutvā madhura|saṃbhāṣaṃ Sugrīvaṃ manasā gataḥ:
«bhavyo rājy'|āgamas tasya Sugrīvasya mah"|ātmanaḥ.
yad ayaṃ kṛtyavān prāptaḥ kṛtyaṃ c' âitad upāgatam.»
tataḥ parama|saṃhṛṣṭo Hanūmān plavaga'|rṣabhaḥ
pratyuvāca tato vākyaṃ Rāmaṃ vākya|viśāradaḥ:
«kim arthaṃ tvaṃ vanaṃ ghoraṃ
Pampā|kānana|maṇḍitam
āgataḥ s'|ânujo durgaṃ
nānā|vyāla|mṛg'|āyutam?»
4.5 tasya tad vacanaṃ śrutvā Lakṣmaṇo Rāma|coditaḥ
ācacakṣe mah"|ātmānaṃ Rāmaṃ Daśarath'|ātmajam:
«rājā Daśaratho nāma dyutimān dharma|vatsalaḥ.
tasy' âyaṃ pūrvajaḥ putro Rāmo nāma janaiḥ śrutaḥ.
śaraṇyaḥ sarva|bhūtānāṃ pitur nirdeśa|pāragaḥ
vīro Daśarathasy' âyaṃ putrāṇāṃ guṇavattaraḥ.
rājyād bhraṣṭo vane vastuṃ mayā sārdham ih' āgataḥ.
bhāryayā ca mahā|tejāḥ Sītay" ânugato vaśī
dina|kṣaye mahā|tejāḥ prabhay" êva divā|karaḥ.
aham asy' âvaro bhrātā guṇair dāsyam upāgataḥ
kṛtajñasya bahujñasya Lakṣmaṇo nāma nāmataḥ.
4.10 sukh'|ârhasya mah"|ârhasya sarva|bhūta|hit'|ātmanaḥ.
aiśvaryeṇa vihīnasya vana|vās'|āśritasya ca.
rakṣas" âpahṛtā bhāryā rahite kāma|rūpiṇā

he has come to me. Saumítri, subduer of foes, speak with 3.25
kind words to Sugríva's companion, this friendly monkey skilled in speech."

When Hánuman heard this agreeably worded speech, he 4.1
was delighted that Rama had some purpose, and he thought about Sugríva: "Since this man has come with some purpose, great Sugríva will acquire kingship. And this purpose is nearly accomplished."

Thoroughly delighted, that bull among monkeys, Hánuman, skilled in speech, then replied to Rama:

"Why have you come with your younger brother to this terrible and inaccessible forest, adorned with Pampa's groves and full of all kinds of savage beasts?"

At these words, Lákshmana, urged by Rama, presented 4.5
great Rama, son of Dasha·ratha.

"There was a glorious king named Dasha·ratha, devoted to righteousness. This is his eldest son, named Rama, famous among people. A refuge for all beings, this warrior who has followed his father's command is the most excellent of Dasha·ratha's sons. Deprived of kingship, he came to live here in the forest with me. Self-controlled and splendid, he was followed by his wife, Sita, just as at day's end the splendid sun is followed by its own radiance. I am his younger brother, Lákshmana by name. I have become his devoted servant because of his good qualities; for he is grateful, learned, worthy of happiness, very deserving and kindly 4.10
disposed toward all beings. Deprived of sovereignty, he has taken refuge in forest life. While we were absent, his wife

tac ca na jñāyate rakṣaḥ patnī yen' âsya sā hṛtā.
Danur nāma Śriyaḥ putraḥ śāpād rākṣasatāṃ gataḥ.
ākhyātas tena Sugrīvaḥ samartho vānar'|âdhipaḥ.
‹sa jñāsyati mahā|vīryas tava bhāry"|âpahāriṇam.›
evam uktvā Danuḥ svargaṃ bhrājamāno gataḥ sukham.
etat te sarvam ākhyātaṃ yāthātathyena pṛcchataḥ;
ahaṃ c' âiva hi Rāmaś ca Sugrīvaṃ śaraṇaṃ gatau.
4.15 eṣa dattvā ca vittāni prāpya c' ânuttamaṃ yaśaḥ
loka|nāthaḥ purā bhūtvā Sugrīvaṃ nātham icchati.
śok'|âbhibhūte Rāme tu śok'|ārte śaraṇaṃ gate
kartum arhati Sugrīvaḥ prasādaṃ saha yūthapaiḥ.»
evaṃ bruvāṇaṃ Saumitriṃ karuṇaṃ s'|âśru|pātanam
Hanūmān pratyuvāc' êdaṃ vākyaṃ vākya|viśāradaḥ:
«īdṛśā buddhi|saṃpannā jita|krodhā jit'|êndriyāḥ
draṣṭavyā vānar'|êndreṇa. diṣṭyā darśanam āgatāḥ!
sa hi rājyāc ca vibhraṣṭaḥ kṛta|vairaś ca Vālinā.
hṛta|dāro vane trasto bhrātrā vinikṛto bhṛśam.
4.20 kariṣyati sa sāhāyyaṃ yuvayor Bhāskar'|ātmajaḥ
Sugrīvaḥ saha c' âsmābhiḥ Sītāyāḥ parimārgaṇe.»
ity evam uktvā Hanumāñ ślakṣṇaṃ madhurayā girā
babhāṣe so, «'bhigacchāmaḥ Sugrīvam iti» Rāghavam.
evaṃ bruvāṇaṃ dharm'|ātmā Hanūmantaṃ sa Lakṣmaṇaḥ
pratipūjya yathā|nyāyam idaṃ provāca Rāghavam:

was carried off by a *rákshasa* who can change form at will, but we do not know the *rákshasa* who stole his wife.

There was a son of Shri named Danu who through a curse became a *rákshasa*. It was he who informed us about powerful Sugríva. 'The heroic king of the monkeys will know your wife's abductor,' he said. Then radiant Danu went happily to heaven. I have stated all of this truthfully to you, since you ask; for Rama and I have both come to Sugríva for help. Rama, who gave away his riches and achieved 4.15
the highest glory, was formerly a protector of people, but now he needs Sugríva as his protector. And since Rama, overcome and tormented by grief, has come for refuge, Sugríva and his troop leaders should be gracious to him."

Saumítri's tears flowed as he spoke in this piteous way; and Hánuman, skilled in speech, made this reply:

"The lord of monkeys must receive men such as you, for you are intelligent and have subdued both your anger and your passions. How fortunate that you have appeared! For his brother Valin has become hostile toward him and stripped him of royal sovereignty as well. Greatly mistreated and robbed of his wife, he lives frightened in the forest. Su- 4.20
gríva, the son of the sun god, along with us, will help you in your search for Sita."

After speaking in this way, Hánuman with his sweet voice gently said to Rághava: "Let us go to Sugríva." In keeping with custom, righteous Lákshmana respectfully saluted Hánuman, who had spoken in that way, and said this to Rághava:

«kapiḥ kathayate hṛṣṭo yath" âyaṃ Mārut'|ātmajaḥ.
kṛtyavān so 'pi saṃprāptaḥ kṛta|kṛtyo 'si, Rāghava.
prasanna|mukha|varṇaś ca vyaktaṃ hṛṣṭaś ca bhāṣate
n' ânṛtaṃ vakṣyate vīro Hanūmān Mārut'|ātmajaḥ.»

4.25 tataḥ sa tu mahā|prājño Hanūmān Mārut'|ātmajaḥ
jagām' ādāya tau vīrau hari|rājāya Rāghavau.
sa tu vipula|yaśāḥ kapi|pravīraḥ
Pavana|sutaḥ kṛta|kṛtyavat prahṛṣṭaḥ
giri|varam uru|vikramaḥ prayātaḥ
sa śubha|matiḥ saha Rāma|Lakṣmaṇābhyām.

"This cheerful monkey, son of the wind god, is telling the truth. Sugríva, too, has a purpose, so you have achieved your purpose, Rághava. Hánuman is cheerful, his countenance is clear, and he speaks candidly. The warrior son of the wind god would not tell a lie."

Then Hánuman, the wise son of the wind god, went with 4.25
the two Rághava warriors to the king of the monkeys. And now the son of the wind god, that most heroic monkey whose fame was widespread, whose valor was great, and whose mind was pure, set out for that best of mountains with Rama and Lákshmana, rejoicing as if he had already accomplished his purpose.

5–8
RAMA'S ALLIANCE WITH SUGRÍVA

5.1 Ṛśyamūkāt tu Hanumān gatvā taṃ Malayaṃ girim
ācacakṣe tadā vīrau kapi|rājāya Rāghavau:
«ayaṃ Rāmo mahā|prājñaḥ saṃprāpto dṛḍha|vikramaḥ.
Lakṣmaṇena saha bhrātrā Rāmo 'yaṃ satya|vikramaḥ.
Ikṣvākūṇāṃ kule jāto Rāmo Daśarath'|ātmajaḥ.
dharme nigaditaś c' âiva pitur nirdeśa|pālakaḥ.
tasy' âsya vasato 'raṇye niyatasya mah"|ātmanaḥ
rakṣas" âpahṛtā bhāryā sa tvāṃ śaraṇam āgataḥ;
5.5 Rāja|sūy'|Âśva|medhaiś ca Vahnir yen' âbhitarpitaḥ
dakṣiṇāś ca tath" ôtsṛṣṭā gāvaḥ śata|sahasraśaḥ.
tapasā satya|vākyena vasudhā yena pālitā.
strī|hetos tasya putro 'yaṃ Rāmas tvāṃ śaraṇaṃ gataḥ.
bhavatā sakhya|kāmau tau bhrātarau Rāma|Lakṣmaṇau.
pratigṛhy' ârcayasv' êmau pūjanīyatamāv ubhau.»
śrutvā Hanumato vākyaṃ Sugrīvo hṛṣṭa|mānasaḥ.
bhayaṃ sa Rāghavād ghoraṃ prajahau vigata|jvaraḥ.
sa kṛtvā mānuṣaṃ rūpaṃ Sugrīvaḥ plavag'|âdhipaḥ
darśanīyatamo bhūtvā prītyā provāca Rāghavam:
5.10 «bhavān dharma|vinītaś ca vikrāntaḥ sarva|vatsalaḥ.
ākhyātā Vāyu|putreṇa tattvato me bhavad|guṇāḥ.
tan mam' âiv' âiṣa satkāro lābhaś c' âiv' ôttamaḥ, prabho,
yat tvam icchasi sauhārdaṃ vānareṇa mayā saha.
rocate yadi vā sakhyaṃ bāhur eṣa prasāritaḥ.
gṛhyatāṃ pāṇinā pāṇir maryādā vadhyatāṃ dhruvā.»

HÁNUMAN WENT from Rishya·muka to Mount Málaya 5.1
and then announced the two Rághava warriors to the
king of the monkeys.
"This is wise Rama, whose valor is unfailing. This truly
valiant Rama has arrived with his brother Lákshmana. Rama, son of Dasha·ratha, was born in the House of the Ikshvákus. Known for his righteousness, he is carrying out his
father's command. While this great, self-controlled man was
living in the forest, his wife was carried off by a *rákshasa*.
And so he has come to you for help. His father gratified the 5.5
god of fire with the *Raja·suya* and Horse Sacrifices, giving
hundreds of thousands of cows as sacrificial fees. He also
protected the earth through his asceticism and truthfulness.
On account of a woman, this son of his, Rama, has come to
you for help. These brothers, Rama and Lákshmana, desire
friendship with you. Receive them and show honor to them,
for they are both most worthy of respect."
When he heard Hánuman's words, Sugríva was delighted
at heart. Freed from anxiety, he gave up his terrible fear of
Rághava. Sugríva, lord of monkeys, took on a very handsome human form and spoke in a friendly way to Rághava:
"You are valiant, instructed in righteousness, and kind to 5.10
all. Your good qualities have been accurately described to
me by the wind god's son. For me it is indeed an honor and
also a great advantage, lord, that you desire friendship with
me, a monkey. And if such an alliance is agreeable to you,
here is my outstretched arm. Take my hand in yours and let
us make a firm pact."

etat tu vacanaṃ śrutvā Sugrīvasya subhāṣitam
saṃprahṛṣṭa|manā hastaṃ pīḍayām āsa pāṇinā.
hṛdyaṃ sauhṛdam ālambya paryaṣvajata pīḍitam.

tato Hanūmān saṃtyajya bhikṣu|rūpam ariṃ|damaḥ
kāṣṭhayoḥ svena rūpeṇa janayām āsa pāvakam.
5.15 dīpyamānaṃ tato vahniṃ puṣpair abhyarcya satkṛtam.
tayor madhye tu suprīto nidadhe susamāhitaḥ.
tato 'gniṃ dīpyamānaṃ tau cakratuś ca pradakṣiṇam
Sugrīvo Rāghavaś c' âiva vayasyatvam upāgatau.
tataḥ suprīta|manasau tāv ubhau hari|Rāghavau
anyonyam abhivīkṣantau na tṛptim upajagmatuḥ.
tataḥ sarv'|ârtha|vidvāṃsaṃ Rāmaṃ Daśarath'|ātmajam
Sugrīvaḥ prāha tejasvī vākyam eka|manās tadā:

6.1 «Ayam ākhyāti me, Rāma, sacivo mantri|sattamaḥ
Hanumān yan|nimittaṃ tvaṃ nirjanaṃ vanam āgataḥ.
Lakṣmaṇena saha bhrātrā vasataś ca vane tava
rakṣas" âpahṛtā bhāryā Maithilī Janak'|ātmajā.
tvayā viyuktā rudatī Lakṣmaṇena ca dhīmatā
antaraṃ prepsunā tena hatvā gṛdhraṃ Jaṭāyuṣam.

bhāryā|viyoga|jaṃ duḥkhaṃ na cirāt tvaṃ vimokṣyase.
ahaṃ tām ānayiṣyāmi naṣṭāṃ Veda|śrutiṃ yathā.
6.5 rasā|tale vā vartantīṃ vartantīṃ vā nabhas|tale
aham ānīya dāsyāmi tava bhāryām, ariṃ|dama.
idaṃ tathyaṃ mama vacas tvam avehi ca, Rāghava.
tyaja śokaṃ, mahā|bāho, tāṃ kāntām ānayāmi te.

Now, when Rama heard Sugríva's eloquent speech, he was delighted at heart and grasped his hand with his own. Accepting cordial friendship, he embraced him tightly.

Then Hánuman, subduer of foes, gave up his mendicant form and in his own form kindled a fire with two pieces
of wood. He honored the blazing fire, worshiping it with 5.15
flowers. Pleased and composed, he placed it between those two. Then Sugríva and Rághava entered into an alliance by reverently circling the blazing fire. Delighted at heart, the monkey and Rághava could not get their fill of looking at each other. Afterward powerful Sugríva intently spoke these words to Dasha·ratha's son Rama, who understood all things:

"MY COMPANION, the excellent counselor Hánuman, has 6.1
told me why you have come to this uninhabited forest, Rama. While you and your brother were living in the forest, both you and wise Lákshmana left your wife, Máithili, daughter of Jánaka, by herself. A *rákshasa* who was longing for such an opportunity carried her off weeping, after he had first killed the vulture Jatáyus.

You shall soon be released from the sorrow born of this separation from your wife. For I shall bring her back like the
lost Vedas. Whether she is down in the underworld or up 6.5
in the heavens, I shall bring back your wife and give her to you, subduer of your foes. Know that these words of mine are true, Rághava. Give up your grief, great-armed man: I shall bring back your beloved.

anumānāt tu jānāmi Maithilī sā na saṃśayaḥ
hriyamāṇā mayā dṛṣṭā rakṣasā krūra|karmaṇā.
krośantī ‹Rāma, Rām' êti› ‹Lakṣmaṇ' êti› ca visvaram
sphurantī Rāvaṇasy' âṅke pannag'|êndra|vadhūr yathā.
ātmanā pañcamaṃ māṃ hi dṛṣṭvā śaila|taṭe sthitam
uttarīyaṃ tayā tyaktaṃ śubhāny ābharaṇāni ca.
6.10 tāny asmābhir gṛhītāni nihitāni ca, Rāghava,
ānayiṣyāmy ahaṃ tāni pratyabhijñātum arhasi.»

tam abravīt tato Rāmaḥ Sugrīvaṃ priya|vādinam:
«ānayasva, sakhe, śīghraṃ! kim arthaṃ pravilambase?»
evam uktas tu Sugrīvaḥ śailasya gahanāṃ guhām
praviveśa tataḥ śīghraṃ Rāghava|priya|kāmyayā.
uttarīyaṃ gṛhītvā tu śubhāny ābharaṇāni ca
«idaṃ paśy' êti» Rāmāya darśayām āsa vānaraḥ.

tato gṛhītvā tad vāsaḥ śubhāny ābharaṇāni ca
abhavad bāṣpa|saṃruddho nīhāreṇ' êva candramāḥ.
6.15 Sītā|sneha|pravṛttena sa tu bāṣpeṇa dūṣitaḥ.
«hā priy" êti» rudan dhairyam utsṛjya nyapatat kṣitau.
hṛdi kṛtvā sa bahuśas tam alaṃkāram uttamam
niśaśvāsa bhṛśaṃ sarpo bila|stha iva roṣitaḥ.
avicchinn'|âśru|vegas tu Saumitriṃ vīkṣya pārśvataḥ
paridevayituṃ dīnaṃ Rāmaḥ samupacakrame:

«paśya, Lakṣmaṇa, Vaidehyā saṃtyaktaṃ hriyamāṇayā
uttarīyam idaṃ bhūmau śarīrād bhūṣaṇāni ca.
śādvalinyāṃ dhruvaṃ bhūmyāṃ Sītayā hriyamāṇayā
utsṛṣṭaṃ bhūṣaṇam idaṃ tathā|rūpaṃ hi dṛśyate.

I now realize that it was Máithili I saw being carried off by a *rákshasa* of cruel deeds. There is no doubt about it. Struggling in Rávana's embrace like the bride of a serpent-king, she was hoarsely crying, 'Rama, Rama! Lákshmana!' When she saw me and my four companions standing on the mountainside, she dropped her shawl and her bright ornaments. These we took and put away, Rághava. I shall 6.10
bring them. You should be able to recognize them."

Then Rama said to Sugríva, the bearer of good news, "Bring them quickly, my friend. Why do you delay?" At these words, Sugríva, who wished to help Rághava, quickly entered a deep cave in the mountain. The monkey took the shawl and the bright ornaments and showed them to Rama, saying, "Look at this."

Then, as Rama took that garment and the bright ornaments, tears covered his face as mist covers the moon. His 6.15
face was stained with the tears he shed for love of Sita. Crying, "Ah, beloved!" he lost his composure and fell to the ground. Repeatedly he pressed those fine ornaments to his heart and sighed deeply like an angry snake in its burrow. Through an unbroken stream of tears, Rama saw Saumítri by his side and began to lament piteously:

"Look, Lákshmana, here are the shawl and ornaments that Vaidéhi let fall from her body to the ground as she was being carried away. As she was being carried off, Sita must surely have dropped these ornaments onto grassy ground, and that is why they look like this.

6.20 brūhi, Sugrīva, kaṃ deśaṃ hriyantī lakṣitā tvayā
rakṣasā raudra|rūpeṇa mama prāṇa|samā priyā?
kva vā vasati tad rakṣo mahad vyasanadaṃ mama
yan|nimittam ahaṃ sarvān nāśayiṣyāmi rākṣasān?
haratā Maithilīṃ yena māṃ ca roṣayatā bhṛśam
ātmano jīvit'|ântāya mṛtyu|dvāram apāvṛtam.
mama dayitatamā hṛtā vanād
rajani|careṇa vimathya yena sā.
kathaya mama ripuṃ tam adya vai,
plavaga|pate, Yama|saṃnidhiṃ nayāmi.»

7.1 EVAṂ UKTAS tu Sugrīvo Rāmeṇ' ārtena vānaraḥ
abravīt prāñjalir vākyaṃ sa|bāṣpaṃ bāṣpa|gadgadaḥ:
«na jāne nilayaṃ tasya sarvathā pāpa|rakṣasaḥ
sāmarthyaṃ vikramaṃ v" âpi dauṣkuleyasya vā kulam.
satyaṃ tu pratijānāmi, tyaja śokam, ariṃ|dama,
kariṣyāmi tathā yatnaṃ yathā prāpsyasi Maithilīm.
Rāvaṇaṃ sagaṇaṃ hatvā paritoṣy' ātma|pauruṣam
tath" âsmi kartā na cirād yathā prīto bhaviṣyasi.
7.5 alaṃ vaiklavyam ālambya, dhairyam ātma|gataṃ smara.
tvad|vidhānāṃ na sadṛśam īdṛśaṃ buddhi lāghavam.
may" âpi vyasanaṃ prāptaṃ bhāryā|haraṇa|jaṃ mahat
na c' âham evaṃ śocāmi na ca dhairyaṃ parityaje.
n' âhaṃ tām anuśocāmi prākṛto vānaro 'pi san.
mah"|ātmā ca vinītaś cā kiṃ punar dhṛtimān bhavān.

Tell me, Sugríva, when you saw my beloved, who is dear as life to me, where was the fierce-looking *rákshasa* taking her? And where does he live, that *rákshasa* who has brought me such calamity? Because of him, I shall destroy all *rákshasas*. By carrying off Máithili and angering me so deeply, he has opened the door of death and brought his own life to an end. Lord of monkeys, tell me about my enemy, the night-stalker who by deceit carried my dearly beloved wife away from the forest. I shall send him this very day into the presence of Yama, the god of death." 6.20

WHEN SORROWFUL Rama had addressed him in this fashion, the monkey Sugríva cupped his palms in supplication. His voice choked with sobs, he tearfully said these words: 7.1

"I know nothing whatever about this lowborn, evil *rákshasa*'s dwelling, his power, his valor or his family. But I solemnly promise I will make an effort such that you shall regain Máithili. Give up your grief, subduer of your foes. Satisfying you by killing Rávana and his followers, I shall
soon exert my strength so that you will be pleased. Enough 7.5
of this yielding to despair. Remember your own natural composure. Such faintheartedness is unworthy of a man like you.

I, too, have met with great misfortune through the abduction of my wife, yet I do not grieve in this fashion, nor do I abandon my composure. Nor do I grieve over her, though I am just an ordinary monkey. How much less should you, who are great, disciplined and resolute?

bāṣpam āpatitaṃ dhairyān nigrahītuṃ tvam arhasi,
maryādāṃ sattva|yuktānāṃ dhṛtiṃ n' ôtsraṣṭum arhasi.
vyasane v" ârtha|kṛcchre vā bhaye vā jīvit'|ântage
vimṛśan vai svayā buddhyā dhṛtimān n' âvasīdati.
7.10 bāliśas tu naro nityaṃ vaiklavyaṃ yo 'nuvartate
sa majjaty avaśaḥ śoke bhār'|ākrānt" êva naur jale.
eṣo 'ñjalir mayā baddhaḥ praṇayāt tvāṃ prasādaye:
pauruṣaṃ śraya śokasya n' ântaraṃ dātum arhasi!
ye śokam anuvartante na teṣāṃ vidyate sukham
tejaś ca kṣīyate teṣāṃ, na tvaṃ śocitum arhasi.
hitaṃ vayasya|bhāvena brūhi n' ôpadiśāmi te.
vayasyatāṃ pūjayan me na tvaṃ śocitum arhasi.»
madhuraṃ sāntvitas tena Sugrīveṇa sa Rāghavaḥ
mukham aśru|pariklinnaṃ vastr'|ântena pramārjayat.
7.15 prakṛtisthas tu Kākutsthaḥ Sugrīva|vacanāt prabhuḥ
saṃpariṣvajya Sugrīvam idaṃ vacanam abravīt:
«kartavyaṃ yad vayasyena snigdhena ca hitena ca
anurūpaṃ ca yuktaṃ ca kṛtaṃ, Sugrīva, tat tvayā.
eṣa ca prakṛtistho 'ham anunītas tvayā, sakhe,
durlabho h' īdṛśo bandhur asmin kāle viśeṣataḥ.
kiṃ tu yatnas tvayā kāryo Maithilyāḥ parimārgaṇe
rākṣasasya ca raudrasya Rāvaṇasya durātmanaḥ.
mayā ca yad anuṣṭheyaṃ visrabdhena tad ucyatām.
varṣāsv iva ca sukṣetre sarvaṃ saṃpadyate tava.
7.20 mayā ca yad idaṃ vākyam abhimānāt samīritam
tat tvayā, hari|śārdūla, tattvam ity upadhāryatām.
anṛtaṃ n' ôkta pūrvaṃ me na ca vakṣye kadā cana.
etat te pratijānāmi satyen' âiva śapāmi te.»

You should firmly hold back the tears that come. You
should not abandon the fortitude demanded of the strong.
In misfortune or loss of wealth or in mortal danger, the
resolute man deliberates with his own judgment and does
not despair. But the foolish man who always gives way to 7.10
despair sinks helplessly in grief, like an overloaded boat in
water. Here, I cup my palms in supplication. I beseech you
out of affection: Rely upon your manliness. You must not
let grief take hold of you. For those who give way to grief,
there is no happiness, and their strength dwindles away.
You must not grieve. It is out of friendship that I offer this
counsel. I am not telling you what to do. But if you honor
my friendship, you should not grieve."

Gently comforted by Sugríva, Rághava wiped his tear-
drenched face with the edge of his garment. And now lord 7.15
Kákutstha, restored to his normal state by Sugríva's words,
embraced him and said this:

"You have done what is right and proper for a loving
and helpful friend to do, Sugríva. Here I am, my friend,
comforted by you and restored to my normal state. Such a
friend is indeed hard to find, particularly at a time like this.
But now you must make an effort to search for Máithili
and the fierce, evil *rákshasa* Rávana. And you must tell me
without reservation what I am to do for you. Everything
will succeed for you, like crops in a good field during the
rains. And you must regard as the truth those words which 7.20
I proudly spoke, tiger among monkeys. I have never spoken
a falsehood before, nor shall I ever speak one. I promise you
this; I swear it to you by truth itself."

tataḥ prahṛṣṭaḥ Sugrīvo vānaraiḥ sacivaiḥ saha
Rāghavasya vacaḥ śrutvā pratijñātaṃ viśeṣataḥ.
mah"|ânubhāvasya vaco niśamya
harir narāṇām ṛṣabhasya tasya
kṛtaṃ sa mene hari|vīra|mukhyas
tadā sva|kāryaṃ hṛdayena vidvān.

8.1 Parituṣṭas tu Sugrīvas tena vākyena vānaraḥ
Lakṣmaṇasy' âgrajaṃ Rāmam idaṃ vacanam abravīt:
«sarvath" âham anugrāhyo devatānām asaṃśayaḥ
upapanna|guṇ'|ôpetaḥ sakhā yasya bhavān mama.
śakyaṃ khalu bhaved, Rāma, sahāyena tvay" ânagha
sura|rājyam api prāptuṃ sva|rājyaṃ kiṃ punaḥ, prabho!
so 'haṃ sabhājyo bandhūnāṃ suhṛdāṃ c' âiva, Rāghava,
yasy' âgni|sākṣikaṃ mitraṃ labdhaṃ Rāghava|vaṃśa|jam.
8.5 aham apy anurūpas te vayasyo jñāsyase śanaiḥ.
na tu vaktuṃ samartho 'haṃ svayam ātma|gatān guṇān.
mah"|ātmanāṃ tu bhūyiṣṭhaṃ
tvad|vidhānāṃ kṛt'|ātmanām
niścalā bhavati prītir
dhairyam ātmavatām iva.
rajataṃ vā suvarṇaṃ vā vastrāṇy ābharaṇāni vā
avibhaktāni sādhūnām avagacchanti sādhavaḥ.
āḍhyo v" âpi daridro vā duḥkhitaḥ sukhito 'pi vā
nirdoṣo vā sadoṣo vā vayasyaḥ paramā gatiḥ.
dhana|tyāgaḥ sukha|tyāgo deha|tyāgo 'pi vā punaḥ
vayasy' ârthe pravartante snehaṃ dṛṣṭvā tathā|vidham.»
8.10 «tat tath" êty» abravīd Rāmaḥ Sugrīvaṃ priya|vādinam
Lakṣmaṇasy' âgrato lakṣmyā Vāsavasy' êva dhīmataḥ.

Sugríva and his monkey companions were delighted to hear Rághava's words, particularly his promise. When the wise monkey Sugríva, foremost of monkey warriors, heard the words of that mighty bull among men, he felt in his heart that his purpose was already accomplished.

DELIGHTED BY this speech, the monkey Sugríva said these 8.1
words to Lákshmana's older brother, Rama:

"Undoubtedly I am favored by the gods in every way, because you who are endowed with every virtue have become my friend. Blameless Rama, with you as my ally I could surely win even the kingdom of the gods, not to mention my own, lord. Rághava, I deserve the honor of my friends and relatives since I have obtained with fire as my witness an
ally born in the House of the Rághavas. You will gradually 8.5
learn that I, too, am a friend worthy of you. But I myself cannot speak of my own good qualities.

The affection of great, magnanimous men like you is altogether unswerving, like the composure of the self-possessed. Good friends regard their own silver, gold, clothes and ornaments as belonging to their good friends as well. Rich or poor, happy or unhappy, guiltless or guilty, a friend is the ultimate refuge. For the sake of a friend, one would sacrifice wealth, happiness or even life itself once one has seen such affection."

"That is so," said Rama to Sugríva, whose welcome words 8.10
were spoken before wise Lákshmana, splendid as Indra Vásava.

tato Rāmaṃ sthitaṃ dṛṣṭvā Lakṣmaṇaṃ ca mahā|balam
Sugrīvaḥ sarvataś cakṣur vane lolam apātayat.
sa dadarśa tataḥ sālam avidūre har'|īśvaraḥ
supuṣpam īṣat|patr'|āḍhyaṃ bhramarair upaśobhitam.
tasy' âikāṃ parṇa|bahulāṃ bhaṅktvā śākhāṃ supuṣpitām
sālasy' āstīrya Sugrīvo niṣasāda sa|Rāghavaḥ.
tāv āsīnau tato dṛṣṭvā Hanūmān api Lakṣmaṇam
sāla|śākhāṃ samutpāṭya vinītam upaveśayat.
8.15 tataḥ prahṛṣṭaḥ Sugrīvaḥ ślakṣṇaṃ madhurayā girā
uvāca praṇayād Rāmaṃ harṣa|vyākulit'|âkṣaram:
«ahaṃ vinikṛto bhrātrā carāmy eṣa bhay'|ârditaḥ
Ṛśyamūkaṃ giri|varaṃ hṛta|bhāryaḥ su|duḥkhitaḥ.
so 'haṃ trasto bhaye magno vasāmy udbhrānta|cetanaḥ
Vālinā nikṛto bhrātrā kṛta|vairaś ca Rāghava.
Vālino me bhay'|ārtasya, sarva|lok'|âbhayaṃ|kara,
mam' âpi tvam anāthasya prasādaṃ kartum arhasi!»
evam uktas tu tejasvī dharmajño dharma|vatsalaḥ
pratyuvāca sa Kākutsthaḥ Sugrīvaṃ prahasann iva:
8.20 «upakāra|phalaṃ mitram apakāro 'ri|lakṣaṇam.
ady' âiva taṃ haniṣyāmi tava bhāry"|âpahāriṇam.
ime hi me mahā|vegāḥ patriṇas tigma|tejasaḥ
Kārtikeya|van'|ôdbhūtāḥ śarā hema|vibhūṣitāḥ
kaṅka|patra|praticchannā Mahendr'|âśani|saṃnibhāḥ
suparvāṇaḥ sutīkṣṇ'|âgrā sa|roṣā bhujagā iva.
bhrātṛ|saṃjñam amitraṃ te Vālinaṃ kṛta|kilbiṣam
śarair vinihataṃ paśya vikīrṇam iva parvatam.»

Then, seeing that Rama and mighty Lákshmana were standing, Sugríva eagerly cast his eyes all about the forest. The lord of monkeys saw a *sala* tree nearby with lovely blossoms, full of leafy shoots and graced with bees. From that *sala* tree Sugríva broke off a beautifully blossoming branch with many leaves. He spread it out and sat down on it with Rama. Then, seeing those two seated, Hánuman as well tore off a *sala* branch and made modest Lákshmana sit down. Then, with a sweet voice, his words agitated 8.15
with excitement, the delighted Sugríva spoke gently and affectionately to Rama:

"Mistreated by my brother, robbed of my wife, here I am, unhappy and tormented by fear, roaming this great mountain Rishya·muka. Wronged and shown hostility by my brother Valin, I live terrified, sunk in fear, my mind distracted, Rághava. You who give freedom from fear to everyone, please be gracious to me, too, for I am oppressed with fear of Valin and have no one to protect me."

Addressed in this fashion, powerful Kákutstha, who was devoted to righteousness and knew what was right, smiled slightly and replied to Sugríva:

"A friend is helpful, an enemy hurtful. This very day I 8.20
shall kill your wife's abductor. For here are my sharp-edged, winged arrows of great speed, born in Kartikéya's bed of reeds, decorated with gold, heron-feathered, well jointed, and with very sharp points, like great Indra's thunderbolts or angry serpents. You shall see your enemy Valin, who calls himself a brother but has wronged you so, brought down by my arrows, like a mountain torn apart."

Rāghavasya vacaḥ śrutvā Sugrīvo vāhinī|patiḥ
praharṣam atulaṃ lebhe «sādhu sādhv iti» c' âbravīt.
8.25 «Rāma, śok'|âbhibhūto 'haṃ śok'|ārtānāṃ bhavān gatiḥ.
vayasya iti kṛtvā hi tvayy ahaṃ paridevaye.
tvaṃ hi pāṇi|pradānena vayasyo so 'gni|sākṣikaḥ
kṛtaḥ prāṇair bahu|mataḥ satyen' âpi śapāmy aham.
vayasya iti kṛtvā ca visrabdhaṃ pravadāmy aham
duḥkham antar|gataṃ yan me mano dahati nityaśaḥ.»

etāvad uktvā vacanaṃ bāṣpa|dūṣita|locanaḥ
bāṣp'|ôpahatayā vācā n' ôccaiḥ śaknoti bhāṣitum.
bāṣpa|vegaṃ tu sahasā nadī|vegam iv' āgatam
dhārayām āsa dhairyeṇa Sugrīvo Rāma|saṃnidhau.
8.30 saṃnigṛhya tu taṃ bāṣpaṃ pramṛjya nayane śubhe
viniḥśvasya ca tejasvī Rāghavaṃ punar abravīt:

«pur" âhaṃ Vālinā, Rāma, rājyāt svād avaropitaḥ
paruṣāṇi ca saṃśrāvya nirdhūto 'smi balīyasā.
hṛtā bhāryā ca me tena prāṇebhyo 'pi garīyasī
suhṛdaś ca madīyā ye saṃyatā bandhaneṣu te.
yatnavāṃś ca suduṣṭ'|ātmā mad|vināśāya, Rāghava,
bahuśas tat|prayuktāś ca vānarā nihatā mayā.
śaṅkayā tv etayā c' âhaṃ dṛṣṭvā tvām api, Rāghava.
n' ôpasarpāmy ahaṃ bhīto bhaye sarve hi bibhyati.
8.35 kevalaṃ hi sahāyā me Hanumat|pramukhās tv ime.
ato 'haṃ dhārayāmy adya prāṇān kṛcchra|gato 'pi san.
ete hi kapayaḥ snigdhā māṃ rakṣanti samantataḥ.
saha gacchanti gantavye nityaṃ tiṣṭhanti ca sthite.

When he heard Rághava's words, the army leader Sugríva
felt unequaled joy and cried, "Excellent! Excellent! Rama, 8.25
I have been overwhelmed by grief, and you are the refuge of the grief-stricken. It is because I regard you as my friend that I lament before you. For by offering me your hand with fire as witness you have become my friend. I swear by truth itself that I value you more than my own life. It is because I regard you as my friend that I confidently express the inner sorrow that constantly torments my mind."

But when with tear-filled eyes and tear-choked voice he had said that much, he could speak no further. Still, since Rama was there, Sugríva resolutely checked the rush of his tears, which had come as suddenly as the rushing of a river.
Holding back his tears, wiping his bright eyes and sighing 8.30
deeply, the powerful monkey addressed Rághava once again:

"Some time ago, Rama, Valin deprived me of kingship. Since he was the stronger, he drove me out with harsh words. He took my wife, who is dearer to me than life itself, and imprisoned my friends. And that evil-minded creature is still trying to destroy me, Rághava. I have often had to kill monkeys he has sent out. So when I saw you, Rághava, I was suspicious and too frightened to approach. For when
danger threatens, everyone is fearful. My only companions 8.35
are these led by Hánuman. Nonetheless, I manage to survive even in these difficult circumstances. For these affectionate monkeys protect me on all sides. When I must go they go along, and when I stay they always stay with me.

saṃkṣepas tv eṣa me, Rāma, kim uktvā vistaraṃ hi te?
sa me jyeṣṭho ripur bhrātā Vālī viśruta|pauruṣaḥ.
tad|vināśādd hi me duḥkhaṃ pranaṣṭaṃ syād anantaram.
sukhaṃ me jīvitaṃ c' âiva tad|vināśa|nibandhanam.
eṣa me, Rāma, śok'|ântaḥ śok'|ārtena niveditaḥ.
duḥkhito 'duḥkhito v" âpi sakhyur nityaṃ sakhā gatiḥ.»
8.40 śrutv" âitac ca vaco Rāmaḥ Sugrīvam idam abravīt:
«kiṃ|nimittam abhūd vairaṃ? śrotum icchāmi tattvataḥ.
sukhaṃ hi kāraṇaṃ śrutvā vairasya tava, vānara,
ānantaryaṃ vidhāsyāmi saṃpradhārya bal'|âbalam.
balavān hi mam' âmarṣaḥ śrutvā tvām avamānitam
vardhate hṛday'|ôtkampī prāvṛḍ|vega iv' âmbhasaḥ.
hṛṣṭaḥ kathaya visrabdho yāvad āropyate dhanuḥ
sṛṣṭaś ca hi mayā bāṇo nirastaś ca ripus tava.»
evam uktas tu Sugrīvaḥ Kākutsthena mah"|ātmanā
praharṣam atulaṃ lebhe caturbhiḥ saha vānaraiḥ.
8.45 tataḥ prahṛṣṭa|vadanaḥ Sugrīvo Lakṣmaṇ'|âgraje
vairasya kāraṇaṃ tattvam ākhyātum upacakrame.

What use is it to tell you the details, Rama? This is the story in brief: My older brother Valin, famed for his great strength, has become my enemy. With his destruction, my suffering would vanish at once. My happiness and even my life itself are bound up with his destruction. Grief-stricken, I have explained how my grief can be ended, Rama. Happy or unhappy, a friend is always the refuge of his friend."

When he had heard this speech, Rama said to Sugríva: "I 8.40
should like to hear the true cause of this hostility. For when I have heard the reason for your hostility and determined your strength or weakness, monkey, I shall willingly do whatever must be done next. For when I hear how you were insulted, the strong indignation that stirs my heart swells, like the rushing water during the rains. Speak freely and in happiness while I string my bow. For the moment I loose my arrow your enemy will be destroyed."

When great Kákutstha addressed them in this way, Sugríva and the other four monkeys felt incomparable joy. Then, 8.45
with joy showing on his face, Sugríva began to explain to Lákshmana's older brother the true cause of the hostility.

9–10
HOSTILITY BETWEEN BROTHERS

9.1 «Vālī nāma mama bhrātā jyeṣṭhaḥ śatru|niṣūdanaḥ
pitur bahu|mato nityaṃ mama c' âpi tathā purā.
pitary uparate 'smākaṃ jyeṣṭho 'yam iti mantribhiḥ
kapīnām īśvaro rājye kṛtaḥ parama|saṃmataḥ.
rājyaṃ praśāsatas tasya pitṛ|paitāmahaṃ mahat
ahaṃ sarveṣu kāleṣu praṇataḥ preṣyavat sthitaḥ.

Māyāvī nāma tejasvī pūrvajo Dundubheḥ sutaḥ
tena tasya mahad vairaṃ strī|kṛtaṃ viśrutaṃ purā.
9.5 sa tu supte jane rātrau Kiṣkindhā|dvāram āgataḥ.
nardati sma susaṃrabdho Vālinaṃ c' āhvayad raṇe.
prasuptas tu mama bhrātā narditaṃ bhairava|svanam
śrutvā na mamṛṣe Vālī niṣpapāta javāt tadā.
sa tu vai niḥsṛtaḥ krodhāt taṃ hantum asur'|ôttamam
vāryamāṇas tataḥ strībhir mayā ca praṇat'|ātmanā.
sa tu nirdhūya sarvān no nirjagāma mahā|balaḥ.
tato 'ham api sauhārdān niḥsṛto Vālinā saha.

sa tu me bhrātaraṃ dṛṣṭvā māṃ ca dūrād avasthitam
asuro jāta|saṃtrāsaḥ pradudrāva tadā bhṛśam.
9.10 tasmin dravati saṃtraste hy āvāṃ drutataraṃ gatau
prakāśo 'pi kṛto mārgaś candreṇ' ôdgacchatā tadā.
sa tṛṇair āvṛtaṃ durgaṃ dharaṇyā vivaraṃ mahat.
praviveś' âsuro vegād āvām āsādya viṣṭhitau.
taṃ praviṣṭaṃ ripuṃ dṛṣṭvā bilaṃ roṣa|vaśaṃ gataḥ.
mām uvāca tadā Vālī vacanaṃ kṣubhit'|êndriyaḥ:

"MY OLDER BROTHER Valin, slayer of his enemies, 9.1
was always highly regarded by our father and by
me as well, in former times. Because he was the elder, the
counselors placed him on the throne as the greatly respected
lord of monkeys when our father died. And while he governed our great ancestral kingdom, I stood by humbly at all times, like a servant.

Now, it is well known that because of a woman there
was great hostility in former times between Valin and the
firstborn son of Dúndubhi, powerful Mayávin. One night 9.5
when people were asleep, he came to the gates of Kishkíndha. Roaring angrily, he challenged Valin to battle. Now, my brother Valin, who was asleep, could not bear it when he heard that frightful-sounding roar, and he quickly rushed out. As he left in a rage to kill that great *ásura*, the women and I respectfully tried to restrain him. But the powerful monkey brushed all of us aside and went out. So out of affection I followed Valin.

Now, when the *ásura* saw from afar my brother and me
taking a stand, he grew frightened and quickly ran away.
And though he ran in terror, the two of us ran faster still, 9.10
for the road was well lit by the rising moon. But the *ásura* plunged into a great cavern in the ground which was hard to reach and covered with grass. The two of us reached the entrance and stopped. When he saw his enemy enter that cavern, Valin gave way to anger. With passions churning, he said these words to me:

‹iha tvaṃ tiṣṭha, Sugrīva, bila|dvāri samāhitaḥ
yāvad atra praviśy' âhaṃ nihanmi samare ripum.›
mayā tv etad vacaḥ śrutvā yācitaḥ sa, paraṃ|tapa,
śāpayitvā ca māṃ padbhyāṃ praviveśa bilaṃ tadā.
9.15 tasya praviṣṭasya bilaṃ s'|âgraḥ saṃvatsaro gataḥ
sthitasya ca mama dvāri sa kālo vyatyavartata.
ahaṃ tu naṣṭaṃ taṃ jñātvā snehād āgata|saṃbhramaḥ
bhrātaraṃ na hi paśyāmi pāpa|śaṅki ca me manaḥ.
atha dīrghasya kālasya bilāt tasmād viniḥsṛtam
sa|phenaṃ rudhiraṃ raktam ahaṃ dṛṣṭvā su|duḥkhitaḥ.
nardatām asurāṇāṃ ca dhvanir me śrotram āgataḥ
nirastasya ca saṃgrāme krośato niḥsvano guroḥ.
ahaṃ tv avagato buddhyā cihnais tair bhrātaraṃ hatam
pidhāya ca bila|dvāraṃ śilayā giri|mātrayā.
śok'|ārtaś c' ôdakaṃ kṛtvā Kiṣkindhām āgataḥ, sakhe.
9.20 gūhamānasya me tattvaṃ yatnato mantribhiḥ śrutam.
tato 'haṃ taiḥ samāgamya sametair abhiṣecitaḥ.
rājyaṃ praśāsatas tasya nyāyato mama, Rāghava,
ājagāma ripuṃ hatvā Vālī tam asur'|ôttamam.
abhiṣiktaṃ tu māṃ dṛṣṭvā krodhāt saṃrakta|locanaḥ
madīyān mantriṇo baddhvā paruṣaṃ vākyam abravīt.
nigrahe 'pi samarthasya taṃ pāpaṃ prati, Rāghava,
na prāvartata me buddhir bhrātṛ|gaurava|yantritā.
mānayaṃs taṃ mah"|ātmānaṃ yathāvac c' âbhyavādayam
uktāś ca n' āśiṣas tena saṃtuṣṭen' ântar|ātmanā.»

'Wait here attentively at the entrance to this cavern, Sugríva, while I go in there and kill my enemy in battle.'

When I heard his words, scorcher of foes, I begged him not to go; but he made me swear by his feet and then entered
the cavern. An entire year passed while he was inside the 9.15
cavern, and I remained at the entrance as that time went by. In my affection for him, I became anxious and believed my brother was dead, for I did not see him, and my mind feared the worst.

Then, after a long time, I saw red foaming blood gush from the cavern, and I was in anguish. And to my ears came the echo of *ásuras* roaring and the sound of my elder brother crying out. Now, judging by these signs that my brother was slain, I blocked the entrance to the cavern with a rock the size of a mountain. Grief-stricken, I offered funeral libations for him and returned to Kishkíndha, my friend.

With effort his counselors got the truth from me, though 9.20
I tried to conceal it. Then they assembled and together had me consecrated. But while I was lawfully governing his kingdom, Rághava, back came Valin, having in fact killed his enemy the great *ásura*. Now, when he saw I had been consecrated, his eyes turned red with anger. He imprisoned my counselors and spoke abusively to me. Though I could have had him punished, Rághava, my heart was restrained by respect for a brother, and I could not act against that evil creature. Honoring that great monkey, I greeted him respectfully, as was proper; but he was not satisfied and would not pronounce blessings on me."

10.1 «TATAḤ KRODHA|samāviṣṭaṃ saṃrabdhaṃ tam upāgatam
aham prasādayām cakre bhrātaram priya|kāmyayā:
‹diṣṭy" âsi kuśalī prāpto nihataś ca tvayā ripuḥ!
anāthasya hi me nāthas tvam eko 'nātha|nandanaḥ.
idaṃ bahu|śalākaṃ te pūrṇa|candram iv' ôditam
chatraṃ sa|vāla|vyajanaṃ pratīcchasva may" ôdyatam.
tvam eva rājā mān'|ârhaḥ sadā c' âhaṃ yathā purā,
nyāsa|bhūtam idaṃ rājyaṃ tava niryātayāmy aham.
10.5 mā ca roṣaṃ kṛthāḥ, saumya, mayi, śatru|nibarhaṇa,
yāce tvāṃ śirasā, rājan, mayā baddho 'yam añjaliḥ.
balād asmi samāgamya mantribhiḥ pura|vāsibhiḥ
rāja|bhāve niyukto 'haṃ śūnya|deśa|jigīṣayā.›
snigdham evaṃ bruvāṇaṃ māṃ
sa tu nirbhartsya vānaraḥ
‹dhik tvām iti› ca māṃ uktvā
bahu tat tad uvāca ha.
prakṛtīś ca samānīya mantriṇaś c' âiva saṃmatān
mām āha suhṛdāṃ madhye vākyaṃ parama|garhitam:
‹viditaṃ vo yathā rātrau Māyāvī sa mah"|âsuraḥ
māṃ samāhvayata krūro yuddh'|ākāṅkṣī su|durmatiḥ.
10.10 tasya tad garjitaṃ śrutvā niḥsṛto 'haṃ nṛp'|ālayāt
anuyātaś ca māṃ tūrṇam ayaṃ bhrātā sudāruṇaḥ.
sa tu dṛṣṭv" âiva māṃ rātrau sadvitīyaṃ mahā|balaḥ
prādravad bhaya|saṃtrasto vīkṣy' āvāṃ tam anudrutau
anudrutas tu vegena praviveśa mahā|bilam.
taṃ praviṣṭaṃ viditvā tu sughoraṃ sumahad bilam
ayam ukto 'tha me bhrātā mayā tu krūra|darśanaḥ:

"Hoping to please him, I tried to appease my enraged 10.1
brother who had arrived so filled with anger.

'Fortunately, you have killed your enemy and arrived
safely! For you, joy of the unprotected, are the only protector
for me, who has no one to protect me. Accept this many-
ribbed umbrella like a full moon on high and these yak-tail
fans, which I offer you. You alone are king and worthy of
honor. I am just as I always was before. I restore to you this
kingdom, which I merely held in trust. Do not be angry with 10.5
me, gentle king, slaughterer of your enemies. I beg you with
bowed head and with palms cupped in supplication.

I was forcibly appointed to the rank of king by the assembled counselors and people of the city, lest the kingless country tempt someone.'

But though I spoke affectionately, that monkey abused me and said to me, 'Damn you!' and many other things of that sort. He brought together citizens and respected counselors, and in the midst of my close friends he said the vilest things about me:

'You all know how cruel, wicked-minded Mayávin, the
great *ásura*, wishing to do battle, challenged me that night.
When I heard his roar, I came out of my palace, and this 10.10
fearsome brother of mine quickly followed me. But as soon
as the mighty *ásura* saw me in the night with a companion,
he ran off terrified. When he saw the two of us running
after him, he rushed, pursued by us, into a great cavern.
When I realized that he had entered that great and terrible
cavern, I spoke to this brother of mine who was plotting a
cruel deed:

«ahatvā n' âsti me śaktiḥ pratigantum itaḥ purīm.
bila|dvāri pratīkṣa tvaṃ yāvad enaṃ nihanmy aham.»
  sthito 'yam iti matvā tu praviṣṭo 'haṃ durāsadam.
taṃ ca me mārgamāṇasya gataḥ saṃvatsaras tadā.
10.15 sa tu dṛṣṭo mayā śatrur anirvedād bhay'|āvahaḥ
nihataś ca mayā tatra so 'suro bandhubhiḥ saha.
tasy' âsyāt tu pravṛttena rudhir'|âugheṇa tad bilam
pūrṇam āsīd durākrāmaṃ stanatas tasya bhū|tale.
sūdayitvā tu taṃ śatruṃ vikrāntaṃ Dundubheḥ sutam
niṣkrāmann eva paśyāmi bilasya pihitaṃ mukham.
vikrośamānasya tu me, «Sugrīv' êti,» punaḥ punaḥ.
yadā prativaco n' âsti tato 'haṃ bhṛśa|duḥkhitaḥ.
pāda prahārais tu mayā bahuśas tad vidāritam.
tato 'haṃ tena niṣkramya yathā punar upāgataḥ.
10.20 tatr' ânen' âsmi saṃruddho rājyaṃ mārgayat" ātmanaḥ
Sugrīveṇa nṛśaṃsena vismṛtya bhrātṛ|sauhṛdam.›
  evam uktvā tu māṃ tatra vastreṇ' âikena vānaraḥ
tadā nirvāsayām āsa Vālī vigata|sādhvasaḥ.
ten' âham apaviddhaś ca hṛta|dāraś ca, Rāghava,
tad|bhayāc ca mahī kṛtsnā krānt" êyaṃ sa|van'|ârṇavā.
Ṛśyamūkaṃ giri|varaṃ bhāryā|haraṇa|duḥkhitaḥ
praviṣṭo 'smi durādharṣaṃ Vālinaḥ kāraṇ'|ântare.
etat te sarvam ākhyātaṃ vair'|ânukathanaṃ mahat,
anāgasā mayā prāptaṃ vyasanaṃ paśya, Rāghava!
10.25 Vālinas tu bhay'|ārtasya, sarva|lok'|âbhayaṃ|kara,
kartum arhasi me, vīra, prasādaṃ tasya nigrahāt.»

"I cannot return to the city without destroying the *ásura*. Wait at the entrance to the cavern while I kill him."

Thinking that Sugríva was standing by, I went into that
formidable cavern. And while I was searching for Mayávin,
a year went by. But because I did not despair, I found and 10.15
killed that fearsome *ásura* enemy together with his kinsmen.
Then the cavern became impassable, filled with a stream of
blood flowing from his mouth as he roared underground.
As I made my way out after killing my enemy, Dúndubhi's
valiant son, I could not see the mouth of the cavern at all,
for it had been blocked. I cried out, "Sugríva!" again and
again. When there was no response, I was deeply distressed.
But with repeated kicks I managed to break through. Then
I came out that way and returned here. I was shut in there 10.20
by this malicious Sugríva who, unmindful of brotherly affection, sought the kingdom for himself.'

And with those words the monkey Valin, unperturbed,
then banished me with nothing but a single garment. He
drove me away and took my wife, Rághava; and in fear of
him I have traversed this entire earth with its forests and
oceans. Sorrowing on account of the abduction of my wife,
I came to Rishya·muka, best of mountains, which for an un-
related reason Valin cannot approach. Now I have told you
the whole long story of our quarrel. Just see, Rághava, the
calamity that has befallen me though I am blameless. Hero, 10.25
you grant freedom from fear to everyone. Please be gracious
to me and punish Valin, for fear of him oppresses me."

evam uktaḥ sa tejasvī dharmajño dharma|saṃhitam
vacanaṃ vaktum ārebhe Sugrīvaṃ prahasann iva:
«amoghāḥ sūrya|saṃkāśā mam' ême niśitāḥ śarāḥ
tasmin Vālini durvṛtte patiṣyanti ruṣ" ânvitāḥ.
yāvat taṃ na hi paśyeyaṃ tava bhāry"|âpahāriṇam,
tāvat sa jīvet pāp'|ātmā Vālī cāritra|dūṣakaḥ.
ātm' ânumānāt paśyāmi magnaṃ tvāṃ śoka|sāgare
tvām ahaṃ tārayiṣyāmi kāmaṃ prāpsyasi puṣkalam.»

Addressed in this way, the powerful knower of righteousness smiled slightly and began to speak to Sugríva words consistent with righteousness:

"These unfailing arrows of mine, sharp, angry, bright as the sun, shall fall on that evildoer Valin. Sinful Valin has violated all decency by taking your wife. He shall remain alive only as long as I do not see him. I realize from my own experience that you are plunged in an ocean of grief. But I will rescue you from it, and you shall attain all that you desire."

11–13
CONFUSION IN COMBAT

11.1 RĀMASYA VACANAṂ śrutvā harṣa|pauruṣa|vardhanam
Sugrīvaḥ pūjayāṃ cakre Rāghavaṃ praśaśaṃsa ca:
«asaṃśayaṃ prajvalitais tīkṣṇair marm'|âtigaiḥ śaraiḥ
tvaṃ daheḥ kupito lokān yug'|ânta iva bhāskaraḥ.
Vālinaḥ pauruṣaṃ yat tad yac ca vīryaṃ dhṛtiś ca yā
tan mam' âika|manāḥ śrutvā vidhatsva yad anantaram.
samudrāt paścimāt pūrvaṃ dakṣiṇād api c' ôttaram
krāmaty anudite sūrye Vālī vyapagata|klamaḥ.
11.5 agrāṇy āruhya śailānāṃ śikharāṇi mahānty api
ūrdhvam utkṣipya tarasā pratigṛhṇāti vīryavān.
bahavaḥ sāravantaś ca vaneṣu vividhā drumāḥ
Vālinā tarasā bhagnā balaṃ prathayat" ātmanaḥ.
mahiṣo Dundubhir nāma Kailāsa|śikhara|prabhaḥ
balaṃ nāga|sahasrasya dhārayām āsa vīryavān.
vīry'|ôtsekena duṣṭ'|ātmā vara|dānāc ca mohitaḥ
jagāma sa mahā|kāyaḥ samudraṃ saritāṃ patim.
ūrmimantam atikramya sāgaraṃ ratna|saṃcayam
‹mama yuddhaṃ prayacch' êti› tam uvāca mah"|ârṇavam.
11.10 tataḥ samudro dharm'|ātmā samutthāya mahā|balaḥ
abravīd vacanaṃ, rājann, asuraṃ kāla|coditam.
‹samartho n' âsmi te dātuṃ yuddhaṃ, yuddha|viśārada,
śrūyatām abhidhāsyāmi yas te yuddhaṃ pradāsyati.
śaila|rājo mah"|âraṇye tapasvi|śaraṇaṃ param
Śaṃkara|śvaśuro nāmnā Himavān iti viśrutaḥ.
guhā|prasravaṇ'|ôpeto bahu|kandara|nirjharaḥ
sa samarthas tava prītim atulāṃ kartum āhave.›

When he had heard Rama's words, which increased 11.1
both his joy and his courage, Sugríva honored Rághava and praised him:
"With your blazing, sharp arrows, which can pierce vital organs, you could no doubt, when angry, burn up the
three worlds, like the sun at the end of the cosmic cycle.
Listen attentively as I describe Valin's manliness, heroism
and fortitude. Then afterward do what must be done.
Before the sun rises, Valin strides from the western to
the eastern ocean and from the southern to the northern
ocean without tiring. Mighty Valin climbs to the tops of 11.5
mountains, swiftly tosses even their huge peaks upward and
then catches them again. And in forests Valin displays his
strength by swiftly shattering all sorts of mighty trees.
There was a mighty buffalo-*ásura* named Dúndubhi, big
as the peak of Mount Kailása, who possessed the strength
of a thousand elephants. Corrupted by pride in his might
and deluded by a boon granted to him, that gigantic creature went to the ocean, the lord of rivers. Confronting the
billowing sea with its hoard of gems, he said to that great
ocean, 'Come, fight with me!' Then, king, the righteous 11.10
mighty ocean rose up and said these words to that *ásura*
who was driven by fate:
'I cannot do battle with you, who are skillful in battle.
But listen; I shall name one who will give you battle. In
a great forest stands the king of mountains, the father-in-
law of Shánkara, the supreme refuge of ascetics known as
Himálaya. With his caverns and cascades, with his many
caves and waterfalls, he is capable of giving you unrivaled
satisfaction in battle.'

tam bhītam iti vijñāya samudram asur'|ôttamaḥ
Himavad|vanam āgacchac charaś cāpād iva cyutaḥ.
11.15 tatas tasya gireḥ śvetā gaj'|êndra|vipulāḥ śilāḥ
cikṣepa bahudhā bhūmau Dundubhir vinanāda ca.
tataḥ śvet'|âmbud'|ākāraḥ saumyaḥ prīti|kar'|ākṛtiḥ
Himavān abravīd vākyaṃ sva eva śikhare sthitaḥ:
‹kleṣṭum arhasi māṃ na tvaṃ, Dundubhe dharma|vatsala,
raṇa|karmasv akuśalas tapasvi|śaraṇaṃ hy aham.›
tasya tad vacanaṃ śrutvā giri|rājasya dhīmataḥ
uvāca Dundubhir vākyaṃ krodhāt saṃrakta|locanaḥ:
‹yadi yuddhe 'samarthas tvaṃ mad|bhayād vā nirudyamaḥ
tam ācakṣva pradadyān me yo 'dya yuddhaṃ yuyutsataḥ!›
11.20 Himavān abravīd vākyaṃ śrutvā vākya|viśāradaḥ
an|ukta|pūrvaṃ dharm'|ātmā krodhāt tam asur'|ôttamam:
‹Vālī nāma mahā|prājñaḥ Śakra|tulya|parākramaḥ
adhyāste vānaraḥ śrīmān Kiṣkindhām atula|prabhām.
sa samartho mahā|prājñas tava yuddha|viśāradaḥ
dvandva|yuddhaṃ mahad dātum Namucer iva Vāsavaḥ.
taṃ śīghram abhigaccha tvaṃ yadi yuddham ih' êcchasi
sa hi durdharṣaṇo nityaṃ śūraḥ samara|karmaṇi.›
śrutvā Himavato vākyaṃ krodh'|āviṣṭaḥ sa Dundubhiḥ
jagāma tāṃ purīṃ tasya Kiṣkindhāṃ Vālinas tadā.
11.25 dhārayan māhiṣaṃ rūpaṃ tīkṣṇa|śṛṅgo bhay'|āvahaḥ
prāvṛṣ' îva mahā|meghas toya|pūrṇo nabhas|tale.
tatas tu dvāram āgamya Kiṣkindhāyā mahā|balaḥ
nanarda kampayan bhūmiṃ Dundubhir dundubhir yathā;

Considering the ocean to be frightened, that best of *á-*
suras went like an arrow loosed from a bow to the forest
of the mountain Himálaya. With a roar Dúndubhi hurled 11.15
from that mountain to the earth many white boulders, as
big as the king of elephants. Then gentle Himálaya, in the
form of a friendly-looking white cloud resting on his own
summit, spoke these words: 'Dúndubhi, you are devoted
to righteousness. You should not trouble me, the refuge of
ascetics, for I am unskilled in warfare.'

Hearing this speech of the wise king of mountains, Dúndubhi, red-eyed with anger, spoke these words: 'If you are
incapable of battle or paralyzed through fear of me, name
someone who can give battle to me today, for I am eager
to fight.'

When righteous Himálaya, skilled in speech, heard that 11.20
unprecedented speech, he replied in anger to that best of
ásuras: 'In Kishkíndha, unequaled in splendor, there dwells
a wise and majestic monkey named Valin, whose prowess is
equal to Shakra's. Wise and skilled in battle, he is capable
of offering you great single combat, just as Indra Vásava did
to Námuchi. Go to him quickly if you desire battle now,
for he is invincible and always heroic in warfare.'

When he heard Himálaya's words, Dúndubhi went in
a fury to Valin's city, Kishkíndha. Taking the form of a 11.25
terrifying, sharp-horned buffalo, he looked like a huge cloud
laden with rain in the monsoon sky. Then mighty Dúndubhi reached Kishkíndha's gate and roared like a great
kettledrum, making the earth tremble; and he broke the
trees growing nearby, tearing up the ground with his hooves,

samīpajān drumān bhañjan vasudhāṃ dārayan khuraiḥ
viṣāṇen' ôllekhan darpāt tad dvāraṃ dvirado yathā.
antaḥ|pura|gato Vālī śrutvā śabdam amarṣaṇaḥ
niṣpapāta saha strībhis tārābhir iva candramāḥ.
mitaṃ vyakt'|âkṣara|padaṃ tam uvāca sa Dundubhim
harīṇām īśvaro Vālī sarveṣāṃ vana|cāriṇām:
11.30 ‹kim arthaṃ nagara|dvāram idaṃ ruddhvā vinardasi?
Dundubhe vidito me 'si. rakṣa prāṇān mahā|bala!›
tasya tad vacanaṃ śrutvā vānar'|êndrasya dhīmataḥ
uvāca Dundubhir vākyaṃ krodhāt saṃrakta|locanaḥ:
‹na tvaṃ strī|saṃnidhau, vīra, vacanaṃ vaktum arhasi.
mama yuddhaṃ prayaccha! tvaṃ tato jñāsyāmi te balam.
athavā dhārayiṣyāmi krodham adya niśām imām?
gṛhyatām udayaḥ svairaṃ kāma|bhogeṣu, vānara!
yo hi mattaṃ pramattaṃ vā suptaṃ vā rahitaṃ bhṛśam
hanyāt sa bhrūṇa|hā loke tvad|vidhaṃ mada|mohitam.›
11.35 sa prahasy' âbravīn mandaṃ krodhāt tam asur'|ôttamam
visṛjya tāḥ striyaḥ sarvās Tārā|prabhṛtikās tadā:
‹matto 'yam iti mā maṃsthā yady a|bhīto 'si saṃyuge.
mado 'yaṃ saṃprahāre 'smin vīra|pānaṃ samarthyatām.›
tam evam uktvā saṃkruddho mālām utkṣipya kāñcanīm
pitrā dattāṃ Mahendreṇa yuddhāya vyavatiṣṭhata.
viṣāṇayor gṛhītvā taṃ Dundubhiṃ giri|saṃnibham
Vālī vyāpātayāṃ cakre nanarda ca mahā|svanam.
yuddhe prāṇa|hare tasmin niṣpiṣṭo Dundubhis tadā,

and boldly slashing the gate with his horns, like a two-tusked elephant.

Valin, who was in the women's quarters, could not bear hearing the noise, so out he rushed with his women, like the moon appearing with the stars. Valin, lord of all the forest-dwelling monkeys, said to Dúndubhi in measured and clearly articulated words: 'Why do you roar and besiege 11.30
this city gate? I know you, mighty Dúndubhi. Protect your own life!'

When he heard the speech of the wise monkey-king, Dúndubhi, red-eyed with anger, said these words:

'Warrior, you should not make speeches in front of women. Give me battle. Then I shall know your strength. Or perhaps I should restrain my anger for tonight? Let us agree on sunrise as the limit to your free enjoyment of love, monkey. For whoever kills anyone who is drunk or heedless or asleep or without weapons or, like you, completely stupefied by passion is regarded in this world as the murderer of an unborn child.'

Laughing quietly, Valin then dismissed Tará and all the 11.35
other women and angrily said to that best of *ásuras*: 'Unless you are afraid of battle, don't think that I am drunk. Consider my intoxication as a warrior's customary drinking before our encounter.'

With these words, angry Valin put on a gold necklace he had received from great Indra, his father, and stood ready for battle. Valin seized that mountainous Dúndubhi by his two horns, threw him to the ground and roared loudly. In that mortal conflict, Dúndubhi was then crushed. As he was

śrotrābhyām atha raktaṃ tu tasya susrāva pātyataḥ
papāta ca mahā|kāyaḥ kṣitau pañcatvam āgataḥ.
11.40 taṃ tolayitvā bāhubhyāṃ gata|sattvam acetanam
cikṣepa vegavān Vālī vegen' âikena yojanam.
tasya vega praviddhasya vaktrāt kṣataja|bindavaḥ
prapetur mārut' ôtkṣiptā Mataṅgasy' āśramaṃ prati.
tān dṛṣṭvā patitāṃs tatra muniḥ śoṇita|vipruṣaḥ
utsasarja mahā|śāpaṃ kṣeptāraṃ Vālinaṃ prati:
‹iha ten' âpraveṣṭavyam praviṣṭasya vadho bhavet.›
sa maha"|ṛṣiṃ samāsādya yācate sma kṛt'|âñjaliḥ.
tataḥ śāpa|bhayād bhīta Ṛśyamūkaṃ mahā|girim
praveṣṭuṃ n' êcchati harir draṣṭuṃ v" âpi, nar'|ēśvara.
11.45 tasy' âpraveśaṃ jñātv" âham idaṃ, Rāma, mahā|vanam
vicarāmi sah'|âmātyo viṣādena vivarjitaḥ.
eṣo 'sthi|nicayas tasya Dundubheḥ saṃprakāśate
vīry'|ôtsekān nirastasya giri|kūṭa|nibho mahān.
ime ca vipulāḥ sālāḥ sapta|śākh"|âvalambinaḥ
yatr' âikaṃ ghaṭate Vālī niṣpatrayitum ojasā.
etad asy' âsamaṃ vīryaṃ mayā, Rāma, prakāśitam
kathaṃ taṃ Vālinaṃ hantuṃ samare śakṣyase, nṛpa?
yadi bhindyād bhavān sālān imāṃs tv ek'|êṣuṇā tataḥ
jānīyāṃ tvāṃ mahā|bāho samarthaṃ Vālino vadhe.»
11.50 tasya tad vacanaṃ śrutvā Sugrīvasya mah"|ātmanaḥ
Rāghavo Dundubheḥ kāyaṃ pād'|âṅguṣṭhena līlayā
tolayitvā mahā|bāhuś cikṣepa daśa|yojanam.
kṣiptaṃ dṛṣṭvā tataḥ kāyaṃ Sugrīvaḥ punar abravīt
Lakṣmaṇasy' âgrato Rāmam idaṃ vacanam arthavat:

flung to the ground, blood flowed from his ears, and the gigantic *ásura* fell to earth, dead. With both arms, impetuous 11.40
Valin lifted that *ásura*, now without life or consciousness, and with one quick toss hurled him a league away.

As he was violently flung away, drops of blood from his mouth were scattered by the wind and fell on Matánga's hermitage. Seeing the drops of blood fall there, the sage pronounced a terrible curse on Valin for throwing the body: 'He must not enter here. It will be death for him to enter.' With palms cupped in reverence, Valin approached the great seer and begged forgiveness.

Frightened by the threat of that curse, lord of men, that monkey therefore refuses to enter here, or even to look at the great mountain Rishya·muka. Knowing that he cannot 11.45
enter here, Rama, I roam this great forest with my ministers, free from care. Here, one can see the skeleton of that Dúndubhi, high as a mountain, hurled away by Valin in the exuberance of his strength.

And here are seven thick *sala* trees with branches hanging down, any one of which Valin with his strength could pierce through with an arrow. I have made clear to you his unequaled strength, Rama. How then will you be able to kill Valin in battle, king? If, however, you could split these *sala* trees with a single arrow, then, great-armed man, I would know you were capable of killing Valin."

When great-armed Rághava heard those words of great 11.50
Sugríva, he easily lifted Dúndubhi's body with his big toe and hurled it ten leagues. And when Sugríva saw the body flung away, he spoke these reasonable words to Rama in Lákshmana's presence:

«ārdraḥ sa|māṃsa|pratyagraḥ kṣiptaḥ kāyaḥ purā, sakhe,
laghuḥ saṃprati nirmāṃsas tṛṇa|bhūtaś ca Rāghava.
n' âtra śakyaṃ balaṃ jñātuṃ tava vā tasya v" âdhikam.»

12.1 Etac ca vacanaṃ śrutvā Sugrīveṇa subhāṣitam
pratyay'|ârthaṃ mahā|tejā Rāmo jagrāha kārmukam.
sa gṛhītvā dhanur ghoraṃ śaram ekaṃ ca mānadaḥ
sālān uddiśya cikṣepa jyā|svanaiḥ pūrayan diśaḥ.
sa visṛṣṭo balavatā bāṇaḥ svarṇa|pariṣkṛtaḥ
bhittvā sālān giri|prasthe sapta, bhūmiṃ viveśa ha.
praviṣṭas tu muhūrtena rasāṃ bhittvā mahā|javaḥ
niṣpatya ca punas tūrṇaṃ sva|tūṇīṃ praviveśa ha.
12.5 tān dṛṣṭvā sapta nirbhinnān sālān vānara|puṃgavaḥ
Rāmasya śara|vegena vismayaṃ paramaṃ gataḥ.
sa mūrdhnā nyapatad bhūmau pralambī|kṛta|bhūṣaṇaḥ
Sugrīvaḥ parama|prīto Rāghavāya kṛt'|âñjaliḥ.
idaṃ c' ôvāca dharmajñaṃ karmaṇā tena harṣitaḥ
Rāmaṃ sarv'|âstra|viduṣāṃ śreṣṭhaṃ śūram avasthitam:
«s'|Êndrān api surān sarvāṃs tvaṃ bāṇaiḥ, puruṣa'|rṣabha,
samarthaḥ samare hantuṃ kiṃ punar Vālinaṃ, prabho.
yena sapta mahā|sālā girir bhūmiś ca dāritāḥ
bāṇen' âikena, Kākutstha, sthātā te ko raṇ'|âgrataḥ?
12.10 adya me vigataḥ śokaḥ prītir adya parā mama
suhṛdaṃ tvāṃ samāsādya Mahendra|Varuṇ'|ôpamam.

"When the body was thrown before, my friend, it was fresh and had flesh and blood. But now it has become like straw, light and without flesh, Rághava. So in this case it is impossible to know whether your strength or Valin's is superior."

When he heard those words so well spoken by Sugríva, mighty Rama took up his bow to inspire confidence. The bestower of honor seized his terrible bow and a single arrow, took aim at the *sala* trees, and shot, filling every quarter with the sound of his bowstring. Released by powerful Rama, the gold-adorned arrow split the seven *sala* trees, passed through the mountaintop and entered the earth. In an instant, the swift arrow split the earth, entered it, flew out again and quickly returned to its quiver. When that bull among monkeys saw those seven *sala* trees pierced by the force of Rama's arrow, he was greatly amazed. Highly pleased, Sugríva cupped his palms in reverence before Rághava and then threw himself down with his head to the ground, so that his ornaments hung down. In his delight at that feat, Sugríva spoke to the heroic knower of righteousness, foremost of those skilled in every weapon, who was standing there: 12.1 12.5

"My lord, bull among men, with your arrows you are capable of killing in battle all the gods, including Indra, to say nothing of Valin. Kákutstha, who can stand in the forefront of battle before you, who with a single arrow have split open seven great *sala* trees, the mountain and the earth? Now my sorrow is gone, now my joy is supreme, for I have 12.10
gained you, the equal of great Indra and Váruna, as my close

tam ady' âiva priy'|ârthaṃ me vairiṇaṃ bhrātṛ|rūpiṇam
Vālinaṃ jahi, Kākutstha! mayā baddho 'yam añjaliḥ.»
tato Rāmaḥ pariṣvajya Sugrīvaṃ priya|darśanam
pratyuvāca mahā|prājño Lakṣmaṇ'|ânumataṃ vacaḥ:
«asmād gacchāma Kiṣkindhāṃ!
kṣipraṃ gaccha tvam agrataḥ.
gatvā c' āhvaya, Sugrīva,
Vālinaṃ bhrātṛ|gandhinam.»
sarve te tvaritaṃ gatvā Kiṣkindhāṃ Vālinaḥ purīm
vṛkṣair ātmānam āvṛtya vyatiṣṭhan gahane vane.
12.15 Sugrīvo vyanadad ghoraṃ Vālino hvāna|kāraṇāt
gāḍhaṃ parihito vegān nādair bhindann iv' âmbaram.
taṃ śrutvā ninadaṃ bhrātuḥ kruddho Vālī mahā|balaḥ
niṣpapāta susaṃrabdho bhāskaro 'sta|taṭād iva.
tataḥ sutumulaṃ yuddhaṃ Vāli|Sugrīvayor abhūt
gagane grahayor ghoraṃ Budh'|Âṅgārakayor iva.
talair aśani|kalpaiś ca vajra|kalpaiś ca muṣṭibhiḥ
jaghnatuḥ samare 'nyonyaṃ bhrātarau krodha|mūrchitau.
tato Rāmo dhanuṣ|pāṇis tāv ubhau samudīkṣya tu
anyonya|sadṛśau vīrāv ubhau devāv iv' Âśvinau.
12.20 yan n' âvagacchat Sugrīvaṃ Vālinaṃ v" âpi Rāghavaḥ
tato na kṛtavān buddhiṃ moktum anta|karaṃ śaram.
etasminn antare bhagnaḥ Sugrīvas tena Vālinā
apaśyan Rāghavaṃ nātham Ṛśyamūkaṃ pradudruve.
klānto rudhira|sikt'|âṅgaḥ prahārair jarjarī|kṛtaḥ
Vālin" âbhidrutaḥ krodhāt praviveśa mahā|vanam.
taṃ praviṣṭaṃ vanaṃ dṛṣṭvā Vālī śāpa|bhayāt tataḥ
«mukto hy asi tvam ity» uktvā sa nivṛtto mahā|balaḥ.

friend. As a favor to me, Kákutstha, you must this very day kill Valin, my enemy in the form of a brother. See, I cup my hands in reverence."

Then wise Rama embraced handsome Sugríva and with Lákshmana's approval responded in these words: "Let us go from here to Kishkíndha. You, Sugríva, go swiftly before us. And when you get there, challenge Valin, that brother in name only."

Proceeding quickly to Valin's city, Kishkíndha, they all stopped in the dense forest, concealing themselves behind trees. Girding his loins, Sugríva, as a challenge to Valin, 12.15
bellowed horribly, seeming to split the sky with his furious roaring. Angered at hearing his brother's roars, mighty Valin, enraged, rushed out, like the sun from behind the slope of the sunset-mountain. Then a tumultuous battle took place between Valin and Sugríva, like a dreadful clash in the sky between the planets Mercury and Mars. In the conflict, the two brothers, beside themselves with rage, struck each other with fists like thunderbolts and with palms like lightning.

Then, bow in hand, Rama looked carefully at those two warriors who were as similar to one another as the twin gods, the Ashvins. And since he could not distinguish Su- 12.20
gríva from Valin, Rághava could not make up his mind to loose his deadly arrow.

Meanwhile, routed by Valin, Sugríva did not see his protector, Rághava, so he fled to Rishya·muka. Exhausted, his body spattered with blood, battered by blows, he fled into the great forest, angrily pursued by Valin. But when mighty Valin saw him enter that forest, he turned back in fear of the curse, saying, "You have escaped, then!"

Rāghavo 'pi saha bhrātrā saha c' âiva Hanūmatā
tad eva vanam āgacchat Sugrīvo yatra vānaraḥ.
12.25 taṃ samīkṣy' āgataṃ Rāmaṃ Sugrīvaḥ saha|Lakṣmaṇam
hrīmān dīnam uvāc' êdaṃ vasudhām avalokayan:

«‹āhvayasv' êti› māṃ uktvā darśayitvā ca vikramam.
vairiṇā ghātayitvā ca kim idānīṃ tvayā kṛtam?
tām eva velāṃ vaktavyaṃ tvayā, Rāghava, tattvataḥ
‹Vālinaṃ na nihanm' îti›, tato n' âham ito vraje.»

tasya c' âivaṃ bruvāṇasya Sugrīvasya mah"|ātmanaḥ
karuṇaṃ dīnayā vācā Rāghavaḥ punar abravīt:

«Sugrīva, śrūyatāṃ, tāta, krodhaś ca vyapanīyatām
kāraṇaṃ yena bāṇo 'yaṃ na mayā sa visarjitaḥ.
12.30 alaṃkāreṇa veṣeṇa pramāṇena gatena ca
tvaṃ ca, Sugrīva, Vālī ca sadṛśau sthaḥ parasparam.
svareṇa varcasā c' âiva prekṣitena ca, vānara,
vikrameṇa ca vākyaiś ca vyaktiṃ vāṃ n' ôpalakṣaye.
tato 'haṃ rūpa|sādṛśyān mohito, vānar'|ôttama,
n' ôtsṛjāmi mahā|vegaṃ śaraṃ śatru|nibarhaṇam.

etan|muhūrte tu mayā paśya Vālinam āhave
nirastam iṣuṇ" âikena veṣṭamānaṃ mahī|tale.
abhijñānaṃ kuruṣva tvam ātmano, vānar'|ēśvara,
yena tvām abhijānīyāṃ dvandva|yuddham upāgatam.
12.35 gaja|puṣpīm imāṃ phullāṃ utpāṭya śubha|lakṣaṇām
kuru, Lakṣmaṇa, kaṇṭhe 'sya Sugrīvasya mah"|ātmanaḥ.»

Rághava, too, with his brother and Hánuman as well, came back to that same forest where the monkey Sugríva was. When he saw Rama arriving with Lákshmana, Sugríva 12.25
was ashamed. With his eyes fixed on the ground, he spoke dejectedly:

"First you showed me your prowess and said I should challenge my enemy. Then you let him beat me. Why do you act like this now? Right then, Rághava, you should have said honestly, 'I will not kill Valin.' Then I would never have budged from here."

But when great Sugríva spoke so pitifully in a dejected voice, Rághava replied:

"Poor Sugríva, listen to the reason that I did not shoot
this arrow, and let your anger be dispelled. In ornaments, in 12.30
your dress, your size and your movements, you and Valin are very similar to each other, Sugríva. Monkey, I cannot tell the difference between the two of you in voice, splendor, glance, valor or speech. And so, best of monkeys, bewildered by this similarity of appearance, I did not loose my swift, foe-destroying arrow.

But soon you will see Valin writhing on the ground, struck down by me in battle with a single arrow. Lord of monkeys, you must place on yourself some distinguishing mark by which I may recognize you when you are engaged in
single combat. Lákshmana, pluck that auspicious flowering 12.35
gaja·pushpi creeper and place it around great Sugríva's neck."

tato giri|taṭe jātām utpāṭya kusum'|āyutām
Lakṣmaṇo gaja|puṣpīṃ tāṃ tasya kaṇṭhe vyasarjayat.
sa tathā śuśubhe śrīmāl̄ latayā kaṇṭha|saktayā
mālay" êva balākānāṃ sa|saṃdhya iva toyadaḥ.
vibhrājamāno vapuṣā Rāma|vākya samāhitaḥ
jagāma saha Rāmeṇa Kiṣkindhāṃ Vāli|pālitām.

13.1 Ṛśyamūkāt sa dharm'|ātmā Kiṣkindhāṃ Lakṣmaṇ'|âgrajaḥ
jagāma saha|Sugrīvo Vāli|vikrama|pālitām.
samudyamya mahac cāpaṃ Rāmaḥ kāñcana|bhūṣitam
śarāṃś c' āditya|saṃkāśān gṛhītvā raṇa|sādhakān.
agratas tu yayau tasya Rāghavasya mah"|ātmanaḥ
Sugrīvaḥ saṃhata|grīvo Lakṣmaṇaś ca mahā|balaḥ.
pṛṣṭhato Hanumān vīro Nalo Nīlaś ca vānaraḥ
Tāraś c' âiva mahā|tejā hari|yūthapa|yūthapāḥ.
13.5 te vīkṣamāṇā vṛkṣāṃś ca puṣpa|bhār'|âvalambinaḥ
prasann'|âmbu vahāś c' âiva saritaḥ sāgaraṃ|gamāḥ
kandarāṇi ca śailāṃś ca nirjharāṇi guhās tathā
śikharāṇi ca mukhyāni darīś ca priya|darśanāḥ.
vaidūrya|vimalaiḥ parṇaiḥ padmaiś c' ākāśa|kuḍmalaiḥ
śobhitān sajalān mārge taṭākāṃś ca vyalokayan
kāraṇḍaiḥ sārasair haṃsair vañjulair jala|kukkuṭaiḥ
cakravākais tathā c' ânyaiḥ śakunaiḥ pratināditān.
mṛdu|śaṣp'|âṅkur'|āhārān nirbhayān vana|gocarān
carataḥ sarvato 'paśyan sthalīṣu hariṇān sthitān
13.10 taṭāka|vairiṇaś c' âpi śukla|danta|vibhūṣitān
ghorān eka|carān vanyān dviradān kūla|ghātinaḥ.
vane vana|carāṃś c' ânyān khe|carāṃś ca vihaṃ|gamān
paśyantas tvaritā jagmuḥ Sugrīva vaśa|vartinaḥ.

Then Lákshmana plucked a blossoming *gaja·pushpi* that was growing on the mountainside and draped it around Sugríva's neck. With the creeper fastened about his neck, majestic Sugríva resembled a rain cloud at twilight with a garland of cranes. Radiant in body, intent on Rama's words, he went with Rama to Kishkíndha, which Valin protected.

AND SO, TAKING up his great gold-adorned bow and with 13.1
it his arrows, bright as the sun and potent in battle, Rama, the righteous elder brother of Lákshmana, went with
Sugríva from Rishya·muka to Kishkíndha, which was protected by Valin's prowess. Before great Rághava went strong-
necked Sugríva and mighty Lákshmana. Behind came heroic
Hánuman, Nala, the monkey Nila, and also glorious Tara,
all leaders among the leaders of the monkey troops.
They saw trees bending down under the burden of their 13.5
blossoms, and rivers flowing to the sea bearing their clear
waters, and gorges and mountains and waterfalls and caves
and high peaks and caverns lovely to behold. And on their
way they beheld ponds whose waters were splendid with lotuses, whose leaves were bright as emeralds and whose buds
were fully opened ponds resounding with *karánda* ducks,
cranes, geese, *váñjulas*, waterfowl, *chakra·vakas* and other
birds. They saw deer ranging in the forest eating tender
shoots of grass, fearlessly wandering everywhere or standing on dry ground; and also fearsome, solitary wild ele- 13.10
phants adorned with white tusks, enemies of the ponds
whose banks they shattered. And thus observing the other
wild animals in the forest and the birds moving in the sky,
they hurried along, obedient to Sugríva's will.

teṣāṃ tu gacchatāṃ tatra tvaritaṃ Raghu|nandanaḥ
druma|ṣaṇḍaṃ vanaṃ dṛṣṭvā Rāmaḥ Sugrīvam abravīt:
«eṣa megha iv' ākāśe vṛkṣa|ṣaṇḍaḥ prakāśate
megha|saṃghāta|vipulaḥ paryanta|kadalī|vṛtaḥ.
kim etaj? jñātum icchāmi, sakhe, kautūhalaṃ mama
kautūhal'|âpanayanaṃ kartum icchāmy ahaṃ tvayā.»
13.15 tasya tad vacanaṃ śrutvā Rāghavasya mah"|ātmanaḥ
gacchann ev' ācacakṣe 'tha Sugrīvas tan mahad vanam:
«etad, Rāghava, vistīrṇam āśramaṃ śrama|nāśanam.
udyāna|vana|saṃpannaṃ svādu|mūla|phal'|ôdakam.
atra Saptajanā nāma munayaḥ saṃśita|vratāḥ
sapt' âiv' āsann adhaḥ|śīrṣā niyataṃ jala|śāyinaḥ.
sapta|rātra|kṛt'|āhārā vāyunā vana|vāsinaḥ
divaṃ varṣa|śatair yātāḥ saptabhiḥ sa|kalevarāḥ.
teṣām evaṃ prabhāvena druma|prākāra|saṃvṛtam
āśramaṃ su|durādharṣam api s' Êndraiḥ sur'|âsuraiḥ.
13.20 pakṣiṇo varjayanty etat tath" ânye vana|cāriṇaḥ
viśanti mohād ye 'py atra nivartante na te punaḥ.
vibhūṣaṇa|ravāś c' âtra śrūyante sa|kal'|âkṣarāḥ
tūrya|gīta|svanāś c' âpi gandho divyaś ca, Rāghava.
tret"|âgnayo 'pi dīpyante dhūmo hy eṣa pradṛśyate.
veṣṭayann iva vṛkṣ'|âgrān kapot'|âṅg'|âruṇo ghanaḥ.
kuru praṇāmaṃ, dharm'|ātmaṃs, tān samuddiśya, Rāghava,
Lakṣmaṇena saha bhrātrā prayataḥ saṃyat'|âñjaliḥ.
praṇamanti hi ye teṣām ṛṣīṇāṃ bhāvit'|ātmanām
na teṣām aśubhaṃ kiṃ cic charīre, Rāma, dṛśyate.»

Now, as they went swiftly on, Rama, joy of the Raghus, noticed a dense grove of trees, and he said to Sugríva:

"There, dark as a rain cloud and massive as a cloud bank in the sky, stands a grove entirely surrounded by plantain trees. I want to know what it is, my friend. I am curious, and I would like you to satisfy my curiosity."

When he heard great Rághava's words, Sugríva told him 13.15
about that large grove as he walked along.

"That is an immense ashram where all weariness is removed, Rághava. For it has gardens and parks, with sweet-tasting roots, fruit and water. There the seven sages called the Sapta·janas once lived. They were strict in their vows and always slept upside down in the water. After seven hundred years of living in the forest, existing solely on the air they took in once every seven days, they went to heaven in their own bodies. By virtue of this power of theirs, their ashram, surrounded by a wall of trees, is unapproachable
even for the gods or demons, including Indra. Birds and 13.20
other forest creatures avoid it. Those who enter it even by mistake do not come out again.

But from within one hears the jingling of ornaments and the sweet sounds of instruments and singing, and there is also a divine fragrance, Rághava. The three sacred fires are also burning there. You can see the dense smoke, gray as a dove's body, shrouding the treetops. Restrained and with palms cupped in reverence, you and your brother Lákshmana must bow humbly to the sages, righteous Rághava. For no ill can befall people who bow humbly to these contemplative seers, Rama."

13.25 tato Rāmaḥ saha bhrātrā Lakṣmaṇena kṛt'|âñjaliḥ
samuddiśya mah"|ātmānas tān ṛṣīn abhyavādayat.
abhivādya ca dharm'|ātmā Rāmo bhrātā ca Lakṣmaṇaḥ
Sugrīvo vānarāś c' âiva jagmuḥ saṃhṛṣṭa|mānasāḥ.
te gatvā dūram adhvānaṃ tasmāt Saptajan'|āśramāt
dadṛśus tāṃ durādharṣāṃ Kiṣkindhāṃ Vāli|pālitām.

So, with their palms cupped in reverence, Rama and his brother Lákshmana respectfully saluted those great seers. 13.25
When they had saluted respectfully, righteous Rama, his brother Lákshmana, and Sugríva and the other monkeys went on, delighted at heart. Then, when they had traveled a long way from the ashram of the Sapta·janas, they saw unassailable Kishkíndha, which Valin protected.

14–18
RAMA REPROACHED

14.1 SARVE TE TVARITAM gatvā Kiṣkindhāṃ Vāli|pālitām
vṛkṣair ātmānam āvṛtya vyatiṣṭhan gahane vane.
vicārya sarvato dṛṣṭiṃ kānane kānana|priyaḥ
Sugrīvo vipula|grīvaḥ krodham āhārayad bhṛśam.
tataḥ sa ninadaṃ ghoraṃ kṛtvā yuddhāya c' āhvayat
parivāraiḥ parivṛto nādair bhindann iv' âmbaram.
atha bāl'|ârka|sadṛśo dṛpta|siṃha|gatis tadā
dṛṣṭvā Rāmaṃ kriyā|dakṣaṃ Sugrīvo vākyam abravīt:

14.5 «hari|vāgurayā vyāptaṃ
tapta|kāñcana|toraṇām
prāptāḥ sma dhvaja|yantr'|
āḍhyāṃ Kiṣkindhāṃ Vālinaḥ purīm.
pratijñā yā tvayā, vīra, kṛtā Vāli|vadhe purā
saphalāṃ tāṃ kuru kṣipraṃ latāṃ kāla iv' āgataḥ!»

evam uktas tu dharm'|ātmā Sugrīveṇa sa Rāghavaḥ
tam ath' ôvāca Sugrīvaṃ vacanaṃ śatru|sūdanaḥ:

«kṛt'|âbhijñāna|cihnas tvam anayā gaja|sāhvayā
viparīta iv' ākāśe sūryo nakṣatra|mālayā.
adya Vāli|samutthaṃ te bhayaṃ vairaṃ ca, vānara,
eken' âhaṃ pramokṣyāmi bāṇa|mokṣeṇa saṃyuge.
14.10 mama darśaya, Sugrīva, vairiṇaṃ bhrātṛ|rūpiṇam!
Vālī vinihato yāvad vane pāṃsuṣu veṣṭate.
yadi dṛṣṭi|pathaṃ prāpto jīvan sa vinivartate
tato doṣeṇa mā gacchet sadyo garhec ca mā bhavān.
pratyakṣaṃ sapta te sālā mayā bāṇena dāritāḥ.
tato vetsi balen' âdya Vālinaṃ nihataṃ mayā.
anṛtaṃ n' ôkta|pūrvaṃ me, vīra, kṛcchre 'pi tiṣṭhatā
dharma|lobha|parītena na ca vakṣye kathaṃ cana.

When they had all gone quickly to Kishkíndha, which 14.1
Valin protected, they stopped in the dense forest,
concealing themselves behind trees. Broad-necked Sugríva,
who loved the forest, glanced about the forest and summoned up his great anger. Then, surrounded by his attendants, he challenged Valin to battle with a dreadful roar,
nearly splitting the skies with his roaring. Now, like the
newly risen sun, Sugríva, who moved like a proud lion,
looked at Rama, skillful in action, and spoke these words:

"We have reached Valin's city Kishkíndha, with its gate- 14.5
way of pure gold, surrounded by a monkey-snare, and
bristling with banners and engines of war. Just as the proper
season arrives to make the vine bear fruit, so should you,
warrior, make good at once your earlier promise to kill
Valin."

Addressed in this way by Sugríva, righteous Rághava, destroyer of his enemies, then said these words to Sugríva:

"Wearing those flowers called *gaja·pushpi*, you are now
easy to recognize: You look like some extraordinary sun up
in the heavens within a garland of stars. By loosing a single
arrow in battle, monkey, I shall today deliver you from fear
and from Valin's enmity. Just show me that enemy in the 14.10
guise of a brother, Sugríva. Then Valin, struck down here in
the forest, will writhe in the dust. If he comes within range
of my sight and leaves again alive, then you may come to
me at once and reproach me with my guilt. Before your very
eyes I split the seven *sala* trees. Know therefore that by my
might I shall kill Valin today. Filled with a desire for right,
I have never before spoken a falsehood even when I was in
danger, warrior, and I shall by no means speak one now.

saphalāṃ ca kariṣyāmi pratijñāṃ, jahi saṃbhramam!
prasūtaṃ kalamaṃ kṣetre varṣen' êva Śatakratuḥ.
14.15 tad|āhvāna|nimittaṃ tvaṃ Vālino hema|mālinaḥ,
Sugrīva, kuru taṃ śabdaṃ niṣpated yena vānaraḥ.
jita|kāśī jaya|ślāghī tvayā c' âdharṣitaḥ purāt
niṣpatiṣyaty asaṃgena Vālī sa priya|saṃyugaḥ.
ripūṇāṃ dharṣaṇaṃ śūrā marṣayanti na saṃyuge
jānantas tu svakaṃ vīryaṃ strī|samakṣaṃ viśeṣataḥ.»
sa tu Rāma|vacaḥ śrutvā Sugrīvo hema|piṅgalaḥ
nanarda krūra|nādena vinirbhindann iv' âmbaram.
tasya śabdena vitrastā gāvo yānti hata|prabhāḥ
rāja|doṣa|parāmṛṣṭāḥ kula|striya iv' ākulāḥ.
14.20 dravanti ca mṛgāḥ śīghraṃ bhagnā iva raṇe hayāḥ
patanti ca khagā bhūmau kṣīṇa|puṇyā iva grahāḥ.
Tataḥ sa jīmūta|gaṇa|praṇādo
nādaṃ vyamuñcat tvarayā pratītaḥ
Sūry'|ātmajaḥ śaurya|vivṛddha|tejāḥ
sarit|patir v" ânila|cañcal'|ōrmiḥ.

15.1 ATHA TASYA ninādaṃ taṃ Sugrīvasya mah"|ātmanaḥ
śuśrāv' ântaḥ|pura|gato Vālī bhrātur amarṣaṇaḥ.
śrutvā tu tasya ninadaṃ sarva|bhūta|prakampanam
madaś c' âika|pade naṣṭaḥ krodhaś c' āpatito mahān.
sa tu roṣa|parīt'|âṅgo Vālī saṃdhy"|ātapa|prabhaḥ
uparakta iv' ādityaḥ sadyo niṣprabhatāṃ gataḥ.
Vālī daṃṣṭrā|karālas tu krodhād dīpt'|âgni saṃnibhaḥ
bhāty utpatita padm'|ābhaḥ sa|mṛṇāla iva hradaḥ.
15.5 śabdaṃ durmarṣaṇaṃ śrutvā niṣpapāta tato hariḥ

Don't worry! For I shall make my promise fruitful, just as Indra of a hundred sacrifices with his rain makes fruitful the rice sprouting in a field. Therefore, Sugríva, in order 14.15
to summon gold-garlanded Valin, you must make such a noise that that monkey will rush out. Challenged by you, Valin, with his air of a conqueror, boastful of his victories and fond of battle, will rush out from the city without delay. Heroes who know their own prowess do not tolerate their enemies' insults in battle, particularly when their women are present."

Upon hearing Rama's speech, tawny-gold Sugríva roared a savage roar, nearly splitting the skies. Terrified by the noise, cattle ran off, like dazed noblewomen who through some failure of their king are ravished and lose their bright beauty. And deer ran swiftly away like horses breaking in battle, and 14.20
birds fell to earth like planets whose merit is exhausted. And then, his power enhanced by valor, his roar like that of a host of clouds, the sun's renowned son suddenly let loose a roar like the ocean when its waves are lashed by the wind.

Now, WHEN VALIN, who was in the women's quarters, 15.1
heard the roaring of his brother, great Sugríva, he could not bear it. But when he heard that roaring which made all beings tremble, his desire vanished at once and great rage arose in him. At one moment radiant as the sun at twilight, now, suddenly, Valin darkened like an eclipsed sun, as his body filled with fury. Like a blazing fire because of his anger, Valin looked like a pool radiant with red lotuses, his terrifying fangs white as lotus fibers. As he heard the 15.5
intolerable sound, the monkey rushed out, nearly shattering

vegena caraṇa|nyāsair dārayann iva medinīm.
taṃ tu Tārā pariṣvajya snehād darśita|sauhṛdā
uvāca trasta|saṃbhrāntā hit'|ôdarkam idaṃ vacaḥ:

«sādhu, krodham imaṃ, vīra, nadī|vegam iv' āgatam
śayanād utthitaḥ kālyaṃ tyaja bhuktām iva srajam.
sahasā tava niṣkrāmo mama tāvan na rocate.
śrūyatām abhidhāsyāmi yan|nimittaṃ nivāryase.
pūrvam āpatitaḥ krodhāt sa tvām āhvayate yudhi.
niṣpatya ca nirastas te hanyamāno diśo gataḥ.
15.10 tvayā tasya nirastasya pīḍitasya viśeṣataḥ
ih' âitya punar āhvānaṃ śaṅkāṃ janayat' îva me.
darpaś ca vyavasāyaś ca yādṛśas tasya nardataḥ
ninādasya ca saṃrambho n' âitad alpaṃ hi kāraṇam!
n' âsahāyam ahaṃ manye Sugrīvaṃ tam ih' āgatam.
avaṣṭabdha|sahāyaś ca yam āśrity' âiṣa garjati.
prakṛtyā nipuṇaś c' âiva buddhimāṃś c' âiva vānaraḥ.
aparīkṣita|vīryeṇa Sugrīvaḥ saha n' âiṣyati.

pūrvam eva mayā, vīra, śrutaṃ kathayato vacaḥ
Aṅgadasya kumārasya vakṣyāmi tvā hitaṃ vacaḥ.
15.15 tava bhrātur hi vikhyātaḥ sahāyo raṇa|karkaśaḥ
Rāmaḥ para|bal'|āmardī yug'|ânt'|âgnir iv' ôtthitaḥ.
nivāsa|vṛkṣaḥ sādhūnām āpannānāṃ parā gatiḥ
ārtānāṃ saṃśrayaś c' âiva yaśasaś c' âika|bhājanam.
jñāna|vijñāna|saṃpanno nideśo nirataḥ pituḥ
dhātūnām iva śail'|êndro guṇānām ākaro mahān.
tat kṣamaṃ na virodhas te saha tena mah"|ātmanā

the earth with the force of his footsteps. But his wife Tará, agitated and frightened, showed her affection by lovingly embracing him and speaking words meant for his own good:

"Come, warrior, give up this anger, which has arisen like the flood of a river, just as one gives up a used garland upon rising from bed at daybreak. I really do not like your rushing out this way. Listen, and I shall tell you why I am holding you back. The last time, Sugríva suddenly appeared and angrily challenged you to battle. When you hurried out,
injured, and defeated him, he ran away. After you defeated 15.10
him and above all injured him, his coming back here to challenge you again really arouses my suspicion. There is some significant reason for such insolence and determination, and for the arrogance of his shouting as he roars. I do not believe that Sugríva has come here without an ally. He is bellowing now because he has obtained an ally on whom he can rely. The monkey Sugríva is by nature clever and intelligent. He would not have come with someone whose prowess was untested.

Let me tell you the useful information I heard Prince Ángada reporting earlier, warrior. Your brother's ally is the cel- 15.15
ebrated Rama, harsh in battle, crushing his enemy's forces, like the fire sprung up at the end of the world. But he is also a sheltering tree for the virtuous, the final refuge for the unfortunate and a resting place for the afflicted. Sole repository of fame, endowed with knowledge and learning, and devoted to his father's command, he is a great mine of virtues, just as the lord of mountains is a mine of minerals. Therefore it is not fitting for you to be in conflict with immeasurably great Rama, who is unconquerable in battle. I

durjayen' âprameyena Rāmeṇa raṇa|karmasu.
śūra, vakṣyāmi te kiṃ cin na c' êcchāmy abhyasūyitum.
śrūyatāṃ kriyatāṃ c' âiva tava vakṣyāmi yadd hitam!

15.20 yauvarājyena Sugrīvaṃ tūrṇaṃ sādhv abhiṣecaya,
vigrahaṃ mā kṛthā, vīra, bhrātrā, rājan, balīyasā.
ahaṃ hi te kṣamaṃ manye tava Rāmeṇa sauhṛdam
Sugrīveṇa ca saṃprītiṃ vairam utsṛjya dūrataḥ.
lālanīyo hi te bhrātā yavīyān eṣa vānaraḥ.
tatra vā sann ihastho vā sarvathā bandhur eva te
yadi te mat|priyaṃ kāryaṃ yadi c' âvaiṣi māṃ hitām
yācyamānaḥ prayatnena sādhu vākyaṃ kuruṣva me!»

16.1 TĀM EVAṂ BRUVATĪṂ Tārāṃ tār"|âdhipa|nibh'|ānanām
Vālī nirbhartsayām āsa vacanaṃ c' êdam abravīt:

«garjato 'sya ca saṃrambhaṃ bhrātuḥ śatror viśeṣataḥ
marṣayiṣyāmy ahaṃ kena kāraṇena, var'|ānane?
adharṣitānāṃ śūrāṇāṃ samareṣv anivartinām
dharṣaṇ'|âmarṣaṇaṃ, bhīru, maraṇād atiricyate.
soḍhuṃ na ca samartho 'haṃ yuddha|kāmasya saṃyuge
Sugrīvasya ca saṃrambhaṃ hīna|grīvasya garjataḥ.
16.5 na ca kāryo viṣādas te Rāghavaṃ prati mat|kṛte.
dharmajñaś ca kṛtajñaś ca kathaṃ pāpaṃ kariṣyati?
nivartasva saha strībhiḥ! kathaṃ bhūyo 'nugacchasi?
sauhṛdaṃ darśitaṃ, Tāre, mayi bhaktiḥ kṛtā tvayā.
pratiyotsyāmy ahaṃ gatvā Sugrīvaṃ, jahi saṃbhramam!
darpaṃ c' âsya vineṣyāmi na ca prāṇair vimokṣyate.

shall tell you something, hero, and I do not want you to be angry. You must listen to the good advice I shall give you and act upon it.

You must consecrate Sugríva immediately as heir appar- 15.20
ent in the proper fashion. You should not make war with
your mighty brother, valiant king. I believe it would be
proper for you to put your hostility aside and have friendship with Rama and affection for Sugríva. This monkey
is your younger brother, deserving your fond indulgence.
Whether here or there, he is after all your kinsman. If you
regard me as well disposed to you and if you wish to do what
pleases me, I beg of you: Please carry out my good advice."

But even as Tará, her face bright as the moon, the lord 16.1
of stars, spoke in this fashion, Valin reproached her and said
these words:

"Why, fair-faced woman, must I suffer the arrogance of
my roaring brother, especially since he is my enemy? For
invincible heroes who never turn back in battle, to endure
insolence is worse than death, timid woman. Thus I cannot tolerate the arrogance of weak-necked, roaring Sugríva,
who wants to fight a battle. Nor should you despair on my 16.5
account because of Rághava. He knows what is right and
his conduct is correct, so how could he do wrong? You have
shown your affection, Tará, and displayed your devotion to
me. Now go back with the other women. Why do you still
follow me? I shall go and fight Sugríva. Do not be anxious:
I shall take away his pride, but I shall not deprive him of
his life. I implore you by my life: Go back, with a prayer for

śāpit" âsi mama prāṇair nivartasva jayena ca.
ahaṃ jitvā nivartiṣye tam alaṃ bhrātaraṃ raṇe.»
taṃ tu Tārā pariṣvajya Vālinaṃ priya|vādinī
cakāra rudatī mandaṃ dakṣiṇā sā pradakṣiṇam.
16.10 tataḥ svasty|ayanaṃ kṛtvā mantravad vijay'|âiṣiṇī
antaḥ|puraṃ saha strībhiḥ praviṣṭā śoka|mohitā.
praviṣṭāyāṃ tu Tārāyāṃ saha strībhiḥ svam ālayam
nagarān niryayau kruddho mahā|sarpa iva śvasan.
sa niḥśvasya mahā|vego Vālī parama|roṣaṇaḥ
sarvataś cārayan dṛṣṭiṃ śatru|darśana|kāṅkṣayā.
sa dadarśa tataḥ śrīmān Sugrīvaṃ hema|piṅgalam
susaṃvītam avaṣṭabdhaṃ dīpyamānam iv' ânalam.
sa taṃ dṛṣṭvā mahā|vīryaṃ Sugrīvaṃ paryavasthitam
gāḍhaṃ paridadhe vāso Vālī parama|roṣaṇaḥ.
16.15 sa Vālī gāḍha|saṃvīto muṣṭim udyamya vīryavān
Sugrīvam ev' âbhimukho yayau yoddhuṃ kṛta|kṣaṇaḥ.
śliṣṭa|muṣṭiṃ samudyamya saṃrabdhataram āgataḥ
Sugrīvo 'pi samuddiśya Vālinaṃ hema|mālinam.
taṃ Vālī krodha|tāmr'|âkṣaḥ Sugrīvaṃ raṇa|paṇḍitam
āpatantaṃ mahā|vegam idaṃ vacanam abravīt:
«eṣa muṣṭir mayā baddho gāḍhaḥ sunihit'|âṅguliḥ
mayā vega|vimuktas te prāṇān ādāya yāsyati!»
evam uktas tu Sugrīvaḥ kruddho Vālinam abravīt:
«tav' âiva ca haran prāṇān muṣṭiḥ patatu mūrdhani!»
16.20 tāḍitas tena saṃkruddhaḥ samabhikramya vegataḥ
abhavac choṇit'|ôdgārī s' ôtpīḍa iva parvataḥ.
Sugrīveṇa tu niḥsaṃgaṃ sālam utpāṭya tejasā
gātreṣv abhihato Vālī vajreṇ' êva mahā|giriḥ.

my victory. When I have sufficiently humbled my brother in battle, I shall return."

Then sweet-speaking, compliant Tará embraced Valin
and circled him reverently, weeping softly. Desiring his vic- 16.10
tory, she offered a blessing accompanied with mantras and
then entered the women's quarters with the other women,
dazed with grief.

Once Tará had entered her own dwelling with the other
women, Valin went out from the city in a rage, hissing like
a great angry snake. Breathing hard in his towering rage,
impetuous Valin cast his glance all about, eagerly seeking his
enemy. Then majestic Valin saw tawny-gold Sugríva, who
was standing his ground with his loins girded, blazing like
fire. Seeing mighty Sugríva stationed there, in a towering
rage Valin girded his loins. Mighty Valin, his loins tightly 16.15
girded, advanced toward Sugríva with his fist raised, eager to
fight. Sugríva, too, raised his clenched fist and ran furiously
toward gold-garlanded Valin. His eyes copper-red with rage,
Valin spoke these words to Sugríva, skilled in battle, who
came rushing at him with tremendous speed:

"This tightly clenched fist of mine, with fingers well positioned, will take your life with it when I let it fly with full force!"

Addressed in that way, Sugríva angrily replied to Valin,
"It is on your head that my fist shall fall, robbing you of
life!" And struck by Valin, who attacked with such force, 16.20
angry Sugríva vomited blood, resembling a mountain with
a waterfall. But Sugríva violently uprooted an entire *sala* tree
and struck Valin on the limbs, as lightning strikes a great
mountain. And now Valin, staggered by the blows of the *sala*

sa tu Vālī pracaritaḥ sāla|tāḍana vihvalaḥ
guru|bhāra|samākrāntā sāgare naur iv' âbhavat.
tau bhīma|bala|vikrāntau Suparṇa|sama|veginau
pravṛddhau ghora|vapuṣau candra|sūryāv iv' âmbare.
Vālinā bhagna|darpas tu Sugrīvo manda|vikramaḥ
Vālinaṃ prati sāmarṣo darśayām āsa lāghavam.
16.25 tato dhanuṣi saṃdhāya śaram āśīviṣ'|ôpamam
Rāghaveṇa mahā|bāṇo Vāli|vakṣasi pātitaḥ.
vegen' âbhihato Vālī nipapāta mahī|tale.
ath' ôkṣitaḥ śoṇita|toya|visravaiḥ
supuṣpit'|âśoka iv' ânil'|ôddhataḥ
vicetano Vāsava|sūnur āhave
prabhraṃśit'|Êndra|dhvajavat kṣitiṃ gataḥ.

17.1 Tataḥ śareṇ' âbhihato Rāmeṇa raṇa|karkaśaḥ
papāta sahasā Vālī nikṛtta iva pādapaḥ.
sa bhūmau nyasta|sarv'|âṅgas tapta|kāñcana|bhūṣaṇaḥ
apatad deva|rājasya mukta|raśmir iva dhvajaḥ.
tasmin nipatite bhūmau hary|ṛkṣāṇāṃ gaṇ'|ēśvare
naṣṭa|candram iva vyoma na vyarājata bhū|talam.
bhūmau nipatitasy' âpi tasya dehaṃ mah"|ātmanaḥ
na śrīr jahāti na prāṇā na tejo na parākramaḥ.
17.5 Śakra|dattā varā mālā kāñcanī ratna|bhūṣitā
dadhāra hari|mukhyasya prāṇāṃs tejaḥ śriyaṃ ca sā.
sa tayā mālayā vīro haimayā hari|yūthapaḥ
saṃdhy"|ânugata|paryantaḥ payo|dhara iv' âbhavat.
tasya mālā ca dehaś ca marma|ghātī ca yaḥ śaraḥ
tridh" êva racitā lakṣmīḥ patitasy' âpi śobhate.
tad astraṃ tasya vīrasya svarga|mārga|prabhāvanam
Rāma|bāṇ'|âsana|kṣiptam āvahat paramāṃ gatim.

tree, lurched like a boat at sea overwhelmed by a heavy load. With their terrible strength and valor, with their frightening appearance, those two, swift as Supárna, seemed as huge as the sun and the moon in the sky. Though his pride had been broken by Valin and his strength was failing, Sugríva, enraged at Valin, demonstrated his agility.

Then Rághava placed on his bow a shaft like a poisonous 16.25
snake and loosed the great arrow at Valin's chest. Violently struck, Valin fell to the ground. Now, spattered by the flowing blood, like a crimson-flowered *ashóka* tree uprooted by the wind, the son of Vásava fell in battle unconscious to the ground, like Indra's flagstaff overthrown.

THEN, STRUCK by Rama's arrow, Valin, harsh in battle, 17.1
fell suddenly like a tree cut down. Adorned with pure gold, his whole body toppled to the ground, like the flagstaff of the king of gods when its ropes are released. As that lord of the hosts of monkeys and apes fell to the ground, the earth grew dim, like the sky when the moon vanishes.

And yet, though he had fallen to the ground, the great monkey's majesty, life, power and valor did not leave his
body. For the wonderful jewel-studded gold necklace that 17.5
Shakra had given him sustained the life, power and majesty of the monkey-chief. With his gold necklace, the heroic leader of the monkey troops looked like a rain cloud edged by the glowing light of evening. Though he had fallen, it was as if his lingering splendor had been broken into three shining parts: his necklace, his body and the arrow piercing his vital organs. For that missile, shot from Rama's bow, had

tam tathā patitaṃ saṃkhye gat'|ârciṣam iv' ânalam
Yayātim iva puṇy'|ânte deva|lokāt paricyutam
17.10 ādityam iva kālena yug'|ânte bhuvi pātitam
Mahendram iva durdharṣaṃ Mahendram iva duḥsaham
Mahendra|putraṃ patitaṃ Vālinaṃ hema|mālinam
siṃh'|ôraskaṃ mahā|bāhuṃ dīpt'|āsyaṃ hari|locanam.
Lakṣmaṇ'|ânugato Rāmo dadarś' ôpasasarpa ca.

sa dṛṣṭvā Rāghavaṃ Vālī Lakṣmaṇaṃ ca mahā|balam
abravīt praśritaṃ vākyaṃ paruṣaṃ dharma|saṃhitam:

«parāṅ|mukha|vadhaṃ kṛtvā ko nu prāptas tvayā guṇaḥ
yad ahaṃ yuddha|saṃrabdhas tvat|kṛte nidhanaṃ gataḥ?
‹kulīnaḥ sattva|sampannas tejasvī carita|vrataḥ
Rāmaḥ karuṇa|vedī ca prajānāṃ ca hite rataḥ.
17.15 s'|ânukrośo mah"|ôtsāhaḥ sama|yajño dṛḍha|vrataḥ.›
iti te sarva|bhūtāni kathayanti yaśo bhuvi.
tān guṇān saṃpradhāry' âham agryaṃ c' âbhijanaṃ tava
Tārayā pratiṣiddhaḥ san Sugrīveṇa samāgataḥ.
na mām anyena saṃrabdhaṃ pramattaṃ veddhum arhasi
iti me buddhir utpannā babhūv' âdarśane tava.

na tvāṃ vinihat'|ātmānaṃ dharma|dhvajam adhārmikam
jāne pāpa|samācāraṃ tṛṇaiḥ kūpam iv' āvṛtam.
satāṃ veṣa|dharaṃ pāpam pracchannam iva pāvakam
n' âhaṃ tvām abhijānāmi dharma|cchadm'|âbhisaṃvṛtam.

opened the path to heaven for that warrior and gained for him the highest state.

Like unassailable great Indra, like irresistible great Indra, great Indra's fallen son, gold-garlanded Valin, lion-chested, long-armed, blazing-faced, tawny-eyed, lay fallen thus in battle, resembling a fire whose flame has gone out, like Yayáti fallen from the world of the gods through exhaustion
of his merit, or the sun cast down to earth by Time at the 17.10
end of the world. Followed closely by Lákshmana, Rama approached and looked at him.

Now, when Valin saw Ràghava and mighty Lákshmana, he spoke these words, which, though harsh, were civil and consistent with righteousness:

"Because of you, I have met my death while in the heat of battle with someone else. What possible merit have you gained by killing me when I wasn't looking? 'Rama is wellborn, virtuous, powerful, compassionate and energetic. He 17.15
has observed vows, knows pity, is devoted to the welfare of the people, knows when to act, and is firm in his vows.' That is how everyone spreads your good reputation throughout the world. Considering those good qualities of yours and your exalted lineage as well, I engaged in battle with Sugríva though Tará tried to stop me. Since I didn't see you, I had no idea you would strike me when I was in the heat of battle with another, heedless of you.

I did not know that your judgment was destroyed and that you were a vicious evildoer hiding under a banner of righteousness, like a well overgrown with grass. I did not know that you were a wicked person wearing the trappings of virtue, concealed by a disguise of righteousness like a

17.20 viṣaye vā pure vā te yadā n' âpakaromy aham
na ca tvāṃ pratijāne 'haṃ kasmāt tvaṃ haṃsy akilbiṣam
phala|mūl'|âśanaṃ nityaṃ vānaraṃ vana|gocaram
mām ih' âpratiyudhyantam anyena ca samāgatam?

tvaṃ nar'|âdhipateḥ putraḥ pratītaḥ priya|darśanaḥ
liṅgam apy asti te, rājan, dṛśyate dharma|saṃhitam.
kaḥ kṣatriya|kule jātaḥ śrutavān naṣṭa|saṃśayaḥ
dharma|liṅga|praticchannaḥ krūraṃ karma samācaret?
Rāma, rāja|kule jāto dharmavān iti viśrutaḥ
abhavyo bhavya|rūpeṇa kim|arthaṃ paridhāvasi?
17.25 sāma dānaṃ kṣamā dharmaḥ satyaṃ dhṛti|parākramau
pārthivānāṃ guṇā, rājan, daṇḍaś c' âpy apakāriṣu.
vayaṃ vana|carā, Rāma, mṛgā mūla|phal'|âśanāḥ.
eṣā prakṛtir asmākaṃ puruṣas tvaṃ nar'|ēśvaraḥ.

bhūmir hiraṇyaṃ rūpyaṃ ca nigrahe kāraṇāni ca.
tatra kas te vane lobho madīyeṣu phaleṣu vā?
nayaś ca vinayaś c' ôbhau nigrah'|ânugrahāv api
rāja|vṛttir asaṃkīrṇā na nṛpāḥ kāma|vṛttayaḥ.
tvaṃ tu kāma|pradhānaś ca kopanaś c' ânavasthitaḥ.
rāja|vṛttaiś ca saṃkīrṇaḥ śar'|āsana|parāyaṇaḥ.
17.30 na te 'sty apacitir dharme n' ârthe buddhir avasthitā
indriyaiḥ kāma|vṛttaḥ san kṛṣyase, manuj'|ēśvara!
hatvā bāṇena, Kākutstha, mām ih' ânaparādhinam
kiṃ vakṣyasi satāṃ madhye karma kṛtvā jugupsitam?

smoldering fire. I did no harm either in your kingdom or 17.20
in your city, nor did I insult you; so why did you kill me, an
innocent forest-ranging monkey, living only on fruit and
roots, when I had joined battle here with someone else and
was not fighting against you?

You are the handsome, renowned son of a ruler of men.
You also have the visible signs associated with righteousness,
king. What man, born in a kshatriya family, learned, free of
doubts, and bearing signs of righteousness, would perform
such a cruel deed? Born in a royal family, reputed to be virtuous, why do you go about with the appearance of decency
when you are in fact not decent, Rama? Conciliation, gen- 17.25
erosity, forbearance, righteousness, truthfulness, steadiness
and courage, as well as punishment of wrongdoers, are the
virtues of kings, Your Majesty. We are but forest-dwelling
beasts, Rama, living on roots and fruit. That is our nature,
while you are a man and a lord of men.

Land, gold and silver are reasons for conquest. But what
possible profit could there be for you in the fruit belonging
to me in this forest? Both statesmanship and restraint as well
as punishing and rewarding are royal functions that must
not be confused. Kings must not act capriciously. But you,
instead, care only for your own desire. You are wrathful,
unsteady, confused about your royal functions and interested only in shooting your arrows. You have no reverence 17.30
for what is right, no settled judgment concerning statecraft;
and because you are addicted to pleasures, you are driven
by your passions, lord of men. Now that you have done this
despicable deed and killed me, an innocent creature, with

rāja|hā brahma|hā go|ghnaś coraḥ prāṇi|vadhe rataḥ
nāstikaḥ parivettā ca sarve niraya|gāminaḥ.
adhāryaṃ carma me sadbhī romāṇy asthi ca varjitam
abhakṣyāṇi ca māṃsāni tvad|vidhair dharma|cāribhiḥ.
pañca pañca|nakhā bhakṣyā brahma|kṣatreṇa, Rāghava,
śalyakaḥ śvā vidho godhā śaśaḥ kūrmaś ca pañcamaḥ.
17.35 carma c' âsthi ca me rājan na spṛśanti manīṣiṇaḥ
abhakṣyāṇi ca māṃsāni so 'haṃ pañca|nakho hataḥ.
tvayā nāthena, Kākutstha, na sa|nāthā vasuṃ|dharā
pramadā śīla|saṃpannā dhūrtena patinā yathā.
śaṭho naikṛtikaḥ kṣudro mithyā|praśrita|mānasaḥ
kathaṃ Daśarathena tvaṃ jātaḥ pāpo mah"|ātmanā?
chinna|cāritrya|kakṣyeṇa satāṃ dharm'|âtivartinā
tyakta|dharm'|âṅkuśen' âhaṃ nihato Rāma|hastinā.
dṛśyamānas tu yudhyethā mayā yudhi nṛp'|ātmaja
adya Vaivasvataṃ devaṃ paśyes tvaṃ nihato mayā.
17.40 tvay" âdṛśyena tu raṇe nihato 'haṃ durāsadaḥ
prasuptaḥ pannagen' êva naraḥ pāna|vaśaṃ gataḥ.
Sugrīva|priya|kāmena yad ahaṃ nihatas tvayā
kaṇṭhe baddhvā pradadyāṃ te 'nihataṃ Rāvaṇaṃ raṇe.

your arrow, what will you say in the presence of virtuous men, Kákutstha?

A king-killer, a brahman-killer, a cow-killer, a thief, a man who delights in killing, an atheist, a man who marries before his elder brother—all of them go to hell. Virtuous people cannot wear my skin, my fur and bones are forbidden, and my flesh cannot be eaten by people like you who observe the law. Only five among the five-clawed creatures can be eaten by brahmans and kshatriyas, Rághava: the hedgehog, the porcupine, the lizard, the rabbit and, fifth, the turtle.
Wise men do not touch my skin or bones, king, and my 17.35
flesh must not be eaten; yet I, a five-clawed creature, have been killed.

With you as her protector, Kákutstha, the earth has no protector and is like a virtuous young wife with a deceitful husband. Treacherous, dishonest, mean, with false humility, how could a wretch like you be born of the great Dasha·ratha? I have been killed by this mad elephant Rama, who has broken the fetters of good conduct, overstepped the laws of virtuous men, and disregarded the goad of lawfulness. If you had fought openly in battle, prince, I would have killed you, and you would now be gazing on Vaivásvata,
god of death. But I, who am unassailable in battle, have 17.40
been struck down by you when you could not be seen, as a man sleeping under the influence of drink may be killed by a snake. I could have given you Rávana, not killed in battle but bound around the neck; yet for that same outcome you killed me, wishing to please Sugríva.

nyastāṃ sāgara|toye vā pātāle v" âpi Maithilīm
jānayeyaṃ tav' ādeśāc chvetām aśvatarīm iva.
yuktaṃ yat prāpnuyād rājyaṃ Sugrīvaḥ svar|gate mayi.
ayuktaṃ yad adharmeṇa tvay" âhaṃ nihato raṇe.
kāmam evaṃ|vidhaṃ lokaḥ kālena viniyujyate.
kṣamaṃ ced bhavatā prāptam uttaraṃ sādhu cintyatām!»

17.45 ity evam uktvā pariśuṣka|vaktraḥ
śar'|âbhighātād vyathito mah"|ātmā
samīkṣya Rāmaṃ ravi|saṃnikāśaṃ
tūṣṇīṃ babhūv' âmara|rāja|sūnuḥ.

18.1 Ity uktaḥ praśritaṃ vākyaṃ dharm'|ârtha|sahitaṃ hitam
paruṣaṃ Vālinā Rāmo nihatena vicetasā.
taṃ niṣprabham iv' ādityaṃ mukta|toyam iv' âmbudam
ukta|vākyaṃ hari|śreṣṭham upaśāntam iv' ânalam
dharm'|ârtha|guṇa|saṃpannaṃ har'|īśvaram anuttamam
adhikṣiptas tadā Rāmaḥ paścād Vālinam abravīt:
«dharmam arthaṃ ca kāmaṃ ca samayaṃ c' âpi laukikam
avijñāya kathaṃ bālyān mām ih' âdya vigarhase?
18.5 apṛṣṭvā buddhi|saṃpannān vṛddhān ācārya|saṃmatān,
saumya, vānara|cāpalyāt tvaṃ māṃ vaktum ih' êcchasi?
Ikṣvākūṇām iyaṃ bhūmiḥ sa|śaila|vana|kānanā
mṛga|pakṣi|manuṣyāṇāṃ nigrah'|ânugrahāv api.
tāṃ pālayati dharm'|ātmā Bharataḥ satya|vāg ṛjuḥ
dharma|kām'|ârtha|tattvajño nigrah'|ânugrahe rataḥ.

Had Máithili been hidden in the ocean waters or even in the underworld, at your command I would have brought her back like the white she-mule. It is fitting that when I have gone to heaven, Sugríva should obtain the kingdom. But for you to have killed me unjustly in battle is not fitting. Granted, all people, being what they are, are destined for death. But if what you have accomplished is proper, think of a good defense."

When he had spoken in this way, the great son of the 17.45
king of the gods, pained by the arrow that had wounded him, his mouth dry, looked at Rama, radiant as the sun, and fell silent.

STRICKEN AND losing consciousness, Valin had addressed 18.1
to Rama those words that were civil, beneficial, consistent with righteousness and statecraft, yet harsh. As he finished speaking, that best of monkeys was like a darkened sun, like a rain cloud that has given up its water, or like an extinguished fire. Rama, having been censured, at last addressed Valin, lord of monkeys, with unsurpassed words distinguished by righteousness and statecraft:

"How can you, who do not understand righteousness, statecraft, pleasure or even worldly conduct, in your foolishness, reproach me here today? My friend, in your monkey 18.5
frivolousness, you wish to revile me here without consulting elders endowed with judgment and respected as teachers. This earth, with its mountains, woods and forests, belongs to the Ikshvákus, as does the right of punishing and rewarding its beasts, birds and men. It is protected by righteous Bharata, who is truthful and upright, who knows the true

nayaś ca vinayaś c' ôbhau yasmin satyaṃ ca susthitam
vikramaś ca yathā dṛṣṭaḥ sa rājā deśa|kālavit.
tasya dharma|kṛt'|ādeśā vayam anye ca pārthivāḥ
carāmo vasudhāṃ kṛtsnāṃ dharma|saṃtānam icchavaḥ.
18.10 tasmin nṛpati|śārdūle Bharate dharma|vatsale
pālayaty akhilāṃ bhūmiṃ kaś cared dharma|nigraham?
te vayaṃ mārga|vibhraṣṭaṃ svadharme parame sthitāḥ
Bharat'|ājñāṃ puras|kṛtya nigṛhṇīmo yathā|vidhi.
tvaṃ tu saṃkliṣṭa|dharmā ca karmaṇā ca vigarhitaḥ
kāma|tantra|pradhānaś ca na sthito rāja|vartmani.
jyeṣṭho bhrātā pitā c' âiva yaś ca vidyāṃ prayacchati:
trayas te pitaro jñeyā dharme ca pathi vartinaḥ.
yavīyān ātmanaḥ putraḥ śiṣyaś c' âpi guṇ'|ôditaḥ:
putravat te trayaś cintyā dharmaś ced atra kāraṇam.
18.15 sūkṣmaḥ parama|durjñeyaḥ satāṃ dharmaḥ, plavaṃ|gama,
hṛdi|sthaḥ sarva|bhūtānām ātmā veda śubh'|âśubham.
capalaś capalaiḥ sārdhaṃ vānarair akṛt'|ātmabhiḥ
jāty|andha iva jāty|andhair mantrayan drakṣyase nu kim?
ahaṃ tu vyaktatām asya vacanasya bravīmi te
na hi māṃ kevalaṃ roṣāt tvaṃ vigarhitum arhasi.

nature of righteousness, pleasure and statecraft, and who
devotes himself to punishing and rewarding. He is a king
who knows the proper place and time for action. In him are
well established both statesmanship and humility, as well as
truth and valor, as prescribed in sacred texts. With his command given for the sake of righteousness, we and the other
princes go about the entire world seeking the continuance
of righteousness. While that tiger among kings, Bhárata, de- 18.10
voted to righteousness, protects the whole earth, who could
suppress righteousness?

Firm in our own high duty, honoring Bharata's command, we duly chastise whoever strays from the path of righteousness. But you violate righteousness and are condemned by your actions. You are engrossed in the pursuit of pleasures, and you have not kept to the path of kings. An older brother, a father and a bestower of learning—these three are to be regarded as fathers by one who walks the path of righteousness. A younger brother, one's own son and also a pupil with good qualities—these three are to be thought of as one's sons, if righteousness is the standard here.

Righteousness is subtle, monkey, and extremely difficult 18.15
to understand even for good people. The self in the heart of
all beings knows good and evil. You are frivolous and consult
with frivolous, weak-minded monkeys, like someone blind
from birth who consults with others blind from birth. What
then can you possibly see? But I shall tell you clearly the
meaning of my statement, for you should not condemn me
simply because you are angry.

tad etat kāraṇaṃ paśya yad|arthaṃ tvaṃ mayā hataḥ:
bhrātur vartasi bhāryāyāṃ tyaktvā dharmaṃ sanātanam.
asya tvaṃ dharamāṇasya Sugrīvasya mah"|ātmanaḥ
Rumāyāṃ vartase kāmāt snuṣāyāṃ, pāpa|karmakṛt.
18.20 tad vyatītasya te dharmāt kāma|vṛttasya, vānara.
bhrātṛ|bhāry"|âbhimarśe 'smin daṇḍo 'yaṃ pratipāditaḥ.
na hi dharma|viruddhasya loka|vṛttād apeyuṣaḥ
daṇḍād anyatra paśyāmi nigrahaṃ, hari|yūthapa.
aurasīṃ bhaginīṃ v" âpi bhāryāṃ v" âpy anujasya yaḥ
pracareta naraḥ kāmāt tasya daṇḍo vadhaḥ smṛtaḥ.
Bharatas tu mahī|pālo vayaṃ tv ādeśa|vartinaḥ.
tvaṃ ca dharmād atikrāntaḥ kathaṃ śakyam upekṣitum?
guru|dharma|vyatikrāntaṃ prājño dharmeṇa pālayan
Bharataḥ kāma|vṛttānāṃ nigrahe paryavasthitaḥ.
18.25 vayaṃ tu Bharat'|ādeśaṃ vidhiṃ kṛtvā, har'|īśvara,
tvad|vidhān bhinna|maryādān niyantuṃ paryavasthitāḥ.
Sugrīveṇa ca me sakhyaṃ Lakṣmaṇena yathā tathā.
dāra|rājya|nimittaṃ ca niḥśreyasi rataḥ sa me.
pratijñā ca mayā dattā tadā vānara|saṃnidhau,
pratijñā ca kathaṃ śakyā mad|vidhen' ânavekṣitum?
tad ebhiḥ kāraṇaiḥ sarvair mahadbhir dharma|saṃhitaiḥ
śāsanaṃ tava yad yuktaṃ tad bhavān anumanyatām.
sarvathā dharma ity eva draṣṭavyas tava nigrahaḥ.
vayasyasy' ôpakartavyaṃ dharmam ev' ânupaśyatā.

Learn therefore the reason that I have killed you: You have forsaken everlasting morality and live in sin with your brother's wife. Out of lust you committed a sinful deed: While great Sugríva is alive, you lived in sin with your daughter-in-law Ruma. You acted according to your desires, 18.20
monkey, and in violating your brother's wife you departed from righteousness. That is why this punishment was administered to you. Leader of monkey troops, I see no way other than punishment to chastise someone who is opposed to righteousness and deviates from universal custom. Death is the punishment prescribed for a man who out of lust approaches his daughter, sister or younger brother's wife. Now Bharata is the ruler of the earth, and we merely carry out his commands. How then can we overlook your violation of righteousness?

Wise Bharata is intent on chastising those addicted to sensual pleasures, righteously disciplining whoever transgresses major laws. And we have made Bhárata's command 18.25
our sacred law, lord of monkeys, and are intent on punishing those who, like you, transgress the proper limits. My friendship with Sugríva is just like my friendship with Lákshmana. And for the sake of his wife and kingdom he is devoted to my highest good. Moreover, I made a promise at that time in the presence of the other monkeys. And how can someone like me disregard a promise?

Therefore, for all those important reasons which are consistent with righteousness, you must agree that your punishment is appropriate. Your chastisement must be viewed as righteous in every way. A person who keeps righteousness clearly in view must assist his friend. Then, too, men who 18.30

18.30 rājabhir dhṛta|daṇḍās tu kṛtvā pāpāni mānavāḥ
nirmalāḥ svargam āyānti santaḥ sukṛtino yathā.
āryeṇa mama Māndhātrā vyasanaṃ ghoram īpsitam
śramaṇena kṛte pāpe yathā pāpaṃ kṛtaṃ tvayā.
anyair api kṛtaṃ pāpaṃ pramattair vasudh"|âdhipaiḥ.
prāyaś|cittaṃ ca kurvanti tena tac chāmyate rajaḥ.
tad alaṃ paritāpena! dharmataḥ parikalpitaḥ
vadho, vānara|śārdūla, na vayaṃ sva|vaśe sthitāḥ.
vāgurābhiś ca pāśaiś ca kūṭaiś ca vividhair narāḥ
praticchannāś ca dṛśyāś ca gṛhṇanti subahūn mṛgān
pradhāvitān vā vitrastān visrabdhān ativiṣṭhitān.
18.35 pramattān apramattān vā narā māṃs'|ârthino bhṛśam
vidhyanti vimukhāṃś c' âpi na ca doṣo 'tra vidyate.
yānti rāja'|rṣayaś c' âtra mṛgayāṃ dharma|kovidāḥ
tasmāt tvaṃ nihato yuddhe mayā bāṇena, vānara,
ayudhyan pratiyudhyan vā yasmāc chākhā|mṛgo hy asi.
durlabhasya ca dharmasya jīvitasya śubhasya ca
rājāno, vānara|śreṣṭha, pradātāro na saṃśayaḥ.
tān na hiṃsyān na c' ākrośen n' ākṣipen n' âpriyaṃ vadet:
devā mānuṣa|rūpeṇa caranty ete mahī|tale.
tvaṃ tu dharmam avijñāya kevalaṃ roṣam āsthitaḥ
pradūṣayasi māṃ dharme pitṛ|paitāmahe sthitam.»
18.40 evam uktas tu Rāmeṇa Vālī pravyathito bhṛśam
pratyuvāca tato Rāmaṃ prāñjalir vānar'|ēśvaraḥ:

have done evil but have been punished by kings become pure and go to heaven just as do virtuous men.

My noble ancestor Mandhátri inflicted a terrible punishment on a mendicant who committed a sin like the sin you committed. Sins have been committed as well by other heedless rulers of the earth. But when they made atonement, that taint was removed. So enough of this sorrow! Your death was decided upon justly, tiger among monkeys: We were not being arbitrary.

By snares, nooses and various traps, men in hiding or out in the open catch all kinds of beasts who run away
terrified or confidently stand still. Men seeking meat shoot 18.35
animals that are attentive or inattentive or even facing the other way, and there is nothing wrong with this. Even royal seers who fully understand righteousness go hunting here. And so, monkey, I struck you down with an arrow in battle regardless of whether you fought back or not. After all, you are only a monkey.

There is no doubt, best of monkeys, that it is kings who give life and prosperity and otherwise unattainable religious merit. One should not harm them, nor censure them, nor insult them, nor say displeasing things to them: They are gods in human form going about on earth. Yet you, who know nothing of righteousness and simply follow your passions, rebuke me for abiding by my sacred ancestral laws."

Addressed by Rama in that way, Valin, lord of monkeys, 18.40
was deeply disturbed. Joining his palms in supplication, he replied to Rama:

«yat tvam āttha, nara|śreṣṭha, tad evaṃ, n' âtra saṃśayaḥ
prativaktuṃ prakṛṣṭe hi n' âpakṛṣṭas tu śaknuyāt.
yad ayuktaṃ mayā pūrvaṃ pramādād vākyam apriyam
tatr' âpi khalu me doṣaṃ kartuṃ n' ârhasi, Rāghava.
tvaṃ hi dṛṣṭ'|ârtha|tattva|jñaḥ prajānāṃ ca hite rataḥ.
kārya|kāraṇa|siddhau te prasannā buddhir avyayā.
mām apy avagataṃ dharmād vyatikrānta|puras|kṛtam
dharma|saṃhitayā vācā, dharmajña, paripālaya!»

18.45 bāṣpa|saṃruddha|kaṇṭhas tu Vālī s'|ārta|ravaḥ śanaiḥ.
uvāca Rāmaṃ saṃprekṣya paṅka|lagna iva dvipaḥ:

«na tv ātmānam ahaṃ śoce na Tārāṃ n' âpi bāndhavān
yathā putraṃ guṇa|śreṣṭham Aṅgadaṃ kanak'|âṅgadam.
sa mam' âdarśanād dīno bālyāt prabhṛti lālitaḥ
taṭāka iva pīt'|âmbur upaśoṣaṃ gamiṣyati.
Sugrīve c' Âṅgade c' âiva vidhatsva matim uttamām
tvaṃ hi śāstā ca goptā ca kāry'|âkārya|vidhau sthitaḥ.
yā te, nara|pate, vṛttir Bharate Lakṣmaṇe ca yā
Sugrīve c' Âṅgade rājaṃs tāṃ cintayitum arhasi.

18.50 mad|doṣa|kṛta|doṣāṃ tāṃ yathā Tārāṃ tapasvinīm
Sugrīvo n' âvamanyeta tath" âvasthātum arhasi.
tvayā hy anugṛhītena śakyaṃ rājyam upāsitum
tvad|vaśe vartamānena tava citt'|ânuvartinā.»

"Best of men, there is no doubt that what you have said is true. Indeed, a lowly person should not talk back to an exalted one. Please do not find fault with me even for the unseemly, displeasing words I spoke before by mistake, Rághava. For you understand worldly interests and know the truth, and you are devoted to the well-being of the people. Your immutable judgment about determining crime and punishment is correct. You know righteousness. Therefore, with righteous words, comfort even me, known to be a flagrant violator of righteousness."

Like an elephant mired in mud, Valin cried out in distress, 18.45
his voice choked with tears. Then, looking at Rama, he said softly:

"I do not grieve as much for myself, or Tará, or even my kinsmen as I do for my eminently virtuous son Ángada of the golden armbands. Cherished since his childhood, he will be so wretched at not seeing me that he will dry up like a pond whose waters have been drunk. Show the same high regard to Ángada as to Sugríva, for you are their teacher and protector, abiding by the rules of what must be done and what must not be done. And, king and lord of men, you should think of Sugríva and Ángada with the
same affection as you have for Bharata and Lákshmana. And 18.50
please arrange it so that Sugríva will not think ill of poor Tará, who is guilty only through my guilt. For the kingdom can be served only by someone you favor, who is under your control and obedient to your wishes."

sa tam āśvāsayad Rāmo Vālinaṃ vyakta|darśanam:
«na vayaṃ bhavatā cintyā n' âpy ātmā, hari|sattama,
vayaṃ bhavad|viśeṣeṇa dharmataḥ kṛta|niścayāḥ.
daṇḍye yaḥ pātayed daṇḍaṃ daṇḍyo yaś c' âpi daṇḍyate
kārya|kāraṇa|siddh'|ârthāv ubhau tau n' âvasīdataḥ.
18.55 tad bhavān daṇḍa|saṃyogād asmād vigata|kalmaṣaḥ
gataḥ svāṃ prakṛtiṃ dharmyāṃ dharma|dṛṣṭena vartmanā.»
sa tasya vākyaṃ madhuraṃ mah"|ātmanaḥ
samāhitaṃ dharma|path'|ânuvartinaḥ
niśamya Rāmasya raṇ'|âvamardino
vacaḥ suyuktaṃ nijagāda vānaraḥ:
«śar'|âbhitaptena vicetasā mayā
pradūṣitas tvaṃ yad ajānatā, prabho,
idaṃ, Mahendr'|ôpama|bhīma|vikrama,
prasāditas tvaṃ kṣama me, mah"|īśvara!»

Rama then consoled Valin, who now saw things clearly:

"You must not worry about us, or even about yourself, best of monkeys, for we made our determination with regard to you according to the law. Neither he who inflicts punishment on one who deserves punishment nor he who is punished when he deserves punishment perishes: Each
serves the due process of justice. Therefore, freed from sin 18.55
by meeting with this punishment, you have returned to your own righteous nature by the path determined by righteousness."

When he heard the sweet, calm speech of great Rama, who followed the path of righteousness and crushed his enemies in battle, the monkey said these very fitting words:

"If when I was half-unconscious with the pain of the arrow, lord, I unwittingly censured you, whose fearful prowess is equal to great Indra's, please be gracious and forgive me, ruler of the earth."

19–25
SUGRÍVA IS KING

19.1 SA VĀNARA|mahā|rājaḥ śayānaḥ śara|vikṣataḥ
pratyukto hetumad|vākyair n' ôttaraṃ pratyapadyata.
aśmabhiḥ paribhinn'|âṅgaḥ pādapair āhato bhṛśam
Rāma|bāṇena c' ākrānto jīvit'|ânte mumoha saḥ.
tam bhāryā bāṇa|mokṣeṇa Rāma|dattena saṃyuge
hataṃ plavaga|śārdūlaṃ Tārā śuśrāva Vālinam.
sā sa|putr" âpriyaṃ śrutvā vadhaṃ bhartuḥ sudāruṇam
niṣpapāta bhṛśaṃ trastā vividhād giri|gahvarāt.
19.5 ye tv Aṅgada|parīvārā vānarā hi mahā|balāḥ
te sa|kārmukam ālokya Rāmaṃ trastāḥ pradudruvuḥ.
sā dadarśa tatas trastān harīn āpatato drutam
yūthād iva paribhraṣṭān mṛgān nihata|yūthapān.
tān uvāca samāsādya duḥkhitān duḥkhitā satī
Rāma|vitrāsitān sarvān anubaddhān iv' êṣubhiḥ:
«vānarā, rāja|siṃhasya yasya yūyaṃ puraḥ|sarāḥ
taṃ vihāya suvitrastāḥ kasmād dravata durgatāḥ?
rājya|hetoḥ sa ced bhrātā bhrātrā raudreṇa pātitaḥ
Rāmeṇa prasṛtair dūrān mārgaṇair dūra|pātibhiḥ?»
19.10 kapi|patnyā vacaḥ śrutvā kapayaḥ kāma|rūpiṇaḥ
prāpta|kālam aviśliṣṭam ūcur vacanam aṅganām:
«jīva|putre, nivartasva putraṃ rakṣasva c' Âṅgadam!
Antako Rāma|rūpeṇa hatvā nayati Vālinam.
kṣiptān vṛkṣān samāvidhya vipulāś ca śilās tathā
Vālī vajra|samair bāṇair vajreṇ' êva nipātitaḥ.

Answered with well-reasoned words, that great king of 19.1
monkeys made no reply as he lay deeply wounded by
the arrow. He had been beaten with trees, and his limbs were
completely shattered by stones. Pierced by Rama's arrow, he
lost consciousness as his life neared its end.

His wife Tará heard that Valin, tiger among monkeys,
had been killed in battle by an arrow shot by Rama. When
she heard the painful news of her husband's terrible death,
she was greatly frightened and rushed out with her son from
the many-chambered mountain cave. Now at the sight of 19.5
Rama with his bow, those mighty monkeys who were Ángada's attendants ran off terrified. Tará saw those mighty
monkeys running away swiftly, like deer bolting from their
herd when their herd leader is struck down. All of them
were anguished and as fearful of Rama as if they were being
pursued by his arrows. Anguished herself, she approached
them and said:

"Monkeys, attendants of the lion among kings, why have
you abandoned him and run off in distress and terror? Is it
because, for the sake of the kingdom, a fierce brother has
had Rama strike down his brother with arrows shot from
afar, striking from afar?"

When the monkeys, who could change form at will, heard 19.10
the speech of that lovely woman, the monkey's wife, they
spoke timely words with one voice:

"You have a living son Ángada, so turn back and protect
him. For Death in the form of Rama has killed Valin and
is leading him away. As if by a thunderbolt, Valin has been
felled by arrows like thunderbolts, which shattered the trees

abhidrutam idaṃ sarvaṃ vidrutaṃ prasṛtaṃ balam
asmin plavaga|śārdūle hate Śakra|sama|prabhe.
rakṣyatāṃ nagaraṃ śūrair Aṅgadaś c' âbhiṣicyatām
padasthaṃ Vālinaḥ putraṃ bhajiṣyanti plavaṃ|gamāḥ.
19.15 athavā ruciraṃ sthānam iha te, rucir'|ānane,
āviśanti hi durgāṇi kṣipram ady' âiva vānarāḥ?
abhāryāḥ saha|bhāryāś ca
santy atra vana|cāriṇaḥ
lubdhebhyo viprayuktebhyaḥ
svebhyo nas tumulaṃ bhayam.»

alp'|ântara|gatānāṃ tu śrutvā vacanam aṅganā
ātmanaḥ pratirūpaṃ sā babhāṣe cāru|hāsinī:
«putreṇa mama kiṃ kāryaṃ, kiṃ rājyena, kim ātmanā
kapi|siṃhe mahā|bhāge tasmin bhartari naśyati?
pāda|mūlaṃ gamiṣyāmi tasy' âiv' âhaṃ mah"|ātmanaḥ
yo 'sau Rāma|prayuktena śareṇa vinipātitaḥ.»
19.20 evam uktvā pradudrāva rudatī śoka|karśitā
śiraś c' ôraś ca bāhubhyāṃ duḥkhena samabhighnatī.
āvrajantī dadarś' âtha patiṃ nipatitaṃ bhuvi
hantāraṃ dānav'|êndrāṇāṃ samareṣv anivartinām
kṣeptāraṃ parvat'|êndrāṇāṃ vajrāṇām iva Vāsavam
mahā|vāta|samāviṣṭaṃ mahā|megh'|âugha|niḥsvanam
Śakra|tulya|parākrāntaṃ vṛṣṭv" êv' ôparataṃ ghanam
nardantaṃ nardatāṃ bhīmaṃ śūraṃ śūreṇa pātitam
śārdūlen' āmiṣasy' ârthe mṛga|rājaṃ yathā hatam
arcitaṃ sarva|lokasya sa|patākaṃ sa|vedikam
nāga|hetoḥ Suparṇena caityam unmathitaṃ yathā.

and large rocks he hurled. Now that that tiger among monkeys, splendid as Shakra, has been killed, this entire army, which had advanced, has scattered and fled. Let the warriors protect the city, and let Valin's son Ángada be consecrated as king. Once he has assumed his rank, the monkeys will serve him. Or perhaps you wish to remain here, fair-faced 19.15
woman, since this very day hostile monkeys will quickly take over our citadels? There are forest-dwelling monkeys out there, both with and without wives. We are in great danger from our destitute and covetous kinsmen."

But when the sweet-smiling woman heard the words of those who were close by, she spoke in a way befitting her:

"What use have I for a son, or a kingdom, or myself, now that my illustrious husband, that lion among monkeys, has perished? I shall go to the feet of that great monkey who was felled by the arrow Rama shot."

With these words she ran, weeping and haggard with 19.20
grief, sorrowfully beating her breast and her head with both hands. As she approached, she saw on the ground her fallen husband, that slayer of *dánava* lords who never turned their backs in battle, him who hurled the highest mountains as Vásava hurls thunderbolts, impetuous as a storm wind, thundering like a mass of great clouds, roaring fearfully among other roarers, valiant as Shakra. Now he was like a cloud stilled once it has rained, a hero felled by a hero as a great stag is slain by a tiger for its flesh, or like a sacred tree with banners and railing, worshiped by all the people, uprooted by Supárna in his search for snakes.

19.25 avaṣṭabhy' âvatiṣṭhantaṃ dadarśa dhanur ūrjitam
Rāmaṃ Rām'|ânujaṃ c' âiva bhartuś c' âiv' ânujaṃ śubhā.
tān atītya samāsādya bhartāraṃ nihataṃ raṇe
samīkṣya vyathitā bhūmau saṃbhrāntā nipapāta ha.
supt" êva punar utthāya, «ārya|putr' êti» krośatī
ruroda sā patiṃ dṛṣṭvā saṃditaṃ mṛtyu|dāmabhiḥ.
tāṃ avekṣya tu Sugrīvaḥ krośantīṃ kurarīm iva
viṣādam agamat kaṣṭaṃ dṛṣṭvā c' Âṅgadam āgatam.

20.1 Rāma|cāpa|visṛṣṭena śareṇ' ânta|kareṇa tam
dṛṣṭvā vinihataṃ bhūmau Tārā tār"|âdhip'|ānanā
sā samāsādya bhartāraṃ paryaṣvajata bhāminī
iṣuṇ" âbhihataṃ dṛṣṭvā Vālinaṃ kuñjar'|ôpamam.
vānar'|êndraṃ Mahendr'|ābhaṃ śoka|saṃtapta|mānasā
Tārā tarum iv' ônmūlaṃ paryadevayad āturā:
«raṇe dāruṇa|vikrānta pravīra plavatāṃ vara,
kiṃ dīnām a|puro|bhāgām adya tvaṃ n' âbhibhāṣase?
20.5 uttiṣṭha, hari|śārdūla, bhajasva śayan'|ôttamam!
n' âivaṃ|vidhāḥ śerate hi bhūmau nṛpati|sattamāḥ.
atīva khalu te kāntā vasudhā, vasudh"|âdhipa,
gat'|âsur api yāṃ gātrair māṃ vihāya niṣevase.
vyaktam anyā tvayā, vīra, dharmataḥ saṃpravartatā
Kiṣkindh" êva purī ramyā svarga|mārge vinirmitā.
yāny asmābhis tvayā sārdhaṃ vaneṣu madhu|gandhiṣu
vihṛtāni tvayā kāle teṣām uparamaḥ kṛtaḥ.
nirānandā nirāś" âhaṃ nimagnā śoka|sāgare
tvayi pañcatvam āpanne mahā|yūthapa|yūthape.

The lovely woman saw Rama standing there, leaning on 19.25
his strong bow, and also the younger brothers of both Rama and her husband. She passed them by, but as she drew near and saw her husband, who had been struck down in battle, she fell to the ground, suffering and bewildered. Then she rose up again as if asleep, crying out, "My husband!" and wept as she saw her lord caught in the bonds of death. Now, as Sugríva watched her crying like an osprey and saw Ángada, who had also come, he became deeply despondent.

When passionate Tará, her face like the lord of stars, 20.1
saw her husband on the ground, killed by a death-dealing shaft loosed from Rama's bow, like an elephant struck by an arrow, she went to him and embraced him. Seeing the monkey-lord Valin, splendid as great Indra, brought down like an uprooted tree, Tará was anguished. With her heart tortured by grief, she lamented:

"Warrior with your fierce prowess in battle, best of leaping monkeys, why do you now not speak to me, a wretched
woman who has done no wrong? Rise up, tiger among mon- 20.5
keys! Go to your own fine bed. Great kings like you do not sleep on the ground. How deep your love for the earth must be, lord of earth, that even in death you abandon me and embrace her with your limbs. By living righteously, warrior, you must have created on the path to heaven some other city as charming as Kishkíndha.

Now you have brought to an end those pleasures we enjoyed with you in the honey-scented woodlands. Without joy, without hope, I am sunk in a sea of grief since you, great leader among troop leaders, have gone to your death.

20.10 hṛdayaṃ susthiraṃ mahyaṃ dṛṣṭvā vinihataṃ bhuvi
yan na śok'|âbhisaṃtaptaṃ sphuṭate 'dya sahasradhā.
Sugrīvasya tvayā bhāryā hṛtā sa ca vivāsitaḥ
yat tat tasya tvayā vyuṣṭiḥ prāpt" êyaṃ, plavag'|âdhipa.
niḥśreyasa|parā mohāt tvayā c' âhaṃ vigarhitā
y" âiṣ" âbruvaṃ hitaṃ vākyaṃ, vānar'|êndra, hit'|âiṣiṇī.
kālo niḥsaṃśayo nūnaṃ jīvit'|ânta|karas tava
balād yen' âvapanno 'si Sugrīvasy' âvaśo vaśam.
vaidhavyaṃ śoka|saṃtāpaṃ kṛpaṇaṃ kṛpaṇā satī
a|duḥkh'|ôpacitā pūrvaṃ vartayiṣyāmy anāthavat.
20.15 lālitaś c' Âṅgado vīraḥ sukumāraḥ sukh'|ôcitaḥ
vatsyate kām avasthāṃ me pitṛvye krodha|mūrchite?
kuruṣva pitaraṃ, putra, sudṛṣṭaṃ dharma|vatsalam
durlabhaṃ darśanaṃ tv asya tava, vatsa, bhaviṣyati!
samāśvāsaya putraṃ tvaṃ saṃdeśaṃ saṃdiśasva ca
mūrdhni c' âinaṃ samāghrāya pravāsaṃ prasthito hy asi!
Rāmeṇa hi mahat karma kṛtaṃ tvām abhinighnatā
ānṛṇyaṃ tu gataṃ tasya Sugrīvasya pratiśrave.
sa|kāmo bhava, Sugrīva, Rumāṃ tvaṃ pratipatsyase
bhuṅkṣva rājyam anudvignaḥ śasto bhrātā ripus tava.
20.20 kiṃ māṃ evaṃ vilapatīṃ premṇā tvaṃ n' âbhibhāṣase?
imāḥ paśya varā bahvīr bhāryās te, vānar'|ēśvara!»
tasyā vilapitaṃ śrutvā vānaryaḥ sarvataś ca tāḥ
parigṛhy' Âṅgadaṃ dīnaṃ duḥkh'|ārtāḥ paricukruśuḥ:

My grief-tortured heart must be hard indeed that it does 20.10
not break into a thousand pieces though I see you on the
ground, destroyed.

This is the fruit you harvest, king of monkeys, for having
exiled Sugríva and taken his wife. Lord of monkeys, you
foolishly rebuked me when I, intent on your happiness and
wishing you well, offered you good advice. It is surely inex-
orable Time that forced you down powerless under Sugríva's
power and put an end to your life.

Once I was filled with joy, but now, in my wretchedness,
I must helplessly lead the life of a wretched, grief-anguished
widow. And the delicate young warrior Ángada, used to 20.15
pleasure, indulged by me—what kind of life will he lead,
when his father's brother is beside himself with anger? Son,
look carefully at your father so fond of righteousness, for you
will never see him again, dear child. And you, console your
son, kiss him on his head, and give him your instructions,
for you are starting on your final journey. By killing you,
Rama has done a great deed and has acquitted himself of
his promise to Sugríva. Be content, Sugríva: You shall have
Ruma back again. Enjoy the kingship without anxiety. Your
brother, who was your enemy, has been cut down. Why do 20.20
you not reply lovingly to me as I lament this way? Lord of
monkeys, behold these many excellent wives of yours."

Hearing her lament, those monkey women, afflicted with
sorrow, surrounded wretched Ángada on all sides and wailed.

«kim Aṅgadaṃ s'|âṅgada|vīra|bāho
vihāya yāsy adya cira|pravāsam?
na yuktam evaṃ guṇa|saṃnikṛṣṭaṃ
vihāya putraṃ, priya|putra, gantuṃ!
kim apriyaṃ te, priya|cāru|veṣa,
kṛtaṃ mayā, nātha, sutena vā te?
sahāyinīm adya vihāya, vīra,
Yama|kṣayaṃ gacchasi durvinītam.
yady apriyaṃ kiṃ cid asaṃpradhārya
kṛtaṃ mayā syāt tava, dīrgha|bāho,
kṣamasva me tadd, hari|vaṃśa|nātha,
vrajāmi mūrdhnā tava, vīra, pādau.»

20.25 tathā tu Tārā karuṇaṃ rudantī
bhartuḥ samīpe saha vānarībhiḥ
vyavasyata prāyam anindya|varṇā
upopaveṣṭuṃ bhuvi yatra Vālī.

21.1 Tato nipatitāṃ Tārāṃ cyutāṃ tārām iv' âmbarāt
śanair āśvāsayām āsa Hanūmān hari|yūthapaḥ:
«guṇa|doṣa|kṛtaṃ jantuḥ sva|karma|phala|hetukam
avyagras tad avāpnoti sarvaṃ pretya śubh'|âśubham.
śocyā śocasi kaṃ śocyaṃ dīnaṃ dīn" ânukampase?
kaś ca kasy' ânuśocyo 'sti dehe 'smin budbud'|ôpame?
Aṅgadas tu kumāro 'yaṃ draṣṭavyo jīva|putrayā
āyatyā ca vidheyāni samarthāny asya cintaya!
21.5 jānāsy aniyatām evaṃ bhūtānām āgatiṃ gatim
tasmāc chubhaṃ hi kartavyaṃ, paṇḍite, n' āihalaukikam.
yasmin hari|sahasrāṇi prayutāny arbudāni ca
vartayanti kṛt'|âṃśāni so 'yaṃ diṣṭ'|ântam āgataḥ.
yad ayaṃ nyāya|dṛṣṭ'|ârthaḥ sāma|dāna|kṣamā|paraḥ
gato dharma|jitāṃ bhūmiṃ n' âinaṃ śocitum arhasi.

"With your braceleted arms worthy of a hero, why do you now abandon Ángada and go on this long journey? You have a beloved son with qualities like your own. It is not right to abandon your son like this and go away. Beloved lord, what displeasing thing has been done by me or your son that you so discourteously abandon me, your companion, and go to Yama's abode, fine-robed warrior? Forgive me, long-armed lord of the monkey race, if I have unknowingly done something to displease you. Warrior, I prostrate myself at your feet."

Accompanied by the other monkey women, fair Tará, 20.25
weeping piteously in this way beside her husband, determined to sit fasting to death at the place where Valin lay.

THEN HÁNUMAN, leader of monkey troops, gently con- 21.1
soled Tará, who had dropped like a star falling from the sky.

"When he dies, a living being unfailingly reaches the good or evil end produced as the fruit of his actions and brought about by his virtues or faults. What person deserving lamentation do you lament, when you yourself deserve our lamentation? When you yourself are pitiable, for what pitiable person do you grieve? And who should mourn for whom, since the body is no more than a bubble? You must instead look after the boy Ángada, since you have this living son. You must think about the proper things to do for him in
the future. You know that the coming and going of beings is 21.5
uncertain. Therefore, wise woman, do what is auspicious, not what is worldly. He upon whom thousands, millions and hundreds of millions of monkeys once subsisted, each obtaining a share, has now reached the end of his allotted

sarve ca hari|śārdūlāḥ putraś c' âyaṃ tav' Âṅgadaḥ
hary|ṛkṣa|pati rājyaṃ ca tvat|sanātham, anindite.
tāv imau śoka|saṃtaptau śanaiḥ preraya, bhāmini,
tvayā parigṛhīto 'yam Aṅgadaḥ śāstu medinīm!
21.10 saṃtatiś ca yathā|dṛṣṭā kṛtyaṃ yac c' âpi sāmpratam
rājñas tat kriyatāṃ sarvam. eṣa kālasya niścayaḥ.
saṃskāryo hari|rājas tu Aṅgadaś c' âbhiṣicyatām.
siṃh'|āsana|gataṃ putraṃ paśyantī śāntim eṣyasi.»

sā tasya vacanaṃ śrutvā bhartṛ|vyasana|pīḍitā
abravīd uttaraṃ Tārā Hanūmantam avasthitam:

«Aṅgada|pratirūpāṇāṃ putrāṇām ekataḥ śatam
hatasy' âpy asya vīrasya gātra|saṃśleṣaṇaṃ varam.
na c' âhaṃ hari|rājasya prabhavāmy Aṅgadasya vā.
pitṛ|vyastasya Sugrīvaḥ sarva|kāryeṣv anantaraḥ.
21.15 na hy eṣā buddhir āstheyā, Hanūmann, Aṅgadaṃ prati;
pitā hi bandhuḥ putrasya na mātā, hari|sattama.
na hi mama hari|rāja|saṃśrayāt
kṣamataram asti paratra c' êha vā
abhimukha|hata|vīra|sevitaṃ
śayanam idaṃ mama sevituṃ kṣamam.»

time. This monkey saw things rightly and was devoted to conciliation, giving and forbearance. Since he has gone to the world of those who conquer through righteousness, you should not grieve for him.

But now, blameless woman, your son Ángada, the other tigers among monkeys, and the kingdom of the lord of apes and monkeys all have you as their protector. Gently direct these two who are tormented by grief, lovely woman. Let Ángada here, supported by you, rule the earth. And since 21.10
there is a male offspring, you must do everything that must now be done for the king. That is the proper decision for this time. The king of monkeys must be purified by cremation, and Ángada must be consecrated. You will find peace of mind once you see your son upon the throne."

When she heard his words, Tará, crushed by her husband's disastrous end, made this reply to Hánuman, who stood near:

"Even if I had a hundred sons like Ángada, I would rather embrace the body of this warrior, though he is dead. I have no power over the king of monkeys or Ángada. His father's brother Sugríva is at hand for all that must be done. Nor 21.15
can your idea concerning Ángada be carried out, Hánuman: A son's true kinsman is his father, not his mother, best of monkeys. There is surely nothing more fitting for me in this world or in the next than to join the king of monkeys. It is fitting for me to rest on this bed where rests my warrior, killed while facing his enemy."

22.1 Vīkṣamāṇas tu mand'|âsuḥ sarvato mandam ucchvasan
ādāv eva tu Sugrīvaṃ dadarśa tv ātmaj'|âgrataḥ.
taṃ prāpta|vijayaṃ Vālī Sugrīvaṃ plavag'|ēśvaram
ābhāṣya vyaktayā vācā sa|sneham idam abravīt:

«Sugrīva, doṣeṇa na māṃ gantum arhasi kilbiṣāt
kṛṣyamāṇaṃ bhaviṣyeṇa buddhi|mohena māṃ balāt.
yugapad vihitaṃ, tāta, na manye sukham āvayoḥ
sauhārdaṃ bhrātṛ|yuktaṃ hi tad idaṃ jātam anyathā.
22.5 pratipadya tvam ady' âiva rājyam eṣāṃ van'|âukasām
mām apy ady' âiva gacchantaṃ viddhi Vaivasvata|kṣayam.
jīvitaṃ ca hi rājyaṃ ca śriyaṃ ca vipulām imām
prajahāmy eṣa vai tūrṇaṃ mahac c' âgarhitaṃ yaśaḥ.
asyāṃ tv aham avasthāyāṃ, vīra, vakṣyāmi yad vacaḥ
yady apy a|sukaraṃ, rājan, kartum eva tad arhasi.

sukh'|ârhaṃ sukha|saṃvṛddhaṃ bālam enam abāliśam
bāṣpa|pūrṇa|mukhaṃ paśya bhūmau patitam Aṅgadam.
mama prāṇaiḥ priyataraṃ putraṃ putram iv' āurasam
mayā hīnam ahīn'|ârthaṃ sarvataḥ paripālaya.
22.10 tvam apy asya hi dātā ca paritrātā ca sarvataḥ
bhayeṣv a|bhaya|daś c' âiva yath" âhaṃ, plavag'|ēśvara.
eṣa Tār"|ātmajaḥ śrīmāṃs tvayā tulya|parākramaḥ
rakṣasāṃ tu vadhe teṣām agratas te bhaviṣyati.
anurūpāṇi karmāṇi vikramya balavān raṇe
kariṣyaty eṣa Tāreyas tarasvī taruṇo 'ṅgadaḥ.

Barely breathing, his life ebbing, Valin looked all about 22.1
and saw first Sugríva, who stood in front of his son. In a clear voice he addressed Sugríva, the victorious lord of monkeys, and said affectionately:

"Sugríva, please do not think me guilty because of my sin: I was forcibly carried away by some predestined confusion of mind. I think that happiness was not ordained for both of us at the same time, dear child. Thus the friendship proper
for brothers turned out quite otherwise. Receive this very 22.5
day sovereignty over these forest-dwelling monkeys. As for me, know that this very day I am going to the abode of Vaivásvata, lord of the dead. For I am rapidly giving up my life, my sovereignty, this vast majesty, and my great reputation, which was beyond reproach. Since I am in this condition, you must carry out the instructions I am about to give you, heroic king, though they will not be easy to follow.

Here is Ángada who, although a child, is not childish. Worthy of happiness, raised in happiness, he has fallen to the ground, his face covered with tears. Look upon my son, who is dearer to me than life, as if he were your own flesh-and-blood son. Protect him in every way so that although he is deprived of me, he will not be otherwise deprived.
You must also be his provider and defender in every way 22.10
and his protector from all dangers, lord of monkeys, just as I was. Your equal in prowess, this majestic son of Tará will stand before you in the slaughter of the *rákshasas*. Advancing valorously in battle, this powerful young son of Tará, mighty Ángada, will perform worthy deeds.

Suṣeṇa|duhitā c' êyam artha|sūkṣma|viniścaye
autpātike ca vividhe sarvataḥ pariniṣṭhitā.
yad eṣā ‹sādhv iti› brūyāt kāryaṃ tan mukta|saṃśayam,
na hi Tārā|mataṃ kiṃ cid anyathā parivartate.
22.15 Rāghavasya ca te kāryaṃ kartavyam aviśaṅkayā,
syād adharmo hy akaraṇe tvāṃ ca hiṃsyād vimānitaḥ.
imāṃ ca mālām ādhatsva divyāṃ, Sugrīva, kāñcanīm,
udārā śrīḥ sthitā hy asyāṃ saṃprajahyān mṛte mayi.»

ity evam uktaḥ Sugrīvo Vālinā bhrātṛ|sauhṛdāt
harṣaṃ tyaktvā punar dīno graha|grasta iv' ôḍu|rāṭ.
tad Vāli|vacanāc chāntaḥ kurvan yuktam atandritaḥ
jagrāha so 'bhyanujñāto mālāṃ tāṃ c' âiva kāñcanīm.
tāṃ mālāṃ kāñcanīṃ dattvā Vālī dṛṣṭv" ātmajaṃ sthitam
saṃsiddhaḥ pretya bhāvāya snehād Aṅgadam abravīt:
22.20 «deśa|kālau bhajasv' âdya kṣamamāṇaḥ priy'|âpriye
sukha|duḥkha|sahaḥ kāle Sugrīva|vaśago bhava.
yathā hi tvaṃ mahā|bāho lālitaḥ satataṃ mayā
na tathā vartamānaṃ tvāṃ Sugrīvo bahu maṃsyate.
m" âsy' âmitrair gataṃ gaccher mā śatrubhir, ariṃ|dama,
bhartur artha|paro dāntaḥ Sugrīva|vaśago bhava.
na c' âtipraṇayaḥ kāryaḥ kartavyo 'praṇayaś ca te
ubhayaṃ hi mahā|doṣaṃ tasmād antara|dṛg bhava.»

And Tará, this daughter of Sushéna, is thoroughly knowledgeable about deciding subtle matters and about various portents. Whatever she says is right should be done without doubt, for nothing Tará believes turns out to be otherwise.
And you must accomplish Rághava's purpose without hes- 22.15
itation; for it would be unrighteous not to do it, and if he were slighted he would harm you. Now take this divine golden garland, Sugríva, for the exalted Shri abiding in it will leave it once I am dead."

But Valin addressed him with such brotherly affection that Sugríva put aside his delight and became wretched again, like the moon swallowed up by Rahu, the planet that eclipses it. Sobered by Valin's words, carefully doing what was proper, he took with permission that golden garland. When Valin had given him that golden garland and was prepared for death, he turned his gaze to his son Ángada standing nearby and said affectionately to him:

"Be attentive to time and place now, enduring the agree- 22.20
able and the disagreeable. Bearing happiness and sorrow in their turn, be submissive to Sugríva's will. Sugríva will not think well of you, great-armed son, if you act as you did when constantly indulged by me. Don't associate with his enemies or with associates of his adversaries, subduer of foes. Restrained and devoted to your master's interests, be submissive to Sugríva's will. You must not show either excessive affection or lack of affection: both are serious faults, so observe moderation."

ity uktv" âtha vivṛtt'|âkṣaḥ śara|saṃpīḍito bhṛśam
vivṛtair daśanair bhīmair babhūv' ôtkrānta|jīvitaḥ.

22.25 hate tu vīre plavag'|âdhipe tadā
plavaṃ|gamās tatra na śarma lebhire
vane|carāḥ siṃha|yute mahā|vane
yathā hi gāvo nihate gavāṃ patau.
tatas tu Tārā vyasan'|ârṇava|plutā
mṛtasya bhartur vadanaṃ samīkṣya sā
jagāma bhūmiṃ parirabhya Vālinaṃ
mahā|drumaṃ chinnam iv' āśritā latā.

23.1 TATAḤ SAMUPAJIGHRANTĪ kapi|rājasya tan mukham
patiṃ lokāc cyutaṃ Tārā mṛtaṃ vacanam abravīt:
«śeṣe tvaṃ viṣame duḥkham akṛtvā vacanaṃ mama
upal'|ôpacite, vīra, su|duḥkhe vasudhā|tale.
mattaḥ priyatarā nūnaṃ, vānar'|êndra, mahī tava
śeṣe hi tāṃ pariṣvajya māṃ ca na pratibhāṣase.
Sugrīva eva vikrānto, vīra sāhasika priya,
ṛkṣa|vānara|mukhyās tvāṃ balinaṃ paryupāsate.
23.5 eṣāṃ vilapitaṃ kṛcchram Aṅgadasya ca śocataḥ
mama c' êmāṃ giraṃ śrutvā kiṃ tvaṃ na pratibudhyase?
idaṃ tac chūra|śayanaṃ yatra śeṣe hato yudhi
śāyitā nihatā yatra tvay" âiva ripavaḥ purā.
viśuddha|sattv'|âbhijana priya|yuddha mama priya,
mām anāthāṃ vihāy' âikāṃ gatas tvam asi, mānada.
śūrāya na pradātavyā kanyā khalu vipaścitā
śūra|bhāryāṃ hatāṃ paśya sadyo māṃ vidhavāṃ kṛtām.
avabhagnaś ca me māno bhagnā me śāśvatī gatiḥ
agādhe ca nimagn" âsmi vipule śoka|sāgare.

Then, with these words, in intense pain from the arrow, rolling his eyes and baring his dreadful fangs, he departed this life. Now, when that heroic lord of monkeys 22.25
was dead, the monkeys there could find no happiness, like forest-dwelling cattle in a great forest full of lions, when their bull has been struck down. Then Tará, plunged in a sea of misfortune, looked at her dead husband's face and sank to the ground, embracing Valin like a vine clinging to a mighty tree that has been cut down.

THEN TARÁ kissed the monkey-king's face and said these 23.1
words to her dead husband, who had gone from this world:

"You would not do as I said, warrior, and so you lie painfully on the rough, rocky ground. The earth must surely be dearer to you than I, lord of monkeys, since you lie embracing her and do not answer me. Sugríva is attacking, my beloved, reckless warrior, and the leaders of the apes and monkeys seek protection from you, mighty one. Hearing 23.5
their painful lament, that of grieving Ángada, and these words of mine, why do you not awaken? Slain in battle, you lie on this hero's bed where once you made your slain enemies lie.

My battle-loving, proud beloved, born in a family of impeccable courage, you have gone away, leaving me alone and without a protector. A wise man should surely never give his daughter to a warrior. Look at me, a warrior's wife, suddenly destroyed and made a widow. My pride is broken, my everlasting happiness is shattered, and I am plunged into a vast, bottomless ocean of grief.

23.10 aśma|sāra|mayaṃ nūnam idaṃ me hṛdayaṃ dṛḍham
bhartāraṃ nihataṃ dṛṣṭvā yan n' âdya śatadhā gatam.
suhṛc c' âiva hi bhartā ca prakṛtyā ca mama priyaḥ
āhave ca parākrāntaḥ śūraḥ pañcatvam āgataḥ.
pati|hīnā tu yā nārī kāmaṃ bhavatu putriṇī
dhana|dhānyaiḥ supūrṇ" âpi vidhav" êty ucyate budhaiḥ.
sva|gātra|prabhave, vīra, śeṣe rudhira|maṇḍale
kṛmi|rāga|paristome tvam evaṃ śayane yathā.
reṇu|śoṇita|saṃvītaṃ gātraṃ tava samantataḥ
parirabdhuṃ na śaknomi bhujābhyāṃ, plavaga'|rṣabha!
23.15 kṛta|kṛtyo 'dya Sugrīvo vaire 'sminn atidāruṇe
yasya Rāma|vimuktena hṛtam ek'|êṣuṇā bhayam.
śareṇa hṛdi lagnena gātra|saṃsparśane tava
vāryāmi tvāṃ nirīkṣantī tvayi pañcatvam āgate.»
udbabarha śaraṃ Nīlas tasya gātra|gataṃ tadā
giri|gahvara|saṃlīnaṃ dīptam āśī|viṣaṃ yathā
tasya niṣkṛṣyamāṇasya bāṇasya ca babhau dyutiḥ
asta|mastaka|saṃruddho raśmir dina|karād iva.
petuḥ kṣataja|dhārās tu vraṇebhyas tasya sarvaśaḥ
tāmra|gairika|saṃpṛktā dhārā iva dharā|dharāt.
23.20 avakīrṇaṃ vimārjantī bhartāraṃ raṇa|reṇunā
asrair nayana|jaiḥ śūraṃ siṣec' âstra|samāhatam.
rudhir'|ôkṣita|sarv'|âṅgaṃ dṛṣṭvā vinihataṃ patim
uvāca Tārā piṅg'|âkṣaṃ putram Aṅgadam aṅganā:

Surely this hard heart of mine is made of stone since it does not break into a hundred pieces now, as I behold my slain husband. 23.10

For he was my friend and my husband and, by his very nature, my beloved. Conquered in battle, my warrior has gone to his death. When a woman has lost her husband, wise men call her a widow, even though she may have sons and abundant wealth and grain.

Warrior, you are lying in a pool of blood spreading from your body, as if on a bed with a crimson cover. I cannot clasp in my arms your body covered all over with dust and
blood, bull among monkeys. Today Sugríva has achieved 23.15
his purpose in this dreadful feud, for a single arrow shot by Rama has dispelled his fear. Now that you have gone to your death, I gaze at you, but the arrow fixed in your heart keeps me from touching your body."

Then Nila drew out the arrow lodged in Valin's body as one might draw out a gleaming poisonous snake lurking in a mountain cave. And the radiance of that shaft as it was drawn out was as bright as a sunbeam caught on the summit of the sunset mountain. And from his wounds streams of blood poured down on all sides, like floodwaters mingled with dark red earth rushing down a mountain.
As she caressed her warrior husband, who had been struck 23.20
down by the arrow and was covered with the dust of battle, she bathed him with tears flowing from her eyes. Then the lovely woman Tará, still gazing at her slain lord, his limbs all spattered with blood, spoke to her tawny-eyed son Ángada:

«avasthāṃ paścimāṃ paśya pituḥ, putra, sudāruṇām
saṃprasaktasya vairasya gato 'ntaḥ pāpa|karmaṇā.
bāla|sūry'|ôdaya|tanuṃ prayāntaṃ Yama|sādanam
abhivādaya rājānaṃ pitaraṃ, putra, mānadam.»
evam uktaḥ samutthāya jagrāha caraṇau pituḥ
bhujābhyāṃ pīna|vṛtābhyām «Aṅgado 'ham iti» bruvan.
23.25 «abhivādayamānaṃ tvām Aṅgadaṃ tvaṃ yathā purā
‹dīrgh'|āyur bhava, putr' êti› kim arthaṃ n' âbhibhāṣase?
ahaṃ putra|sahāyā tvām upāse gata|cetanam
siṃhena nihataṃ sadyo gauḥ sa|vats" êva go|vṛṣam.
iṣṭvā saṃgrāma|yajñena nānā|praharaṇ'|âmbhasā
asminn avabhṛthe snātaḥ kathaṃ patnyā mayā vinā?
yā dattā deva|rājena tava tuṣṭena saṃyuge
śātakumbhamayīṃ mālāṃ tāṃ te paśyāmi n' êha kim?
rāja|śrīr na jahāti tvāṃ gat'|āsum api, mānada,
sūryasy' āvartamānasya śaila|rājam iva prabhā.
23.30 na me vacaḥ pathyam idaṃ tvayā kṛtaṃ,
na c' âsmi śaktā hi nivāraṇe tava,
hatā sa|putr" âsmi hatena saṃyuge,
saha tvayā śrīr vijahāti mām iha.»

24.1 GAT'|ÂSUṂ VĀLINAṂ dṛṣṭvā Rāghavas tad|anantaram
abravīt praśritaṃ vākyaṃ Sugrīvaṃ śatru|tāpanaḥ:
«na śoka|paritāpena śreyasā yujyate mṛtaḥ:
yad atr' ânantaraṃ kāryaṃ tat samādhātum arhatha.
loka|vṛttam anuṣṭheyaṃ kṛtaṃ vo bāṣpa|mokṣaṇam
na kālād uttaraṃ kiṃ cit karma śakyam upāsitum.

"My son, behold your father's dreadful final state. The end has come to an enmity caused by an evil deed. My son, salute the proud king, your father, whose body was like the newly risen sun, for he has set out for Yama's abode."

Addressed in this fashion, he rose and embraced his father's feet with his well-rounded arms, saying: "It is I, Ángada." Tará continued:

"Ángada salutes you. Why do you not say to him as 23.25
before, 'Long life to you, my son!'? Though you are without consciousness, I shall stay by you with my son, just as a cow with her calf stays by her bull when he is suddenly struck down by a lion. How is it that without me, your wife, you first offered the sacrifice of battle and then, using many blows as water, took the concluding bath? Why do I not see here that golden garland of yours, which was given to you by the king of gods when you pleased him in battle? Though your life is gone, proud monkey, royal Shri does not abandon you, just as the radiance of the setting sun
does not leave the king of mountains. You did not follow 23.30
my good advice, nor was I able to hold you back. Destroyed in battle, you have destroyed me and my son. Along with you, Shri now abandons me."

As SOON AS he saw that Valin had expired, Rághava, 24.1
tormentor of his enemies, spoke these courteous words to Sugríva:

"A dead person derives no benefit from grief and lamentation: You should all attend to what must be done next for him. Worldly practice must be followed. But enough of your tears: No religious rite can be undertaken after its

niyatiḥ kāraṇaṃ loke niyatiḥ karma|sādhanam
niyatiḥ sarva|bhūtānāṃ niyogeṣv iha kāraṇam.
24.5 na kartā kasya cit kaś cin niyoge c' âpi n' ēśvaraḥ
sva|bhāve vartate lokas tasya kālaḥ parāyaṇam.
na kālaḥ kālam atyeti na kālaḥ parihīyate
sva|bhāvaṃ vā samāsādya na kaś cid ativartate.
na kālasy' âsti bandhutvaṃ na hetur na parākramaḥ
na mitra|jñāti|saṃbandhaḥ kāraṇaṃ n' ātmano vaśaḥ.
kiṃ tu kāla|pariṇāmo draṣṭavyaḥ sādhu paśyatā
dharmaś c' ârthaś ca kāmaś ca kāla|krama|samāhitāḥ.

itaḥ svāṃ prakṛtiṃ Vālī gataḥ prāptaḥ kriyā|phalam
dharm'|ârtha|kāma|saṃyogaiḥ pavitraṃ, plavag'|ēśvara.
24.10 svadharmasya ca saṃyogāj jitas tena mah"|ātmanā
svargaḥ parigṛhītaś ca prāṇān aparirakṣatā.
eṣā vai niyatiḥ śreṣṭhā yāṃ gato hari|yūthapaḥ
tad alaṃ paritāpena prāpta|kālam upāsyatām!»

vacan'|ânte tu Rāmasya Lakṣmaṇaḥ para|vīra|hā
avadat praśritaṃ vākyaṃ Sugrīvaṃ gata|cetasam:

«kuru tvam asya, Sugrīva, preta|kāryam anantaram
Tār"|Âṅgadābhyāṃ sahito Vālino dahanaṃ prati.
samājñāpaya kāṣṭhāni śuṣkāṇi ca bahūni ca
candanāni ca divyāni Vāli|saṃskāra|kāraṇāt.
24.15 samāśvāsaya c' âinaṃ tvam Aṅgadaṃ dīna|cetasam.

proper time. Fate is the prime mover in this world. Fate brings about action. Fate is the prime mover controlling
all beings here on earth. No one is truly in control of any 24.5
action; nor is anyone capable of compelling anyone else. People are ruled by their inherent nature, and fate is their final resort. Fate does not violate fate. Fate is inevitable. Nor can anyone resist his inherent nature and pass beyond it. Fate has no kinship, no connection with friends or relations. There is no means to combat it or prevail over it. It is the prime mover, and no one can master it. But he who sees clearly should recognize in everything the unfolding of fate. Religious merit, wealth and pleasure are all determined by the workings of fate.

Valin has gone from this world and attained his own true nature. He has obtained the fruit of his actions purified by timely attention to gaining religious merit, wealth and
pleasure, lord of monkeys. By losing his life in battle, that 24.10
great monkey has now reached the heaven that he won through attention to his own duty. It is surely to the highest destiny that the leader of troops of monkeys has gone. So enough of this lamenting! Attend to the duties at hand."

At the end of Rama's speech, Lákshmana, slayer of enemy warriors, spoke these courteous words to Sugríva, who was distraught:

"You must perform Valin's funeral rites without delay, Sugríva. Together with Tará, and Ángada, arrange for his cremation. Order many dry logs and fine sandalwood for
performing Valin's funeral rites. And comfort Ángada, who 24.15
is despondent. You must not be foolish: The city is depending on you. Ángada must bring garlands, various garments,

mā bhūr bāliśa|buddhis tvaṃ! tvad|adhīnam idaṃ puram.
Aṅgadas tv ānayen mālyaṃ vastrāṇi vividhāni ca
ghṛtaṃ tailam atho gandhān yac c' âtra samanantaram.
tvaṃ, Tāra, śibikāṃ śīghram ādāy' āgaccha saṃbhramāt
tvarā guṇavatī yuktā hy asmin kāle viśeṣataḥ.
sajjī|bhavantu plavagāḥ śibikā|vāhan'|ôcitāḥ
samarthā balinaś c' âiva nirhariṣyanti Vālinam.»

evam uktvā tu Sugrīvaṃ Sumitr"|ānanda|vardhanaḥ
tasthau bhrātṛ|samīpa|stho Lakṣmaṇaḥ para|vīrahā.
24.20 Lakṣmaṇasya vacaḥ śrutvā Tāraḥ saṃbhrānta|mānasaḥ
praviveśa guhāṃ śīghraṃ śibik"|āsakta|mānasaḥ.
ādāya śibikāṃ Tāraḥ sa tu paryāpayat punaḥ
vānarair uhyamānāṃ tāṃ śūrair udvahan'|ôcitaiḥ.
tato Vālinam udyamya Sugrīvaḥ śibikāṃ tadā
āropayata vikrośann Aṅgadena sah' âiva tu.
āropya śibikāṃ c' âiva Vālinaṃ gata|jīvitam
alaṃkāraiś ca vividhair mālyair vastraiś ca bhūṣitam
ājñāpayat tadā rājā Sugrīvaḥ plavag'|ēśvaraḥ:
«aurdhvadehikam āryasya kriyatām anurūpataḥ!
24.25 viśrāṇayanto ratnāni vividhāni bahūni ca
agrataḥ plavagā yāntu śibikā tad|anantaram!»
rājñām ṛddhi|viśeṣā hi dṛśyante bhuvi yādṛśāḥ
tādṛśaṃ Vālinaḥ kṣipraṃ prākurvann aurdhvadehikam.

Aṅgadam parigṛhy' āśu Tāra|prabhṛtayas tathā
krośantaḥ prayayuḥ sarve vānarā hata|bāndhavāḥ.
Tārā|prabhṛtayaḥ sarvā vānaryo hata|yūthapāḥ
anujagmur hi bhartāraṃ krośantyaḥ karuṇa|svanāḥ.
tāsāṃ rudita|śabdena vānarīṇāṃ van'|ântare
vanāni girayaḥ sarve vikrośant' îva sarvataḥ.
24.30 puline giri|nadyās tu vivikte jala|saṃvṛte

clarified butter, oil, perfumes and whatever else is immediately required. And you, Tara, make haste. Bring a bier quickly, for speed is always advantageous and is especially appropriate at a time like this. Let monkeys fit to carry the bier be made ready. Capable and strong, they shall bear Valin away."

After speaking thus to Sugríva, Lákshmana, delight of
Sumítra, killer of enemy warriors, remained standing near
his brother. Tara was thrown into a flurry at hearing Láksh- 24.20
mana's words, and he quickly entered the cave, intent on
getting a bier. Then Tara rushed back bringing with him a
bier borne by monkey warriors fit to bear it. Crying aloud,
Sugríva and Ángada then lifted Valin up and placed him on
the bier. Then, when the lord of the monkeys, King Sugríva, had placed on the bier the lifeless Valin, adorned with
various ornaments, garlands and garments, he commanded,
"Let the funeral rites of this noble monkey be carried out
in a suitable fashion. Let monkeys scattering many jewels 24.25
of every kind precede the bier." Then without delay they
performed Valin's funeral rites with the same extraordinary
pomp that is shown on earth for human kings.

Tara and all the other monkeys who had lost their kinsman surrounded Ángada and quickly set out, crying aloud.
And Tará and all the other monkey women who had lost
their lord followed after their husband crying aloud, making a pitiful sound. Echoing the sound of those monkey
women weeping in the forest, all the woods and mountains
seemed to cry out on every side. On a solitary sandbank of 24.30
the mountain stream, entirely surrounded by water, a large
number of forest-dwelling monkeys built a pyre. Then those

citāṃ cakruḥ subahavo vānarā vana|cāriṇaḥ.
avaropya tataḥ skandhāc chibikāṃ vahan'|ôcitāḥ
tasthur ek'|ântam āśritya sarve śoka|samanvitāḥ.
tatas Tārā patiṃ dṛṣṭvā śibikā|tala|śāyinam
āropy' âṅke śiras tasya vilalāpa su|duḥkhitā:

«janaṃ na paśyas' îmaṃ tvaṃ kasmāc chok'|âbhipīḍitam?
prahṛṣṭam iva te vaktraṃ gat'|âsor api, mānada,
ast'|ârka|sama|varṇaṃ ca lakṣyate jīvato yathā.
eṣa tvāṃ Rāma|rūpeṇa Kālaḥ karṣati, vānara,
yena sma vidhavāḥ sarvāḥ kṛtā ek'|êṣuṇā raṇe.
24.35 imās tās tava, rāj'|êndra, vānaryo vallabhāḥ sadā.
pādair vikṛṣṭam adhvānam āgatāḥ. kiṃ na budhyase?
tav' êṣṭā nanu nām' âitā bhāryāś candra|nibh'|ānanāḥ
idānīṃ n' ēkṣase kasmāt Sugrīvaṃ plavag'|ēśvaram?
ete hi sacivā, rājaṃs, Tāra|prabhṛtayas tava
pura|vāsi|janaś c' âyaṃ parivāry' āsate, 'nagha.
visarjay' âinān pravalān yath'' ôcitam, ariṃ|dama,
tataḥ krīḍāmahe sarvā vaneṣu madir'|ôtkaṭāḥ.»

evaṃ vilapatīṃ Tārāṃ pati|śoka|pariplutām
utthāpayanti sma tadā vānaryaḥ śoka|karśitāḥ.
24.40 Sugrīveṇa tataḥ sārdham Aṅgadaḥ pitaraṃ rudan
citām āropayām āsa śoken' âbhihat'|êndriyaḥ.
tato 'gniṃ vidhivad dattvā so 'pasavyaṃ cakāra ha
pitaraṃ dīrgham adhvānaṃ prasthitaṃ vyākul'|êndriyaḥ.

serving as bearers lowered the bier from their shoulders and stood to one side, all of them filled with grief. Now, when Tará saw her husband lying on the bier, she placed his head on her lap and lamented sorrowfully:

"Why do you not look at me, when I am so grief-stricken? Though you are dead, proud monkey, your face seems joyful and radiant as the setting sun, just as it looked when you were alive. It is Death in the form of Rama who is dragging you away, monkey: With a single arrow in battle, he has made widows of us all. Here are your monkey 24.35
women, always dear to you. They have traveled this long path on foot, lord of kings. Why do you not awake? Why do you not gaze now upon these wives whom you surely love, with their faces bright as the moon, or at Sugríva, the lord of monkeys? Here surrounding you are your ministers, Tara and the others, and the people who dwell in your city, blameless king. Dismiss these monkeys as you always do, tamer of your foes, so that all of us women, drunk with wine, can make love with you in the woods."

Plunged in grief for her husband, Tará lamented in this way until the other monkey women, haggard with grief, raised her up. Then Ángada, distraught with grief, wept for 24.40
his father as he placed him on the pyre with Sugríva's help. Beside himself with sorrow, he then lit the fire according to the ritual prescriptions, and reverently circled his father, who had set out on his long journey.

saṃskṛtya Vālinaṃ te tu vidhi|pūrvaṃ plavaṃ|gamāḥ
ājagmur udakaṃ kartuṃ nadīṃ śīta|jalāṃ śubhām.
tatas te sahitās tatra Aṅgadaṃ sthāpya c' âgrataḥ
Sugrīva|Tārā|sahitāḥ siṣicur Vāline jalam.
Sugrīven' âiva dīnena dīno bhūtvā mahā|balaḥ
samāna|śokaḥ Kākutsthaḥ preta|kāryāṇy akārayat.

25.1 Tataḥ śok'|âbhisaṃtaptaṃ Sugrīvaṃ klinna|vāsanam
śākhā|mṛga|mahā|mātrāḥ parivāry' ôpatasthire.
abhigamya mahā|bāhuṃ Rāmam akliṣṭa|kāriṇam
sthitāḥ prāñjalayaḥ sarve Pitāmaham iva' ṛṣayaḥ.
tataḥ kāñcana|śail'|ābhas taruṇ'|ârka|nibh'|ānanaḥ
abravīt prāñjalir vākyaṃ Hanumān Mārut'|ātmajaḥ:
«bhavat|prasādāt Sugrīvaḥ pitṛ|paitāmahaṃ mahat
vānarāṇāṃ suduṣprāpaṃ prāpto rājyam idaṃ, prabho.
25.5 bhavatā samanujñātaḥ praviśya nagaraṃ śubham
saṃvidhāsyati kāryāṇi sarvāṇi sa|suhṛj|janaḥ.
snāto 'yaṃ vividhair gandhair auṣadhaiś ca yathā|vidhi
arcayiṣyati ratnaiś ca mālyaiś ca tvāṃ viśeṣataḥ.
imāṃ giri|guhāṃ ramyām abhigantum ito 'rhasi.
kuruṣva svāmi|saṃbandhaṃ vānarān saṃpraharṣayan.»
evam ukto Hanumatā Rāghavaḥ para|vīrahā
pratyuvāca Hanūmantaṃ buddhimān vākya|kovidaḥ:

When the monkeys had cremated Valin in keeping with the ritual prescriptions, they went to make water-offerings in that auspicious river with its cool waters. Then, gathered together there, they placed Ángada in front and, along with Sugríva and Tará, sprinkled water for Valin. And thus did mighty Kákutstha and Sugríva, dejected and sharing the same grief, have the funeral rites performed.

THEN THE CHIEF ministers of the monkeys surrounded 25.1
grief-stricken Sugríva, whose garments were still wet, and waited in attendance upon him. Approaching great-armed Rama, tireless in action, they all stood with palms cupped in reverence, like the seers before Grandfather Brahma. Then, his palms cupped in reverence, the wind god's son Hánuman, bright as the golden Mount Meru, his face like the newly risen sun, spoke these words:

"Through your grace, lord, Sugríva has obtained this great ancestral monkey kingdom, so difficult to obtain.
With your permission, he will enter his fair city with his 25.5
friends and attend to all his duties. When he is anointed with various perfumes and herbs in accordance with the ritual prescriptions, he will specially honor you with jewels and garlands. Please proceed from here to the delightful mountain cave Kishkíndha. Make the monkeys rejoice by uniting them with their king."

Thus addressed by Hánuman, wise and eloquent Rama, slayer of enemy warriors, replied to Hánuman:

«caturdaśa|samāḥ, saumya, grāmaṃ vā yadi vā puram
na pravekṣyāmi, Hanuman, pitur nirdeśa|pālakaḥ.
25.10 susamṛddhāṃ guhāṃ divyāṃ Sugrīvo vānara'|ṛṣabhaḥ
praviṣṭo vidhivad vīraḥ kṣipraṃ rājye 'bhiṣicyatām.»
evam uktvā Hanūmantaṃ Rāmaḥ Sugrīvam abravīt:
«imam apy Aṅgadaṃ, vīra, yauvarājye 'bhiṣecaya.
pūrvo 'yaṃ vārṣiko māsaḥ Śrāvaṇaḥ salil'|āgamaḥ,
pravṛttāḥ, saumya, catvāro māsā vārṣika|saṃjñitāḥ.
n' âyam udyoga|samayaḥ. praviśa tvaṃ purīṃ śubhām,
asmin vatsyāmy ahaṃ, saumya, parvate saha|Lakṣmaṇaḥ.
iyaṃ giri|guhā ramyā viśālā yukta|mārutā
prabhūta|salilā, saumya, prabhūta|kamal'|ôtpalā.
25.15 Kārtike samanuprāpte tvaṃ Rāvaṇa|vadhe yata
eṣa naḥ samayaḥ, saumya. praviśa tvaṃ svam ālayam
abhiṣiñcasva rājye ca suhṛdaḥ saṃpraharṣaya!»
iti Rām'|âbhyanujñātaḥ Sugrīvo vānara'|ṛṣabhaḥ
praviveśa purīṃ ramyāṃ Kiṣkindhāṃ Vāli|pālitām.
taṃ vānara|sahasrāṇi praviṣṭaṃ vānar'|ēśvaram
abhivādya prahṛṣṭāni sarvataḥ paryavārayan.
tataḥ prakṛtayaḥ sarvā dṛṣṭvā hari|gaṇ'|ēśvaram
praṇamya mūrdhnā patitā vasudhāyāṃ samāhitāḥ.
Sugrīvaḥ prakṛtīḥ sarvāḥ saṃbhāṣy' ôtthāpya vīryavān
bhrātur antaḥ|puraṃ saumyaṃ praviveśa mahā|balaḥ.

"Observing my father's command, gentle Hánuman, I
shall not enter a village or a city for fourteen years. But let 25.10
the heroic bull among monkeys Sugríva enter his wonderful,
luxurious cave at once and be consecrated king according
to the ritual prescriptions."

Then, when Rama had spoken in this fashion to Hánuman, he said to Sugríva: "Warrior, have Ángada, too,
consecrated as heir apparent. It is now Shrávana, the first of
the rainy months, bringing the onset of the monsoon. Now
begin the four months called the rainy season, my friend.
This is not the time for undertakings. So enter your fair city,
my friend; I shall dwell on this mountain with Lákshmana. Here is a pleasant mountain cave, my friend, spacious
and airy, with abundant water and many lotuses and lilies
nearby. When the month of Kártika has arrived, you must 25.15
try to kill Rávana, for this was our agreement. But for now,
my friend, enter your dwelling, be consecrated as king and
make your friends rejoice."

Dismissed in this way by Rama, Sugríva, bull among monkeys, entered the charming city Kishkíndha once protected by Valin. Thousands of monkeys respectfully greeted the lord of monkeys as he entered and joyfully surrounded him. Then, when they saw the lord of the troops of monkeys, all his assembled subjects bowed their heads and then prostrated themselves on the ground. After addressing all his subjects and making them rise, Sugríva, vigorous and mighty, entered the lovely women's quarters, which had been his brother's.

25.20 praviśya tv abhiniṣkrāntaṃ Sugrīvaṃ vānara'|rṣabham
abhyaṣiñcanta suhṛdaḥ Sahasrākṣam iv' âmarāḥ.
tasya pāṇḍuram ājahruś chatraṃ hema|pariṣkṛtam
śukle ca bāla|vyajane hema|daṇḍe yaśas|kare
tathā sarvāṇi ratnāni sarva|bīj'|āuṣadhāni ca
sa|kṣīrāṇāṃ ca vṛkṣāṇāṃ prarohān kusumāni ca
śuklāni c' âiva vastrāṇi śvetaṃ c' âiv' ânulepanam
sugandhīni ca mālyāni sthala|jāny ambu|jāni ca
candanāni ca divyāni gandhāṃś ca vividhān bahūn
akṣataṃ jāta|rūpaṃ ca priyaṅgu|madhu|sarpiṣī
25.25 dadhi carma ca vaiyāghraṃ vārāhī c' âpy upāna|hau
samālaṃbhanam ādāya rocanāṃ sa|manaḥśilām
ājagmus tatra muditā varāḥ kanyās tu ṣoḍaśa.

tatas te vānara|śreṣṭhaṃ yathā|kālaṃ yathā|vidhi
ratnair vastraiś ca bhakṣyaiś ca toṣayitvā dvija'|rṣabhān
tataḥ kuśa|paristīrṇaṃ samiddhaṃ jāta|vedasam
mantra|pūtena haviṣā hutvā mantravido janāḥ.
tato hema|pratiṣṭhāne var'|āstaraṇa|saṃvṛte
prāsāda|śikhare ramye citra|māly'|ôpaśobhite.

prāṅ|mukhaṃ vividhair mantraiḥ sthāpayitvā var'|āsane
nadī|nadebhyaḥ saṃhṛtya tīrthebhyaś ca samantataḥ
25.30 āhṛtya ca samudrebhyaḥ sarvebhyo vānara'|rṣabhāḥ
apaḥ kanaka|kumbheṣu nidhāya vimalāḥ śubhāḥ
śubhair vṛṣabha|śṛṅgaiś ca kalaśaiś c' âpi kāñcanaiḥ
śāstra|dṛṣṭena vidhinā maha"|rṣi|vihitena ca

When he had gone in there and come out again, his 25.20
friends consecrated Sugríva, bull among monkeys, as the
immortals consecrated thousand-eyed Indra. They brought
him the gold-adorned white umbrella and the two gold-
handled white yak-tail fans, which confer glory, as well as
all kinds of jewels and every kind of seed and herb, shoots
and blossoms of succulent trees, white garments, white
unguent and very fragrant garlands of flowers that grow
on dry ground and in water. And they also brought the
finest sandalwood and many kinds of fragrant things, and
gold-colored unhusked grain, *priyángu* honey and clarified 25.25
butter, curds, a tiger skin and boar-skin sandals. And sixteen
beautiful, joyous maidens came there bringing yellow and
red unguents.

According to prescribed rule, first the brahmans were
gratified with gifts of jewels and garments and things to
eat. Then people who knew the mantras made an offering
with an oblation purified by mantras into the lighted fire
encircled by *kusha* grass. Then, with various mantras, they
installed that best of monkeys, who was facing east, on
a gold-footed throne that was covered with fine cushions
and standing on a lovely turret of the palace adorned with
colorful garlands.

From rivers and streams, from sacred bathing places all
around and from all the oceans, those bulls among monkeys had brought pure, auspicious waters, which they mixed
together and placed in gold pitchers. Then, at the proper 25.30
moment, by the rule prescribed in the scriptures and ordained by the great sages, using auspicious bulls' horns and

Gajo Gavākṣo Gavayaḥ Śarabho Gandhamādanaḥ
Maindaś ca Dvividaś c' âiva Hanūmān Jāmbavān Nalaḥ
abhyaṣiñcanta Sugrīvaṃ prasannena sugandhinā
salilena Sahasrākṣaṃ Vasavo Vāsavaṃ yathā.
abhiṣikte tu Sugrīve sarve vānara|puṃgavāḥ
pracukruśur mah"|ātmāno hṛṣṭās tatra sahasraśaḥ.
25.35 Rāmasya tu vacaḥ kurvan Sugrīvo hari|puṃgavaḥ
Aṅgadaṃ saṃpariṣvajya yauvarājye 'bhiṣecayat.
Aṅgade c' âbhiṣikte tu s'|ânukrośāḥ plavaṃ|gamāḥ
«sādhu sādhv iti» Sugrīvaṃ mah"|ātmāno 'bhyapūjayan.
hṛṣṭa|puṣṭa|jan'|ākīrṇā patākā|dhvaja|śobhitā
babhūva nagarī ramyā Kiṣkindhā giri|gahvare.
nivedya Rāmāya tadā mah"|ātmane
mah"|âbhiṣekaṃ kapi|vāhinī|patiḥ
Rumāṃ ca bhāryāṃ pratilabhya vīryavān
avāpa rājyaṃ tridaś'|âdhipo yathā.

golden jars, Gaja, Gaváksha, Gávaya, Shárabha, Gandha·mádana, Mainda, Dvívida, Hánuman, Jámbavan and Nala consecrated Sugríva with clear, fragrant water, just as the Vasus consecrated thousand-eyed Vásava.

Once Sugríva was consecrated, all those thousands of
great bulls among monkeys shouted for joy. And following 25.35
Rama's advice, Sugríva, bull among monkeys, embraced Ángada and had him consecrated as heir apparent. Now, when Ángada was consecrated, the great monkeys, full of compassion, showed their approval of Sugríva, crying, "Excellent! Excellent!" Within the mountain cave, the city of Kishkíndha was delightful, filled with happy, thriving people and resplendent with flags and banners. Then, once the vigorous leader of the monkey army had informed great Rama of his solemn consecration, he recovered his wife Ruma and took possession of his kingdom as did Indra, the lord of the thirty gods.

26–33
AUTUMN REMINDER

26.1 ABHIṢIKTE TU Sugrīve praviṣṭe vānare guhām
ājagāma saha bhrātrā Rāmaḥ Prasravaṇaṃ girim
śārdūla|mṛga|saṃghuṣṭaṃ siṃhair bhīma|ravair vṛtam
nānā|gulma|latā|gūḍhaṃ bahu|pādapa|saṃkulam
ṛkṣa|vānara|gopucchair mārjāraiś ca niṣevitam
megha|rāśi|nibhaṃ śailaṃ nityaṃ śuci|jal'|āśrayam.
tasya śailasya śikhare mahatīm āyatāṃ guhām
pratyagṛhṇata vās'|ârthaṃ Rāmaḥ Saumitriṇā saha.
26.5 avasat tatra dharm'|ātmā Rāghavaḥ saha|Lakṣmaṇaḥ
bahu|dṛśya|darī|kuñje tasmin Prasravaṇe girau.
su|sukhe 'pi bahu|dravye tasmin hi dharaṇī|dhare
vasatas tasya Rāmasya ratir alp" âpi n' âbhavat
hṛtāṃ hi bhāryāṃ smarataḥ prāṇebhyo 'pi garīyasīm.
uday'|âbhyuditaṃ dṛṣṭvā śaś'|âṅkaṃ ca viśeṣataḥ
āviveśa na taṃ nidrā niśāsu śayanaṃ gatam.
tat|samutthena śokena bāṣp'|ôpahata|cetasam
taṃ śocamānaṃ Kākutsthaṃ nityaṃ śoka|parāyaṇam
tulya|duḥkho 'bravīd bhrātā Lakṣmaṇo 'nunayan vacaḥ:
«alaṃ, vīra, vyathāṃ gatvā! na tvaṃ śocitum arhasi!
śocato hy avasīdanti sarv'|ârthā viditaṃ hi te.
26.10 bhavān kriyā|paro loke bhavān deva|parāyaṇaḥ
āstiko dharma|śīlaś ca vyavasāyī ca, Rāghava.
na hy avyavasitaḥ śatruṃ rākṣasaṃ taṃ viśeṣataḥ
samarthas tvaṃ raṇe hantuṃ vikramair jihma|kāriṇam.
samunmūlaya śokaṃ tvaṃ vyavasāyaṃ sthiraṃ kuru
tataḥ saparivāraṃ taṃ nirmūlaṃ kuru rākṣasam!

Now, when the monkey Sugríva had been consecrated 26.1
and had entered his cave, Rama went with his brother
to Mount Prasrávana, which resounded with the cries of
tigers and wild beasts and was full of lions roaring frightfully.
Covered with all kinds of bushes and vines, thick with trees,
it was inhabited by apes, monkeys, langurs and forest-cats.
Always abounding in pure water, the mountain towered like
a mass of clouds. Rama and Saumítri chose as their dwelling
a large, deep cave on the peak of that mountain. And there 26.5
righteous Rághava dwelt with Lákshmana on Mount Prasrávana, with its many lovely caves and bowers.

But though that mountain was very pleasant and full of
valuable things, Rama did not feel the least delight living
there, for he was thinking of his abducted wife, who was
more precious to him than his life's breath. Nor would sleep
come to him when he had gone to bed at night, especially
when he saw the moon rising in the east. Grieving for Sita, his mind weakened by all his tears, sorrowful Kákutstha
was constantly absorbed in his grief. Equally unhappy, his
brother Lákshmana said these words, entreating him:

"Enough of this yielding to anguish, warrior. You should
not grieve. Surely you know that when a person grieves, all
his endeavors fail. You are attentive to your duties in this 26.10
world, you are devoted to the gods, and you are a believer,
Rághava. You are also virtuous and resolute. Without resolve you cannot by acts of valor kill your enemy in battle,
particularly that devious *rákshasa*. You must first put aside
your grief and make a firm resolve. Then you can crush
that *rákshasa* and his followers. For you could overturn the
very earth together with her oceans, forests and mountains,

pṛthivīm api, Kākutstha, sa|sāgara|van'|âcalām
parivartayituṃ śaktaḥ kim aṅga punā Rāvaṇam.
ahaṃ tu khalu te vīryaṃ prasuptaṃ pratibodhaye
dīptair āhutibhiḥ kāle bhasma|cchannam iv' ânalam.»
26.15 Lakṣmaṇasya tu tad vākyaṃ pratipūjya hitaṃ śubham
Rāghavaḥ suhṛdaṃ snigdham idam vacanam abravīt:
«vācyaṃ yad anuraktena snigdhena ca hitena ca
satya|vikrama|yuktena tad uktaṃ, Lakṣmaṇa, tvayā.
eṣa śokaḥ parityaktaḥ sarva|kāry'|âvasādakaḥ
vikrameṣv apratihataṃ tejaḥ protsāhayāmy aham.
śarat|kālaṃ pratīkṣe 'ham iyaṃ prāvṛḍ upasthitā
tataḥ sa|rāṣṭraṃ sa|gaṇaṃ rākṣasaṃ taṃ nihanmy aham.»
tasya tad vacanaṃ śrutvā hṛṣṭo Rāmasya Lakṣmaṇaḥ
punar ev' âbravīd vākyaṃ Saumitrir mitra|nandanaḥ:
26.20 «etat te sadṛśaṃ vākyam uktaṃ, śatru|nibarhaṇa.
idānīm asi, Kākutstha, prakṛtiṃ svām upāgataḥ.
vijñāya hy ātmano vīryaṃ tathyaṃ bhavitum arhasi.
etat sadṛśam uktaṃ te śrutasy' âbhijanasya ca.
tasmāt, puruṣa|śārdūla, cintayañ śatru|nigraham
varṣā|rātram anuprāptam atikrāmaya, Rāghava!
niyamya kopaṃ pratipālyatāṃ śarat
kṣamasva māsāṃś caturo mayā saha
vas' âcale 'smin mṛga|rāja|sevite
saṃvardhayañ śatru|vadhe|samudyataḥ!»

27.1 Sa tadā Vālinaṃ hatvā Sugrīvam abhiṣicya ca
vasan Mālyavataḥ pṛṣṭhe Rāmo Lakṣmaṇam abravīt:

Kákutstha, let alone Rávana. With fiery words I shall surely arouse your slumbering courage, as one would rekindle with timely oblations a fire smoldering beneath its ashes."

Commending Lákshmana's useful and suitable speech, 26.15
Rághava spoke these warm, affectionate words:

"You have said what should be said by someone devoted, affectionate, helpful and truly valiant, Lákshmana. Here, I have forsaken my grief, which makes all undertakings fail. I shall call forth my irresistible fierceness in deeds of valor. But the rainy season is now at hand, and I must wait for autumn. Then I shall destroy that *rákshasa* together with his kingdom and his troops."

Lákshmana Saumítri, delight of his friends, was overjoyed to hear Rama's words, and he spoke once again:

"The words you have just spoken are worthy of you, 26.20
slaughterer of your enemies. Now, Kákutstha, you have returned to your own nature. Recognizing your own heroism, you must be true to it. This speech is worthy of you and of your renowned family. Therefore, Rághava, tiger among men, pass the rainy season at hand thinking about the defeat of your enemy. Hold back your anger and await the autumn. Endure these four months with me. Live on this mountain, haunt of the king of beasts, passing the time and preparing to destroy your enemy."

AND SO, AFTER he had killed Valin and had Sugríva con- 27.1
secrated, Rama, who was living on top of Mount Mályavan, said to Lákshmana:

«ayaṃ sa kālaḥ saṃprāptaḥ samayo 'dya jal'|āgamaḥ.
saṃpaśya tvaṃ nabho meghaiḥ saṃvṛtaṃ giri|saṃnibhaiḥ.
nava|māsa|dhṛtaṃ garbhaṃ bhāskarasya gabhastibhiḥ
pītvā rasaṃ samudrāṇāṃ dyauḥ prasūte ras'|âyanam.
śakyam ambaram āruhya megha|sopāna|paṅktibhiḥ
kuṭaj'|ârjuna|mālābhir alaṃkartuṃ divā|karam.
27.5 saṃdhyā|rāg'|ôtthitais tāmrair anteṣv adhika|pāṇḍuraiḥ
snigdhair abhra|paṭa|cchadair baddha|vraṇam iv' âmbaram.
manda|māruta|niḥśvāsaṃ saṃdhyā|candana|rañjitam
āpāṇḍu|jaladaṃ bhāti kām'|āturam iv' âmbaram.
eṣā dharma|parikliṣṭā nava|vāri|pariplutā
Sīt" êva śoka|saṃtaptā mahī bāṣpaṃ vimuñcati.
megh'|ôdara|vinirmuktāḥ kahlāra|sukha|śītalāḥ
śakyam añjalibhiḥ pātuṃ vātāḥ ketaki|gandhinaḥ.
eṣa phull'|ârjunaḥ śailaḥ ketakair adhivāsitaḥ
Sugrīva iva śānt'|ârir dhārābhir abhiṣicyate.
27.10 megha|kṛṣṇ'|âjina|dharā dhārā|yajñ'|ôpavītinaḥ
mārut'|āpūrita|guhāḥ prādhītā iva parvatāḥ.
kaśābhir iva haimībhir vidyudbhir iva tāḍitam
antaḥ|stanita|nirghoṣaṃ savedanam iv' âmbaram.
nīla|megh'|āśritā vidyut sphurantī pratibhāti me
sphurantī Rāvaṇasy' âṅke Vaideh" îva tapasvinī.
imās tā manmathavatāṃ hitāḥ pratihatā diśaḥ
anuliptā iva ghanair naṣṭa|graha|niśā|karāḥ.

"Now the time has come, the season when the rains arrive. See, the sky is covered with clouds as big as mountains. The heavens, which drank the oceans' water through the sun's rays, are giving birth to the elixir of life, their embryo carried for nine months. On a stairway of clouds, one could climb the sky to ornament the sun with garlands of *kútaja* and
árjuna blossoms. The sky seems to have wounds bound up 27.5
with dressings of soft clouds, red with the color of sunset but very pale at the edges. Sighing with gentle winds, the sky, pale with clouds yet tinged by the sunset, resembles a lovesick man anointed with red sandal-paste.

And like Sita burning with grief, this heat-stricken earth, newly flooded with water, sheds tears. Soft and cool as a white lotus, fragrant with *kétaki* blossoms, these breezes loosed from the heart of the clouds might be sipped from the hollow of one's hand. And this mountain, perfumed by *kétaka* flowers and with its *árjuna* trees in full bloom, is anointed by showers just as Sugríva was, once his enemy
was subdued. Wearing clouds as their black antelope skins 27.10
and streams as their sacred threads, the mountains, with wind murmuring in their caves, are like brahmans reciting.

The sky, lashed by lightning as if by golden whips, makes thundering sounds within, as if in pain. Flickering against dark clouds, the lightning looks to me like poor Vaidéhi trembling in Rávana's grasp. Spread with clouds so that the moon and planets have vanished, the sky is darkened in all directions, favoring lovers.

kva cid bāṣp'|âbhisaṃruddhān varṣ'|āgama|samutsukān
kuṭajān paśya, Saumitre, puṣṭitān giri|sānuṣu!
mama śok'|âbhibhūtasya kāma|saṃdīpanān sthitān.

27.15 rajaḥ praśāntaṃ sa|himo 'dya vāyur
nidāgha|doṣa|prasarāḥ praśāntāḥ
sthitā hi yātrā vasudh"|âdhipānāṃ
pravāsino yānti narāḥ sva|deśān.

saṃprasthitā mānasa|vāsa|lubdhāḥ
priy'|ânvitāḥ saṃprati cakravākāḥ
abhīkṣṇa|varṣ'|ôdaka|vikṣateṣu
yānāni mārgeṣu na saṃpatanti.

kva cit prakāśaṃ kva cid aprakāśaṃ
nabhaḥ prakīrṇ'|âmbu|dharaṃ vibhāti
kva cit kva cit parvata|saṃniruddhaṃ
rūpaṃ yathā śānta|mah"|ârṇavasya.

vyāmiśritaṃ sarja|kadamba|puṣpair
navaṃ jalaṃ parvata|dhātu|tāmraṃ
mayūra|kekābhir anuprayātaṃ
śail'|âpagāḥ śīghrataraṃ vahanti.

ras'|ākulaṃ ṣaṭpada|saṃnikāśaṃ
prabhujyate jambu|phalaṃ prakāmaṃ
aneka|varṇaṃ pavan'|âvadhūtam
bhūmau pataty āmra|phalaṃ vipakvaṃ.

27.20 vidyut|patākāḥ sa|balāka|mālāḥ
śail'|êndra|kūṭ'|ākṛti|saṃnikāśāḥ
garjanti meghāḥ samudīrṇa|nādā
matta|gaj'|êndrā iva saṃyugasthāḥ.

And look at the flowering *kútaja* trees standing on the mountainsides, veiled in places by mist, delighted by the coming of the rain. They inflame my love, Saumítri, though I am overcome by grief.

Now the dust has settled, the breeze is cool, the spread of summer's ills has ceased, the expeditions of kings have halted, and men absent from home return to their own countries. 27.15

The geese who yearn to live on Lake Mánasa have started off. The *chakra·vaka* birds are now united with their beloved mates. On roads damaged by constant rains, carts can no longer move about. Here visible, there invisible, the sky scattered with clouds looks like a calm sea obscured here and there by mountains.

To the accompaniment of peacocks' cries, the hill streams swiftly bear along the fresh rainwater, red with ore from the mountains, and mingled with *sarja* and *kadámba* blossoms. Black as bees, the succulent fruit of the *jambu* tree can be eaten to one's heart's content, while the many-colored mango fruits shaken by the wind fall to the ground, fully ripe.

With lightning for banners and rows of cranes for garlands, the clouds, resembling majestic mountain peaks, emit deep rumblings like maddened elephants trumpeting excitedly in battle. 27.20

megh'|âbhikāmī parisaṃpatantī
sammoditā bhāti balāka|paṅktiḥ
vāt'|âvadhūtā vara|pauṇḍarīkī
lamb" êva mālā racit" âmbarasya.
nidrā śanaiḥ Keśavam abhyupaiti
drutaṃ nadī sāgaram abhyupaiti
hṛṣṭā balākā ghanam abhyupaiti
kāntā sakāmā priyam abhyupaiti.
jātā van'|ântāḥ śikhi|supranṛttā
jātāḥ kadambāḥ sa|kadamba|śākhāḥ
jātā vṛṣā goṣu samāna|kāmā
jātā mahī sasya|van'|âbhirāmā.
vahanti varṣanti nadanti bhānti
dhyāyanti nṛtyanti samāśvasanti
nadyo ghanā matta|gajā van'|ântāḥ
priyā|vihīnāḥ śikhinaḥ plavaṃgāḥ.
27.25 praharṣitāḥ ketaka|puṣpa|gandhaṃ
āghrāya hṛṣṭā vana|nirjhareṣu
prapāta|śabd'|ākulitā gaj'|êndrāḥ
sārdhaṃ mayūraiḥ samadā nadanti.
dārā|nipātair abhihanyamānāḥ
kadamba|śākhāsu vilambamānāḥ
kṣaṇ'|ârjitaṃ puṣpa|ras'|âvagāḍhaṃ
śanair madaṃ ṣaṭ|caraṇās tyajanti.
aṅgāra|cūrṇ'|ôtkara|saṃnikāśaiḥ
phalaiḥ suparyāpta|rasaiḥ samṛddhaiḥ
jambū|drumāṇāṃ pravibhānti śākhā
nilīyamānā iva ṣaṭpad'|âughaiḥ.
taḍit|patākābhir alaṃkṛtānāṃ
udīrṇa|gambhīra|mahā|ravāṇām

Longing for clouds, a row of joyous cranes flying along together looks like a hanging garland of the finest white lotuses strung across the sky, swaying in the breeze.

Gently sleep approaches Késhava, swiftly the river approaches the sea, joyfully the she-crane approaches the cloud, eagerly the woman in love approaches her beloved.

The forests are now filled with peacocks dancing, the boughs of the *kadámba* tree are now filled with blossoms, bulls and their cows alike are now filled with desire, and the earth is now filled with the beauty of its crops and forests. Rivers flow, clouds rain, rutting elephants trumpet, forests glisten, parted lovers pine, peacocks dance and monkeys rejoice.

Overjoyed at smelling the fragrance of *kétaka* flowers, 27.25
stirred by the sound of cascading water in forest waterfalls, rutting elephants cry excitedly along with the peacocks.

Battered by the downpour of rain, bees clinging to *kadámba* branches gradually lose the deep intoxication so quickly gained from flower nectar. The boughs of the *jambu* tree, with their full-grown fruits brimming with juice and dark as mounds of charcoal, look as if swarms of black bees had alighted on them.

Making loud, deep roars, the storm clouds decked with lightning-banners are like elephants ready for battle. Wandering in mountain forests, the majestic elephant in rut

vibhānti rūpāṇi balāhakānāṃ
ran'|ôdyatānām iva vāraṇānāṃ.
mārg'|ânugaḥ śaila|van'|ânusārī
saṃprasthito megha|ravaṃ niśamya
yuddh'|âbhikāmaḥ pratināga|śaṅkī
matto gaj'|êndraḥ pratisaṃnivṛttaḥ.
27.30 muktā sakāśaṃ salilaṃ patad vai
sunirmalaṃ patra|puṭeṣu lagnaṃ
hṛṣṭā vivarṇa|cchadanā vihaṃgāḥ
sur'|êndra|dattaṃ tṛṣitāḥ pibanti.
nīleṣu nīlā nava|vāri|pūrṇā
megheṣu meghāḥ pravibhānti saktāḥ
dav'|âgni|dagdheṣu dav'|âgni|dagdhāḥ
śaileṣu śailā iva baddha|mūlāḥ.
mattā gaj'|êndrā muditā gav'|êndrā
vaneṣu viśrāntatarā mṛg'|êndrāḥ
ramyā nag'|êndrā nibhṛtā nar'|êndrāḥ
prakrīḍito vāri|dharaiḥ sur'|êndraḥ.
vṛttā yātrā nar'|êndrāṇāṃ senā pratinivartate.
vairāṇi c' âiva mārgāś ca salilena samī|kṛtāḥ.
māsi Prauṣṭhapade Brahma brāhmaṇānāṃ vivakṣatām
ayam adhyāya|samayaḥ Sāmagānām upasthitaḥ.
27.35 nivṛtta|karm'|āyatano nūnaṃ saṃcita|saṃcayaḥ
Āṣāḍhīm abhyupagato Bharataḥ Kosal'|âdhipaḥ.
nūnam āpūryamāṇāyāḥ Sarayvā vardhate rayaḥ
māṃ samīkṣya samāyāntam Ayodhyāyā iva svanaḥ.
imāḥ sphīta|guṇā varṣāḥ Sugrīvaḥ sukham aśnute
vijit'|âriḥ sa|dāraś ca rājye mahati ca sthitaḥ.
ahaṃ tu hṛta|dāraś ca rājyāc ca mahataś cyutaḥ
nadī|kūlam iva klinnam avasīdāmi, Lakṣmaṇa.

who has set out on his way eager for battle turns back upon hearing the roar of the clouds, thinking he hears a rival elephant.

Falling like pearls bestowed by the lord of gods, bright 27.30
raindrops cling in leaf-cups, where thirsty birds with faded wings drink with delight. Massed against other dark clouds, dark clouds full of fresh water look like firmly rooted mountains burned by forest fires seen against other mountains burned by forest fires. Lords of elephants are in rut, lords of cattle are overjoyed, lords of forest beasts are tranquil, lords of mountains are charming, lords of men are at rest, and the lord of gods is at play with the water-bearing clouds.

The expeditions of kings have ceased, their armies turn back. Hostilities and roads are equally blocked by water. In the month of Praushtha·pada, the time for study has now come for Sámaga brahmans wishing to learn the Veda.
With work completed on his dwellings and with his stores 27.35
assembled, Bharata, lord of Kósala, has surely undertaken some vow on the full-moon day of Ashádha. As the Sárayu River now becomes full, its current swells, as will the cheers of Ayódhya's people when they see me return. During these bountiful rains, Sugríva, established in his great kingdom, his enemy conquered, is enjoying pleasure with his wives.

But deprived of my great kingdom and robbed of my wife, I have been broken like a sodden riverbank, Lákshmana. Thus my vast grief and these rains, which are slow

śokaś ca mama vistīrṇo varṣāś ca bhṛśa|durgamāḥ
Rāvaṇaś ca mahāñ śatrur apāraṃ pratibhāti me.
27.40 ayātrāṃ c' âiva dṛṣṭv" êmāṃ mārgāṃś ca bhṛśa|durgamān
praṇate c' âiva Sugrīve na mayā kiṃ cid īritam.
api c' âtiparikliṣṭaṃ cirād dāraiḥ samāgatam
ātma|kārya|garīyastvād vaktuṃ n' êcchāmi vānaram.
svayam eva hi viśramya jñātvā kālam upāgatam
upakāraṃ ca Sugrīvo vetsyate n' âtra saṃśayaḥ.
tasmāt kāla|pratīkṣo 'haṃ sthito 'smi, śubha|lakṣaṇa,
Sugrīvasya nadīnāṃ ca prasādam anupālayan.
upakāreṇa vīro hi pratikāreṇa yujyate
a|kṛtajño 'pratikṛto hanti sattvavatāṃ manaḥ.»
27.45 ath' âivam uktaḥ praṇidhāya Lakṣmaṇaḥ
kṛt'|âñjalis tat pratipūjya bhāṣitaṃ
uvāca Rāmaṃ sv|abhirāma|darśanaṃ
pradarśayan darśanam ātmanaḥ śubhaṃ:
«yath"|ôktam etat tava sarvam īpsitaṃ,
nar'|êndra, kartā na cirādd har'|īśvaraḥ.
śarat|pratīkṣaḥ kṣamatām imaṃ bhavāñ
jala|prapātaṃ ripu|nigrahe dhṛtaḥ.»

28.1 Samīkṣya vimalaṃ vyoma gata|vidyud|balāhakam,
sāras'|ārava|saṃghuṣṭaṃ, ramya|jyotsn"|ânulepanam,
samṛddh'|ârthaṃ ca Sugrīvaṃ
manda|dharm'|ârtha|saṃgraham
atyartham asatāṃ mārgam
ek'|ânta|gata|mānasam
nivṛtta|kāryaṃ siddh'|ârthaṃ pramad"|âbhirataṃ sadā
prāptavantam abhipretān sarvān eva mano|rathān
svāṃ ca patnīm abhipretāṃ Tārāṃ c' âpi samīpsitām

to pass, and my mighty enemy Rávana all seem without
end to me. When I saw that roads were impassable and an 27.40
expedition impossible, I asked for nothing, even though Sugríva bowed in submission. Moreover, given the magnitude
of my undertaking, I did not wish to ask anything of the
exhausted monkey who was at long last reunited with his
wives. No doubt when he has rested, Sugríva himself will
realize that the time has come and will recognize his obligation. Therefore, you who bear auspicious marks, I keep
awaiting the proper time, watching for both Sugríva and the
rivers to become favorable. For a service rendered obliges a
warrior to repay the service. The ungrateful man who does
not do so wounds the heart of virtuous people."

Thus addressed, Lákshmana reflected and approved that 27.45
speech and then, with palms cupped, spoke to handsome
Rama, showing his own correct view: "Lord of men, before
long the king of monkeys will do all that you desire, just as
you have said. You must endure the falling rain, waiting for
autumn, intent upon the destruction of your enemy."

HÁNUMAN OBSERVED the clear sky free of clouds and 28.1
lightning, spread with lovely light, and resounding with the
cries of cranes. He also observed Sugríva with his abundant
wealth, doing little to accumulate wealth or religious merit,
his mind entirely given over to wicked ways; his objective
complete, his goals accomplished; always taking pleasure
in women, obtaining all his cherished wishes and his own
cherished wife, and also Tará, whom he had coveted. Divert-
ing himself night and day, his object achieved, his suffering
ended, he was enjoying himself like the lord of gods in the 28.5

viharantam aho|rātraṃ kṛt'|ârthaṃ vigata|jvaram
28.5 krīḍantam iva dev'|ēśaṃ Nandane 'psarasāṃ gaṇaiḥ
mantriṣu nyasta|kāryaṃ ca mantriṇām anavekṣakam
utsanna|rājya|saṃdeśaṃ kāma|vṛttam avasthitam
niścit'|ârtho 'rtha|tattva|jñaḥ kāla|dharma|viśeṣa|vit
prasādya vākyair madhurair hetumadbhir mano|ramaiḥ
vākyavid vākya|tattva|jñaṃ har'|īśaṃ Mārut'|ātmajaḥ
hitaṃ tathyaṃ ca pathyaṃ ca sāma|dharm'|ârtha|nīti|mat
praṇaya|prīti|saṃyuktaṃ viśvāsa|kṛta|niścayam
har'|īśvaram upāgamya Hanumān vākyam abravīt:

«rājyaṃ prāptaṃ yaśaś c' âiva kaulī śrīr abhivardhitā.
mitrāṇāṃ saṃgrahaḥ śeṣas, tad bhavān kartum arhati!
28.10 yo hi mitreṣu kālajñaḥ satataṃ sādhu vartate
tasya rājyaṃ ca kīrtiś ca pratāpaś c' âbhivardhate.
yasya kośaś ca daṇḍaś ca mitrāṇy ātmā ca, bhūmipa,
samavetāni sarvāṇi sa rājyaṃ mahad aśnute.
tad bhavān vṛtta|saṃpannaḥ sthitaḥ pathi niratyaye.
mitr'|ârtham abhinīt'|ârthaṃ yathāvat kartum arhati!
yas tu kāla|vyatīteṣu mitra|kāryeṣu vartate
sa kṛtvā mahato 'py arthān na mitr'|ârthena yujyate.

kriyatāṃ Rāghavasy' âitad Vaidehyāḥ parimārgaṇam
tad idaṃ, vīra, kāryaṃ te kāl'|âtītam, ariṃ|dama!
28.15 na ca kālam atītaṃ te nivedayati kālavit
tvaramāṇo 'pi san prājñas tava, rājan, vaś'|ânugaḥ.

Nándana garden with the hosts of *ápsaras*es. Addicted to sensual behavior, relegating his duties to his ministers and not overseeing his ministers, his command over the kingdom was destroyed. So the son of Máruta, who knew the real nature of things and had decided what needed to be done, who knew what was right for particular occasions, and who knew correct speech, propitiated with sweet, pleasing and well-reasoned words the lord of monkeys who knew true speech. He approached the lord of monkeys, who was full of love and affection for him and was convinced of his trustworthiness, and then spoke these words, which were beneficial, true and salutary, and were conciliatory, righteous, meaningful and politic:

"You have obtained kingship and fame and increased
the royal majesty of your family. It only remains for you
to support your allies, and this you must do. For if one 28.10
always deals with allies correctly and at the proper time,
then one's kingdom and glory and splendor increase. He
who has treasury, scepter, allies and self united in proper
balance enjoys great sovereignty, lord of the earth. Your
conduct is virtuous and you keep to a path free of danger.
Therefore you should duly accomplish your ally's purpose
for the sake of what is proper. But he who attends to his
ally's purpose when the right time has passed does not serve
his ally's purpose even if he accomplishes great things.

Therefore you must conduct a search for Vaidéhi. You
must do this for Rághava, heroic foe-tamer, for time is passing. Even though he is in a hurry and knows that time is of 28.15
the essence, that wise man does not remind you that time
is passing, for he is obedient to your will, king. Rághava is

kulasya ketuḥ sphītasya dīrgha|bandhuś ca Rāghavaḥ
aprameya|prabhāvaś ca svayaṃ c' âpratimo guṇaiḥ.
tasya tvaṃ kuru vai kāryaṃ pūrvaṃ tena kṛtaṃ tava,
har'|īśvara, hari|śreṣṭhān ājñāpayitum arhasi!
na hi tāvad bhavet kālo vyatītaś codanād ṛte.
coditasya hi kāryasya bhavet kāla|vyatikramaḥ.
akartur api kāryasya bhavān kartā, har'|īśvara,
kiṃ punaḥ pratikartus te rājyena ca dhanena ca.
28.20 śaktimān asi vikrānto, vānara'|ṛkṣa|gaṇ'|ēśvara.
kartuṃ Dāśaratheḥ prītim ājñāyāṃ kiṃ nu sajjase?
kāmaṃ khalu śarair śaktaḥ sur'|âsura|mah"|ôragān
vaśe Dāśarathiḥ kartuṃ tvat|pratijñāṃ tu kāṅkṣate.
prāṇa|tyāg'|âviśaṅkena kṛtaṃ tena tava priyam.
tasya mārgāma Vaidehīṃ pṛthivyām api c' âmbare.
na devā na ca gandharvā n' âsurā na marud|gaṇāḥ
na ca yakṣā bhayaṃ tasya kuryuḥ kim uta rākṣasāḥ.
tad evaṃ śakti|yuktasya pūrvaṃ priya|kṛtas tathā
Rāmasy' ârhasi, piṅg'|ēśa, kartuṃ sarv'|ātmanā priyam.
28.25 n' âdhastād avanau n' âpsu gatir n' ôpari c' âmbare
kasya cit sajjate 'smākaṃ, kap'|īśvara, tav' ājñayā.
tad ājñāpaya kaḥ kiṃ te kṛte vasatu kutra cit?
harayo hy apradhṛṣyās te santi koṭy|agrato, 'nagha.»

the head of his flourishing family and is an enduring friend. His might is immeasurable and he himself is incomparable in his virtues. Attend to his interests, then; he has already attended to yours. Lord of monkeys, you should give orders to the chief monkeys. For the proper time has not yet run out if only you act without further urging. But if the undertaking must still be urged upon you, then the right time will have passed. You should attend to the interests even of someone who does nothing for you, lord of monkeys, not to mention someone who has obligated you by giving
you kingship and wealth. Lord of the hosts of apes and 28.20
monkeys, you are powerful and valiant. Why then do you hesitate about ordering this favor to be done for Dásharathi?

Granted, with his own arrows Dásharathi can subdue gods, demons and great snakes. Still, he is waiting for your promise to be kept. Risking his life without hesitation, he did a favor for you. So for him, we must search this earth or the very heavens for Vaidéhi. Neither gods nor *gandhárvas* nor demons nor *yakshas* nor the host of Maruts could frighten him, much less *rákshasas*. You had a favor done for you first by powerful Rama; therefore, lord of tawny monkeys, you should with all your heart do a favor for him.
If you so command, lord of monkeys, none of us will slacken 28.25
his pace, whether on earth or on water, in the underworld or even up in the sky. Therefore command who is to stay where to do what for you. For you have more than ten million unassailable monkeys, blameless king."

tasya tad vacanaṃ śrutvā kāle sādhu niveditam
Sugrīvaḥ sattva|saṃpannaś cakāra matim uttamām.
sa saṃdideś' âbhimataṃ Nīlaṃ nitya|kṛt'|ôdyamam
dikṣu sarvāsu sarveṣāṃ sainyānām upasaṃgrahe.
«yathā senā samagrā me yūtha|pālāś ca sarvaśaḥ
samāgacchanty asaṃgena sen"|âgrāṇi tathā kuru!
28.30 ye tv anta|pālāḥ plavagāḥ śīghragā vyavasāyinaḥ
samānayantu te sainyaṃ tvaritāḥ śāsanān mama!
svayaṃ c' ânantaraṃ sainyaṃ bhavān ev' ânupaśyatu.
tri|pañca|rātrād ūrdhvaṃ yaḥ prāpnuyān n' êha vānaraḥ
tasya prāṇ'|ântiko daṇḍo n' âtra kāryā vicāraṇā.
harīṃś ca vṛddhān upayātu s'|Âṅgado
bhavān mam' ājñām adhikṛtya niścitām.»
iti vyavasthāṃ hari|puṃgav'|ēśvaro
vidhāya veśma praviveśa vīryavān.

29.1 Guhāṃ praviṣṭe Sugrīve vimukte gagane ghanaiḥ
varṣa|rātr'|ôṣito Rāmaḥ kāma|śok'|âbhipīḍitaḥ.
pāṇḍuraṃ gaganaṃ dṛṣṭvā vimalaṃ candra|maṇḍalam
śāradīṃ rajanīṃ c' âiva dṛṣṭvā jyotsn'|ânulepanām.
kāma|vṛttaṃ ca Sugrīvaṃ naṣṭāṃ ca Janak'|ātmajām
buddhvā kālam atītaṃ ca mumoha param'|āturaḥ.
sa tu saṃjñām upāgamya muhūrtān matimān punaḥ
manaḥsthām api Vaidehīṃ cintayām āsa Rāghavaḥ.
29.5 āsīnaḥ parvatasy' âgre hema|dhātu|vibhūṣite
śāradaṃ gaganaṃ dṛṣṭva jagāma manasā priyām.
dṛṣṭvā ca vimalaṃ vyoma gata|vidyud|balāhakam
sāras'|ārava|saṃghuṣṭaṃ vilalāp' ārtayā girā:

Upon hearing this correct speech communicated at the proper time, mighty Sugríva made an excellent decision. He ordered respected Nila, always diligent, to gather all his armies from every quarter.

"See to it that my entire army with its vanguards and all the troop leaders assemble without delay. And let the 28.30
swift and resolute monkeys who guard the outposts quickly assemble the troops at my command. And afterward you yourself must review the troops. Any monkey who has not reached here in fifteen days will be punished by death. Let there be no doubt about this. You and Ángada are to go to the monkey-elders concerning the orders upon which I have decided." Then, when the vigorous lord of those bulls among monkeys had made these arrangements, he entered his dwelling.

After Sugríva had entered his cave and when the sky 29.1
was free of clouds, Rama, who had waited through the rainy season, was oppressed by grief and desire. He gazed at the clear sky and the white circle of the moon and the autumn night washed with moonlight. Realizing that Sugríva was given over to lust, that Jánaka's daughter was lost, and that the proper time had passed by, he was so deeply tormented that he fainted. Then, after a moment, wise Rághava regained consciousness and thought about Vaidéhi,
who was always in his heart. Seated on the mountaintop 29.5
bright with gold and minerals, he gazed at the autumn sky, and his thoughts were fixed on his beloved. And as he gazed at that clear sky free of clouds and lightning, resounding with the cries of cranes, he lamented in a pained voice:

«sāras'|ārava|saṃnādaiḥ sāras'|ārava|nādinī
y" āśrame ramate bālā s" âdya me ramate katham?
puṣpitāṃś c' āsanān dṛṣṭvā kāñcanān iva nirmalān
kathaṃ sā ramate bālā paśyantī mām apaśyatī?
yā purā kala|haṃsānāṃ svareṇa kala|bhāṣiṇī
budhyate cāru|sarv'|âṅgī s" âdya me budhyate katham?
29.10 niḥsvanaṃ cakravākānāṃ niśamya saha|cāriṇām
puṇḍarīka|viśāl'|âkṣī katham eṣā bhaviṣyati?
sarāṃsi sarito vāpīḥ kānanāni vanāni ca
tāṃ vinā mṛga|śāv'|âkṣīṃ caran n' âdya sukhaṃ labhe.
api tāṃ mad|viyogāc ca saukumāryāc ca bhāminīm
na dūraṃ pīḍayet kāmaḥ śarad|guṇa|nirantaraḥ.»
evam|ādi nara|śreṣṭho vilalāpa nṛp'|ātmajaḥ
vihaṃga iva sāraṅgaḥ salilaṃ tridaś'|ēśvarāt.
tataś cañcūrya ramyeṣu phal'|ârthī giri|sānuṣu
dadarśa paryupāvṛtto lakṣmīvāl Lakṣmaṇo 'grajam.
29.15 taṃ cintayā duḥsahayā parītaṃ
visaṃjñam ekaṃ vijane manasvī
bhrātur viṣādāt paritāpa dīnaḥ
samīkṣya Saumitrir uvāca Rāmaṃ:
«kim, ārya, kāmasya vaśaṃ gatena?
kim ātma|pauruṣya parābhavena?
ayaṃ sadā saṃhriyate samādhiḥ.
kim atra yogena nivartitena?
kriy"|âbhiyogaṃ manasaḥ prasādaṃ
samādhi|yog'|ânugataṃ ca kālaṃ

"My young wife, whose voice is like the crying of cranes, used to enjoy the crying of cranes in our hermitage; how can she find enjoyment now? And how can my young wife enjoy the sight of flowering *ásana* trees bright as gold, when she looks about and doesn't see me? Soft-voiced, lovely in every limb, she used to awaken at the sound of the geese. What
wakes her now? When she hears the call of the *chakra·vaka* 29.10
birds and their mates, how can my lotus-eyed wife survive? Without that fawn-eyed woman, I find no happiness now in wandering through woods and forests, near lakes, rivers and ponds. I hope that lovely woman, so young and far from me, is not deeply tormented by love endlessly renewed by autumn's charms."

The king's son, best of men, kept lamenting in this way, like a *saránga* bird asking for water from Indra, lord of the thirty gods.

Then fortunate Lákshmana, who had been ranging over the beautiful mountainsides in search of fruit, returned and
saw his elder brother. When he saw him alone in that solitary 29.15
place, distraught and filled with unbearable cares, wise Saumítri was wretched with anguish because of his brother's dejection, and he said to Rama:

"Elder brother, what is the use of submitting to love? What is the good of defeating your own manliness? Composure can always be achieved. What is the good of turning away from endeavor now? Undaunted warrior, exert yourself in your task, make your mind serene, use your time for concentration and exertion, and make these things and your ally's strength a cause of success, achieved by your own actions. Nor can another easily possess Jánaki when you

sahāya|sāmarthyam, adīna|sattva,
svā|karma|hetuṃ ca kuruṣva hetuṃ!
na Jānakī, mānava|vaṃśa|nātha,
tvayā sa|nāthā sulabhā pareṇa:
na c' âgni|cūḍāṃ jvalitām upetya
na dahyate, vīra|var'|ârha, kaś cit.»
sa|lakṣmaṇaṃ Lakṣmaṇam apradhṛṣyaṃ
svabhāva|jaṃ vākyam uvāca Rāmaḥ
hitaṃ ca pathyaṃ ca naya|prasaktaṃ
sa|sāma|dharm'|ârtha|samāhitaṃ ca:
29.20 «niḥsaṃśayaṃ kāryam avekṣitavyaṃ.
kriyā|viśeṣo hy anuvartitavyaḥ.
nanu pravṛttasya durāsadasya,
kumāra, kāryasya phalaṃ na cintyaṃ?»
atha padma|palāś'|âkṣīṃ Maithilīm anucintayan
uvāca Lakṣmaṇaṃ Rāmo mukhena pariśuṣyatā:
«tarpayitvā Sahasr'|âkṣaḥ salilena vasuṃ|dharām
nirvartayitvā sasyāni kṛta|karmā vyavasthitaḥ.
snigdha|gambhīra|nirghoṣāḥ śaila|druma|puro|gamāḥ
visṛjya salilaṃ meghāḥ pariśrāntā, nṛp'|ātmaja.
nīl'|ôtpala|dala|śyāmāḥ śyāmī|kṛtvā diśo daśa,
vimadā iva mātaṅgāḥ śānta|vegāḥ payo|dharāḥ.
29.25 jala|garbhā mahā|vegāḥ kuṭaj'|ârjuna|gandhinaḥ
caritvā viratāḥ, saumya, vṛṣṭi|vātāḥ samudyatāḥ.
ghanānāṃ vāraṇānāṃ ca mayūrāṇāṃ ca, Lakṣmaṇa,
nādaḥ prasravaṇānāṃ ca praśāntaḥ sahas", ânagha.
abhivṛṣṭā mahā|meghair nirmalāś citra|sānavaḥ
anuliptā iv' ābhānti girayaś candra|raśmibhiḥ.
darśayanti śaran|nadyaḥ pulināni śanaiḥ śanaiḥ
nava|saṃgama|savrīḍā jaghanān' îva yoṣitaḥ.

are her protector, protector of the race of men: No one approaches the blazing flame of a fire without being burned, most worthy of warriors."

Rama then addressed unassailable Lákshmana, who bore
auspicious marks, with these characteristic words that were
beneficial, salutary, consistent with statesmanship, conciliatory, righteous, and full of meaning: "Undoubtedly we must 29.20
look after our undertaking. We must carry out specific actions. We must certainly give thought to the outcome of the
difficult undertaking we have begun, prince." Then Rama
spoke to Lákshmana, his mouth becoming dry with grief as
he thought again of lotus-eyed Máithili:

"Thousand-eyed Indra has satisfied the earth with water
and ripened the crops. Now he has settled down, his work
accomplished. Passing before mountains and trees with a
deep, pleasing sound, the clouds released their water and
are now exhausted, prince. Water-bearing clouds dark as
blue-lotus petals had darkened the ten directions. Now, like
elephants no longer in rut, their violence is calmed. High up, 29.25
the violent water-bearing storm-winds fragrant with *kútaja*
and *árjuna* blossoms have passed by and now are still, gentle
brother. Clouds, elephants, peacocks and waterfalls have
all at once ceased their sounds, blameless Lákshmana. The
mountains have been washed spotless by great clouds and
their glittering peaks now shine as if bathed in moonbeams.

Little by little the autumn rivers reveal their sandbanks, just as young women, bashful in their first sexual encounter, reveal their loins. With their waters now clear, resounding

prasanna|salilāḥ, saumya, kurarībhir vināditāḥ
cakravāka|gaṇ'|ākīrṇā vibhānti salil'|āśayāḥ.
29.30 anyonya|baddha|vairāṇāṃ jigīṣūṇāṃ, nṛp'|ātmaja,
udyoga|samayaḥ, saumya, pārthivānām upasthitaḥ.
iyaṃ sā prathamā yātrā pārthivānāṃ, nṛp'|ātmaja,
na ca paśyāmi Sugrīvam udyogaṃ vā tathā|vidham.

catvāro vārṣikā māsā gatā varṣa|śat'|ôpamāḥ
mama śok'|âbhitaptasya, saumya, Sītām apaśyataḥ.
priyā|vihīne duḥkh'|ārte hṛta|rājye vivāsite
kṛpāṃ na kurute rājā Sugrīvo mayi, Lakṣmaṇa.
‹anātho hṛta|rājyo 'yaṃ Rāvaṇena ca dharṣitaḥ
dīno dūra|gṛhaḥ kāmī māṃ c' âiva śaraṇaṃ gataḥ.›
29.35 ity etaiḥ kāraṇaiḥ, saumya, Sugrīvasya durātmanaḥ
ahaṃ vānara|rājasya paribhūtaḥ, paraṃ|tapa.
sa kālaṃ parisaṃkhyāya Sītāyāḥ parimārgaṇe
kṛt'|ârthaḥ samayaṃ kṛtvā durmatir n' âvabudhyate.

tvaṃ praviśya ca Kiṣkindhāṃ brūhi vānara|puṃgavam
mūrkhaṃ grāmya|sukhe saktaṃ Sugrīvaṃ vacanān mama.
arthināṃ upapannānāṃ pūrvaṃ c' âpy upakāriṇām
āśāṃ saṃśrutya yo hanti sa loke puruṣ'|âdhamaḥ.
śubhaṃ vā yadi vā pāpaṃ yo hi vākyam udīritam
satyena parigṛhṇāti sa vīraḥ puruṣ'|ôttamaḥ.
29.40 kṛt'|ârthā hy akṛt'|ârthānāṃ mitrāṇāṃ na bhavanti ye
tān mṛtān api kravy'|âdaḥ kṛtaghnān n' ôpabhuñjate.

with the cries of ospreys and crowded with hosts of *chakra·vaka* birds, the lakes look lovely, gentle brother. For kings 29.30
eager to conquer and bitterly hostile toward one another, the time for exertion has arrived, gentle prince. Now is the time when kings make their first military expeditions, prince, yet I see neither Sugríva nor any such preparation by him.

I am tormented with grief at not seeing Sita, so for me the four rainy months have passed as if they were a hundred years, gentle brother. Although I am tortured by sorrow, deprived of my beloved, robbed of my kingdom, and in exile, King Sugríva shows me no compassion, Lákshmana. 'Without a protector, deprived of his kingdom, far from home, assailed by Rávana, miserable and lovesick, Rama has come to me for help.' Such thoughts as these are the 29.35
reason that the wicked-minded king of monkeys, Sugríva, slights me, gentle brother, scorcher of your foes. Now that he has achieved his own object, this evil-minded monkey, who himself specified the time for Sita's search, disregards the agreement he made.

Enter Kishkíndha and speak in my name to that bull among monkeys, Sugríva, that fool intent on vulgar pleasures. He who promises and then destroys the hopes of worthy suppliants who have moreover previously rendered services is the vilest man in the world. But he who accepts as an oath his own spoken word, whether for good or for evil,
is a hero and the best of men. Even carrion-eaters will not 29.40
consume the dead bodies of those ingrates who, once their own object is achieved, will not assist their friends whose objects are still unachieved.

nūnaṃ kāñcana|pṛṣṭhasya vikṛṣṭasya mayā raṇe
draṣṭum icchanti cāpasya rūpaṃ vidyud|gaṇ'|ôpamam.
ghoraṃ jyā|tala|nirghoṣaṃ kruddhasya mama saṃyuge
nirghoṣam iva vajrasya punaḥ saṃśrotum icchati.
kāmam evaṃ|gate 'py asya parijñāte parākrame
tvat|sahāyasya me, vīra, na cintā syān, nṛp'|ātmaja.

yad artham ayam ārambhaḥ kṛtaḥ, para|puraṃ|jaya,
samayaṃ n' âbhijānāti kṛt'|ârthaḥ plavag'|ēśvaraḥ.
29.45 varṣā|samaya|kālaṃ tu pratijñāya har'|īśvaraḥ
vyatītāṃś caturo māsān viharan n' âvabudhyate.
s'|âmātya|pariṣat krīḍan pānam ev' ôpasevate
śoka|dīneṣu n' âsmāsu Sugrīvaḥ kurute dayām.
ucyatāṃ, gaccha, Sugrīvas tvayā, vatsa mahā|bala,
mama roṣasya yad rūpaṃ, brūyāś c' âinam idaṃ vacaḥ:

‹na ca saṃkucitaḥ panthā yena Vālī hato gataḥ.
samaye tiṣṭha, Sugrīva, mā Vāli|patham anvagāḥ.
eka eva raṇe Vālī śareṇa nihato mayā
tvāṃ tu satyād atikrāntaṃ haniṣyāmi sa|bāndhavam.›
29.50 tad evaṃ|vihite kārye yadd hitaṃ, puruṣa'|rṣabha,
tat tad brūhi, nara|śreṣṭha, tvara kāla|vyatikramaḥ.
‹kuruṣva satyaṃ mayi, vānar'|ēśvara,
pratiśrutaṃ dharmam avekṣya śāśvatam!
mā Vālinaṃ pretya gato Yama|kṣayaṃ
tvam adya paśyer mama coditaiḥ śaraiḥ!›»

He must want to see my golden-backed bow flash like a streak of lightning when I bend it in combat. He must want to hear again the terrible clash of the bowstring against my arm-guard, which booms like a thunderbolt when I am angry in battle. Granted that his valor is known to be so great; still, with you as my companion, heroic prince, I should have no worry.

Now that his object is achieved, the lord of monkeys
does not acknowledge the agreement on account of which
I made this effort, conqueror of enemy cities. Though he 29.45
promised the end of the rains as the agreed-upon time, the
lord of monkeys is enjoying himself and does not notice
that the four months have passed. Amusing himself with
his ministers and his council, Sugríva spends all his time
drinking. He has no pity on us, though we are wretched
with grief. Go, dear boy, and tell Sugríva the nature of my
anger. And, mighty one, you should say these words to him:

'The path Valin traveled when he died is not closed. Stand
by your agreement, Sugríva, lest you follow in Valin's path. I
slew Valin alone with my arrow in battle. But if you neglect
your oath, I shall kill your entire family along with you.' So, 29.50
bull among men, say to him whatever is helpful given the
state of affairs. Make haste, best of men: Time is running
out. 'Keep the promise you made me, lord of monkeys,
heeding the immemorial code of righteous conduct, lest
I shoot you dead with my arrows and send you today to
Yama's abode to see Valin.'"

sa pūrvajaṃ tīvra|vivṛddha|kopaṃ
lālapyamānaṃ prasamīkṣya dīnaṃ
cakāra tīvrāṃ matim ugra|tejā
har'|īśvare mānava|vaṃśa|nāthaḥ.

30.1 SA KĀMINAṂ dīnam adīna|sattvaḥ
śok'|âbhipannaṃ samudīrṇa|kopaṃ
nar'|êndra|sūnur nara|deva|putraṃ
Rām'|ânujaḥ pūrvajam ity uvāca:
«na vānaraḥ sthāsyati sādhu|vṛtte.
na maṃsyate kārya|phal'|ânuṣaṅgān.
na bhakṣyate vānara|rājya|lakṣmīṃ
tathā hi n' âbhikramate 'sya buddhiḥ.
mati|kṣayād grāmya|sukheṣu saktas
tava prasād'|âpratikāra|buddhiḥ.
hato 'grajaṃ paśyatu Vālinaṃ sa.
na rājyam evaṃ viguṇasya deyam.
na dhāraye kopam udīrṇa|vegaṃ
nihanmi Sugrīvam asatyam adya.
hari|pravīraiḥ saha Vāli|putro
nar'|êndra|patnyā vicayaṃ karotu.»
30.5 tam ātta|bāṇ'|āsanam utpatantaṃ
nivedit'|ârthaṃ raṇa|caṇḍa|kopaṃ.
uvāca Rāmaḥ para|vīra|hantā
sv|avekṣitaṃ s'|ânunayaṃ ca vākyaṃ:

When this lord of the race of men, whose might was terrible, saw that his dejected older brother was addressing him repeatedly with sharply increasing anger, he made a harsh decision about the lord of monkeys.

Rama's high-spirited younger brother, son of the lord of men, replied to his dejected, lovesick elder brother, son of a king of men, who was overcome with grief and whose anger had greatly increased: 30.1

"The monkey will not keep to virtuous conduct. He will not keep in mind the connection between your efforts and his rewards. And so it is that he does not get started. He will not long enjoy the royal power of the monkey kingdom. Attached to vulgar pleasures because his mind is corrupted, he has no inclination to repay your favor, warrior. Let him die and behold his older brother Valin. A kingdom should not be given to someone so devoid of virtues. I cannot contain my violent anger. I shall kill faithless Sugríva today. Let Valin's son and the chief monkeys conduct the search for the king's wife."

After announcing his intention, he seized his bow and was rushing off in a terrible rage for battle. But Rama, slayer of enemy warriors, addressed him with these circumspect and courteous words: 30.5

«na hi vai tvad|vidho loke pāpam evaṃ samācaret.
pāpam āryeṇa yo hanti sa vīraḥ puruṣ'|ôttamaḥ.
n' êdam adya tvayā grāhyaṃ sādhu|vṛttena, Lakṣmaṇa,
tāṃ prītim anuvartasva pūrva|vṛttaṃ ca saṃgatam.
sām'|ôpahitayā vācā rūkṣāṇi parivarjayan
vaktum arhasi Sugrīvaṃ vyatītaṃ kāla|paryaye.»
so 'grajen' ânuśiṣṭ'|ârtho yathāvat puruṣa'|rṣabhaḥ
praviveśa purīṃ vīro Lakṣmaṇaḥ para|vīra|hā.
30.10 tataḥ śubha|matiḥ prājño bhrātuḥ priya|hite rataḥ
Lakṣmaṇaḥ pratisaṃrabdho jagāma bhavanaṃ kapeḥ.
Śakra|bāṇ'|āsana|prakhyaṃ dhanuḥ kāl'|ântak'|ôpamaḥ
pragṛhya giri śṛṅg'|ābhaṃ Mandaraḥ sānumān iva.
yath"|ôkta|kārī vacanam uttaraṃ c' âiva s'|ôttaram
Bṛhaspati|samo buddhyā mattvā Rām'|ânujas tadā.
kāma|krodha|samutthena bhrātuḥ kop'|âgninā vṛtaḥ
prabhañjana iv' âprītaḥ prayayau Lakṣmaṇas tadā.
sāla|tāl'|âśvakarṇāṃś ca tarasā pātayan bahūn
paryasyan giri|kūṭāni drumān anyāṃś ca vegataḥ
30.15 śilāś ca śakalī|kurvan padbhyāṃ gaja iv' āśugaḥ
dūram eka|padaṃ tyaktvā yayau kārya|vaśād drutam.
tām apaśyad bal'|ākīrṇāṃ hari|rāja|mahā|purīm
durgām Ikṣvāku|śārdūlaḥ Kiṣkindhāṃ giri|saṃkaṭe.
roṣāt prasphuramāṇ'|âuṣṭhaḥ Sugrīvaṃ prati Lakṣmaṇaḥ
dadarśa vānarān bhīmān Kiṣkindhāyā bahiś|carān.
śaila|śṛṅgāṇi śataśaḥ pravṛddhāṃś ca mahī|ruhān
jagṛhuḥ kuñjara|prakhyā vānarāḥ parvat'|ântare.

"Surely someone like you should not do such evil in this world. He who destroys evil by virtue is a hero and the best of men. As a man of honorable conduct, Lákshmana, you must not choose this evil now. Pursue toward Sugríva that affection and friendship we previously followed. With conciliatory words, avoiding harshness, you must tell Sugríva that time has run out."

Duly instructed in this matter by his elder brother, Lákshmana, that bull among men, slayer of enemy warriors,
entered the city. Then Lákshmana, wise, honest-minded, 30.10
devoted to his brother's pleasure and well-being, went to
the monkey's dwelling in a fury, resembling death-dealing
Time. Like Mount Mándara with its high peak, he bore a
bow like a mountain peak, bright as a rainbow. Equal to
Brihas·pati in intelligence, Rama's younger brother Lákshmana, doing as he was told, reflected on the speech he would
make, the reply to it, and his reply to that. Then, enveloped
by the fire of his own wrath aroused by his brother's desire and anger, he advanced like a raging tempest. Violently
toppling many *sala*, *tala* and *ashva·karna* trees, impetuously
overturning other trees and mountain peaks, and crushing 30.15
rocks with his feet like a swift-moving elephant, he raced
on, making long strides in keeping with his mission.

There, in a gap in the mountains, that tiger of the Ikshvákus saw Kishkíndha, the monkey-king's great and inaccessible citadel, crowded with troops. His lip trembling with anger at Sugríva, Lákshmana saw dreadful monkeys moving about outside Kishkíndha. In the space between the mountains, monkeys as big as elephants clutched mountain peaks and full-grown trees by the hundred. Now, when

tān gṛhīta|praharaṇān harīn dṛṣṭvā tu Lakṣmaṇaḥ
babhūva dvi|guṇaṃ kruddho bahv|indhana iv' ânalaḥ.
30.20 taṃ te bhaya|parīt'|âṅgāḥ kruddhaṃ dṛṣṭvā plavaṃ|gamāḥ
kāla|mṛtyu|yug'|ânt'|ābhaṃ śataśo vidrutā diśaḥ.
tataḥ Sugrīva|bhavanaṃ praviśya hari|puṃgavāḥ
krodham āgamanaṃ c' âiva Lakṣmaṇasya nyavedayan.
Tārayā sahitaḥ kāmī saktaḥ kapi|vṛṣo rahaḥ
na teṣāṃ kapi|vīrāṇāṃ śuśrāva vacanaṃ tadā.
tataḥ saciva|saṃdiṣṭā harayo roma|harṣaṇāḥ
giri|kuñjara|megh'|ābhā nagaryā niryayus tadā.
nakha|daṃṣṭr"|āyudhā ghorāḥ sarve vikṛta|darśanāḥ
sarve śārdūla|darpāś ca sarve ca vikṛt'|ānanāḥ.
30.25 daśa|nāga|balāḥ ke cit ke cid daśa|guṇ'|ôttarāḥ
ke cin nāga|sahasrasya babhūvus tulya|vikramāḥ.

kṛtsnāṃ hi kapibhir vyāptāṃ druma|hastair mahā|balaiḥ
apaśyal Lakṣmaṇaḥ kruddhaḥ Kiṣkindhāṃ tāṃ durāsadam.
tatas te harayaḥ sarve prākāra|parikh'|ântarāt
niṣkramy' ôdagra|sattvās tu tasthur āviṣkṛtaṃ tadā.
Sugrīvasya pramādaṃ ca pūrvajaṃ c' ārtam ātmavān
buddhvā kopa|vaśaṃ vīraḥ punar eva jagāma saḥ.
sa dīrgh'|ôṣṇa|mah"|ôcchvāsaḥ kopa|saṃrakta|locanaḥ
babhūva nara|śārdūlaḥ sadhūma iva pāvakaḥ.
30.30 bāṇa|śalya|sphurajj|jihvaḥ sāyak'|āsana|bhogavān
sva|tejo viṣa|saṃghātaḥ pañc'|āsya iva pannagaḥ.
taṃ dīptam iva kāl'|âgniṃ nāg'|êndram iva kopitam
samāsādy' Âṅgadas trāsād viṣādam agamad bhṛśam.

he saw that the monkeys had seized weapons, Lákshmana's
anger redoubled, like a fire with ample fuel.

When those monkeys saw that he was furious and that he 30.20
resembled Time, Death and the end of the world, they ran
off by the hundred in every direction, their limbs gripped
by fear. Then those bulls among monkeys entered Sugríva's
dwelling and reported Lákshmana's arrival and his wrath.
But the lustful, infatuated bull among monkeys was se-
cluded with Tará and did not hear the words of those monkey warriors. Instructed by the ministers, terrifying monkeys as big as mountains, elephants or clouds then went
forth from the city. With claws and fangs for weapons, all
were terrible, all were hideous with deformed faces, and all
were as bold as tigers. Some had the strength of ten ele- 30.25
phants, some ten times that, and some had the valor of a
thousand elephants.

In his anger, Lákshmana gazed upon unassailable Kishkíndha, entirely surrounded by mighty monkeys with trees
in their hands. Then all those immensely powerful monkeys
came out beyond the moat surrounding the ramparts and
stood there in full view. That self-possessed warrior, recall-
ing Sugríva's dereliction and the suffering of his own elder
brother, once again gave way to anger. Red-eyed with anger
and sighing long, hot sighs, that tiger among men resembled
a smoking fire. With his arrowheads like darting tongues, his 30.30
bow like coils and his inner strength like a store of venom, he
resembled a five-headed snake. As he approached this man
who was enflamed like the fire of universal destruction and
who was like some angry serpent-lord, Ángada was terrified
and greatly dismayed.

so 'ṅgadaṃ roṣa|tāmr'|âkṣaḥ saṃdideśa mahā|yaśāḥ
«Sugrīvaḥ kathyatāṃ, vatsa, mam' āgamanam ity uta:
‹eṣa Rām'|ânujaḥ prāptas tvat|sakāśam ariṃ|damaḥ
bhrātur vyasana|saṃtapto dvāri tiṣṭhati Lakṣmaṇaḥ›»
Lakṣmaṇasya vacaḥ śrutvā śok'|āviṣṭo 'ṅgado 'bravīt
pituḥ samīpam āgamya: «Saumitrir ayam āgataḥ.»
30.35 te mah"|âugha|nibhaṃ dṛṣṭvā vajr'|âśani|sama|svanam
siṃha|nādaṃ samaṃ cakrur Lakṣmaṇasya samīpataḥ.
tena śabdena mahatā pratyabudhyata vānaraḥ
mada|vihvala|tāmr'|âkṣo vyākula|srag|vibhūṣaṇaḥ.
ath' Âṅgada|vacaḥ śrutvā ten' âiva ca samāgatau
mantriṇau vānar'|êndrasya saṃmat'|ôdāra|darśinau.
Plakṣaś c' âiva Prabhāvaś ca mantriṇāv artha|dharmayoḥ
vaktum ucc'|âvacaṃ prāptaṃ Lakṣmaṇaṃ tau śaśaṃsatuḥ.
prasādayitvā Sugrīvaṃ vacanaiḥ sāma|niścitaiḥ
āsīnaṃ paryupāsīnau yathā Śakraṃ Marut|patim:
30.40 «satya|saṃdhau mahā|bhāgau bhrātarau Rāma|Lakṣmaṇau
vayasya|bhāvaṃ saṃprāptau rājy'|ârhau rājya|dāyinau.
tayor eko dhanuṣ|pāṇir dvāri tiṣṭhati Lakṣmaṇaḥ
yasya bhītāḥ pravepante nādān muñcanti vānarāḥ.
sa eṣa Rāghava|bhrātā Lakṣmaṇo vākya|sārathiḥ
vyavasāya|rathaḥ prāptas tasya Rāmasya śāsanāt.

His eyes reddened with anger, Lákshmana, whose fame was great, instructed Ángada, "Dear child, announce my arrival to Sugríva with these words:

'Rama's younger brother Lákshmana, subduer of his foes, is here to see you. Tormented by his brother's misfortune, he is standing at the gate.'"

When he heard Lákshmana's speech, Ángada, overcome with grief, approached his father and said, "Saumítri is here."

But when the monkey warriors saw Lákshmana, all at 30.35
once, right before him they roared a roar like that of a lion or of a mighty stream, or like the sound of a thunderbolt. At that loud noise the monkey awoke, red-eyed and unsteady with drunkenness, his garlands and ornaments in disarray.

Now, when they heard Ángada's words, two of the monkey-king's counselors, who were respected and noble to behold, accompanied him. Those two counselors, Plaksha and Prabháva, announced that Lákshmana had arrived to speak of various matters concerning righteousness and statecraft. Soothing him with speeches certain to be conciliatory, they respectfully attended the seated Sugríva as if he were Shakra, lord of the Maruts:

"The illustrious brothers Rama and Lákshmana, true to 30.40
their promise, worthy of kingship and conferring kingship, have become your friends. One of them, Lákshmana, is standing at the gate, bow in hand. Trembling in fear of him, the monkeys are screeching. Rághava's brother Lákshmana is here. He has arrived at Rama's command, with Rama's words as his charioteer and with his own determination as his chariot. You and your son and your kinsmen must bow

tasya mūrdhnā praṇamya tvaṃ sa|putraḥ saha bandhubhiḥ
rājaṃs tiṣṭha sva|samaye bhava satya|pratiśravaḥ!»

31.1 Aṅgadasya vacaḥ śrutvā Sugrīvaḥ sacivaiḥ saha
Lakṣmaṇaṃ kupitaṃ śrutvā mumoc' āsanam ātmavān.
sacivān abravīd vākyaṃ niścitya guru|lāghavam
mantrajñān mantra|kuśalo mantreṣu pariniṣṭhitaḥ:
«na me durvyāhṛtaṃ kiṃ cin, n' âpi me duranuṣṭhitam.
Lakṣmaṇo Rāghava|bhrātā kruddhaḥ kim iti cintaye?
asuhṛdbhir mam' âmitrair nityam antara|darśibhiḥ
mama doṣān asaṃbhūtāñ śrāvito Rāghav'|ânujaḥ.
31.5 atra tāvad yathā|buddhi sarvair eva yathā|vidhi
bhavadbhir niścayas tasya vijñeyo nipuṇaṃ śanaiḥ.
na khalv asti mama trāso Lakṣmaṇān n' âpi Rāghavāt
mitraṃ tv asthāna|kupitaṃ janayaty eva saṃbhramam.
sarvathā sukaraṃ mitraṃ duṣkaraṃ paripālanam.
anityatvāt tu cittānāṃ prītir alpe 'pi bhidyate
ato|nimittaṃ trasto 'haṃ Rāmeṇa tu mah"|ātmanā
yan mam' ôpakṛtaṃ śakyaṃ pratikartuṃ na tan mayā.»
Sugrīveṇ' âivam uktas tu Hanumān hari|puṃgavaḥ
uvāca svena tarkeṇa madhye vānara|mantriṇām:
31.10 «sarvathā n' âitad āścaryaṃ yat tvaṃ, hari|gaṇ'|ēśvara,
na vismarasi susnigdham upakāra|kṛtaṃ śubham.
Rāghaveṇa tu śūreṇa bhayam utsṛjya dūrataḥ
tvat|priy'|ârthaṃ hato Vālī Śakra|tulya|parākramaḥ.

your heads to him. You must stand by your agreement, king. You must be faithful to your promise."

WHEN SELF-POSSESSED Sugríva, along with his ministers, 31.1
heard Ángada's words and heard that Lákshmana was angry, he rose from his seat. Experienced and thoroughly versed in counsel, weighing his alternatives, he spoke these words to his ministers who understood counsel:

"I have said nothing wrong nor have I done anything wrong. I wonder, then, why Rághava's brother Lákshmana is so angry? Evil-hearted enemies, always looking for my weak spots, must have reported nonexistent misdeeds of
mine to Rághava's younger brother. So, to start with, all 31.5
of you must reach some conclusion about this, using your own judgment, gradually, cleverly and in keeping with the rules of proper conduct. I am by no means afraid of Lákshmana or of Rághava, but a friend angry without grounds does give rise to alarm. It is always easy to make a friend but hard to keep one. Since feelings do not endure, affection breaks down over small things. It is for this reason that I am frightened, for I really cannot repay the service rendered to me by great Rama."

Thus addressed by Sugríva, Hánuman, bull among monkeys, stated his own conjecture in the midst of the monkey counselors:

"It is no wonder at all that you cannot forget the affec- 31.10
tionate good deed done as a service to you. For in order to please you, heroic Rághava cast fear far away and killed Valin, who was equal in prowess to Shakra. There is no doubt that it is entirely due to his affection that Rághava is an-

sarvathā praṇayāt kruddho Rāghavo n' âtra saṃśayaḥ
bhrātaraṃ sa prahitavāl̄ Lakṣmaṇaṃ lakṣmi|vardhanam.
tvaṃ pramatto na jānīṣe kālaṃ, kalavidāṃ vara.
phulla|sapta|cchada|śyāmā pravṛttā tu śarac chivā.
nirmala|graha|nakṣatrā dyauḥ pranaṣṭa|balāhakā.
prasannāś ca diśaḥ sarvāḥ saritaś ca sarāṃsi ca.
31.15 prāptam udyoga|kālaṃ tu n' âvaiṣi, hari|puṃgava.
tvaṃ pramatta iti vyaktaṃ Lakṣmaṇo 'yam ih' āgataḥ.
ārtasya hṛta|dārasya paruṣaṃ puruṣ'|ântarāt
vacanaṃ marṣaṇīyaṃ te Rāghavasya mah"|ātmanaḥ.
kṛt'|âparādhasya hi te n' ânyat paśyāmy ahaṃ kṣamam
antareṇ' âñjaliṃ baddhvā Lakṣmaṇasya prasādanāt.
niyuktair mantribhir vācyo avaśyaṃ pārthivo hitam.
ata eva bhayaṃ tyaktvā bravīmy avadhṛtaṃ vacaḥ.
abhikruddhaḥ samartho hi cāpam udyamya Rāghavaḥ
sa|dev'|âsura|gandharvaṃ vaśe sthāpayituṃ jagat.
31.20 na sa kṣamaḥ kopayituṃ yaḥ prasādya punar bhavet
pūrv'|ôpakāraṃ smaratā kṛtajñena viśeṣataḥ.
tasya mūrdhnā praṇamya tvaṃ sa|putraḥ sa|suhṛj|janaḥ,
rājaṃs, tiṣṭha sva|samaye bhartur bhāry" êva tad|vaśe!
na Rāma|Rām'|ânuja|śāsanaṃ tvayā,
kap'|îndra, yuktaṃ manas" âpy apohitum
mano hi te jñāsyati mānuṣaṃ balaṃ
sa|Rāghavasy' âsya sur'|êndra|varcasaḥ!»

gry and has sent his brother Lákshmana, bestower of good fortune. Best of those who understand time, you have been inattentive and did not realize the time: Propitious autumn has begun, lush with flowering *sapta·cchada* trees. There are bright planets and stars in the heavens now that the clouds have disappeared. The sky is clear in all directions, and so
are the rivers and lakes. But still you do not realize that the 31.15
time for your endeavor has arrived, bull among monkeys. Since you are clearly negligent, Lákshmana has come.

So now you must tolerate from the mouth of another man the harsh words of great Rághava, who is suffering because his wife has been taken. And since you have committed an offense, I see no alternative for you but to propitiate Lákshmana with cupped palms. A king needs to be told what is beneficial by his appointed counselors. For that reason, I have put aside fear to speak these well-considered words. For when Rághava is angered, he can, by raising his bow, bring under his power the whole world with its gods, *ásuras* and *gandhárvas*.

It is not proper, particularly for someone who is grateful, 31.20
who remembers a past favor, to anger a person who must be propitiated again. You, your son and your close friends must bow your heads to him. Then you must honor your agreement, king, as submissive to him as a wife to her husband. King of monkeys, it is not right for you to reject the instruction of Rama and his younger brother, even in your mind. For your mind surely knows the human strength of Rághava and Lákshmana, powerful as the gods."

32.1 ATHA PRATISAMĀDIṢṬO Lakṣmaṇaḥ para|vīra|hā
praviveśa guhāṃ ghorāṃ Kiṣkindhāṃ Rāma|śāsanāt.
dvāra|sthā harayas tatra mahā|kāyā mahā|balāḥ
babhūvur Lakṣmaṇaṃ dṛṣṭvā sarve prāñjalayaḥ sthitāḥ.
niḥśvasantaṃ tu taṃ dṛṣṭvā kruddhaṃ Daśarath'|ātmajam
babhūvur harayas trastā na c' âinaṃ paryavārayan.
sa taṃ ratna|mayīṃ śrīmān divyāṃ puṣpita|kānanām
ramyāṃ ratna|samākīrṇāṃ dadarśa mahatīṃ guhām
32.5 harmya|prāsāda|saṃbādhāṃ nānā|paṇy'|ôpaśobhitām
sarva|kāma|phalair vṛkṣaiḥ puṣpitair upaśobhitām
deva|gandharva|putraiś ca vānaraiḥ kāma|rūpibhiḥ
divya|māly'|âmbara|dharaiḥ śobhitāṃ priya|darśanaiḥ
candan'|âgaru|padmānāṃ gandhaiḥ surabhi|gandhināṃ
maireyāṇāṃ madhūnāṃ ca saṃmodita|mahā|pathām
Vindhya|Meru|giri|prasthaiḥ prāsādair naika|bhūmibhiḥ
dadarśa giri|nadyaś ca vimalās tatra Rāghavaḥ.
Aṅgadasya gṛhaṃ ramyaṃ Maindasya Dvividasya ca
Gavayasya Gavākṣasya Gajasya Śarabhasya ca
32.10 Vidyunmāleś ca Saṃpāteḥ Sūryākṣasya Hanūmataḥ
Vīrabāhoḥ Subāhoś ca Nalasya ca mah"|ātmanaḥ
Kumudasya Suṣeṇasya Tāra|Jāmbavatos tathā
Dadhivaktrasya Nīlasya Supāṭala|Sunetrayoḥ.
eteṣāṃ kapi|mukhyānāṃ rāja|mārge mah"|ātmanām
dadarśa gṛha|mukhyāni mahā|sārāṇi Lakṣmaṇaḥ
pāṇḍur'|âbhra|prakāśāni divya|mālya|yutāni ca
prabhūta|dhana|dhānyāni strī|ratnaiḥ|śobhitāni ca.

THEN, WHEN HE was summoned, Lákshmana, slayer of 32.1
enemy warriors, entered the terrible cave Kishkíndha as Rama had commanded. At the sight of Lákshmana, the huge
and powerful monkey gatekeepers all stood with their hands
cupped in reverence. Perceiving that Dasha·ratha's son was
breathing heavily in anger, the monkeys were frightened
and did not close in around him.

Majestic Lákshmana saw that delightful, heavenly, great
cave made of jewels, filled with jewels, crowded with man- 32.5
sions and palaces, resplendent with all sorts of wares. The
cave with its blossoming groves was resplendent with blossoming trees, whose fruits satisfied every desire. It was splendid with beautiful monkeys wearing heavenly garlands and
clothing, for these were the sons of gods and *gandhárvas*
and could change form at will. The principal streets were
fragrant with the scents of sweet-smelling sandal, aloes and
padma, and of *mairéya* and *madhu* wines; and there were
many-storied palaces as solid as Mount Meru or the Vindhya mountains. And Rághava saw there unsullied mountain
streams.

On the royal highway Lákshmana saw Ángada's lovely
house and the fine, substantial houses of those great and em-
inent monkeys Mainda, Dvívida, Gávaya, Gaváksha, Gaja
and Shárabha; Vidyun·mala, Sampáti, Suryáksha, Hánu- 32.10
man, Vira·bahu and great Nala; Kúmuda, Sushéna, Tara,
and Jámbavan, too; Dadhi·vaktra, Nila, Supátala and Suné-
tra. Their houses were as bright as white clouds and strung
with heavenly garlands. They were full of wealth and grain
and splendid with the most beautiful women.

pāṇḍureṇa tu śailena parikṣiptaṃ durāsadam
vānar'|êndra|gṛhaṃ ramyaṃ Mahendra|sadan'|ôpamam
32.15 śulkaiḥ prāsāda|śikharaiḥ Kailāsa|śikhar'|ôpamaiḥ
sarva|kāma|phalair vṛkṣaiḥ puṣpitair upaśobhitam
Mahendra|dattaiḥ śrīmadbhir nīla|jīmūta|saṃnibhaiḥ
divya|puṣpa|phalair vṛkṣaiḥ śīta|cchāyair mano|ramaiḥ.
haribhiḥ saṃvṛta|dvāraṃ balibhiḥ śastra|pāṇibhiḥ.
divya|māly'|āvṛtaṃ śubhraṃ tapta|kāñcana|toraṇam.
Sugrīvasya gṛhaṃ ramyaṃ praviveśa mahā|balaḥ
avāryamāṇaḥ Saumitrir mah"|âbhram iva bhāskaraḥ.
sa sapta|kakṣyā dharm'|ātmā yān'|āsana|samāvṛtāḥ
praviśya sumahad guptaṃ dadarś' ântaḥ|puraṃ mahat
32.20 haima|rājata|paryaṅkair bahubhiś ca var'|āsanaiḥ
mah"|ârh'|āstaraṇ'|ôpetais tatra tatr' ôpaśobhitam.
praviśann eva satataṃ śuśrāva madhura|svaram
tantrī|gīta|samākīrṇaṃ sama|gīta|pad'|âkṣaram.
bahvīś ca vividh'|ākārā rūpa|yauvana|garvitāḥ
striyaḥ Sugrīva|bhavane dadarśa sa mahā|balaḥ.
dṛṣṭv" âbhijana|saṃpannāś citra|mālya|kṛta|srajaḥ
vara|mālya|kṛta|vyagrā bhūṣaṇ'|ôttama|bhūṣitāḥ
n' âtṛptān n' âti ca vyagrān n' ânudātta|paricchadān
Sugrīv'|ânucarāṃś c' âpi lakṣayām āsa Lakṣmaṇaḥ.

Enclosed by a white stone rampart was the lovely but unapproachable house of the lord of monkeys, which was like
great Indra's abode, with white palace turrets like Kailása's 32.15
peaks, resplendent with blossoming trees whose fruits satisfied every desire, with majestic trees given by great Indra. It had trees with heavenly blossoms and fruits, which were delightful, like dark clouds, giving cool shade. Its doorways were flanked by powerful monkeys with weapons in hand. It was bright, covered with heavenly garlands, and had an arched gateway of pure gold.

Unhindered, mighty Saumítri entered Sugríva's lovely house as the bright sun enters a great cloud. Passing seven enclosures filled with chariots and seats, righteous Lákshmana
saw the large, well-guarded women's quarters, resplendent 32.20
everywhere with beds of gold and silver and with many fine seats furnished with expensive cushions.

As he entered, he heard continuous sweet music, accompanied by the sound of stringed instruments, in which words and syllables were matched to the singing. And within Sugríva's palace mighty Lákshmana saw many women of every description, proud of their beauty and youth. Noble in birth, they were adorned with the finest ornaments. Their garlands were made of bright-colored flowers, and they were absorbed in making exquisite garlands. Lákshmana saw them and noticed also Sugríva's satisfied, attentive servants wearing elegant clothing.

32.25 tataḥ Sugrīvam āsīnaṃ kāñcane param'|āsane
mah"|ârh'|āstaraṇ'|ôpete dadarś' āditya|saṃnibham
divy'|ābharaṇa|citr'|âṅgaṃ divya|rūpaṃ yaśasvinam
divya|māly'|âmbara|dharaṃ Mahendram iva durjayam
divy'|ābharaṇa|mālyābhiḥ pramadābhiḥ samāvṛtam.
Rumāṃ tu vīraḥ parirabhya gāḍhaṃ
var'|āsana|stho vara|hema|varṇaḥ
dadarśa Saumitrim adīna|sattvaṃ
viśāla|netraḥ su|viśāla|netram.

33.1 TAM APRATIHATAṂ kruddhaṃ praviṣṭaṃ puruṣa'|rṣabham
Sugrīvo Lakṣmaṇaṃ dṛṣṭvā babhūva vyathit'|êndriyaḥ.
kruddhaṃ niḥśvasamānaṃ taṃ pradīptam iva tejasā
bhrātur vyasana|saṃtaptaṃ dṛṣṭvā Daśarath'|ātmajam
utpapāta hari|śreṣṭho hitvā sauvarṇam āsanam
mahān Mahendrasya yathā sv|alaṃkṛta iva dhvajaḥ.
utpatantam anūtpetū Rumā|prabhṛtayaḥ striyaḥ
Sugrīvaṃ gagane pūrṇaṃ candraṃ tārā|gaṇā iva.
33.5 saṃrakta|nayanaḥ śrīmān vicacāla kṛt'|âñjaliḥ
babhūv' âvasthitas tatra kalpa|vṛkṣo mahān iva.
Rumā|dvitīyaṃ Sugrīvaṃ nārī|madhya|gataṃ sthitam
abravīl Lakṣmaṇaḥ kruddhaḥ sa|tāraṃ śaśinaṃ yathā:
«sattv'|âbhijana|saṃpannaḥ s'|ânukrośo jit'|êndriyaḥ
kṛtajñaḥ satya|vādī ca rājā loke mahīyate.
yas tu rājā sthito 'dharme mitrāṇām upakāriṇām
mithyā|pratijñāṃ kurute ko nṛśaṃsataras tataḥ?
śatam aśv'|ânṛte hanti, sahasraṃ tu gav'|ânṛte.

Then he saw glorious Sugríva seated on a splendid golden throne furnished with expensive cushions. He was as bright as the sun, his appearance was heavenly, and his body glittered with heavenly ornaments. Surrounded by beautiful women who were decked in heavenly ornaments and garlands, and wearing heavenly garlands and clothing himself, he was as invincible as great Indra. Tightly embracing Ruma, seated on his throne, his color that of finest gold, the large-eyed hero Sugríva gazed at large-eyed, dauntless Saumítri. 32.25

When Sugríva saw Lákshmana, that bull among men, 33.1
enter unchecked and angry, his mind was troubled. The great monkey chief saw Dasha·ratha's son, blazing with power and breathing hard in his rage, aggrieved at his brother's misfortune. And so he left his golden throne, rising up like great Indra's beautifully adorned staff. As Sugríva arose, the women led by Ruma rose with him, like the host
of stars following the full moon into the heavens. Majestic, 33.5
his eyes reddened, he swayed. Then, with palms cupped, he stood firm, like the great wish-fulfilling tree.

Lákshmana spoke angrily to Sugríva, who stood with Ruma in the midst of the women, like the moon among the stars:

"A wellborn, powerful king whose passions are controlled, who is grateful, compassionate and truthful, is much esteemed in this world. But who is more malicious than that king bent on unrighteousness who makes a false promise to friends who have helped him? By lying about a horse, a man in effect kills a hundred. By lying about a cow, he kills a

ātmānaṃ sva|janaṃ hanti puruṣaḥ puruṣ'|ânṛte.
33.10 pūrvaṃ kṛt'|ârtho mitrāṇāṃ na tat pratikaroti yaḥ
kṛtaghnaḥ sarva|bhūtānāṃ sa vadhyaḥ, plavag'|ēśvara!
gīto 'yaṃ Brahmaṇā ślokaḥ sarva|loka|namas|kṛtaḥ
dṛṣṭvā kṛtaghnaṃ kruddhena taṃ nibodha, plavaṃ|gama!
brahmaghne ca surā|pe ca core bhagna|vrate tathā
niṣkṛtir vihitā sadbhiḥ kṛtaghne n' âsti niṣkṛtiḥ.
an|āryas tvaṃ kṛtaghnaś ca mithyā|vādī ca, vānara,
pūrvaṃ kṛt'|ârtho Rāmasya na tat pratikaroṣi yat.
nanu nāma kṛt'|ârthena tvayā Rāmasya, vānara,
Sītāyā mārgaṇe yatnaḥ kartavyaḥ kṛtam icchatā.
33.15 sa tvaṃ grāmyeṣu bhogeṣu sakto mithyā|pratiśravaḥ.
na tvāṃ Rāmo vijānīte sarpaṃ maṇḍūka|rāviṇam.
mahā|bhāgena Rāmeṇa pāpaḥ karuṇa|vedinā
harīṇāṃ prāpito rājyaṃ tvaṃ durātmā mah"|ātmanā.
kṛtaṃ cen n' âbhijānīṣe Rāmasy' âkliṣṭa|karmaṇaḥ
sadyas tvaṃ niśitair bāṇair hato drakṣyasi Vālinam.
na ca saṃkucitaḥ panthā yena Vālī hato gataḥ;
samaye tiṣṭha, Sugrīva, mā Vāli|patham anvagāḥ!
na nūnam Ikṣvāku|varasya kārmukāc
cyutāñ śarān paśyasi vajra|saṃnibhān
tataḥ sukhaṃ nāma niṣevase sukhī
na Rāma|kāryaṃ manas" âpy avekṣase.»

thousand. But it is himself and his kinsmen he kills when he
lies about another man. He who does not repay his friends 33.10
when his own object is already achieved is an ingrate, fit to
be killed by all beings, lord of monkeys. This *shloka* verse
revered by all people was sung by Brahma, angry at seeing
an ingrate. Listen to it, monkey.

Virtuous men have prescribed atonements for the brahman-killer, the drinker of wine, the thief and the breaker
of vows; but for the ingrate there is no atonement. You are
ignoble, monkey, an ingrate and a liar; for you do not repay
Rama though your own object is already achieved. Surely,
monkey, since your own object is achieved, you must make
an effort to look for Sita if you wish to repay Rama's service. You are addicted to vulgar pleasures and false to your 33.15
promise. Rama did not realize you were a snake croaking
like a frog. It was through great, illustrious, compassionate Rama that you, who are evil and wicked, obtained the
kingship of the monkeys. If you do not acknowledge the
service rendered by Rama, who is tireless in action, you will
at once, shot dead with sharp arrows, see Valin. The path
Valin traveled when he died is not closed. Stand by your
agreement, Sugríva, lest you follow in Valin's path. It must
be that since you cannot see the arrows that fall like thunderbolts from the bow of that best of Ikshvákus, you are
content to pursue pleasure and do not give even a thought
to what needs to be done for Rama."

34–38
THE MONKEYS GATHER

34.1 TATHĀ BRUVĀṆAṂ Saumitriṃ pradīptam iva tejasā.
abravīl Lakṣmaṇaṃ Tārā tār"|âdhipa|nibh'|ānanā:
«n' âivaṃ, Lakṣmaṇa, vaktavyo n' âyaṃ paruṣam arhati.
harīṇām īśvaraḥ śrotuṃ tava vaktrād viśeṣataḥ.
n' âiv' âkṛtajñaḥ Sugrīvo na śaṭho n' âpi dāruṇaḥ.
n' âiv' ânṛta|katho, vīra, na jihmaś ca kap'|īśvaraḥ.
upakāraṃ kṛtaṃ vīro n' âpy ayaṃ vismṛtaḥ kapiḥ
Rāmeṇa, vīra, Sugrīvo yad anyair duṣkaraṃ raṇe.
34.5 Rāma|prasādāt kīrtiṃ ca kapi|rājyaṃ ca śāśvatam
prāptavān iha Sugrīvo Rumāṃ māṃ ca, paraṃ|tapa.
su|duḥkhaṃ śāyitaḥ pūrvaṃ
prāpy' êdaṃ sukham uttamam
prāpta|kālaṃ na jānīte
Viśvāmitro yathā muniḥ.
Ghṛtācyāṃ kila saṃsakto daśa|varṣāṇi, Lakṣmaṇa,
aho 'manyata dharm'|ātmā Viśvāmitro mahā|muniḥ.
sa hi prāptaṃ na jānīte kālaṃ kālavidāṃ varaḥ
Viśvāmitro mahā|tejāḥ kiṃ punar yaḥ pṛthag|janaḥ?
deha|dharmaṃ gatasy' âsya pariśrāntasya Lakṣmaṇa,
avitṛptasya kāmeṣu Rāmaḥ kṣantum ih'|ârhati.
34.10 na ca roṣa|vaśaṃ, tāta, gantum arhasi, Lakṣmaṇa,
niścay'|ârtham avijñāya sahasā prākṛto yathā.
sattva|yuktā hi puruṣās tvad|vidhāḥ, puruṣa'|rṣabha,
avimṛśya na roṣasya sahasā yānti vaśyatām.
prasādaye tvāṃ, dharmajña, Sugrīv'|ârthe samāhitā.

As Sumítra's son Lákshmana spoke in that fashion, he 34.1
seemed ablaze with power. Then Tará, her face bright as the lord of stars, said to him:

"One should not address the lord of monkeys in this manner, Lákshmana. He does not deserve to hear harsh words, especially from your mouth. Sugríva is not at all ungrateful or deceitful or pitiless. The lord of monkeys does not tell lies, hero, nor is he dishonest. Nor has this heroic monkey Sugríva forgotten that Rama rendered a service impossible
for any other to accomplish in battle, hero. It is through 34.5
Rama's favor that Sugríva has now obtained renown, the everlasting kingship of the monkeys, as well as Ruma and me, scorcher of your foes.

He rested most unhappily before; so now that he has achieved this extreme happiness, like the sage Vishva·mitra he does not realize what the time is. For they say that the great sage, righteous Vishva·mitra, was so attached to the *ápsaras* Ghritáchi that he thought ten years to be but a single day, Lákshmana. If even powerful Vishva·mitra, who best understands time, did not notice the passage of time, what can you expect from an ordinary being? Rama should pardon Sugríva, who is only following his bodily nature, and who, although exhausted, is not yet sated with sensual pleasures, Lákshmana.

And you, my dear Lákshmana, should not rashly suc- 34.10
cumb to anger like a common man, without knowing the true state of affairs. For men of strong character like you, bull among men, do not rashly succumb to the power of anger without reflection. I beseech you earnestly for Sugríva's sake. You know what is right. Please give up your

mahān roṣa|samutpannaḥ saṃrambhas tyajyatām ayam.
Rumāṃ māṃ kapi|rājyaṃ ca dhana|dhānya|vasūni ca
Rāma|priy'|ârthaṃ Sugrīvas tyajed iti matir mama.
samāneṣyati Sugrīvaḥ Sītayā saha Rāghavam
śaś'|âṅkam iva Rohiṇyā nihatvā Rāvaṇaṃ raṇe.
34.15 śata|koṭi|sahasrāṇi Laṅkāyāṃ kila rakṣasām
ayutāni ca ṣaṭ|triṃśat sahasrāṇi śatāni ca.
ahatvā tāṃś ca durdharṣān rākṣasān kāma|rūpiṇaḥ
na śakyo Rāvaṇo hantuṃ yena sā Maithilī hṛtā.
te na śakyā raṇe hantum asahāyena, Lakṣmaṇa,
Rāvaṇaḥ krūra|karmā ca Sugrīveṇa viśeṣataḥ.
evam ākhyātavān Vālī sa hy abhijño har'|īśvaraḥ
āgamas tu na me vyaktaḥ śravāt tasya bravīmy aham.
tvat|sahāya|nimittaṃ vai preṣitā hari|puṃgavāḥ
ānetuṃ vānarān yuddhe subahūn hari|yūthapān.
34.20 tāṃś ca pratīkṣamāṇo 'yaṃ vikrāntān sumahā|balān
Rāghavasy' ârtha|siddhy|arthaṃ na niryāti har'|īśvaraḥ.
kṛtā tu saṃsthā, Saumitre, Sugrīveṇa yathā purā
adya tair vānarair sarvair āgantavyaṃ mahā|balaiḥ.
ṛkṣa|koṭi|sahasrāṇi go|lāṅgūla|śatāni ca
adya tvām upayāsyanti; jahi kopam, ariṃ|dama,
koṭyo 'nekās tu, Kākutstha, kapīnāṃ dīpta|tejasām
tava hi mukham idaṃ nirīkṣya kopāt
ksataja|nibhe nayane nirīkṣamāṇāḥ
hari|vara|vanitā na yānti śāntiṃ
prathama|bhayasya hi śaṅkitāḥ sma sarvāḥ.»

great agitation born of anger. I believe that, to please Rama, Sugríva would give up Ruma, me, the monkey kingdom, and his wealth, grain and riches. Sugríva will kill Rávana in battle and reunite Rághava and Sita, like the hare-marked moon and his consort, the constellation Róhini.

They say that in Lanka there are one thousand times one 34.15
billion and thirty-six times one hundred, thirty-six times one thousand, and thirty-six times ten thousand *rákshasas*. And without killing those unassailable *rákshasas*, who can change form at will, one cannot kill Rávana, who has carried off Máithili. For those *rákshasas* and cruel Rávana cannot be slain in battle without an ally, Lákshmana, particularly Sugríva. That is what Valin, the lord of monkeys, indicated, and he was well informed. But my knowledge is not direct: I am telling you only what I heard from him. In order to provide you with allies in battle, bulls among monkeys have been dispatched to bring many monkeys, the monkey-troop
leaders. And since he is still awaiting those mighty, valiant 34.20
monkeys, the lord of monkeys cannot set out to accomplish Rághava's purpose.

Sugríva already issued a decree according to which all those mighty monkeys should be arriving today, Saumítri. Ten billion apes, a billion langurs and many millions of monkeys with blazing power will come to you today, Kákutstha. So give up your anger, subduer of your foes. For when they see this face of yours and your eyes blood-red with rage, all the wives of the monkey-lord fear their previous danger and can find no peace of mind."

35.1 Ity uktas Tārayā vākyaṃ praśritaṃ dharma|saṃhitam
mṛdu|sva|bhāvaḥ Saumitriḥ pratijagrāha tad vacaḥ.
tasmin pratigṛhīte tu vākye hari|gaṇ'|ēśvaraḥ
Lakṣmaṇāt sumahat trāsaṃ vastraṃ klinnam iv' âtyajat.
tataḥ kaṇṭha|gataṃ mālyaṃ citraṃ bahu|guṇaṃ mahat
ciccheda vimadaś c' āsīt Sugrīvo vānar'|ēśvaraḥ.
sa Lakṣmaṇaṃ bhīma|balaṃ sarva|vānara|sattamaḥ
abravīt praśritaṃ vākyaṃ Sugrīvaḥ saṃpraharṣayan:
35.5 «pranaṣṭā śrīś ca kīrtiś ca kapi|rājyaṃ ca śāśvatam
Rāma|prasādāt, Saumitre, punaḥ prāptam idaṃ mayā.
kaḥ śaktas tasya devasya khyātasya svena karmaṇā
tādṛśaṃ vikramaṃ, vīra, pratikartum, ariṃ|dama?
Sītāṃ prāpsyati dharm'|ātmā vadhiṣyati ca Rāvaṇam
sahāya|mātreṇa mayā Rāghavaḥ svena tejasā
sahāya|kṛtyaṃ hi tasya yena sapta mahā|drumāḥ
śailaś ca vasudhā c' âiva bāṇen' âikena dāritāḥ?
dhanur visphāramāṇasya yasya śabdena, Lakṣmaṇa,
sa|śailā kampitā bhūmiḥ sahāyais tasya kiṃ nu vai?
35.10 anuyātrāṃ nar'|êndrasya kariṣye 'haṃ, nara'|rṣabha,
gacchato Rāvaṇaṃ hantuṃ vairiṇaṃ sa|puraḥ|saram.
yadi kiṃ cid atikrāntaṃ viśvāsāt praṇayena vā
preṣyasya kṣamitavyaṃ me na kaś cin n' âparādhyati.»
iti tasya bruvāṇasya Sugrīvasya mah"|ātmanaḥ
abhaval Lakṣmaṇaḥ prītaḥ premṇā c' êdam uvāca ha:

After Tará had addressed him in those polite words 35.1
consistent with righteousness, Saumítri, who was tender by nature, accepted her words. And once those words had been accepted, the lord of the monkey hosts put aside his great terror of Lákshmana as one might put aside a wet garment. Then Sugríva, lord of monkeys, tore off the great, wonderful garland of many properties which was around his neck, and he was free of his intoxication. Sugríva, best of all monkeys, spoke conciliatory words, delighting Lákshmana, whose power was terrifying.

"My lost majesty and glory and the everlasting kingship of 35.5
the monkeys—all this I have regained through Rama's favor, Saumítri. Heroic tamer of foes, who could ever repay such valor as that of this king renowned for his deeds? Righteous Rághava will regain Sita and will kill Rávana by his own power. I shall be merely his ally. What need has he of an ally when with a single arrow he pierced seven great trees, a mountain and even the earth itself? When the mere sound of his twanging bow makes the earth and its mountains
tremble, Lákshmana, what need has he of allies? When the 35.10
lord of men goes forth to kill his enemy Rávana, along with his attendants, bull among men, I shall merely follow in his train. If I, who am his servant, have committed any transgression, let it be forgiven out of trust or affection. All servants make mistakes."

As great Sugríva spoke in this way, Lákshmana was pleased and said affectionately:

«sarvathā hi mama bhrātā sanātho, vānar'|ēśvara,
tvayā nāthena, Sugrīva, praśritena viśeṣataḥ.
yas te prabhāvaḥ, Sugrīva, yac ca te śaucam uttamam
arhas taṃ kapi|rājyasya śriyaṃ bhoktum anuttamām.
35.15 sahāyena ca, Sugrīva, tvayā Rāmaḥ pratāpavān
vadhiṣyati raṇe śatrūn acirān: n' âtra saṃśayaḥ.
dharmajñasya kṛtajñasya saṃgrāmeṣv anivartinaḥ.
upapannaṃ ca yuktaṃ ca, Sugrīva, tava bhāṣitam
doṣajñaḥ sati sāmarthye ko 'nyo bhāṣitum arhati
varjayitvā mama jyeṣṭhaṃ tvāṃ ca, vānara|sattama.
sadṛśaś c' âsi Rāmasya vikrameṇa balena ca
sahāyo daivatair dattaś cirāya, hari|puṃgava.
kiṃ tu śīghram ito, vīra, niṣkrāma tvaṃ mayā saha
sāntvayasva vayasyaṃ ca bhārya|haraṇa|duḥkhitam
35.20 yac ca śok'|âbhibhūtasya śrutvā Rāmasya bhāṣitam
mayā tvaṃ paruṣāṇy uktas tac ca tvaṃ kṣantum arhasi.»

36.1 Evam uktas tu Sugrīvo Lakṣmaṇena mah"|ātmanā
Hanumantaṃ sthitaṃ pārśve sacivaṃ vākyam abravīt:
«Mahendra|Himavad|Vindhya|Kailāsa|śikhareṣu ca
Mandare pāṇḍu|śikhare pañca|śaileṣu ye sthitāḥ
taruṇ'|āditya|varṇeṣu bhrājamāneṣu sarvaśaḥ
parvateṣu samudr'|ânte paścimasyāṃ tu ye diśi
āditya|bhavane c' âiva girau saṃdhy"|âbhra|saṃnibhe
padma|tāla|vanaṃ bhīmaṃ saṃśritā hari|puṃgavāḥ
36.5 añjan'|âmbuda|saṃkāśāḥ kuñjara|pratim'|âujasaḥ

"With you above all as his courteous protector, lord of
monkeys, my brother has a true protector in every way, Sugríva. By virtue of your dignity and your extreme purity, Sugríva, you are worthy of enjoying the unsurpassed majesty
of the kingship over the monkeys. With you as his ally, 35.15
valorous Rama will soon kill his enemies in battle, Sugríva.
There is no doubt about that. You are grateful and righteous
and never turn back in battle, Sugríva. What you say is
fitting and proper. Apart from you and my elder brother,
what other powerful person who recognizes his own faults
is able to speak of them, best of monkeys? You are Rama's
equal in valor and strength, and the gods have given you to
be his ally for a long time to come, bull among monkeys.
Nevertheless, hero, you must leave this place at once with
me and console your friend, who is suffering because of his
wife's abduction. Please forgive me if, after hearing what 35.20
Rama said when he was overcome with grief, I spoke harsh
words to you."

WHEN GREAT Lákshmana had addressed him in this fash- 36.1
ion, Sugríva said these words to his minister Hánuman, who
stood beside him:

"You must immediately summon all the monkeys on
earth: those who live on the peaks of the five mountains
Mahéndra, Himálaya, Vindhya, Kailása and white-peaked
Mándara; and those who dwell in the west near the seashore
on mountains glittering all over with the color of the newly
risen sun; and those bulls among monkeys who shelter in
the dreadful forests of *padma* and *tala* trees on the mountain
that is the sun's dwelling and that resembles a rain cloud at

Añjane parvate c' âiva ye vasanti plavaṃ|gamāḥ
manaḥśilā|guh"|āvāsā vānarāḥ kanaka|prabhāḥ
Meru|pārśva|gatāś c' âiva ye ca Dhūṃra|giriṃ śritāḥ
taruṇ'|āditya|varṇāś ca parvate ye mah"|Âruṇe
pibanto madhu|maireyaṃ bhīma|vegāḥ plavaṃ|gamāḥ
vaneṣu ca suramyeṣu sugandhiṣu mahatsu ca
tāpasānāṃ ca ramyeṣu van'|ânteṣu samantataḥ
tāṃs tāṃs tvam ānaya kṣipraṃ pṛthivyāṃ sarva|vānarān
sāma|dān'|ādibhiḥ kalpair āśu preṣaya vānarān!
36.10 preṣitāḥ prathamaṃ ye ca mayā dūtā mahā|javāḥ
tvaraṇ'|ârthaṃ tu bhūyas tvaṃ harīn saṃpreṣay' âparān.
ye prasaktāś ca kāmeṣu dīrgha|sūtrāś ca vānarāḥ
ih' ānayasva tān sarvāñ śīghraṃ tu mama śāsanāt.
ahobhir daśabhir ye ca n' āgacchanti mam' ājñayā
hantavyās te durātmāno rāja|śāsana|dūṣakāḥ.

śatāny atha sahasrāṇi koṭyaś ca mama śāsanāt
prayāntu kapi|siṃhānāṃ diśo mama mate sthitāḥ.
megha|parvata|saṃkāśāś chādayanta iv' âmbaram
ghora|rūpāḥ kapi|śreṣṭhā yāntu mac|chāsanād itaḥ.
36.15 te gatijñā gatiṃ gatvā pṛthivyāṃ sarva|vānarāḥ
ānayantu harīn sarvāṃs tvaritāḥ śāsanān mama»

tasya vānara|rājasya śrutvā Vāyu|suto vacaḥ
dikṣu sarvāsu vikrāntān preṣayām āsa vānarān.
te padaṃ Viṣṇu|vikrāntaṃ patatri|jyotir|adhva|gāḥ
prayātāḥ prahitā rājñā harayas tat|kṣaṇena vai.
te samudreṣu giriṣu vaneṣu ca saritsu ca

twilight; and those leaping monkeys strong as elephants, 36.5
black as collyrium or storm clouds, who live on the Áñjana mountain; and those monkeys bright as gold dwelling in caves of red arsenic ore on the flanks of Mount Meru, and those inhabiting the Dhumra mountain; and those leaping monkeys of terrifying power, who are the color of the newly risen sun and drink honey-wine on the great Áruna mountain; and those who inhabit the great, fragrant, delightful forests and everywhere haunt the ascetics' charming forest groves. Using such devices as bribery and conciliation, send forth your monkeys at once.

And send forth other monkeys as well to hasten those 36.10
very swift messengers I dispatched previously. Then quickly bring at my command all those monkeys who, absorbed in pleasures, are too long in coming. Any wicked ones who do not come at my command within ten days are to be executed as transgressors of their king's orders.

Now let the hundreds and thousands and tens of millions of lions among monkeys who abide by my wishes depart in all directions at my command. Let those excellent and frightful-looking monkeys go forth from here at my command, as if blocking out the sky like clouds or mountains.
Let all monkeys who know the way hasten on their way. 36.15
Bring at my command all the monkeys on earth."

Upon hearing the monkey-king's words, the wind god's son dispatched valiant monkeys in every direction. Dispatched by the king, those monkeys set out at that very moment into the sky, where Vishnu stepped, traveling along the path of birds and heavenly bodies. For Rama's sake those monkeys urged on all the monkeys who dwelt by the oceans,

vānarā vānarān sarvān Rāma|hetor acodayan
Mṛtyu|Kāl'|ôpamasy' ājñāṃ rāja|rājasya vānarāḥ
Sugrīvasy' āyayuḥ śrutvā Sugrīva|bhaya|darśinaḥ.
36.20 tatas te 'ñjana|saṃkāśā gires tasmān mahā|javāḥ
tisraḥ koṭyaḥ plavaṃgānāṃ niryayur yatra Rāghavaḥ.
astaṃ gacchati yatr' ârkas tasmin giri|vare ratāḥ
tapta|hema|sam'|ābhāsās tasmāt koṭyo daśa cyutāḥ.
Kailāsa|śikharebhyaś ca siṃha|kesara|varcasām
tataḥ koṭi|sahasrāṇi vānarāṇām upāgaman.
phala|mūlena jīvanto Himavantam upāśritāḥ
teṣāṃ koṭi|sahasrāṇāṃ sahasraṃ samavartata.
Aṅgāraka|samānānāṃ bhīmānāṃ bhīma|karmaṇām
Vindhyād vānara|koṭīnāṃ sahasrāṇy apatan drutam.
36.25 kṣīr'|ôda|velā|nilayās tamāla|vana|vāsinaḥ
nārikel'|âśanāś c' âiva teṣāṃ saṃkhyā na vidyate.
vanebhyo gahvarebhyaś ca saridbhyaś ca mahā|javāḥ
āgacchad vānarī senā pibant' îva divā|karam.

ye tu tvarayituṃ yātā vānarāḥ sarva|vānarān
te vīrā Himavac|chailaṃ dadṛśus taṃ mahā|drumam
tasmin giri|vare ramye yajño Māheśvaraḥ purā
sarva|deva|manas|toṣo babhau divyo mano|haraḥ
anna|viṣyanda|jātāni mūlāni ca phalāni ca
amṛta|svādu|kalpāni dadṛśus tatra vānarāḥ.
36.30 tad|anna|saṃbhavaṃ divyaṃ phalaṃ mūlaṃ mano|haram
yaḥ kaś cit sakṛd aśnāti māsaṃ bhavati tarpitaḥ.
tāni mūlāni divyāni phalāni ca phal'|âśanāḥ

on the mountains, in the forests and near the rivers. When these monkeys heard the orders of Sugríva, their king of kings who was like Death or Time, they came, fearful of Sugríva.

So down from their mountain three times ten million 36.20
very swift leaping monkeys, black as collyrium, came to the spot where Rághava was. And ten times ten million, bright as pure gold, who delighted in that best of mountains where the sun sets, came down from it. And then from the peaks of Mount Kailása there came a thousand times ten million monkeys lustrous as a lion's mane. Then came a thousand thousands of ten millions, who dwelt in the Himálayas, living on fruit and roots. And down from the Vindhya mountains rushed thousands of ten millions of terrifying
monkeys, as red as Mars, whose deeds were frightful. And 36.25
there was an untold number of those who lived on the shore of the ocean of milk, dwelling in forests of *tamála* trees and eating coconuts. From the forests, caves and rivers came a swift monkey army, seeming to swallow up the sun.

Now those heroic monkeys who had gone to hasten all the other monkeys saw the mountain Himálaya with its great trees. On that charming best of mountains there was long ago a lovely, wonderful sacrifice for Mahéshvara which gratified the hearts of all the gods. There the monkeys saw roots and fruit, sweet as the nectar of the gods, which were produced from the overflowing of the food offered at that
sacrifice. Whoever eats even once those delightful, divine 36.30
roots and fruit produced from that sacrificial food remains satisfied for a month. The leaders of the troops of monkeys, who lived on fruit, took those divine roots and fruit

auṣadhāni ca divyāni jagṛhur hari|yūthapāḥ.
tasmāc ca yajñ'|āyatanāt puṣpāṇi surabhīṇi ca
āninyur vānarā gatvā Sugrīva|priya|kāraṇāt.
te tu sarve hari|varāḥ pṛthivyāṃ sarva|vānarān
saṃcodayitvā tvaritaṃ yūthānāṃ jagmur agrataḥ.
te tu tena muhūrtena yūthapāḥ śīghra|kāriṇaḥ
Kiṣkindhāṃ tvarayā prāptāḥ Sugrīvo yatra vānaraḥ.
36.35 te gṛhītv" âuṣadhīḥ sarvāḥ phalaṃ mūlaṃ ca vānarāḥ
taṃ pratigrāhayām āsur vacanaṃ c' êdam abruvan:
«sarve parigatāḥ śailāḥ samudrāś ca vanāni ca.
pṛthivyāṃ vānarāḥ sarve śāsanād upayānti te.»
evaṃ śrutvā tato hṛṣṭaḥ Sugrīvaḥ plavag'|âdhipaḥ
pratijagrāha ca prītas teṣāṃ sarvam upāyanam.

37.1 PRATIGṚHYA ca tat sarvam upānayam upāhṛtam
vānarān sāntvayitvā ca sarvān eva vyasarjayat.
visarjayitvā sa harīñ śūrāṃs tān kṛta|karmaṇaḥ
mene kṛt'|ârtham ātmānaṃ Rāghavaṃ ca mahā|balam.
sa Lakṣmaṇo bhīma|balaṃ sarva|vānara|sattamam
abravīt praśritaṃ vākyaṃ Sugrīvaṃ saṃpraharṣayan:
«Kiṣkindhāyā viniṣkrāma yadi te, saumya, rocate!»
tasya tad vacanaṃ śrutvā Lakṣmaṇasya subhāṣitam
Sugrīvaḥ parama|prīto vākyam etad uvāca ha:
«evaṃ bhavatu. gacchāmaḥ. stheyaṃ tvac|chāsane mayā.»
37.5 tam evam uktvā Sugrīvo Lakṣmaṇaṃ śubha|lakṣmaṇam
visarjayām āsa tadā Tārām anyāś ca yoṣitaḥ.
«et' êty» uccair hari|varān Sugrīvaḥ samudāharat.
tasya tad vacanaṃ śrutvā harayaḥ śīghram āyayuḥ

and divine herbs. And the monkeys who had gone there also brought from that place of sacrifice fragrant flowers in order to please Sugríva. Then, having exhorted all the other monkeys on earth, all those excellent monkeys went off swiftly ahead of their troops.

In a moment those swift-moving troop leaders speedily reached Kishkíndha, where the monkey Sugríva was. Those 36.35
monkeys took all the herbs, fruit and roots and presented them to him with these words: "We have gone around to all the mountains, oceans and forests. All the monkeys on earth are coming at your command." When he heard this, Sugríva, ruler of monkeys, was delighted, and he accepted all their gifts with pleasure.

Sugríva accepted all the gifts that were offered, and 37.1
then, speaking kindly to those monkeys, he dismissed them all. When he had dismissed those heroic monkeys who had accomplished their mission, he felt as though he and mighty Rághava had already achieved their object. Now Lákshmana spoke conciliatory words to Sugríva, whose strength was terrible, delighting that best of all monkeys: "If it pleases you, gentle friend, depart from Kishkíndha." Upon hearing Lákshmana's well-spoken words, Sugríva was highly pleased and said this: "So be it. We shall go. I must abide by your command."

When Sugríva had spoken in this way to Lákshmana 37.5
who bore auspicious marks, he dismissed Tará and the other women. To his chief monkeys Sugríva loudly cried, "Come!" When they heard his words, all those monkeys who were fit to see the women came quickly, their palms cupped in

baddh'|âñjali|puṭāḥ sarve ye syuḥ strī|darśana|kṣamāḥ.
tān uvāca tataḥ prāptān rāj" ârka|sadṛśa|prabhaḥ:
«upasthāpayata kṣipraṃ śibikāṃ mama, vānarāḥ!»
śrutvā tu vacanaṃ tasya harayaḥ śīghra|vikramāḥ
samupasthāpayām āsuḥ śibikāṃ priya|darśanām.
37.10 tām upasthāpitāṃ dṛṣṭvā śibikāṃ vānar'|âdhipaḥ
«Lakṣmaṇ', āruhyatāṃ śīghram iti» Saumitrim abravīt.
ity uktvā kāñcanaṃ yānaṃ Sugrīvaḥ sūrya|saṃnibham
bṛhadbhir haribhir yuktam āruroha sa|Lakṣmaṇaḥ.
pāṇḍureṇ' ātapatreṇa dhriyamāṇena mūrdhani
śuklaiś ca bāla|vyajanair dhūyamānaiḥ samantataḥ
śaṅkha|bherī|ninādaiś ca bandibhiś c' âbhivanditaḥ
niryayau prāpya Sugrīvo rājya|śriyam anuttamām.
sa vānara śatais tīṣkṇair bahubhiḥ śastra|pāṇibhiḥ
parikīrṇo yayau tatra yatra Rāmo vyavasthitaḥ.
37.15 sa taṃ deśam anuprāpya śreṣṭhaṃ Rāma|niṣevitam
avātaran mahā|tejāḥ śibikāyāḥ sa|Lakṣmaṇaḥ.
āsādya ca tato Rāmaṃ kṛt'|âñjali|puṭo 'bhavat.
kṛt'|âñjalau sthite tasmin vānarāś c' âbhavaṃs tathā.
taṭākam iva tad dṛṣṭvā Rāmaḥ kuḍmala|paṅkajam
vānarāṇāṃ mahat sainyaṃ Sugrīve prītimān abhūt.
pādayoḥ patitaṃ mūrdhnā tam utthāpya har'|īśvaram
premṇā ca bahu|mānāc ca Rāghavaḥ pariṣasvaje.
pariṣvajya ca dharm'|ātmā «niṣīd' êti» tato 'bravīt
taṃ niṣaṇṇaṃ tato dṛṣṭvā kṣitau Rāmo 'bravīd vacaḥ:

reverence. Radiant as the sun, the king then said to those
who had come, "Monkeys, bring my palanquin at once!"
Hearing his words, the swift-striding monkeys brought his
beautiful palanquin. When he saw that his palanquin had 37.10
been brought, the king of monkeys said to Saumítri, "Climb
in quickly, Lákshmana!"

Having spoken in this fashion, Sugríva together with
Lákshmana climbed into his golden palanquin bright as
the sun, which was borne by huge monkeys. With a white
umbrella carried over his head, and with white yak-tail fans
waving on all sides, hailed by the sound of conchs and ket-
tledrums, and lauded by bards, Sugríva went forth, having
attained unsurpassed royal majesty. Surrounded by many
hundreds of fierce monkeys with weapons in hand, he proceeded to where Rama was waiting.

But once he reached that pleasant place where Rama 37.15
dwelt, glorious Sugríva descended from his palanquin with
Lákshmana. He approached Rama with his palms cupped
in reverence. And as he stood with palms cupped, the other
monkeys did the same. When Rama saw that vast army of
monkeys like a pond full of lotus buds, he was pleased with
Sugríva. Rághava raised up the lord of monkeys, who had
fallen at his feet with his head to the ground, and embraced
him with great respect and affection. When righteous Rama
had embraced him, he said, "Be seated!" Then, when he saw
him seated on the ground, he said these words:

37.20 «dharmam arthaṃ ca kāmaṃ ca kāle yas tu niṣevate
vibhajya satataṃ, vīra, sa rājā, hari|sattama.
hitvā dharmaṃ tath" ârthaṃ ca kāmaṃ yas tu niṣevate
sa vṛkṣ'|âgre yathā suptaḥ patitaḥ pratibudhyate.
amitrāṇāṃ vadhe yukto mitrāṇāṃ saṃgrahe rataḥ
tri|varga|phala|bhoktā tu rājā dharmeṇa yujyate.
udyoga|samayas tv eṣa prāptaḥ, śatru|vināśana,
saṃcintyatāṃ hi, paṅk'|ēśa, haribhiḥ saha mantribhiḥ!»
evam uktas tu Sugrīvo Rāmaṃ vacanam abravīt:
37.25 «pranaṣṭā śrīś ca kīrtiś ca kapi|rājyaṃ ca śāśvatam
tvat prasādān, mahā|bāho, punaḥ prāptam idaṃ mayā.
tava, deva, prasadāc ca bhrātuś ca, jayatāṃ vara,
kṛtaṃ na pratikuryād yaḥ puruṣāṇāṃ sa dūṣakaḥ.
ete vānara|mukhyāś ca śataśaḥ, śatru|sūdana,
prāptāś c' ādāya balinaḥ pṛthivyāṃ sarva|vānarān.
ṛkṣāś c' âvahitāḥ śūrā go|lāṅgūlāś ca, Rāghava,
kāntāra|vana|durgāṇām abhijñā ghora|darśanāḥ
deva|gandharva|putrāś ca vānarāḥ kāma|rūpiṇaḥ
svaiḥ svaiḥ parivṛtāḥ sainyair vartante pathi, Rāghava.
37.30 śataiḥ śata|sahasraiś ca koṭibhiś ca plavaṃ|gamāḥ
ayutaiś c' āvṛtā vīrā śaṅkubhiś ca, paraṃ|tapa.
arbudair arbuda|śatair madhyaiś c' ântaiś ca vānarāḥ
samudraiś ca par'|ârdhaiś ca harayo hari|yūthapāḥ
āgamiṣyanti te, rājan, Mahendra|sama|vikramāḥ

"He who distinguishes righteousness, wealth and pleasure and always pursues each one at the proper time is indeed a king, heroic monkey. But he who neglects righteousness and wealth to pursue pleasure awakens only after he has fallen, like a man who sleeps on top of a tree. On the other hand, a king intent on killing his enemies and devoted to supporting his friends gains religious merit and enjoys the fruit of all three goals of life. Now the time has come for effort, destroyer of enemies. Please consider this carefully with your monkey counselors, lord of tawny monkeys." 37.20

Addressed in this way, Sugríva said these words to Rama:

"My lost majesty and glory and the everlasting kingship of 37.25
the monkeys—all this I have regained through your favor, great-armed man. King and best of conquerors, he who would not repay what was done through your favor and your brother's would be infamous among men. Now the monkey chieftains have come by the hundred, bringing all the powerful monkeys on earth, slayer of your enemies. Vigilant apes and heroic langurs of frightful appearance, well-acquainted with wildernesses, forests and inaccessible places, Rághava, and forest monkeys who are the sons of gods and *gandhárva*s and can change their form at will—all are on the way, Rághava, surrounded by their respective armies.

Scorcher of your foes, heroic leaping monkeys surrounded 37.30
by hundreds and by ten thousands and by hundreds of thousands and by ten millions and by ten trillions; and forest monkeys surrounded by hundreds of millions and by hundreds of hundreds of millions, and by a thousand trillions and by ten thousand trillions; and tawny monkeys, leaders

Meru|Mandara|saṃkāśā Vindhya|Meru|kṛt'|ālayāḥ.
te tvām abhigamiṣyanti rākṣasaṃ ye sa|bāndhavam
nihatya Rāvaṇaṃ saṃkhye hy ānayiṣyanti Maithilīm.»
tatas tam udyogam avekṣya buddhimān
hari|pravīrasya nideśa|vartinaḥ
babhūva harṣād vasudh"|âdhip'|ātmajaḥ
prabuddha|nīl'|ôtpala|tulya|darśanaḥ.

38.1 Iti bruvāṇaṃ Sugrīvaṃ Rāmo dharma|bhṛtāṃ varaḥ
bāhubhyāṃ saṃpariṣvajya pratyuvāca kṛt'|âñjalim:
«yad Indro varṣate varṣaṃ na tac citraṃ bhaved bhuvi
ādityo vā sahasr'|âṃśuḥ kuryād vi|timiraṃ nabhaḥ
candramā raśmibhiḥ kuryāt pṛthivīṃ saumya|nirmalām
tvad|vidho v" âpi mitrāṇāṃ pratikuryāt, paraṃ|tapa.
evaṃ tvayi na tac citraṃ bhaved yat, saumya, śobhanam.
jānāmy ahaṃ tvāṃ, Sugrīva, satataṃ priya|vādinam.
38.5 tvat|sanāthaḥ, sakhe, saṃkhye jet" âsmi sakalān arīn
tvam eva me suhṛn|mitraṃ! sāhāyyaṃ kartum arhasi.
jahār' ātma|vināśāya Vaidehīṃ rākṣas'|âdhamaḥ
vañcayitvā tu Paulomīm Anuhlādo yathā Śacīm.
na cirāt taṃ haniṣyāmi Rāvaṇaṃ niśitaiḥ śaraiḥ
Paulomyāḥ pitaraṃ dṛptaṃ Śatakratur iv' ârihā.»

of tawny monkey troops, surrounded by one hundred trillions and by one hundred thousand trillions, who make their home on the Vindhya and Meru mountains, who themselves resemble Mount Meru and Mount Mándara, who possess the valor of great Indra—all these are coming, king. And those who come to you will surely kill the *rákshasa* Rávana and his kinsmen in battle and will bring back Máithili."

Then, as he considered this effort on the part of the great monkey-hero who was obedient to his orders, the wise son of the ruler of the earth resembled in his joy a full-blown blue lotus.

As SUGRÍVA was speaking in this way with his palms 38.1
cupped in reverence, Rama, best of those who uphold righteousness, embraced him with both arms and replied:

"It is not surprising, dear friend, that Indra showers rain upon the earth, that the thousand-rayed sun should drive the darkness from the sky, that the moon with its beams should illuminate the earth, or that someone like you, scorcher of your foes, should repay his friends. In the same way it is not surprising that what is best should be found in you, dear Sugríva. I know that you always say
what is pleasing. With you, my friend, as my protector, I 38.5
shall conquer all my enemies in battle. You alone are my friend and ally. Please help me. That evil *rákshasa* has seized Vaidéhi only to destroy himself, just as Anuhláda treacherously seized Pulóman's daughter Shachi. Before long I shall kill Rávana with sharp arrows, just as Indra of a hundred

etasminn antare c' âiva rajaḥ samabhivartata
uṣṇāṃ tīvrāṃ sahasr'|âṃśoś chādayad gagane prabhām.
diśaḥ paryākulāś c' āsan rajasā tena mūrchitāḥ
cacāla ca mahī sarvā sa|śaila|vana|kānanā.

38.10 tato nag'|êndra|saṃkāśais tīkṣṇa|daṃṣṭrair mahā|balaiḥ
kṛtsnā saṃchāditā bhūmir asaṃkhyeyaiḥ plavaṃ|gamaiḥ.
nimeṣ'|ântara|mātreṇa tatas tair hari|yūthapaiḥ
koṭī|śata|parīvāraiḥ kāma|rūpibhir āvṛtā
nādeyaiḥ pārvatīyaiś ca sāmudraiś ca mahā|balaiḥ
haribhir megha|nirhrādair anyaiś ca vana|cāribhiḥ
taruṇ'|āditya|varṇaiś ca śaśi|gauraiś ca vānaraiḥ
padma|kesara|varṇaiś ca śvetair Meru|kṛt'|ālayaiḥ.
koṭī|sahasrair daśabhiḥ śrīmān parivṛtas tadā
vīraḥ Śatabalir nāma vānaraḥ pratyadṛśyata.

38.15 tataḥ kāñcana|śail'|ābhas Tārāyā vīryavān pitā
anekair daśa|sāhasraiḥ koṭibhiḥ pratyadṛśyata.
padma|kesara|saṃkāśas taruṇ'|ârka|nibh'|ānanaḥ
buddhimān vānara|śreṣṭhaḥ sarva|vānara|sattamaḥ
anīkair bahu|sāhasrair vānarāṇāṃ samanvitaḥ
pitā Hanumataḥ śrīmān Kesarī pratyadṛśyata.
go|lāṅgūla mahā|rājo Gavākṣo bhīma|vikramaḥ
vṛtaḥ koṭi|sahasreṇa vānarāṇām adṛśyata.
ṛkṣāṇāṃ bhīma|vegānāṃ Dhūmraḥ śatru|nibarhaṇaḥ
vṛtaḥ koṭi|sahasrābhyāṃ dvābhyāṃ samabhivartata.

sacrifices, a slayer of his enemies, killed Pulóman, Shachi's proud father."

As they were conversing, dust began rising into the sky,
veiling the fierce, hot brilliance of the thousand-rayed sun.
All directions were obscured and thick with that dust, and
the whole earth with its mountains, woods and forests trembled. Suddenly the entire land was covered with countless 38.10
mighty, sharp-fanged monkeys as great as mountains. In
the mere twinkling of an eye, it was covered by monkey-
troop leaders with a hundred times ten million followers
who could change form at will; by mighty monkeys from
the rivers, mountains and oceans; and by others who were
forest-dwellers, roaring like rain clouds. Some were the color
of the newly risen sun, while others were as pale as the moon.
And there were monkeys as golden as lotus filaments, and
white ones who made their home on Mount Meru.

Then the majestic monkey hero named Shata·bali appeared, surrounded by ten thousand times ten million monkeys. Next, Tará's mighty father, bright as a mountain of 38.15
gold, appeared with many tens of thousands times ten million. Golden as a lotus filament, his face bright as the newly
risen sun, the intelligent, most excellent of all monkeys,
majestic Késarin, Hánuman's father, best of monkeys, now
appeared, with his army of many thousands of monkeys.
The great king of the langurs, Gaváksha of terrifying valor,
appeared surrounded by a thousand times ten million monkeys. Next came Dhumra, destroyer of his enemies, surrounded by two thousand times ten million apes of terrifying speed. Then came the heroic troop leader named Pána- 38.20

38.20 mah"|âcala nibhair ghoraiḥ Panaso nāma yūthapaḥ
ājagāma mahā|vīryas tisṛbhiḥ koṭibhir vṛtaḥ.
nīl'|âñjana|cay'|ākāro Nīlo nām' âtha yūthapaḥ
adṛśyata mahā|kāyaḥ koṭibhir daśabhir vṛtaḥ.
Darīmukhaś ca balavān yūthapo 'bhyāyayau tadā
vṛtaḥ koṭi|sahasreṇa Sugrīvaṃ samupasthitaḥ.
Maindaś ca Dvividaś c' ôbhāv Aśvi|putrau mahā|balau
koṭi|koṭi|sahasreṇa vānarāṇām adṛśyatām.
tataḥ koṭi|sahasrāṇāṃ sahasreṇa śatena ca
pṛṣṭhato 'nugataḥ prāpto haribhir Gandhamādanaḥ.
38.25 tataḥ padma|sahasreṇa vṛtaḥ śaṅku|śatena ca
yuva|rājo 'ṅgadaḥ prāptaḥ pitṛ|tulya|parākramaḥ.
tatas tārā|dyutis Tāro harir bhīma|parākramaḥ
pañcabhir hari|koṭībhir dūrataḥ pratyadṛśyata.
Indrajānuḥ kapir vīro yūthapaḥ pratyadṛśyata
ekādaśānāṃ koṭīnām īśvaras taiś ca saṃvṛtaḥ.
tato Rambhas tv anuprāptas taruṇ'|āditya|saṃnibhaḥ
ayutena vṛtaś c' âiva sahasreṇa śatena ca.
tato yūtha|patir vīro Durmukho nāma vānaraḥ
pratyadṛśyata koṭibhyāṃ dvābhyāṃ parivṛto balī.
38.30 Kailāsa|śikhar'|ākārair vānarair bhīma|vikramaiḥ
vṛtaḥ koṭi|sahasreṇa Hanumān pratyadṛśyata.
Nalaś c' âpi mahā|vīryaḥ saṃvṛto druma|vāsibhiḥ
koṭī|śatena saṃprāptaḥ sahasreṇa śatena ca.
Śarabhaḥ Kumudo Vahnir vānaro Rambha eva ca
ete c' ânye ca bahavo vānarāḥ kāma|rūpiṇaḥ

sa, surrounded by three times ten million terrible monkeys resembling great mountains.

And the huge troop leader named Nila arrived, looking like a dark mound of collyrium and surrounded by ten times ten million. And then the powerful troop leader Dari·mukha, surrounded by a thousand times ten million, came and approached Sugríva. Then Mainda and Dvívida, the two mighty sons of the Ashvins, appeared with a thousand times ten million times ten million monkeys. Then came Gandha·mádana with a hundred and a thousand times a thousand
times ten million monkeys following behind him. Next 38.25
came the heir apparent Ángada, whose prowess equaled his father's, surrounded by a thousand times one trillion and one hundred times ten trillion. Then the monkey Tara, brilliant as a star, terrifying in his prowess, appeared in the distance with five times ten million monkeys.

The heroic troop leader, the monkey Indra·janu, lord of eleven times ten million, appeared along with them. And then came Rambha, bright as the newly risen sun, surrounded by a hundred and a thousand and ten thousand. Then the mighty and heroic monkey-lord of troops named Dúrmukha appeared, encircled by two times ten
million. Surrounded by a thousand times ten million mon- 38.30
keys of terrifying valor and tall as the peaks of Kailása, Hánuman appeared. Heroic Nala came, too, surrounded by one hundred and a thousand and one hundred times ten million tree-dwellers. And Shárabha, Kúmuda, Vahni, and also the monkey Rambha–these and many other monkeys who could change form at will, monkeys leaping and jumping and roaring, advanced toward Sugríva, covering

āvṛtya pṛthivīṃ sarvāṃ parvatāṃś ca vanāni ca
āplavantaḥ plavantaś ca garjantaś ca plavaṃ|gamāḥ
abhyavartanta Sugrīvaṃ sūryam abhra|gaṇā iva.
kurvāṇā bahu|śabdāṃś ca prahṛṣṭā bala|śālinaḥ
śirobhir vānar'|êndrāya Sugrīvāya nyavedayan.
38.35 apare vānara|śreṣṭhāḥ saṃgamya ca yath"|ôcitam
Sugrīveṇa samāgamya sthitāḥ prāñjalayas tadā.
Sugrīvas tvarito Rāme sarvāṃs tān vānara'|rṣabhān
nivedayitvā dharmajñaḥ sthitaḥ prāñjalir abravīt:
«yathā sukhaṃ parvata|nirjhareṣu
vaneṣu sarveṣu ca, vānar'|êndrāḥ,
niveśayitvā vidhivad balāni
balaṃ balajñaḥ pratipattum īṣṭe.»

the whole earth and the mountains and woods, like a host of clouds advancing toward the sun.

Full of strength, making a great noise in their delight, they bowed their heads and reported to Sugríva, lord of monkeys.
And other excellent monkeys, assembling as was proper, 38.35
approached Sugríva and stood with their palms cupped in reverence. Standing with his own palms cupped reverently, righteous Sugríva immediately presented all those bulls among monkeys to Rama, and then he said:

"Monkey-princes! Each troop leader, when he has duly encamped his troops comfortably near the swift mountain streams and in all the forests, should be prepared to review his troops."

39–42
MONKEYS IN SEARCH

39.1 ATHA RĀJĀ SAMṚDDH'|ârthaḥ Sugrīvaḥ plavag'|ēśvaraḥ
uvāca nara|śārdūlaṃ Rāmaṃ para|bal'|ârdanam:
«āgatā viniviṣṭāś ca balinaḥ kāma|rūpiṇaḥ
vānar'|êndrā Mahendr'|ābhā ye mad|viṣaya|vāsinaḥ.
ta ime bahu|sāhasrair haribhir bhīma|vikramaiḥ
āgatā vānarā ghorā daitya|dānava|saṃnibhāḥ.
khyāta|karm'|âpadānāś ca balavanto jita|klamāḥ
parākrameṣu vikhyātā vyavasāyeṣu c' ôttamāḥ
39.5 pṛthivy|ambu|carā, Rāma, nānā|naga|nivāsinaḥ
koṭy|agraśa ime prāptā vānarās tava kiṃkarāḥ.
nideśa|vartinaḥ sarve sarve guru|hite ratāḥ.
abhipretam anuṣṭhātuṃ tava śakṣyanty, ariṃ|dama.
yan manyase, nara|vyāghra, prāpta|kālaṃ tad ucyatām
tat sainyaṃ tvad|vaśe yuktam ājñāpayitum arhasi.
kāmam eṣām idaṃ kāryaṃ viditaṃ mama tattvataḥ
tath" âpi tu yathā|tattvam ājñāpayitum arhasi.»
tathā bruvāṇaṃ Sugrīvaṃ Rāmo Daśarath'|ātmajaḥ
bāhubhyāṃ saṃpariṣvajya idaṃ vacanam abravīt:
39.10 «jñāyatāṃ, saumya, Vaidehī yadi jīvati vā na vā
sa ca deśo, mahā|prājña, yasmin vasati Rāvaṇaḥ.
adhigamya ca Vaidehīṃ nilayaṃ Rāvaṇasya ca
prāpta|kālaṃ vidhāsyāmi tasmin kāle saha tvayā.
n' âham asmin prabhuḥ kārye, vānar'|ēśa, na Lakṣmaṇaḥ.
tvam asya hetuḥ kāryasya prabhuś ca, plavag'|ēśvara.
tvam ev' ājñāpaya, vibho, mama kārya|viniścayam.

Now, the lord of monkeys King Sugríva, his purpose 39.1
accomplished, spoke to Rama, that tiger among men
and tormentor of enemy armies:

"The mighty monkey-princes who dwell in my domain,
splendid as great Indra and able to change form at will,
have come and are now encamped. These terrifying monkeys resembling *daitya*s and *dánava*s have come with many
thousands of tawny monkeys of fearful valor. Celebrated
for their deeds and feats, strong, indefatigable, celebrated
for their prowess and foremost in resolve, traveling by land 39.5
and on water, dwelling on various mountains, these monkeys who have arrived by the tens of millions are at your
service, Rama. All obey orders, all are devoted to the welfare
of their master. They will be able to accomplish your desire,
subduer of your foes. You have only to say what you think
is appropriate to the moment, tiger among men. This army
is under your control. Please command it. It is true that I
know exactly what they are to do, but even so you should
command, as is proper."

Then Rama, the son of Dasha·ratha, embraced Sugríva,
who was speaking in this fashion, and said these words:

"Wise and dear friend, you must find the place where 39.10
Rávana dwells and learn whether or not Vaidéhi is alive.
When I find Vaidéhi and the hiding place of Rávana, I
shall at that time arrange with you what is appropriate.
Neither Lákshmana nor I is master in this undertaking, lord
of monkeys. You are both master and the means of success
for this undertaking, king of leaping monkeys. Knowing
my decision about what is to be done, you alone must
command. For without doubt you understand what has

tvaṃ hi jānāsi yat kāryaṃ mama, vīra, na saṃśayaḥ.
suhṛd dvitīyo vikrāntaḥ prājñaḥ kāla|viśeṣa|vit
bhavān asmadd|hite yuktaḥ sukṛt'|ârtho 'rtha|vittamaḥ.»
39.15 evam uktas tu Sugrīvo Vinataṃ nāma yūthapam
abravīd Rāma|sāṃnidhye Lakṣmaṇasya ca dhīmataḥ
śail'|ābhaṃ megha|nirghoṣam ūrjitaṃ plavag'|ēśvaram:
«soma|sūry'|ātmajaiḥ sārdhaṃ vānarair, vānar'|ôttama,
deśa|kāla|nayair yuktaḥ kāry'|âkārya|viniścaye.
vṛtaḥ śata|sahasreṇa vānarāṇāṃ tarasvinām
adhigaccha diśaṃ pūrvāṃ sa|śaila|vana|kānanām.
tatra Sītāṃ ca Vaidehīṃ nilayaṃ Rāvaṇasya ca
mārgadhvaṃ giri|durgeṣu vaneṣu ca nadīṣu ca.
nadīṃ Bhāgīrathīṃ ramyāṃ Sarayūṃ Kauśikīṃ tathā
Kālindīṃ Yamunāṃ ramyāṃ Yāmunaṃ ca mahā|girim
39.20 Sarasvatīṃ ca Sindhuṃ ca Śoṇaṃ maṇi|nibh'|ôdakam
Mahīṃ Kālamahīṃ c' âiva śaila|kānana|śobhitām
Brahmamālān Videhāṃś ca
Mālavān Kāśi|Kosalān
Māgadhāṃś ca mahā|grāmān
Puṇḍrān Vaṅgāṃs tath" âiva ca
pattanaṃ kośa|kārāṇāṃ bhūmiṃ ca rajat'|ākarām
sarvam etad vicetavyaṃ mṛgayadbhir tatas tataḥ
Rāmasya dayitāṃ bhāryāṃ Sītāṃ Daśaratha|snuṣām.

to be done for me, mighty hero. You are my friend and companion, valiant, intelligent, discriminating about time, intent on our welfare, wise about achieving objectives, with your own objective fully achieved."

Thus addressed, Sugríva spoke in the presence of Rama 39.15
and wise Lákshmana to a powerful troop leader and lord of monkeys named Vínata, who was as big as a mountain and who roared like a thunder cloud:

"Along with the monkeys who are sons of the moon and the sun, you possess the worldly wisdom about time and place necessary for deciding what to do and what not to do, best of monkeys. Accompanied by a hundred thousand swift monkeys, go to the eastern quarter with its mountains, woods and forests. There you must search for Vidéha's daughter Sita and for Rávana's hiding place in the inaccessible mountain regions, in the forests and along the rivers.

The charming rivers Bhagírathi, Sárayu, Káushiki, and the charming Kalíndi and Yamuná rivers, and the great
mountain Yámuna, and the rivers Sarásvati and Sindhu, 39.20
and the Shona with jewel-bright waters, and the Mahi and the Kala·mahi rivers adorned with mountains and woods; the regions of Brahma·mala, Vidéha, Málava, Kashi, and Kósala and the large villages of Mágadha, and Pundra as well as Vanga, the city of silkworms and the land of silver mines—all of this you must search, hunting here, there and everywhere for Rama's beloved wife Sita, the daughter-in-law of Dasha·ratha.

samudram avagāḍhāṃś ca parvatān pattanāni ca
Mandarasya ca ye koṭiṃ saṃśritāḥ ke cid āyatām
Karṇaprāvaraṇāś c' âiva tathā c' âpy Oṣṭhakarṇakāḥ
39.25 ghorā Lohamukhāś c' âiva javanāś c' âika|pādakāḥ
akṣayā balavantaś ca puruṣāḥ puruṣ'|âdakāḥ
Kirātāḥ karṇa|cūḍāś ca hem'|âṅgāḥ priya|darśanāḥ
āma|mīn'|âśanās tatra Kirātā dvīpa|vāsinaḥ
antar|jala|carā ghorā nara|vyāghrā iti śrutāḥ
eteṣām ālayāḥ sarve viceyāḥ, kānan'|âukasaḥ!
giribhir ye ca gamyante plavanena plavena ca
ratnavantaṃ Yavadvīpaṃ sapta|rājy'|ôpaśobhitam
Suvarṇarūpyakaṃ c' âiva suvarṇ'|ākara|maṇḍitam.

Yavadvīpam atikramya Śiśiro nāma parvataḥ
39.30 divaṃ spṛśati śṛṅgeṇa deva|dānava|sevitaḥ
eteṣāṃ giri|durgeṣu pratāpeṣu vaneṣu ca
Rāvaṇaḥ saha Vaidehyā mārgitavyas tatas tataḥ
tataḥ samudra|dvīpāṃś ca subhīmān draṣṭum arhatha.
tatr' âsurā mahā|kāyāś chāyāṃ gṛhṇanti nityaśaḥ
Brahmaṇā samanujñātā dīrgha|kālaṃ bubhukṣitāḥ.

taṃ kāla|megha|pratimaṃ mah"|ôraga|niṣevitam
abhigamya mahā|nādaṃ tīrthen' âiva mah"|ôdadhim
tato rakta|jalaṃ bhīmaṃ Lohitaṃ nāma sāgaram
gatā drakṣyatha tāṃ c' âiva bṛhatīṃ kūṭa|śālmalīm
39.35 gṛhaṃ ca Vainateyasya nānā|ratna|vibhūṣitam
tatra Kailāsa|saṃkāśaṃ vihitaṃ Viśvakarmaṇā.
tatra śaila|nibhā bhīmā Mandehā nāma rākṣasāḥ

Those who shelter on the broad summit of Mount Mán- 39.25
dara and in cities and on mountains immersed in the ocean,
both the Karna·praváranas and the Oshtha·kárnakas, and
the terrible Loha·mukhas, and the swift one-legged men,
and the strong, imperishable man-eating men, and the handsome golden-limbed Kirátas with ear ornaments, and the
terrible Kirátas known as tiger-men who live on islands,
eating raw fish and moving through the water—you must
search all their dwelling places, monkeys! And you must go
to those islands that can be reached from mountains, by
swimming or by boat: to Yava·dvipa, rich in jewels, splendid with its seven kingdoms, and to Suvárna·rúpyaka, ornamented with gold mines.

Beyond Yava·dvipa, there is a mountain named Shíshira. 39.30
Touching the sky with its peaks, it is frequented by gods and
dánavas. In the inaccessible places of the mountains, by the
waterfalls and in the forests of these islands, you must search
for Rávana and Vaidéhi here, there and everywhere. And
then you must explore the dreadful islands in the sea. There
huge *ásuras* constantly seize shadows; they are permitted to
do so by Brahma because they went hungry for a long time.

By some means you must approach that sea, black as a
storm cloud, loudly roaring, infested with great serpents;
and then from there you must go to the dreadful ocean
called Lóhita because of its red waters. There you will see
the giant *kuta·shálmali* tree, and a house built by Vishva· 39.35
karman for Vainatéya, bright as Mount Kailása and adorned
with every kind of jewel. There the dreadful, dangerous *rákshasas* called Mandéhas, big as mountains and with various
forms, hang from the mountain peaks. Every day, toward

śaila|śṛṅgeṣu lambante nānā|rūpā bhay'|āvahāḥ.
te patanti jale nityaṃ sūryasy' ôdayanaṃ prati
abhitaptāś ca sūryeṇa lambante sma punaḥ punaḥ.

tataḥ pāṇḍura|megh'|ābhaṃ Kṣīraudaṃ nāma sāgaram
gatā drakṣyatha, durdharṣā, muktā|hāram iv' ōrmibhiḥ.
tasya madhye mahā|śveta Ṛsabho nāma parvataḥ
divya|gandhaiḥ kusumitai rajataiś ca nagair vṛtaḥ
39.40 saraś ca rājataiḥ padmair jvalitair hema|kesaraiḥ
nāṃnā Sudarśanaṃ nāma rāja|haṃsaiḥ samākulam.
vibudhāś cāraṇā yakṣāḥ kiṃnarāḥ s'|âpsaro|gaṇāḥ
hṛṣṭāḥ samabhigacchanti nalinīṃ tāṃ riraṃsavaḥ.

Kṣīrodaṃ samatikramya tato drakṣyatha, vānarāḥ,
Jalodaṃ sāgara|śreṣṭhaṃ sarva|bhūta|bhay'|āvaham.
tatra tat kopa|jaṃ tejaḥ kṛtaṃ haya|mukhaṃ mahat
asy' āhus tan mahā|vegam odanaṃ sacar'|âcaram.
tatra vikrośatāṃ nādo bhūtānāṃ sāgar'|âukasām
śrūyate c' âsamarthānāṃ dṛṣṭvā tad vaḍavā|mukham.
39.45 svād'|ûdasy' ôttare deśe yojanāni trayodaśa
Jātarūpaśilo nāma mahān kanaka|parvataḥ.
āsīnaṃ parvatasy' âgre sarva|bhūta|namas|kṛtam
sahasra|śirasaṃ devam Anantaṃ nīla|vāsasam.
triśirāḥ kāñcanaḥ ketus tālas tasya mah"|ātmanaḥ
sthāpitaḥ parvatasy' âgre virājati sa|vedikaḥ.

pūrvasyāṃ diśi nirmāṇaṃ kṛtaṃ tat tridaś'|ēśvaraiḥ.
tataḥ paraṃ hema|mayaḥ śrīmān udaya|parvataḥ.
tasya koṭir divaṃ spṛṣṭvā śata|yojanam āyatā
jāta|rūpa|mayī divyā virājati sa|vedikā.

sunrise, they fall into the water, only to hang scorching in the sun again and again.

Then, moving on, unassailable monkeys, you will see the Ocean of Milk, white as a cloud and with waves like necklaces of pearls. In its midst are a great white mountain named Ríshabha, surrounded by divinely fragrant silver 39.40
trees in bloom, and a lake named Sudárshana, crowded with royal geese and shining silver lotuses with gold filaments. With great delight, the gods, celestial singers, *yakshas* and *kim·naras*, eager for sexual pleasure, approach that lotus bed with the hosts of *ápsarases*.

Passing beyond the Ocean of Milk, monkeys, you will then see that excellent Freshwater Ocean, a source of dread to all beings. For in it is placed that great horse-faced fire born of anger, whose food they say is the rushing water with all its animals and plants. And there you can hear the sound of the helpless creatures who live in that ocean,
crying out because they have seen that mare's face. Thirteen 39.45
leagues from the northern part of the freshwater ocean is a great golden mountain named Jata·rupa·shila. On top of the mountain you will see sitting the thousand-headed god Anánta, clothed in blue and worshiped by all beings. And planted on top of the mountain is that great being's shining emblem, a triple-crowned golden palmyra tree resting on a sacred mound.

The thirty gods have made this the limit of the eastern quarter. Beyond it is the majestic sunrise mountain made of gold. Touching the heavens, its heavenly golden summit covered with sacred mounds shines, stretching one hundred

39.50 sālais tālais tamālaiś ca karṇikāraiś ca puṣpitaiḥ
jāta|rūpa|mayair divyaiḥ śobhate sūrya|saṃnibhaiḥ.
tatra yojana|vistāram ucchritaṃ daśa|yojanam
śṛṅgaṃ Saumanasaṃ nāma jāta|rūpa|mayaṃ dhruvam.
tatra pūrvaṃ padaṃ kṛtvā purā Viṣṇus tri|vikrame
dvitīyaṃ śikharaṃ Meroś cakāra Puruṣ'|ôttamaḥ.
uttareṇa parikramya Jambūdvīpaṃ divā|karaḥ
dṛśyo bhavati bhūyiṣṭhaṃ śikharaṃ tan mah"|ôcchrayam.
tatra Vaikhānasā nāma Vālakhilyā maha"|rṣayaḥ
prakāśamānā dṛśyante sūrya|varṇās tapasvinaḥ.

39.55 ayaṃ Sudarśano dvīpaḥ puro yasya prakāśate
yasmiṃs tejaś ca cakṣuś ca sarva|prāṇabhṛtām api.
śailasya tasya kuñjeṣu kandareṣu vaneṣu ca
Rāvaṇaḥ saha Vaidehyā mārgitavyas tatas tataḥ.
kāñcanasya ca śailasya sūryasya ca mah"|ātmanaḥ
āviṣṭā tejasā saṃdhyā pūrvā raktā prakāśate.
tataḥ param agamyā syād dik pūrvā tridaś'|āvṛtā
rahitā candra|sūryābhyām adṛśyā timir'|āvṛtā.

śaileṣu teṣu sarveṣu kandareṣu vaneṣu ca
ye ca n' ôktā mayā deśā viceyā teṣu Jānakī!

39.60 etāvad vānaraiḥ śakyaṃ gantuṃ, vānara|puṃgavāḥ,
abhāskaram amaryādaṃ na jānīmas tataḥ param.
adhigamya tu Vaidehīṃ nilayaṃ Rāvaṇasya ca
māse pūrṇe nivartadhvam udayaṃ prāpya parvatam.
ūrdhvaṃ māsān na vastavyaṃ vasan vadhyo bhaven mama,
siddh'|ârthāḥ saṃnivartadhvam adhigamya ca Maithilīm!

leagues high. It looks splendid with its heavenly, blossoming 39.50
sala, *tala*, *tamála* and *karni·kara* trees made of gold and
bright as the sun. On it is the eternal peak named Saumána-
sa, one league wide, ten leagues high, made of gold. When
he took his three strides long ago, Vishnu, the Supreme
Being, placed his first step there and his second on Mount
Meru's crest. The sun becomes most clearly visible when
it travels around to the north of Jambu·dvipa and reaches
that very lofty peak. And there one sees those great seers,
the ascetics called Vaikhánasas and Vala·khilyas, gleaming
with the color of the sun.

Here is the island Sudárshana, on which shines that light 39.55
in whose presence alone the eyes of all living beings are able
to see. In the bowers, caves and forests of this mountain,
you must hunt for Rávana and Vaidéhi here, there and
everywhere. Suffused with the light of the golden mountain
and of the great sun, the eastern twilight glows red. Beyond
this, one cannot proceed toward the eastern quarter, for it
is invisible, devoid of moon and sun, shrouded in darkness,
and guarded by the thirty gods.

You must search for Jánaki in every mountain, cave and
forest and even in those places I have not mentioned. But 39.60
only this far, bulls among monkeys, can monkeys go. For
we know not what lies beyond, boundless and untouched
by sun. You must reach the sunrise mountain, find Vaidéhi and the hiding place of Rávana, and return within a
month. But you must not stay beyond a month, for I shall
kill anyone who does. You are to find Máithili and return
with your mission accomplished. Go carefully over great
Indra's beloved quarter, graced with forests; and when you

Mahendra|kāntāṃ vana|ṣaṇḍa|maṇḍitāṃ
diśaṃ caritvā nipuṇena, vānarāḥ,
avāpya Sītāṃ Raghu|vaṃśaja|priyām
tato nivṛttāḥ sukhito bhaviṣyatha.»

40.1 TATAḤ PRASTHĀPYA Sugrīvas tan mahad vānaraṃ balam
dakṣiṇāṃ preṣayām āsa vānarān abhilakṣitān.
Nīlam Agni|sutaṃ c' âiva Hanumantaṃ ca vānaram
Pitāmaha|sutaṃ c' âiva Jāmbavantaṃ mahā|kapim
Suhotraṃ ca Śarāriṃ ca Śaragulmaṃ tath" âiva ca
Gajaṃ Gavākṣaṃ Gavayaṃ Suṣeṇam Ṛṣabhaṃ tathā
Maindaṃ ca Dvividaṃ c' âiva Vijayaṃ Gandhamādanam
Ulkāmukham Asaṅgaṃ ca Hutāśana|sutāv ubhau
40.5 Aṅgada|pramukhān vīrān vīraḥ kapi|gaṇ'|ēśvaraḥ
vega|vikrama|saṃpannān saṃdideśa viśeṣavit.
teṣām agre|saraṃ c' âiva mahad balam a|saṃga|gam
vidhāya hari|vīrāṇām ādiśad dakṣiṇāṃ diśam.
ye ke cana samuddeśās tasyāṃ diśi su|durgamāḥ
kap'|īśaḥ kapi|mukhyānāṃ sa teṣāṃ tān udāharat:
«sahasra|śirasaṃ Vindhyaṃ nānā|druma|lat"|āvṛtam
Narmadāṃ ca nadīṃ durgāṃ mah"|ôraga|niṣevitām
tato Godāvarīṃ ramyāṃ Kṛṣṇāveṇīṃ mahā|nadīm
Varadāṃ ca mahā|bhāgāṃ mah"|ôraga|niṣevitām
40.10 Mekhalān Utkalāṃś c' âiva Daśārṇa|nagarāṇy api
Avantīm Abhravantīṃ ca sarvam ev' ânupaśyata!
Vidarbhān Ṛṣikāṃś c' âiva ramyān Māhiṣakān api
tathā Baṅgān Kaliṅgāṃś ca Kauśikāṃś ca samantataḥ
anvīkṣya Daṇḍak'|âraṇyaṃ sa|parvata|nadī|guham
nadīṃ Godāvarīṃ c' âiva sarvam ev' ânupaśyata!
tath" âiv' Āndhrāṃś ca Puṇḍrāṃś
ca Colān Pāṇḍyān sa|Keralān

have found Sita, dear to him who was born in Raghu's line, and returned, you shall live in comfort, monkeys."

THEN, WHEN HE had dispatched that great monkey army, 40.1
Sugríva sent off distinguished monkeys to the south.

The heroic and judicious lord of the monkey hosts gave
orders to swift, valiant heroes headed by Ángada—to Nila, 40.5
son of Agni, and to the monkey Hánuman; and to Grandfather Brahma's son, the great monkey Jámbavan; and to
Suhótra and Sharári and also Shara·gulma; and to Gaja,
Gaváksha, Gávaya, Sushéna and Ríshabha; to Mainda and
Dvívida, Víjaya and Gandha·mádana; and to Ulka·muk-
ha and Asánga, both sons of Agni, the eater of oblations.
And commanding a great army to go without delay ahead of
those monkey heroes, he directed them toward the southern
quarter.

That lord of monkeys mentioned to those chief monkeys all the inaccessible places in that region, saying:

"The thousand-peaked Vindhyas covered with all sorts of
trees and vines, and the inaccessible River Nármada infested
with huge serpents; then the charming Godávari, the great
river Krishna·veni and the blessed Várada infested with huge
serpents; and the Mékhala and Útkala regions as well as 40.10
the cities of Dashárna, and Avánti and Abhravánti—search
them all. After exploring Vidárbha, Ríshika and charming
Mahíshaka, Banga, Kalínga and Káushika all around, as well
as the Dándaka forest with its mountains, rivers and caves,
you must search the River Godávari and Andhra, Pundra,
Chola, Pandya and Kérala—all of them. And you must go
as well to Mount Ayo·mukha, embellished with ore.

Ayomukhaś ca gantavyaḥ
parvato dhātu|maṇḍitaḥ.
vicitra|śikharaḥ śrīmāṃś citra|puṣpita|kānanaḥ
sa|candana|van'|ôddeśo mārgitavyo mahā|giriḥ.
40.15 tatas tām āpagāṃ divyāṃ prasanna|salilāṃ śivām
tatra drakṣyatha Kāverīṃ vihṛtām apsaro|gaṇaiḥ.
tasy' āsīnaṃ nagasy' âgre Malayasya mah"|âujasam
drakṣyath' āditya|saṃkāśam Agastyam ṛṣi|sattamam.
tatas ten' âbhyanujñātāḥ prasannena mah"|ātmanā
Tāmraparṇīṃ grāha|juṣṭāṃ tariṣyatha mahā|nadīm.
sā candana|vanair divyaiḥ pracchannā dvīpa|śālinī
kānt" êva yuvatiḥ kāntaṃ samudram avagāhate.
tato hema|mayaṃ divyaṃ muktā|maṇi|vibhūṣitam
yuktaṃ kavāṭaṃ Pāṇḍyānāṃ gatā drakṣyatha, vānarāḥ!
40.20 tataḥ samudram āsādya saṃpradhāry' ârtha|niścayam
Agastyen' ântare tatra sāgare viniveśitaḥ
citra|nānā|nagaḥ śrīmān Mahendraḥ parvat'|ôttamaḥ
jāta|rūpa|mayaḥ śrīmān avagāḍho mah"|ârṇavam.
nānā|vidhair nagaiḥ phullair latābhiś c' ôpaśobhitam
deva'|rṣi|yakṣa|pravarair apsarobhiś ca sevitam
siddha|cāraṇa|saṃghaiś ca prakīrṇaṃ su|mano|haram
tam upaiti Sahasrākṣaḥ sadā parvasu parvasu.
dvīpas tasy' âpare pāre śata|yojanam āyataḥ
agamyo mānuṣair dīptas taṃ mārgadhvaṃ samantataḥ!
tatra sarv'|ātmanā Sītā mārgitavyā viśeṣataḥ.
40.25 sa hi deśas tu vadhyasya Rāvaṇasya durātmanaḥ
rākṣas'|âdhipater vāsaḥ Sahasrākṣa|sama|dyuteḥ.

You must search that majestic great mountain with its
many-colored peaks, its brightly flowering woods and forest tracts of sandalwood. There you will see that heavenly, 40.15
auspicious river Kavéri with its clear waters in which groups
of *ápsaras*es play. And you will see the best of seers, mighty
Agástya, bright as the sun, seated on the summit of Mount
Málaya.

When that great seer graciously gives you permission to leave, you will cross the broad river Tamra·parni, the haunt of crocodiles. Graced with islands and hidden by heavenly sandalwood forests, it plunges into the ocean as a beloved young woman would rush to her beloved.

Proceeding from there, monkeys, you will see the heavenly gateway made of gold and ornamented with pearls and
jewels, befitting the Pandyas. Then, when you come to the 40.20
sea and consider what best to do, you will find on the shore
majestic Mount Mahéndra, the best of mountains, set there
in that place by Agástya himself. Made of gold and with all
sorts of bright trees, it plunges deep into the great ocean.
Every time the moon enters a new phase, thousand-eyed
Indra comes to this captivating mountain, adorned with all
kinds of blossoming trees and vines, frequented by excellent
gods, seers and *yaksha*s and by *ápsaras*es, and thronged with
multitudes of perfected beings and celestial bards.

On the far side of that ocean, there is a shining island
that no man can reach. It is a hundred leagues wide, yet
you must explore it all: It is there in particular that you
should search for Sita with all your heart. For this country 40.25
is the abode of evil Rávana, overlord of the *rákshasa*s, whose
splendor equals thousand-eyed Indra's, and who must be

dakṣiṇasya samudrasya madhye tasya tu rākṣasī
Aṅgārak' êti vikhyātā chāyām ākṣipya bhojinī.
tam atikramya lakṣmīvān samudre śata|yojane
giriḥ Puṣpitako nāma siddha|cāraṇa|sevitaḥ.
candra|sūry'|âṃśu|saṃkāśaḥ sāgar'|âmbu|samāvṛtaḥ
bhrājate vipulaiḥ śṛṅgair ambaraṃ vilikhann iva.
tasy' âikaṃ kāñcanaṃ śṛṅgaṃ sevate yaṃ divā|karaḥ
śvetaṃ rājatam ekaṃ ca sevate yaṃ niśā|karaḥ.
40.30 na taṃ kṛtaghnāḥ paśyanti na nṛśaṃsā na nāstikāḥ
praṇamya śirasā śailaṃ taṃ vimārgata vānarāḥ!
tam atikramya durdharṣāḥ Sūryavān nāma parvataḥ
adhvanā durvigāhena yojanāni caturdaśa.
tatas tam apy atikramya Vaidyuto nāma parvataḥ
sarva|kāma|phalair vṛkṣaiḥ sarva|kāla|mano|haraiḥ.
tatra bhuktvā var'|ârhāṇi mūlāni ca phalāni ca
madhūni pītvā mukhyāni paraṃ gacchata, vānarāḥ!
tatra netra|manaḥ|kāntaḥ Kuñjaro nāma parvataḥ
Agastya|bhavanaṃ yatra nirmitaṃ Viśvakarmaṇā.
40.35 tatra yojana|vistāram ucchritaṃ daśa|yojanam
śaraṇaṃ kāñcanaṃ divyaṃ nānā|ratna|vibhūṣitam.
tatra Bhogavatī nāma sarpāṇām ālayaḥ purī
viśāla|rathyā durdharṣā sarvataḥ parirakṣitā
rakṣitā pannagair ghorais tīkṣṇa|daṃṣṭrair mahā|viṣaiḥ
sarpa|rājo mahā|ghoro yasyāṃ vasati Vāsukiḥ
niryāya mārgitavyā ca sā ca Bhogavatī purī.

killed. But in the middle of the southern ocean there is a *rá-kshasa* woman known as Angáraka, who feeds by catching shadows. Beyond, in an ocean a hundred leagues across, is a splendid mountain named Pushpítaka, frequented by perfected beings and celestial bards. Bright as the rays of the moon or the sun, surrounded by the waters of the sea, it shines and seems to scrape the sky with its huge peaks. It has one peak of gold, frequented by the sun, bringer of day, and one of bright silver, frequented by the moon, bringer
of night. The ungrateful, the wicked and the unbelieving 40.30
cannot see it. You must bow your heads to that mountain, monkeys, and then search it thoroughly.

Fourteen leagues beyond it by an impenetrable path is a mountain named Súryavan, unassailable monkeys. Then beyond even that there is a mountain named Váidyuta, its trees captivating in every season, their fruits satisfying every desire. When you have eaten the precious roots and fruit and tasted the excellent honey there, monkeys, you must proceed. There is the mountain named Kúñjara, pleasing to the eye and to the mind, where Vishva·karman built a palace
for Agástya. There, a league wide and ten leagues high, is 40.35
his heavenly golden residence, ornamented with every kind of jewel. And there, well protected on all sides, is the city of Bhógavati, the unassailable abode of the serpents. Its wide streets are guarded by fearsome serpents, sharp-fanged and highly venomous. Vásuki, the terrible king of the serpents, lives there. You must go and search that city of Bhógavati.

tam ca deśam atikramya mahān ṛṣabha|saṃsthitaḥ
sarva|ratna|mayaḥ śrīmān Ṛṣabho nāma parvataḥ
go|śīrṣakaṃ padmakaṃ ca hari|śyāmaṃ ca candanam
divyam utpadyate yatra tac c' âiv' âgni sama|prabham.
40.40 na tu tac candanaṃ dṛṣṭvā spraṣṭavyaṃ ca kadā cana
Rohitā nāma gandharvā ghorā rakṣanti tad vanam.
tatra gandharva|patayaḥ pañca|sūrya|sama|prabhāḥ
Śailūṣo Grāmaṇīr Bhikṣuḥ Śubhro Babhrus tath" âiva ca.
ante pṛthivyā durdharṣās tatra svarga|jitaḥ sthitāḥ
tataḥ paraṃ na vaḥ sevyaḥ pitṛ|lokaḥ sudāruṇaḥ
rāja|dhānī Yamasy' âiṣā kaṣṭena tamas" āvṛtā.

etāvad eva yuṣmābhir, vīrā vānara|puṃgavāḥ,
śakyaṃ vicetuṃ gantuṃ vā n' âto gatimatāṃ gatiḥ.
sarvam etat samālokya yac c' ânyad api dṛśyate
gatiṃ viditvā Vaidehyāḥ saṃnivartitum arhatha.
40.45 yas tu māsān nivṛtto 'gre ‹dṛṣṭā Sīt" êti› vakṣyati.
mat|tulya|vibhavo bhogaiḥ sukhaṃ sa vihariṣyati.
tataḥ priyataro n' âsti mama prāṇād viśeṣataḥ.
kṛt'|âparādho bahuśo mama bandhur bhaviṣyati.
amita|bala|parākramā bhavanto
vipula|guṇeṣu kuleṣu ca prasūtāḥ.
manuja|pati|sutāṃ yathā labhadhvaṃ
tad adhiguṇaṃ puruṣ'|ârtham ārabhadhvam!»

41.1 TATAḤ PRASTHĀPYA Sugrīvas tān harīn dakṣiṇāṃ diśam
buddhi|vikrama|saṃpannān vāyu|vega|samāñ jave
ath' āhūya mahā|tejāḥ Suṣeṇaṃ nāma yūthapam
Tārāyāḥ pitaraṃ rājā śvaśuraṃ bhīma|vikramam
abravīt prāñjalir vākyam abhigamya praṇamya ca:

And beyond that place is the great, majestic mountain named Ríshabha, shaped like a bull. It is full of every kind of jewel and on it grows heavenly *go·shirsha*, *padma* and *hari·shyama* sandalwood, bright as fire. But though you see 40.40
that sandalwood, you must under no circumstances touch it; for fearsome *gandhárvas* called the Róhitas guard that forest. In it dwell five *gandhárva* lords, bright as the sun: Shailúsha, Grámani, Bhikshu, Shubhra and Babhru. There at the end of the earth live the unassailable people who have won heaven. Beyond that is the dreadful world of deceased ancestors, which you must not visit. For that is Yama's royal capital, enveloped by awful darkness.

That is as far as you can search or proceed, heroic bulls among monkeys: Beyond it, there is no path for the living. Explore all this and whatever else you may see, and when you have learned Vaidéhi's location you must return. Whoever returns before the month's end and says 'I have 40.45
seen Sita!' will become as wealthy as I am and amuse himself happily with pleasures. No one will be dearer to me than he. I will love him more than life itself. Even if he has committed many offenses, he will become my friend. You have boundless strength and prowess and were born in families of great virtue. Now you must begin this virtuous undertaking so that you may recover the daughter of the king."

WHEN THE GLORIOUS king had dispatched to the south- 41.1
ern quarter those wise and valiant monkeys, who equaled the wind in speed, he summoned his father-in-law, Tará's father, Sushéna by name, a troop leader of terrifying valor. Approaching him, he bowed, his palms cupped in rever-

«sāhāyyaṃ kuru Rāmasya kṛtye 'smin samupasthite.
vṛtaḥ śata|sahasreṇa vānarāṇāṃ tarasvinām
abhigaccha diśaṃ, saumya, paścimāṃ vāruṇīṃ, prabho!
41.5 Surāṣṭrān saha Bāhlīkāñ Śūdr'|Ābhīrāṃs tath" âiva ca
sphīt'|âñjana|padān ramyān vipulāni purāṇi ca
puṃnāga|gahanaṃ Kukṣiṃ bakul'|ôddālak'|ākulam
tathā ketaka|ṣaṇḍāṃś ca mārgadhvaṃ, hari|yūthapāḥ!
pratyak|sroto|gamāś c' âiva nadyaḥ śīta|jalāḥ śivāḥ
tāpasānām araṇyāni kāntārā girayaś ca ye.
giri|jāl'|āvṛtāṃ durgāṃ mārgitvā paścimāṃ diśam
tataḥ paścimam āsādya samudraṃ draṣṭum arhatha
timi|nakr'|āyuta|jalam akṣobhyam atha vānarāḥ!
tataḥ ketaka|ṣaṇḍeṣu tamāla|gahaneṣu ca
kapayo vihariṣyanti nārikela|vaneṣu ca.
41.10 tatra Sītāṃ ca mārgadhvaṃ nilayaṃ Rāvaṇasya ca
Marīci|pattanaṃ c' âiva ramyaṃ c' âiva Jaṭīpuram
Avantīm Aṅgalopāṃ ca tathā c' Âlakṣitaṃ vanam
rāṣṭrāṇi ca viśālāni pattanāni tatas tataḥ.
Sindhu|sāgarayoś c' âiva saṃgame tatra parvataḥ
mahān Hemagirir nāma śata|śṛṅgo mahā|drumaḥ.
tasya prastheṣu ramyeṣu siṃhāḥ pakṣa|gamāḥ sthitāḥ
timi|matsya|gajāṃś c' âiva nīḍāny āropayanti te.
tāni nīḍāni siṃhānāṃ giri|śṛṅga|gatāś ca ye
dṛptās tṛptāś ca mātaṅgās toyada|svana|niḥsvanāḥ
vicaranti viśāle 'smiṃs toya|pūrṇe samantataḥ.
41.15 tasya śṛṅgaṃ diva|sparśaṃ kāñcanaṃ citra|pādapam

ence, and said, "Please assist Rama in the undertaking that is at hand.

Accompanied by one hundred thousand swift monkeys,
please go to Váruna's western quarter, gentle lord. You 41.5
monkey-troop leaders must search Suráshtra, Bahlíka, Shud-
ra and Abhíra, with their lovely and thriving countryside
and large towns. You must also search Kukshi with its thick
forests of *pum·naga* trees, filled with *bákula* and *uddála-*
ka trees; and also the *kétaka* thickets, and the auspicious
westward-flowing rivers with their cool waters, the forests
of ascetics and whatever woods and mountains there may be.

Once you have searched the inaccessible western quarter,
covered by a network of mountains, you will reach the im-
perturbable western ocean, monkeys, and see its waters full
of whales and crocodiles. Then your monkeys will amuse
themselves in *kétaka* thickets, in *tamála* forests and coconut
groves. You must search for Sita and for Rávana's hiding 41.10
place there and in the city of Maríchi, and in charming Jati·
pura; in Avánti, Anga·lopa and in the Alákshita forest, and
throughout those vast kingdoms and cities.

There, where the Sindhu River meets the ocean, stands
a great mountain named Hema·giri, with a hundred peaks
and gigantic trees. On its charming slopes live *simha* birds,
who carry up to their nests whales, fish and elephants. Trumpeting with the sound of storm clouds, the proud and satisfied elephants who live on the mountain peak graze all about
near these *simha* birds' nests in this broad and well-watered
place. You monkeys, who change form at will, must quickly 41.15
explore the whole of its golden peak that is covered with

sarvam āśu vicetavyaṃ kapibhiḥ kāma|rūpibhiḥ!
koṭiṃ tatra samudre tu kāñcanīṃ śata|yojanam
durdarśāṃ pariyātrasya gatā drakṣyatha, vānarāḥ.

koṭyas tatra caturviṃśad gandharvāṇāṃ tarasvinām
vasanty agni|nikāśānāṃ ghorāṇāṃ kāma|rūpiṇām.
n' âty|āsādayitavyās te vānarair bhīma|vikramaiḥ
n' ādeyaṃ ca phalaṃ tasmād deśāt kiṃ cit plavaṃ|gamaiḥ.
durāsadā hi te vīrāḥ sattvavanto mahā|balāḥ
phala|mūlāni te tatra rakṣante bhīma|vikramāḥ.
41.20 tatra yatnaś ca kartavyo mārgitavyā ca Jānakī
na hi tebhyo bhayaṃ kiṃ cit kapitvam anuvartatām.

catur|bhāge samudrasya Cakravān nāma parvataḥ
tatra cakraṃ sahasr'|âraṃ nirmitaṃ Viśvakarmaṇā.
tatra Pañcajanaṃ hatvā Hayagrīvaṃ ca dānavam
ājahāra tataś cakraṃ śaṅkhaṃ ca Puruṣ'|ôttamaḥ.

tasya sānuṣu citreṣu viśālāsu guhāsu ca
Rāvaṇaḥ saha Vaidehyā mārgitavyas tatas tataḥ.
yojanāni catuḥ|ṣaṣṭir Varāho nāma parvataḥ
suvarṇa|śṛṅgaḥ su|śrīmān agādhe Varuṇ'|ālaye.
41.25 tatra Prāgjyotiṣaṃ nāma jāta|rūpa|mayaṃ puram
yasmin vasati duṣṭ'|ātmā Narako nāma dānavaḥ.
tasya sānuṣu citreṣu viśālāsu guhāsu ca
Rāvaṇaḥ saha Vaidehyā mārgitavyas tatas tataḥ.

bright trees and touches the sky. When you get there, monkeys, you will see in that ocean Mount Pariyátra's golden summit one hundred leagues high and rarely seen.

Twenty-four times ten million swift and terrible *gandhárvas* dwell there, bright as fire, changing their forms at will. They must not be approached too closely by you monkeys of fearsome valor, nor are you leaping monkeys to take any fruit whatever from that place. For those unassailable heroes of terrifying valor are courageous and very strong, and they
guard the fruit and roots there. You must exert yourselves 41.20
and hunt for Jánaki there, for they will not present any danger at all if you just behave like ordinary monkeys.

In one quarter of the ocean stands a mountain named Chákravan, where Vishva·karman fashioned a discus with a thousand spokes. There Vishnu, the Supreme Being, killed Pañcha·jana and the *dánava* Haya·griva and took that discus and a conch.

On the mountain's bright-colored slopes and in its large caves, you must search for Rávana and Vaidéhi here, there and everywhere. In Váruna's bottomless abode, the sea, stands a most majestic golden-peaked mountain named Va-
ráha, sixty-four leagues high. On it is a city of pure gold 41.25
named Prag·jyótisha, in which lives an evil-minded *dánava* named Náraka. On the mountain's bright-colored slopes and in its large caves, you must search for Rávana and Vaidéhi here, there and everywhere.

tam atikramya śail'|êndraṃ kāñcan'|āntara|nirdaraḥ.
parvataḥ sarva|sauvarṇo dhārā|prasravaṇ'|āyutaḥ.
taṃ gajāś ca varāhāś ca siṃhā vyāghrāś ca sarvataḥ
abhigarjanti satataṃ tena śabdena darpitāḥ.
tasmin hari|hayaḥ śrīmān Mahendraḥ Pāka|śāsanaḥ
abhiṣiktaḥ surai rājā. Meghavān nāma parvataḥ.
41.30 tam atikramya śail'|êndraṃ Mahendra|paripālitam
ṣaṣṭiṃ giri|sahasrāṇi kāñcanāni gamiṣyatha
taruṇ'|āditya varṇāni bhrājamānāni sarvataḥ
jāta|rūpa|mayair vṛkṣaiḥ śobhitāni supuṣpitaiḥ.
teṣāṃ madhye sthito rājā Merur uttama|parvataḥ
Ādityena prasannena śailo datta|varaḥ purā.
ten' âivam uktaḥ śail'|êndraḥ: ‹sarva eva tvad|āśrayāḥ:
mat|prasādād bhaviṣyanti divā rātrau ca kāñcanāḥ.
tvayi ye c' âpi vatsyanti deva|gandharva|dānavāḥ
te bhaviṣyanti raktāś ca prabhayā kāñcana|prabhāḥ.›
41.35 Ādityā Vasavo Rudrā Marutaś ca div'|âukasaḥ
āgamya paścimāṃ saṃdhyāṃ Merum uttama|parvatam
Ādityam upatiṣṭhanti taiś ca sūryo 'bhipūjitaḥ
adṛśyaḥ sarva|bhūtānām astaṃ gacchati parvatam.
yojanānāṃ sahasrāṇi daśa tāni divā|karaḥ
muhūrt'|ârdhena taṃ śīghram abhiyāti śil'|ôccayam.
śṛṅge tasya mahad divyaṃ bhavanaṃ sūrya|saṃnibham
prāsāda|guṇa|saṃbādhaṃ vihitaṃ Viśvakarmaṇā
śobhitaṃ tarubhiś citrair nānā|pakṣi|samākulaiḥ
niketaṃ pāśa|hastasya Varuṇasya mah"|ātmanaḥ.

Beyond that king of mountains, there is a mountain with
ten thousand streams and waterfalls. It is entirely of gold,
and its caves are golden within. All over it elephants, boars,
lions and tigers roar incessantly, maddened by their own
cries. On it the gods consecrated as their king the majestic
chastiser of Paka, Indra of the tawny horses. The mountain's
name is Méghavan. Passing beyond that king of mountains 41.30
protected by great Indra, you will come upon sixty thousand
golden mountains the color of the newly risen sun, gleaming
on every side, resplendent with beautifully flowering trees
made of pure gold.

In their midst stands Mount Meru, the king and greatest
of mountains, to whom Adítya, the sun god, who had been
propitiated, long ago granted a boon. And he spoke thus
to the king of mountains: 'All who seek refuge on you by
day or by night will by my grace become golden. Moreover,
those gods, *gandhárvas* and *dánavas* who live on you will be
colored by your radiance and thus take on the radiance of
gold.' The Adítyas, Vasus, Rudras, Maruts and gods come 41.35
to Mount Meru, greatest of mountains, at the time of the
evening twilight and worship Adítya, the sun god. Rever-
enced by them, the sun goes to the sunset mountain and
becomes invisible to all beings.

Traversing ten thousand leagues in half an hour, the sun,
bringer of day, quickly reaches the sunset mountain. On its
peak is a large and heavenly dwelling as bright as the sun,
crowded with many palaces and resplendent with wonderful
trees filled with birds of every kind. It was built by Vish-
va·karman and is the abode of great Váruna who holds a
noose in his hand. Between Meru and the sunset mountain 41.40

41.40 antarā Merum astaṃ ca tālo daśa|śirā mahān
jāta|rūpa|mayaḥ śrīmān bhrājate citra|vedikaḥ.
teṣu sarveṣu durgeṣu saraḥsu ca saritsu ca
Rāvaṇaḥ saha Vaidehyā mārgitavyas tatas tataḥ!
yatra tiṣṭhati dharm'|ātmā tapasā svena bhāvitaḥ
Merusāvarṇir ity eva khyāto vai Brahmaṇā samaḥ
praṣṭavyo Merusāvarṇir maha"|rṣiḥ sūrya|saṃnibhaḥ
praṇamya śirasā bhūmau pravṛttiṃ Maithilīṃ prati.
etāvaj jīva|lokasya bhāskaro rajanī|kṣaye
kṛtvā vitimiraṃ sarvam astaṃ gacchati parvatam.
41.45 etāvad vānaraiḥ śakyaṃ gantuṃ, vānara|puṃgavāḥ,
abhāskaram amaryādaṃ na jānīmas tataḥ param.
adhigamya tu Vaidehīṃ nilayaṃ Rāvaṇasya ca
astaṃ parvatam āsādya pūrṇe māse nivartata.
ūrdhvaṃ māsān na vastavyaṃ vasan vadhyo bhaven mama;
sah' âiva śūro yuṣmābhiḥ śvaśuro me gamiṣyati.
śrotavyaṃ sarvam etasya bhavadbhir diṣṭa|kāribhiḥ
gurur eṣa mahā|bāhuḥ śvaśuro me mahā|balaḥ
bhavantaś c' âpi vikrāntāḥ pramāṇaṃ sarva|karmasu
pramāṇam enaṃ saṃsthāpya paśyadhvaṃ paścimāṃ diśam.
41.50 dṛṣṭāyāṃ tu nar'|êndrasya patnyām amita|tejasaḥ
kṛta|kṛtyā bhaviṣyāmaḥ kṛtasya pratikarmaṇā.
ato 'nyad api yat kiṃ cit kāryasy' âsya hitaṃ bhavet
saṃpradhārya bhavadbhiś ca deśa|kāl'|ârtha|saṃhitam.»

shines a great and majestic palmyra tree made of gold, with ten crowns and a splendid sacred mound. Among all the inaccessible lakes and rivers, you must search for Rávana and Vaidéhi here, there and everywhere.

In the place where the great and righteous seer Meru·savárni lives, sanctified by his own asceticism, the equal of Brahma, radiant as the sun, you must bow your heads to the ground and ask him for news about Máithili. Only this much of the world of the living does the sun illuminate when night is over, before moving again to the sunset mountain.
And only so far, bulls among monkeys, can monkeys go. For 41.45
we know not what lies beyond, boundless and untouched by the sun.

You must reach the sunset mountain, find Vaidéhi and the hiding place of Rávana, and return within a month. But you must not stay beyond a month, for I shall kill anyone who does. My heroic father-in-law will go with you. This is my revered elder, my great-armed, mighty father-in-law. You who follow my commands must listen to everything he says. Although you, too, are valiant and are authorities concerning every action, you must make him your authority
and so explore the western quarter. Once you have found 41.50
the wife of the immeasurably powerful king, we will have accomplished our purpose by repaying what was done for us. Also keep in mind anything else that might be helpful to this enterprise, and then do it in accordance with the place, time and goal."

tataḥ Suṣeṇa|pramukhāḥ plavaṃ|gamāḥ
Sugrīva|vākyaṃ nipuṇaṃ niśamya
āmantrya sarve plavag'|âdhipaṃ te
jagmur diśaṃ tāṃ Varuṇ'|âbhiguptām.

42.1 TATAḤ SAṂDIŚYA Sugrīvaḥ śvaśuraṃ paścimāṃ diśam
vīraṃ Śatabaliṃ nāma vānaraṃ vānara'|rṣabhaḥ
uvāca rājā mantrajñaḥ sarva|vānara|saṃmatam
vākyam ātma|hitaṃ c' âiva Rāmasya ca hitaṃ tathā:
«vṛtaḥ śata|sahasreṇa tvad|vidhānāṃ van'|âukasām
Vaivasvata|sutaiḥ sārdhaṃ pratiṣṭhasva sva|mantribhiḥ.
diśaṃ hy udīcīṃ vikrāntāṃ hima|śail'|âvataṃsakām
sarvataḥ parimārgadhvaṃ Rāma|patnīm aninditām.
42.5 asmin kārye vinivṛtte kṛte Dāśaratheḥ priye
ṛṇān muktā bhaviṣyāmaḥ kṛt'|ârth'|ârthavidāṃ varāḥ.
kṛtaṃ hi priyam asmākaṃ Rāghaveṇa mah"|ātmanā
tasya cet pratikāro 'sti sa|phalaṃ jīvitaṃ bhavet.
etāṃ buddhiṃ samāsthāya dṛśyate Jānakī yathā
tathā bhavadbhiḥ kartavyam asmat|priya|hit'|âiṣibhiḥ.
ayaṃ hi sarva|bhūtānāṃ mānyas tu nara|sattamaḥ
asmāsu c' āgata|prītī Rāmaḥ para|puraṃ|jayaḥ.
imāni vana|durgāṇi nadyaḥ śail'|ântarāṇi ca
bhavantaḥ parimārgantu buddhi|vikrama|saṃpadā.
42.10 tatra Mlecchān Pulindāṃś ca Śūrasenāṃs tath" âiva ca
Prasthalān Bharatāṃś c' âiva Kurūṃś ca saha Madrakaiḥ
Kāmbojān Yavanāṃś c' âiva Śakān Āraṭṭakān api

Then, when the monkeys had heard Sugríva's skillful speech, they all took leave of the lord of monkeys and, headed by Sushéna, set out toward the quarter guarded by Váruna.

THEN, WHEN KING Sugríva, bull among monkeys, skilled 42.1
in counsel, had directed his father-in-law to the western quarter, he addressed the heroic monkey named Shata·bali, who was respected by all the monkeys, in words that were to his own benefit as well as Rama's:

"Surrounded by a hundred thousand forest-dwelling monkeys like yourself, you are to depart with your counselors, the sons of Yama Vaivásvata. You are to search for Rama's blameless wife everywhere in the mighty northern
quarter whose crest ornament is the Himálayas. You are 42.5
foremost among those who know their goals and achieve them. Once this task has been completed, once this favor has been done for Dasha·ratha's son, we shall be free of our obligation. For great Rághava did us a favor. If the favor is returned, our own life will have been fruitful. You who desire what is pleasing and beneficial to us must accept this view and act in such a way that Jánaki is found. For Rama, the best of men and a conqueror of enemy cities, is worthy of every being's respect and has entered into friendship with us.

Using your abundance of intelligence and valor, you must thoroughly search the inaccessible forests, rivers and even
inside the mountain caverns. When you have searched re- 42.10
peatedly through the countries of the Mlecchas, the Pulíndas and the Shura·senas; the Prásthalas, the Bharatas, the

Bāhlīkān Ṛṣikāṃś c' âiva Pauravān atha Ṭaṅkaṇān
Cīnān Paramacīnāṃś ca Nīhārāṃś ca punaḥ punaḥ
anviṣya Daradāṃś c' âiva Himavantaṃ vicinvatha!
lodhra|padmaka|ṣaṇḍeṣu deva|dāru|vaneṣu ca
Rāvaṇaḥ saha Vaidehya mārgitavyas tatas tataḥ!

tataḥ Som'|āśramaṃ gatvā deva|gandharva|sevitam
Kālaṃ nāma mahā|sānuṃ parvataṃ taṃ gamiṣyatha.
42.15 mahatsu tasya śṛṅgeṣu nirdareṣu guhāsu ca
vicinudhvaṃ mahā|bhāgāṃ Rāma|patnīṃ yaśasvinīm.
tam atikramya śail'|êndraṃ hema|vargaṃ mahā|girim
tataḥ Sudarśanaṃ nāma parvataṃ gantum arhatha.
tasya kānana|ṣaṇḍeṣu nirdareṣu guhāsu ca
Rāvaṇaḥ saha Vaidehyā mārgitavyas tatas tataḥ!

tam atikramya c' ākāśaṃ sarvataḥ śata|yojanam
a|parvata|nadī|vṛkṣaṃ sarva|sattva|vivarjitam.
taṃ tu śīghram atikramya kāntāraṃ roma|harṣaṇam
Kailāsaṃ pāṇḍuraṃ śailaṃ prāpya hṛṣṭā bhaviṣyatha.
42.20 tatra pāṇḍura|megh'|ābhaṃ jāmbūnada|pariṣkṛtam
Kubera|bhavanaṃ divyaṃ nirmitaṃ Viśvakarmaṇā.
viśālā nalinī yatra prabhūta|kamal'|ôtpalā
haṃsa|kāraṇḍav'|ākīrṇā apsaro|gaṇa|sevitā.
tatra Vaiśravaṇo rājā sarva|bhūta|namas|kṛtaḥ
Dhanado ramate śrīmān guhyakaiḥ saha yakṣa|rāṭ.

Kurus and Mádrakas; the Kambójas, the Yávanas, the Shakas, the Aráttakas, the Bahlíkas, the Ríshikas, the Páuravas and the Tánkanas; the Chinas, the Párama·chinas, the Niháras, and the Dáradas; you must scour the Himálayas. In thickets of *lodhra* and *pádmaka* and through the forests of *deva·daru* pine, you must search for Rávana and Vaidéhi here, there and everywhere.

When you come to the ashram of Soma, frequented by gods and *gandhárvas*, you will have reached the mountain
named Kala, with its mighty peaks. On its great peaks, in 42.15
its caverns and caves, you must hunt for Rama's renowned, illustrious wife. Passing beyond that great mountain, you should then go to the mountain called Sudárshana, a king of mountains filled with gold. In its forest thickets, its caverns and caves, you must search for Rávana and Vaidéhi here, there and everywhere.

Beyond it lies an open space, a hundred leagues on every side, without mountains, rivers or trees, devoid of any living thing. But if you quickly cross that horrifying wasteland, you will be delighted once you reach the white mountain
Kailása. There, bright as a white cloud and embellished 42.20
with gold, stands Kubéra's heavenly dwelling, built by Vishva·karman. Near it is a vast lotus pond filled with red and blue lotuses, crowded with geese and ducks, and frequented by hosts of *ápsaras*es. And there the majestic giver of wealth, King Kubéra Váishravana, king of the *yaksha*s, honored by all beings, enjoys himself along with the *gúhyakas*.

tasya candra|nikaśeṣu parvateṣu guhāsu ca
Rāvaṇaḥ saha Vaidehyā mārgitavyas tatas tataḥ.
Krauñcaṃ tu girim āsādya bilaṃ tasya su|durgamam
apramattaiḥ praveṣṭavyaṃ duṣpraveśaṃ hi tat smṛtam!
42.25 vasanti hi mah"|ātmānas tatra sūrya|sama|prabhāḥ
devair apy arcitāḥ samyag deva|rūpā|maha"|rṣayaḥ.
Krauñcasya tu guhāś c' ânyāḥ sānūni śikharāṇi ca
nirdarāś ca nitambāś ca vicetavyās tatas tataḥ
Krauñcasya śikharaṃ c' âpi nirīkṣya ca tatas tataḥ
avṛkṣaṃ kāma|śailaṃ ca Mānasaṃ vihag'|ālayam.
na gatis tatra bhūtānāṃ deva|dānava|rakṣasām
sa ca sarvair vicetavyaḥ sa|sānu|prastha|bhū|dharaḥ.
Krauñcaṃ girim atikramya Maināko nāma parvataḥ
Mayasya bhavanaṃ tatra dānavasya svayaṃ kṛtam.
42.30 Maināka s tu vicetavyaḥ sa|sānu|prastha|kandaraḥ
strīṇām aśva|mukhīnāṃ ca niketās tatra tatra tu.
taṃ deśaṃ samatikramya āśramaṃ siddha|sevitam
siddhā Vaikhānasās tatra Vālakhilyāś ca tāpasāḥ.
vandyās te tu tapaḥ|siddhās tāpasā vīta|kalmaṣāḥ
praṣṭavyāś c' âpi Sītāyāḥ pravṛttaṃ vinay'|ânvitaiḥ.
hema|puṣkara|saṃchannaṃ tatra Vaikhānasaṃ saraḥ
taruṇ'|āditya|saṃkāśair haṃsair vicaritaṃ śubhaiḥ.
aupavāhyaḥ Kuberasya Sārvabhauma iti smṛtaḥ
gajaḥ paryeti taṃ deśaṃ sadā saha kareṇubhiḥ.

On Kailása's foothills bright as the moon, and in its caves, you must search for Rávana and Vaidéhi here, there and everywhere.

When you reach the Krauñcha mountain, you must cautiously enter its inaccessible opening, for it is said to be very difficult to enter. In it live great seers radiant as the sun; they 42.25
look like gods and are worshiped by the gods themselves.

After exploring Krauncha's peak and the abode of birds, the wish-fulfilling mountain Mánasa, devoid of trees, you must search Krauñcha's other caves, ridges, peaks, caverns and slopes, here, there and everywhere. Great beings such as gods, *dánavas* and *rákshasas* do not go there; still, all of you are to search it, including its ridges, tablelands and foothills.

Beyond Mount Krauñcha lies a mountain called Mai-náka, where stands the *dánava* Maya's palace, which he
fashioned himself. You must search Mainráka including its 42.30
ridges, tablelands and caves, where stand the scattered dwellings of the horse-faced women. Beyond that region stands an ashram frequented by *siddhas*. In it are *siddhas*, Vaikhánasa hermits and Vala·khilya ascetics. You must reverentially greet those ascetics, who are free of sin and perfected by austerities, and politely ask them for news of Sita. The hermits' lake is there, covered with golden lotuses and visited by lovely geese radiant as the newly risen sun. Kubéra's royal mount, the bull elephant Sarva·bhauma, always roams about that region with his cows.

42.35 tat saraḥ samatikramya naṣṭa|candra|divā|karam
a|nakṣatra|gaṇam vyoma niṣpayodam anādimat.
gabhastibhir iv' ârkasya sa tu deśaḥ prakāśate
viśrāmyadbhis tapaḥ|siddhair deva|kalpaiḥ svayam|prabhaiḥ.
taṃ tu deśam atikramya Śailodā nāma nimnagā
ubhayos tīrayor yasyāḥ kīcakā nāma veṇavaḥ.
te nayanti paraṃ tīraṃ siddhān pratyānayanti ca
Uttarāḥ Kuravas tatra kṛta|puṇya|pratiśriyāḥ.
tataḥ kāñcana|padmābhiḥ padminībhiḥ kṛt'|ôdakāḥ
nīla|vaidūrya|patr'|āḍhyā nadyas tatra sahasraśaḥ.
42.40 rakt'|ôtpala|vanaiś c' âtra maṇḍitāś ca hiraṇ|mayaiḥ
taruṇ'|āditya|sadṛśair bhānti tatra jal'|āśayāḥ.
mah"|ârha|maṇi|patraiś ca kāñcana|prabha|kesaraiḥ
nīl'|ôtpala|vanaiś citraiḥ sa deśaḥ sarvato vṛtaḥ.
nistulābhiś ca muktābhir maṇibhiś ca mahā|dhanaiḥ
udbhūta|pulinās tatra jāta|rūpaiś ca nimnagāḥ
sarva|ratna|mayaiś citrair avagāḍhā nag'|ôttamaiḥ
jāta|rūpa|mayaiś c' âpi hut'|âśana|sama|prabhaiḥ.
nitya|puṣpa|phalāś c' âtra nagāḥ patra|rath'|ākulāḥ
divya|gandha|rasa|sparśāḥ sarva|kāmān sravanti ca.
42.45 nān"|ākārāṇi vāsāṃsi phalanty anye nag'|ôttamāḥ
muktā|vaidūrya|citrāṇi bhūṣaṇāni tath" âiva ca
strīṇāṃ yāny anurūpāṇi puruṣāṇāṃ tath" âiva ca.
sarva'|rtu|sukha|sevyāni phalanty anye nag'|ôttamāḥ.
mah"|ârhāṇi vicitrāṇi haimāny anye nag'|ôttamāḥ
śayanāni prasūyante citr'|āstāraṇavanti ca
manaḥ|kāntāni mālyāni phalanty atr' âpare drumāḥ
pānāni ca mah"|ârhāṇi bhakṣyāṇi vividhāni ca.

Beyond that lake the sky is devoid of moon and sun, 42.35
with no hosts of stars, no clouds and no beginning. And yet
that region seems radiant with sunbeams, so self-luminous
are the godlike beings perfected by austerities who repose
there. And beyond that region is a river named Shailóda,
on both of whose banks grow the bamboo canes known as
kíchaka. These carry the *siddha*s to and from the opposite
shore, where lies the country of Úttara·kuru, the refuge of
those who have performed meritorious deeds.

There are rivers by the thousand there, their waters brimming with beds of golden lotuses, rich with leaves sapphire
and emerald. The ponds there sparkle, for they are adorned 42.40
with clusters of red lotuses made of gold, bright as the newly
risen sun. The whole region is covered with bright clusters
of blue lotuses, with leaves like precious jewels, and filaments shining like gold. There splendid, glittering mountains, golden and bright as fire, full of all kinds of jewels,
plunge down to rivers in which shoals of round pearls, precious gems and gold have arisen. And there trees crowded
with birds, always laden with fruit and flowers, whose fragrance, taste and touch are heavenly, yield every desire.

Other magnificent trees bring forth garments of every 42.45
appearance as well as ornaments glittering with pearls and
emeralds, for both women and men. Still others bear fruits
to enjoy in every season. Others yield wonderful precious
golden beds with bright-colored coverings; while other trees
produce garlands that delight the heart, and all sorts of costly
drinks and foods.

striyaś ca guṇa|saṃpannā rūpa|yauvana|lakṣitāḥ
gandharvāḥ kiṃnarā siddhā nāgā vidyā|dharās tathā
ramante sahitās tatra nārībhir bhāskara|prabhāḥ.
42.50 sarve sukṛta|karmāṇaḥ sarve rati|parāyaṇāḥ
sarve kām'|ârtha|sahitā vasanti saha yoṣitaḥ.
gīta|vāditra|nirghoṣaḥ s'|ôtkṛṣṭa|hasita|svanaḥ
śrūyate satataṃ tatra sarva|bhūta|mano|haraḥ.
tatra n' âmuditaḥ kaś cin n' âsti kaś cid asat|priyaḥ.
ahany ahani vardhante guṇās tatra mano|ramāḥ.
samatikramya taṃ deśam uttaras toyasāṃ nidhiḥ.
tatra Somagirir nāma madhye hema|mayo mahān.
Indra|loka|gatā ye ca Brahma|loka|gatāś ca ye
devās taṃ samavekṣante giri|rājaṃ divaṃ gatam.
42.55 sa tu deśo visūryo 'pi tasya bhāsā prakāśate:
sūrya|lakṣmy" âbhivijñeyas tapas" êva Vivasvatā.
bhagavān api viśv'|ātmā śam|bhur ekādaś'|ātmakaḥ
Brahmā vasati dev'|ēśo brahma'|ṛṣi|parivāritaḥ
na kathaṃ cana gantavyaṃ Kurūṇām uttareṇa vaḥ.
anyeṣām api bhūtānāṃ n' âtikrāmati vai gatiḥ.
sā hi Somagirir nāma devānām api durgamaḥ.
tam ālokya tataḥ kṣipram upāvartitum arhatha!
etāvad vānaraiḥ śakyaṃ gantuṃ, vānara|puṃgavāḥ,
abhāskaram amaryādaṃ na jānīmas tataḥ param.

There are splendid women there distinguished by their beauty and youth. There *gandhárvas*, *kim·naras*, perfected beings, great serpents and *vidya·dharas*, all shining like the sun, make love with these women. All have performed virtu- 42.50
ous deeds, all are intent on sexual delight, all live with young women, enjoying pleasures and wealth. Sounds of singing and musical instruments and loud laughter are constantly heard there, delighting the hearts of all beings.

No one is unhappy there, no one lacks a beloved. There virtues that delight the heart increase day by day.

Beyond that country lies the northern ocean. There, in its midst, stands the great golden mountain named Soma·giri. Those gods who have gone to the world of Indra and those who have gone to the world of Brahma behold that king of mountains, for it reaches up to heaven. It is the radiance of 42.55
the mountain which makes this sunless region seem to blaze with sunlight: You can recognize it by a splendor like that of the blazing sun god Vivásvan. And there dwells the blessed one, the soul of the universe, the benevolent elevenfold lord of the gods Brahma, surrounded by brahman-seers. By no means are you to go north of the Kurus. Even for other beings, no path lies beyond. For this mountain called Soma·giri cannot be reached even by the gods. Once you have seen it, you must turn back at once. Only this far, bulls among monkeys, can monkeys go. For we know not what lies beyond, boundless and untouched by sun.

42.60 sarvam etad vicetavyaṃ yan mayā parikīrtitam
yad anyad api n' ôktaṃ ca tatr' âpi kriyatāṃ matiḥ!
tataḥ kṛtaṃ Dāśarather mahat priyaṃ
mahattaraṃ c' âpi tato mama priyaṃ
kṛtaṃ bhaviṣyaty anil'|ânal'|ôpamā
Videha|jā|darśana|jena karmaṇā.
tataḥ kṛt'|ârthāḥ sahitāḥ sabāndhavā
may" ârcitāḥ sarva|guṇair mano|ramaiḥ
cariṣyath' ôrvīṃ pratiśānta|śatravaḥ
saha|priyā bhūta|dharāḥ plavaṃ|gamāḥ.»

You are to search every place that I have mentioned. But 42.60
you must also resolve to search any others that I failed to mention. Then, by acting to find Vidéha's daughter, you who are equal to wind or fire will have done a great favor for Dasha·ratha's son and an even greater favor for me. And so when you have accomplished your mission, monkeys, I will honor you and your kinsmen with pleasing objects full of every virtue. With your enemies subdued, able to support other beings, you shall roam the earth with your beloveds."

43–46
RETURN FROM EAST, WEST AND NORTH

43.1 Viśeṣeṇa tu Sugrīvo Hanumaty artham uktavān
sa hi tasmin hari|śreṣṭhe niścit'|ârtho 'rtha|sādhane.
«na bhūmau n' ântarikṣe vā n' âmbare n' âmar'|ālaye
n' âpsu vā gati|saṃgaṃ te paśyāmi, hari|puṃgava.
s'|âsurāḥ saha|gandharvāḥ sa|nāga|nara|devatāḥ
viditāḥ sarva|lokās te sa|sāgara|dharā|dharāḥ.
gatir vegaś ca tejaś ca lāghavaṃ ca, mahā|kape,
pitus te sadṛśaṃ, vīra, Mārutasya mah"|âujasaḥ.
43.5 tejasā v" âpi te bhūtaṃ samaṃ bhuvi na vidyate
tad yathā labhyate Sītā tat tvam ev' ôpapādaya.
tvayy eva, Hanumann, asti balaṃ buddhiḥ parākramaḥ
deśa|kāl'|ânuvṛttaś ca nayaś ca, naya|paṇḍita.»
tataḥ kārya|samāsaṃgam avagamya Hanūmati
viditvā Hanumantaṃ ca cintayām āsa Rāghavaḥ:
«sarvathā niścit'|ârtho 'yaṃ Hanūmati har'|īśvaraḥ
niścit'|ârthataraś c' âpi Hanūmān kārya|sādhane.
tad evaṃ prasthitasy' âsya parijñātasya karmabhiḥ
bhartrā parigṛhītasya dhruvaḥ kārya|phal'|ôdayaḥ.»
43.10 taṃ samīkṣya mahā|tejā vyavasāy'|ôttaraṃ harim
kṛt'|ârtha iva saṃvṛttaḥ prahṛṣṭ'|êndriya|mānasaḥ.
dadau tasya tataḥ prītaḥ sva|nām'|âṅk'|ôpaśobhitam
aṅgulīyam abhijñānaṃ rāja|putryāḥ paraṃ|tapaḥ.

AND NOW SUGRÍVA stated his purpose to Hánuman in particular, for he was confident that he, the foremost of the monkeys, would achieve it. 43.1

"Neither on earth, nor in the air, nor in the sky, nor in the region of the gods, nor in the waters do I foresee any obstacle to your passage, bull among monkeys. For you know all worlds, together with their oceans and mountains, their *á-suras*, *gandhárvas*, great serpents, men and gods. Great and heroic monkey, your motion, speed, power and quickness are equal to those of your father, the mighty wind god
Máruta. Nor is there any other being on earth to equal 43.5
you in strength. Therefore, if Sita is to be recovered, you yourself must bring this about. In you alone, Hánuman, are strength, intelligence, prowess, regard for time and place, and statesmanship, wisest of statesmen."

Understanding from this that the undertaking had been entrusted to Hánuman, and knowing Hánuman himself, Rághava thought:

"The lord of monkeys has complete confidence in Hánuman, and Hánuman appears even more confident about accomplishing this undertaking. Known by his deeds and chosen by his master, even as he sets out his success in this undertaking is therefore assured."

And as mighty Rama beheld that supremely resolute 43.10
monkey, his senses and heart filled with joy like someone whose object was already achieved. And so Rama, scorcher of his foes, was delighted and gave him a ring engraved with his name as a token of recognition for the princess.

«anena tvāṃ, hari|śreṣṭha, cihnena Janak'|ātmajā
mat|sakāśād anuprāptam anudvign" ânupaśyati.
vyavasāyaś ca te, vīra, sattva|yuktaś ca vikramaḥ
Sugrīvasya ca saṃdeśaḥ siddhiṃ kathayat' îva me.»
sa tad gṛhya hari|śreṣṭhaḥ sthāpya mūrdhni kṛt'|âñjaliḥ
vanditvā caraṇau c' âiva prasthitaḥ plavag'|ôttamaḥ.

43.15 sa tat prakarṣan hariṇāṃ balaṃ mahad
babhūva vīraḥ Pavan'|ātmajaḥ kapiḥ
gat'|âmbude vyomni viśuddha|maṇḍalaḥ
śaś" îva nakṣatra|gaṇ'|ôpaśobhitaḥ.
«atibala, balam āśritas tav' âhaṃ,
hari|vara, vikrama vikramair analpaiḥ,
Pavana|suta, yath" âbhigamyate sā
Janaka|sutā, Hanumaṃs, tathā kuruṣva!»

44.1 TAD UGRA|ŚĀSANAṂ bhartur vijñāya hari|puṃgavāḥ
śalabhā iva saṃchādya medinīṃ saṃpratasthire.
Rāmaḥ Prasravaṇe tasmin nyavasat saha|Lakṣmaṇaḥ
pratīkṣamāṇas taṃ māsaṃ yaḥ Sīt"|âdhigame kṛtaḥ.
uttarāṃ tu diśaṃ ramyāṃ giri|rāja|samāvṛtām
pratasthe sahasā vīro hariḥ Śatabalis tadā.
pūrvāṃ diśaṃ prati yayau Vinato hari|yūthapaḥ.
44.5 Tār'|Âṅgad'|ādi|sahitaḥ plavagaḥ Pavan'|ātmajaḥ
Agastya|caritām āśāṃ dakṣiṇāṃ hari|yūthapaḥ.
paścimāṃ tu diśaṃ ghorāṃ Suṣeṇaḥ plavag'|ēśvaraḥ
pratasthe hari|śārdūlo bhṛśaṃ Varuṇa|pālitām.
tataḥ sarvā diśo rājā codayitvā yathā|tatham

"Jánaka's daughter will see by this sign that you have come from me and she will not be afraid, best of monkeys.

Your determination and your valor combined with strength, together with Sugríva's command, hero, seem to me to foretell success."

Taking the ring, that best of tawny monkeys touched it to his head, his palms cupped in reverence; then, bowing at
Rama's feet, he departed, that finest of leaping monkeys. As 43.15
that heroic monkey, son of the wind god, led away his great army of tawny monkeys, he looked like the unblemished circle of the hare-marked moon adorned by hosts of stars in a cloudless sky.

"Mighty Hánuman, valiant as a lion, I rely on your might, son of the wind. You must perform feats of great valor so that Jánaka's daughter is regained!"

THOSE BULLS among monkeys understood their master's 44.1
stern command and set off, covering the earth like locusts. But Rama remained on Mount Prasrávana with Lákshmana, waiting out the month that had been allotted to recovering Sita. Then the heroic monkey Shata·bali set off at once for the lovely northern quarter guarded by the king of mountains. Vínata, leader of monkey troops, proceeded
to the eastern quarter. The monkey-son of the wind god, 44.5
leader of monkey troops, went with Tara, Ángada and others to the southern quarter, where Agástya journeyed. The lord of monkeys, Sushéna, tiger among monkeys, set out for the terrible western quarter, which Váruna staunchly

kapi|senā|patīn mukhyān mumoda sukhitaḥ sukham.
evaṃ saṃcoditāḥ sarve rājñā vānara|yūthapāḥ
svāṃ svāṃ diśam abhipretya tvaritāḥ saṃpratasthire.
nadantaś c' ônnadantaś ca garjantaś ca plavaṃ|gamāḥ
kṣvelanto dhāvamānāś ca yayuḥ plavaga|sattamāḥ
«ānayiṣyāmahe Sītāṃ haniṣyāmaś ca Rāvaṇam!»
44.10 «aham eko haniṣyāmi prāptaṃ Rāvaṇam āhave
tataś c' ônmathya sahasā hariṣye Janak'|ātmajām
vepamānāṃ śrameṇ' âdya bhavadbhiḥ sthīyatām iti
eka ev' āhariṣyāmi pātālād api Jānakīm!»
«vidhamiṣyāmy ahaṃ vṛkṣān!» «dārayiṣyāmy ahaṃ girīn!»
«dharaṇīṃ dārayiṣyāmi!» «kṣobhayiṣyāmi sāgarān!»
«ahaṃ yojana|saṃkhyāyāḥ plavitā n' âtra saṃśayaḥ
śataṃ!» «yojana|saṃkhyāyāḥ śataṃ samadhikaṃ hy aham!»
«bhū|tale sāgare v" âpi śaileṣu ca vaneṣu ca
pātālasy' âpi vā madhye na mam' ācchidyate gatiḥ!»
44.15 ity ekaikaṃ tadā tatra vānarā bala|darpitāḥ
ūcuś ca vacanaṃ tasmin hari|rājasya saṃnidhau.

45.1 Gateṣu vānar'|êndreṣu Rāmaḥ Sugrīvam abravīt:
«kathaṃ bhavān vijānīte sarvaṃ vai maṇḍalaṃ bhuvaḥ?»
Sugrīvas tu tato Rāmam uvāca praṇat'|ātmavān:
«śrūyatāṃ sarvam ākhyāsye vistareṇa, nara'|rṣabha.

defends. Then, when he had duly dispatched his principal monkey-generals to every quarter, the delighted king rejoiced happily.

Dispatched in this way by the king, all the monkey-
troop leaders set off, each hastening toward his own assigned
quarter. Those monkeys, those extraordinary of monkeys,
advanced, jumping and running, roaring, shouting, and
growling, "We will kill Rávana and recover Sita!" "When I 44.10
find Rávana, I will kill him in battle all by myself. And when
I have crushed him, I will immediately bring back Jánaka's
daughter, trembling in her exhaustion. I will bring back Jánaki all by myself even if it is from the underworld. The
rest of you can wait here!" "I will scatter trees!" "I will split
mountains!" "I will split the earth!" "I will roil the oceans!"
"I will leap a distance of one hundred leagues, without any
doubt!" "And I will leap more than one hundred leagues!"
"On the earth's surface, in the ocean, on mountains or in
forests, or even in the depths of the underworld, nothing
can stop me!" Such were the declarations made by those 44.15
monkeys, proud of their strength, as each spoke in turn in
the presence of the monkey-king.

WHEN THE MONKEY leaders had gone, Rama spoke to 45.1
Sugríva, "How do you happen to know the whole compass
of the earth so well?" Then self-possessed Sugríva bowed
and said to Rama, "Listen, bull among men, and I shall tell
you the whole story in detail.

yadā tu Dundubhiṃ nāma dānavaṃ mahiṣ'|ākṛtim
parikālayate Vālī Malayaṃ prati parvatam
tadā viveśa mahiṣo Malayasya guhāṃ prati
viveśa Vālī tatr' âpi Malayaṃ taj|jighāṃsayā.
45.5 tato 'haṃ tatra nikṣipto guhā|dvāri vinītavat
na ca niṣkramate Vālī tadā saṃvatsare gate.
tataḥ kṣataja|vegena āpupūre tadā bilam.
tad ahaṃ vismito dṛṣṭvā bhrātṛ|śoka|viṣ'|ârditaḥ.
ath' âhaṃ kṛta|buddhis tu suvyaktaṃ nihato guruḥ
śilā parvata|saṃkāśā bila|dvāri mayā kṛtā
‹aśaknuvan niṣkramituṃ mahiṣo vinaśed iti.›
tato 'ham āgāṃ Kiṣkindhāṃ nirāśas tasya jīvite
rājyaṃ ca sumahat prāptaṃ Tārā ca Rumayā saha
mitraiś ca sahitas tatra vasāmi vigata|jvaraḥ.
ājagāma tato Vālī hatvā taṃ dānava'|rṣabham
tato 'ham adadāṃ rājyaṃ gauravād bhaya|yantritaḥ.
45.10 sa māṃ jighāṃsur duṣṭ'|ātmā Vālī pravyathit'|êndriyaḥ
parikālayate krodhād dhāvantaṃ sacivaiḥ saha.
tato 'haṃ Vālinā tena s'|ânubandhaḥ pradhāvitaḥ
nadīś ca vividhāḥ paśyan vanāni nagarāṇi ca.
ādarśa|tala|saṃkāśā tato vai pṛthivī mayā
alāta|cakra|pratimā dṛṣṭā goṣpadavat tadā.
tataḥ pūrvam ahaṃ gatvā dakṣiṇām aham āśritaḥ
diśaṃ ca paścimāṃ bhūyo gato 'smi bhaya|śaṅkitaḥ
uttarāṃ tu diśaṃ yāntaṃ Hanumān mām ath' âbravīt:
‹idānīṃ me smṛtaṃ, rājan, yathā Vālī har'|īśvaraḥ
Mataṅgena tadā śapto hy asminn āśrama|maṇḍale:

When Valin chased Dúndubhi—a *dánava* in the form
of a buffalo—toward Mount Málaya, the buffalo entered
a cave in Málaya. Valin, too, entered the mountain at that
spot, with the intention of killing him. Then I was installed 45.5
obediently at the opening to the cave. But Valin did not
come out even after a year had passed. And then the hole
was filled with a torrent of blood. Dismayed to see that,
I suffered intense grief for my brother. I thought that my
elder brother had surely been killed; so I placed a rock as big
as a mountain over the opening of the hole, thinking that
if the buffalo were unable to come out he would perish.

Then, without hope for Valin's life, I returned to Kishkíndha. The great kingdom became mine, and so did Tará
and Ruma. And there I lived with my friends, free of care.
Then Valin came back, after killing that bull among *dánavas*. So I restored the kingdom to him, driven by fear because
he was my elder. But wicked Valin had taken leave of his 45.10
senses. He wanted to kill me, and in his rage he pursued
me as I fled with my ministers. As Valin chased me and
my companions, I saw all sorts of rivers, forests and cities.
Thus it was that I saw the earth—like the surface of a mirror
or like the circling of a torch—as if it were merely a cow's
hoofprint.

After I had gone east, I took refuge in the south. Then
I went on to the west because I was fearful of the danger.
But then, when I came to the north, Hánuman said to me:
'I now remember, king, how the lord of monkeys, Valin,
was earlier cursed by Matánga, who said, "If Valin should 45.15
enter the confines of this ashram, his head will break into a
hundred pieces." Staying there will be pleasant and free of

45.15 «praviśed yadi vā Vālī mūrdh" âsya śatadhā bhavet»
tatra vāsaḥ sukho 'smākaṃ nirudvigno bhaviṣyati.›
tataḥ parvatam āsādya Ṛśyamūkaṃ, nṛp'|ātmaja,
na viveśa tadā Vālī Mataṅgasya bhayāt tadā.
evaṃ mayā tadā, rājan, pratyakṣam upalakṣitam
pṛthivī|maṇḍalaṃ kṛtsnaṃ guhām asmy āgatas tataḥ.»

46.1 DARŚAN'|ÂRTHAṂ tu Vaidehyāḥ sarvataḥ kapi|yūthapāḥ
vyādiṣṭāḥ kapi|rājena yath"|ôktaṃ jagmur añjasā.
sarāṃsi saritaḥ kakṣān ākāśaṃ nagarāṇi ca
nadī|durgāṃs tathā śailān vicinvanti samantataḥ.
Sugrīveṇa samākhyātān sarve vānara|yūthapāḥ
pradeśān pravicinvanti sa|śaila|vana|kānanān.
vicintya divasaṃ sarve Sīt"|âdhigamane dhṛtāḥ
samāyānti sma medinyāṃ niśā|kāleśu vānarāḥ.
46.5 sarva'|rtukāṃś ca deśeṣu vānarāḥ saphalān drumān
āsādya rajanīṃ śayyāṃ cakruḥ sarveṣv ahaḥsu te.
tad ahaḥ prathamaṃ kṛtvā māse Prasravaṇaṃ gatāḥ
kapi|rājena saṃgamya nirāśāḥ kapi|yūthapāḥ.
vicitya tu diśaṃ pūrvāṃ yath"|ôktāṃ sacivaiḥ saha
adṛṣṭvā Vinataḥ Sītām ājagāma mahā|balaḥ.
uttarāṃ tu diśaṃ sarvāṃ vicitya sa mahā|kapiḥ
āgataḥ saha sainyena vīraḥ Śatabalis tadā.
Suṣeṇaḥ paścimām āśāṃ vicitya saha vānaraiḥ
sametya māse saṃpūrṇe Sugrīvam upacakrame.
46.10 taṃ Prasravaṇa|pṛṣṭha|sthaṃ samāsādy' âbhivādya ca
āsīnaṃ saha Rāmeṇa Sugrīvam idam abruvan:

worry for us.' Therefore, prince, when Valin reached Mount Rishya·muka, he did not enter the ashram on account of fear of Matánga. So it was, king, that at that time I beheld with my own eyes the entire compass of the earth, before I came to the cave."

AT THE COMMAND of the monkey-king, the leaders of the 46.1
monkey troops swiftly departed in every direction, as they had been instructed, in order to find Vaidéhi. They thoroughly searched lakes, rivers, underbrush, open ground, cities, mountains and inaccessible places near rivers. All the monkey-troop leaders scoured the regions Sugríva had mentioned, including their mountains, forests and woods. Intent on finding Sita, all the monkeys searched by day, and at
night gathered in one place. And every day in those coun- 46.5
tries they made their beds for the night in trees bearing fruit in all seasons.

But when a month had passed since that first day, the monkey-troop leaders gave up hope and returned to Mount Prasrávana, where they met with the monkey-king. Mighty Vínata and his companions searched the east as instructed but returned without finding Sita. Then came the great monkey-hero Shata·bali with his army, after searching all of the north. After searching the west, Sushéna and his monkeys reassembled and came to Sugríva when the month
had passed. They approached Sugríva, who was seated with 46.10
Rama on top of Mount Prasrávana, and saluting respectfully they said:

«vicitāḥ parvatāḥ sarve vanāni nagarāṇi ca
nimnagāḥ sāgar'|ântāś ca sarve jana|padās tathā.
guhāś ca vicitāḥ sarvā yās tvayā parikīrtitāḥ
vicitāś ca mahā|gulmā latā|vitata|saṃtatāḥ.
gahaneṣu ca deśeṣu durgeṣu viṣameṣu ca
sattvāny atipramāṇāni vicitāni hatāni ca
ye c' âiva gahanā deśā vicitās te punaḥ punaḥ.

udāra|sattv'|âbhijano mah"|ātmā
sa Maithilīṃ drakṣyati vānar'|êndraḥ;
diśaṃ tu yām eva gatā tu Sītā
tām āsthito Vāyu|suto Hanūmān.»

"We have searched all the lands; all the mountains, forests, cities and rivers flowing to the seas. And we have searched all the caves you mentioned, and all the vast thickets densely overspread with creepers. In impenetrable, inaccessible and impassable places, we have stalked and killed huge beasts. And we have searched those impenetrable places repeatedly.

It is great Hánuman, that lord of monkeys of exalted strength and illustrious lineage, who will find Máithili; for the son of the wind god has gone in the direction that Sita went."

47–52
THE SOUTHERN OCEAN

47.1 Saha Tār'|Âṅgadābhyāṃ tu gatvā sa Hanumān kapiḥ
Sugrīveṇa yath" ôddiṣṭaṃ taṃ deśam upacakrame.
sa tu dūram upāgamya sarvais taiḥ kapi|sattamaiḥ
vicinoti sma Vindhyasya guhāś ca gahanāni ca.
parvat'|âgrān nadī|durgān sarāṃsi vipulān drumān
vṛkṣa|ṣaṇḍāṃś ca vividhān parvatān ghana|pādapān
anveṣamāṇās te sarve vānarāḥ sarvato diśam
na Sītāṃ dadṛśur vīrā Maithilīṃ Janak'|ātmajām.
47.5 te bhakṣayanto mūlāni phalāni vividhāni ca
anveṣamāṇā durdharṣā nyavasaṃs tatra tatra ha
sa tu deśo dur|anveṣo guhā|gahana|vān mahān.
tyaktvā tu taṃ tadā deśaṃ sarve vai hari|yūthapāḥ
deśam anyaṃ durādharṣaṃ viviśuś c' â|kuto|bhayāḥ
yatra vandhya|phalā vṛkṣā vipuṣpāḥ parṇa|varjitāḥ
nistoyāḥ sarito yatra mūlaṃ yatra su|durlabham
na santi mahiṣā yatra na mṛgā na ca hastinaḥ
śārdūlāḥ pakṣiṇo v" âpi ye c' ânye vana|gocarāḥ
snigdha|patrāḥ sthale yatra padminyaḥ phulla|paṅkajāḥ
prekṣaṇīyāḥ sugandhāś ca bhramaraiś c' âpi varjitāḥ.
47.10 Kaṇḍur nāma mahā|bhāgaḥ satya|vādī tapo|dhanaḥ
maha"|rṣiḥ param'|âmarṣī niyamair duṣpradharṣaṇaḥ.
tasya tasmin vane putro bālako daśa|vārṣikaḥ.
pranaṣṭo jīvit'|ântāya kruddhas tatra mahā|muniḥ.
tena dharm'|ātmanā śaptaṃ kṛtsnaṃ tatra mahad vanam
aśaraṇyaṃ durādharṣaṃ mṛga|pakṣi|vivarjitam.
tasya te kānan'|ântāṃs tu girīṇāṃ kandarāṇi ca
prabhavāni nadīnāṃ ca vicinvanti samāhitāḥ.

INDEED, THE monkey Hánuman had set out with Tara 47.1
and Ángada and was advancing toward the region indicated by Sugríva. He journeyed far with all those great
monkeys and explored the caves and impenetrable forests of
the Vindhya mountains. Though all those heroic monkeys
searched everywhere in that quarter—inaccessible places
near rivers, mountaintops, lakes, large trees, different groves
of trees and foothills thick with trees—none of them found
the princess of Míthila, Jánaka's daughter Sita. Eating vari- 47.5
ous roots and fruit as they searched, the unassailable monkeys camped in different places; but that country was vast
and was difficult to search with its caves and deep forests.

Then all those dauntless monkey-troop leaders left that
region and entered another region difficult to approach,
where the trees lacked fruit, flowers and leaves, where the
rivers were without water, where roots were very hard to
find, where there were no buffalo, deer, elephants, tigers,
birds or other forest creatures, and where beautiful, fragrant
lotus beds, with glossy leaves and full-blown lotuses, were
without bees.

There was an illustrious great seer named Kandu, ascetic, 47.10
truthful, highly irascible and unassailable by virtue of his
religious observances. His son, a ten-year-old boy, perished
in that forest. The great sage was angered at his ending his
life there. Cursed then by that righteous sage, the entire
vast forest became inhospitable, unapproachable and devoid of wild animals and birds. Nonetheless, the monkeys
carefully searched its forest regions, its mountain caves and
the sources of its rivers. But even though the great monkeys

tatra c' âpi mah"|ātmāno n' âpaśyan Janak'|ātmajām
hartāraṃ Rāvaṇaṃ v" âpi Sugrīva|priya|kāriṇaḥ.
47.15 te praviśya tu taṃ bhīmaṃ latā|gulma|samāvṛtam
dadṛśuḥ krūra|karmāṇam asuraṃ sura|nirbhayam.
taṃ dṛṣṭvā vānarā ghoraṃ sthitaṃ śailam iv' âparam
gāḍhaṃ parihitāḥ sarve dṛṣṭvā taṃ parvat'|ôpamam.
so 'pi tān vānarān sarvān «naṣṭāḥ sth' êty» abravīd balī
abhyadhāvata saṃkruddho muṣṭim udyamya saṃhitam.
tam āpatantaṃ sahasā Vāli|putro 'ṅgadas tadā
«Rāvaṇo 'yam iti» jñātvā talen' âbhijaghāna ha
sa Vāli|putr'|âbhihato vaktrāc choṇitam udvaman.
47.20 asuro nyapatad bhūmau paryasta iva parvataḥ
te tu tasmin nirucchvāse vānarā jita|kāśinaḥ
vyacinvan prāyaśas tatra sarvaṃ tad giri|gahvaram.
vicitaṃ tu tataḥ kṛtvā sarve te kānanaṃ punaḥ
anyad ev' âparaṃ ghoraṃ viviśur giri|gahvaram
te vicintya punaḥ khinnā viniṣpatya samāgatāḥ
ek'|ânte vṛkṣa|mūle tu niṣedur dīna|mānasāḥ.

48.1 Ath' Âṅgadas tadā sarvān vānarān idam abravīt
pariśrānto mahā|prājñaḥ samāśvāsya śanair vacaḥ:
«vanāni girayo nadyo durgāṇi gahanāni ca
daryo giri|guhāś c' âiva vicitā naḥ samantataḥ
tatra tatra sah' âsmābhir Jānakī na ca dṛśyate
tad vā rakṣo hṛtā yena Sītā sura|sut'|ôpamā.
kālaś ca no mahān yātaḥ Sugrīvaś c' ôgra|śāsanaḥ
tasmād bhavantaḥ sahitā vicinvantu samantataḥ.
48.5 vihāya tandrīṃ śokaṃ ca nidrāṃ c' âiva samutthitām

were eager to please Sugríva, they found neither Jánaka's daughter nor her abductor, Rávana.

However, as they entered a frightful place covered over 47.15
by vines and thickets, they saw an *ásura* of cruel deeds who feared not even the gods. When the monkeys saw him standing like some terrible mountain, when they saw him looking like a mountain, they all girded their loins tightly. Then the mighty *ásura* said to all these monkeys, "You are lost!" and, raising his clenched fist, he charged them furiously. Thinking, "This must be Rávana," Valin's son Ángada struck him with the palm of his hand as he rushed violently upon them. Struck by Valin's son and vomiting blood from his mouth,
the *ásura* fell to the ground like a mountain overturned. 47.20
When he had breathed his last, those monkeys, with an air of victory, searched nearly every cave there in that mountain.

Exhausted after searching again, they came out and sat down all together in a lonely place at the foot of a tree, dejected at heart.

Now wise Ángada, though exhausted, encouraged all 48.1
the monkeys and softly spoke these words to them:

"Together we have searched here there, and everywhere throughout the forests, mountains, rivers, the deep and inaccessible woods, as well as the mountain caves and caverns; and yet we have not seen anywhere Jánaka's daughter Sita, who is like a daughter of the gods, nor have we seen the *rákshasa* who carried her off. Most of our time has gone by, and Sugríva is stern in his commands. Therefore together

vicinudhvaṃ yathā Sītāṃ paśyāmo Janak'|ātmajām.
anirvedaṃ ca dākṣyaṃ ca manasaś c' âparājayam
kārya|siddhi|karāṇy āhus tasmād etad bravīmy aham.
ady' âp' îdaṃ vanaṃ durgaṃ vicinvantu van'|âukasaḥ.
khedaṃ tyaktvā punaḥ sarvaṃ vanam etad vicīyatām.
avaśyaṃ kriyamāṇasya dṛśyate karmaṇaḥ phalam.
alaṃ nirvedam āgamya na hi no malinaṃ kṣamam!
Sugrīvaḥ krodhano rājā tīkṣṇa|daṇḍaś ca, vānarāḥ,
bhetavyaṃ tasya satataṃ Rāmasya ca mah"|ātmanaḥ.
48.10 hit'|ārtham etad uktaṃ vaḥ kriyatāṃ yadi rocate
ucyatāṃ vā kṣamaṃ yan naḥ sarveṣām eva, vānarāḥ.»
Aṅgadasya vacaḥ śrutvā vacanaṃ Gandhamādanaḥ
uvāc' âvyaktayā vācā pipāsā|śrama|khinnayā:
«sadṛśaṃ khalu vo vākyam Aṅgado yad uvāca ha
hitaṃ c' âiv' ânukūlaṃ ca kriyatām asya bhāṣitam.
punar mārgāmahe śailān kandarāṃś ca darīs tathā
kānanāni ca śūnyāni giri|prasravaṇāni ca.
yath" ôddiṣṭāni sarvāṇi Sugrīveṇa mah"|ātmanā
vicinvantu vanaṃ sarve giri|durgāṇi sarvaśaḥ.»
48.15 tataḥ samutthāya punar vānarās te mahā|balāḥ
Vindhya|kānana|saṃkīrṇāṃ vicerur dakṣiṇāṃ diśam.

you must search everywhere. You must shake off the exhaus- 48.5
tion, grief and sleepiness that has arisen and search so that we may find Jánaka's daughter Sita. They say that cheerfulness, perseverance and mental fortitude produce success in an undertaking. That is why I am telling you this. This very day, forest-dwellers, you must search this inaccessible forest. You must banish dejection and search this entire forest again. If one takes action, one inevitably sees its results. So enough of this yielding to despair! It is not right for us to close our eyes.

Then, too, Sugríva is a wrathful king and inflicts harsh punishment, monkeys. He is always to be feared, as is great Rama.

If it pleases you, do what I have said, which is to your 48.10
advantage. Otherwise you say what is right for all of us, monkeys."

When Gandha·mádana heard these words of Ángada, he responded in a voice rendered weary and indistinct through thirst and exhaustion:

"What Ángada says is surely appropriate, beneficial and favorable to you. We should do as he says. We must explore these mountains, caves, caverns, desolate forests and mountain waterfalls yet again. You must all search the forest and all the inaccessible parts of the mountain as specified by great Sugríva."

So once more the mighty monkeys got up and roamed 48.15
over the southern region, which was densely covered with the forests of the Vindhya range.

te śārad'|âbhra|pratimaṃ śrīmad|rajata|parvatam
śṛṅgavantaṃ darīvantam adhiruhya ca vānarāḥ
tatra lodhra|vanaṃ ramyaṃ sapta|parṇa|vanāni ca
vicinvanto hari|varāḥ Sītā|darśana|kāṅkṣiṇaḥ.
tasy' âgram adhirūḍhās te śrāntā vipula|vikramāḥ
na paśyanti sma Vaidehīṃ Rāmasya mahiṣīṃ priyām.
te tu dṛṣṭi|gataṃ kṛtvā taṃ śailaṃ bahu|kandaram
avārohanta harayo vīkṣamāṇāḥ samantataḥ.
48.20 avaruhya tato bhūmiṃ śrāntā vigata|cetasaḥ
sthitvā muhūrtaṃ tatr' âtha vṛkṣa|mūlam upāśritāḥ.
te muhūrtaṃ samāśvastāḥ kiṃ cid bhagna|pariśramāḥ
punar ev' ôdyatāḥ kṛtsnāṃ mārgituṃ dakṣiṇāṃ diśam.
Hanumat|pramukhās te tu prasthitāḥ plavaga'|rṣabhāḥ
Vindhyam ev' āditas tāvad vicerus te samantataḥ.

49.1 Saha Tār"|Âṅgadābhyāṃ tu saṃgamya Hanumān kapiḥ
vicinoti sma Vindhyasya guhāś ca gahanāni ca
siṃha|śārdūla|juṣṭāś ca guhāś ca paritas tathā
viṣameṣu nag'|êndrasya mahā|prasravaṇeṣu ca.
teṣāṃ tatr' âiva vasatāṃ sa kālo vyatyavartata.
sa hi deśo duranveṣo guhā|gahanavān mahān
tatra Vāyu|sutaḥ sarvaṃ vicinoti sma parvatam.
49.5 paraspareṇa rahitā anyonyasy' âvidūrataḥ
Gajo Gavākṣo Gavayaḥ Śarabho Gandhamādanaḥ
Maindaś ca Dvividaś c' âiva Hanumān Jāmbavān api
Aṅgado yuva|rājaś ca Tāraś ca vana|gocaraḥ
giri|jāl'|āvṛtān deśān mārgitvā dakṣiṇāṃ diśam

Those great monkeys climbed a majestic silver mountain that had peaks and caverns and was bright as an autumn cloud; and they searched a grove of *lodhra* trees and groves of *sapta·parna* trees, hoping to find Sita. But when those very valiant monkeys reached the mountaintop exhausted, they still had not found Vaidéhi, Rama's beloved queen. And when those monkeys had examined that mountain and its
many caves, they descended, looking all about. By the time 48.20
they had descended from there to level ground, they were nearly unconscious with exhaustion, so they stopped there for a while, leaning against the roots of a tree.

After a while they recovered, and when their exhaustion was somewhat dispelled they were ready once more to search the entire southern region. Setting off with Hánuman at their head, those bulls among leaping monkeys began ranging over the Vindhyas on all sides all over again.

Now the monkey Hánuman, along with Tara and Án- 49.1
gada, searched the caves and deep forests of the Vindhya ranges, and also the caverns inhabited by lions and tigers all around on precipices and by the great waterfalls of that king of mountains. While they stayed there, the appointed time passed by. For that vast region with its caves and deep forests was hard to search. There the wind god's son searched the whole mountain.

Separated from one another, but not too far, Gaja, Gavák- 49.5
sha, Gávaya, Shárabha, Gandha·mádana, Mainda, Dvívida, Hánuman, Jámbavan, Ángada the heir apparent and Tara the forest-dweller searched the lands of the south, which are overspread with mountain chains. At length, overcome by

kṣut|pipāsā|parītāś ca śrāntāś ca salil'|ârthinaḥ
avakīrṇaṃ latā|vṛkṣair dadṛśus te mahā|bilam.
tataḥ krauñcāś ca haṃsāś ca sārasāś c' âpi niṣkraman
jal'|ārdrāś cakra|vākāś ca rakt'|âṅgāḥ padma|reṇubhiḥ.
tatas tad bilam āsādya sugandhi dur|atikramam
vismaya|vyagra|manaso babhūvur vānara'|rṣabhāḥ.
49.10 saṃjāta|pariśaṅkās te tad bilaṃ plavag'|ôttamāḥ
abhyapadyanta saṃhṛṣṭās tejovanto mahā|balāḥ.
tataḥ parvata|kūṭ'|ābho Hanumān Mārut'|ātmajaḥ
abravīd vānarān sarvān kāntāra|vana|kovidaḥ:
«giri|jāl'|āvṛtān deśān mārgitvā dakṣiṇāṃ diśam
vayaṃ sarve pariśrāntā na ca paśyāmi Maithilīm.
asmāc c' âpi bilādd haṃsāḥ krauñcāś ca saha sārasaiḥ
jal'|ārdrāś cakra|vākāś ca niṣpatanti sma sarvaśaḥ.
nūnaṃ salilavān atra kūpo vā yadi vā hradaḥ.
tathā c' ême bila|dvāre snigdhās tiṣṭhanti pādapāḥ.»
49.15 ity uktās tad bilaṃ sarve viviśus timir'|āvṛtam.
a|candra|sūryaṃ harayo dadṛśū roma|harṣaṇam.
tatas tasmin bile durge nānā|pādapa|saṃkule
anyonyaṃ sampariṣvajya jagmur yojanam antaram.
te naṣṭa|saṃjñās tṛṣitāḥ saṃbhrāntāḥ salil'|ârthinaḥ
paripetur bile tasmin kaṃ cit kālam atandritāḥ.
te kṛśā dīna|vadanāḥ pariśrāntāḥ plavaṃ|gamāḥ
ālokaṃ dadṛśur vīrā nirāśā jīvite tadā.

hunger and thirst, exhausted and desperate for water, they saw an enormous cavern overgrown with vines and trees.

Out of it flew *krauñcha* birds, geese, sarus cranes and *chakra·vaka* birds, dripping with water, their bodies red with lotus pollen. Reaching that fragrant but impenetrable cavern, those bulls among monkeys were amazed and bewildered.
Their expectations aroused, those splendid, mighty, excel- 49.10
lent monkeys approached that cavern with delight. Then Hánuman, son of the wind god Máruta, huge as a mountain peak, who was familiar with forests and jungles, addressed all the monkeys:

"We are all exhausted from searching the lands of the south, which are overspread with mountain chains; yet we still have not found Máithili. Moreover, geese, *krauñcha* birds, sarus cranes and *chakra·vaka* birds are flying out of this cavern on every side, dripping with water. Then, too, lush trees stand at the entrance to the cavern. Surely there must be a well with water or else a pool in there."

Addressed in this fashion, the monkeys all entered the 49.15
cavern, which was shrouded in darkness. Unlit by moon or sun, it looked terrifying to them.

So, clinging to each other, they walked for a league inside that impenetrable cavern all crowded with various trees. Nearly unconscious, thirsty, bewildered and desperate for water, they wandered tirelessly through that cavern for some time. At last, despairing of their lives, those heroic monkeys, thin, sad-faced and exhausted, saw a light.

tatas taṃ deśam āgamya saumyaṃ vitimiraṃ vanam
dadṛśuḥ kāñcanān vṛkṣān dīpta|vaiśvānara|prabhān
49.20 sālāṃs tālāṃś ca puṃnāgān kakubhān vañjulān dhavān
campakān nāga|vṛkṣāṃś ca karṇikārāṃś ca puṣpitān.
taruṇ'|āditya|saṃkāśān vaidūrya|maya|vedikān
nīla|vaidūrya|varṇāś ca padminīḥ patag'|āvṛtāḥ.
mahadbhiḥ kāñcanair vṛkṣair vṛtaṃ bāl'|ârka|saṃnibhaiḥ
jāta|rūpa|mayair matsyair mahadbhiś ca sakacchapaiḥ
nalinīs tatra dadṛśuḥ prasanna|salil'|āyutāḥ
kāñcanāni vimānāni rājatāni tath" âiva ca.
tapanīya|gavākṣāṇi muktā|jāl'|āvṛtāni ca
haima|rājata|bhaumāni vaidūrya|maṇi|manti ca.
49.25 dadṛśus tatra harayo gṛha|mukhyāni sarvaśaḥ
puṣpitān phalino vṛkṣān pravāla|maṇi|saṃnibhān.
kāñcana|bhramarāṃś c' âiva madhūni ca samantataḥ
maṇi|kāñcana|citrāṇi śayanāny āsanāni ca.
mah"|ârhāṇi ca yānāni dadṛśus te samantataḥ
haima|rājata|kāṃsyānāṃ bhājanānāṃ ca saṃcayān
agarūṇāṃ ca divyānāṃ candanānāṃ ca saṃcayān
śucīny abhyavahāryāṇi mūlāni ca phalāni ca
mah"|ârhāṇi ca pānāni madhūni rasavanti ca
divyānām ambarāṇāṃ ca mah"|ârhāṇāṃ ca saṃcayān
kambalānāṃ ca citrāṇām ajinānāṃ ca saṃcayān.
49.30 tatra tatra vicinvanto bile tatra mahā|prabhāḥ
dadṛśur vānarāḥ śūrāḥ striyaṃ kāṃ cid adūrataḥ.
tāṃ dṛṣṭvā bhṛśa|saṃtrastāś cīra|kṛṣṇ'|âjin'|âmbarām
tāpasīṃ niyat'|āhārāṃ jvalantīm iva tejasā.
tato Hanūmān giri saṃnikāśaḥ
kṛt'|âñjalis tām abhivādya vṛddhāṃ

Soon they reached a pleasant spot, a brightly illuminated
forest; they saw golden trees bright as a blazing fire: *salas* 49.20
and *talas*, *pumnágas*, *kákubhas*, *vánjulas*, *dhavas*, *chámpakas*, *naga·vrikshas* and blossoming *karnikáras*, radiant as the
newly risen sun. Around them were sacrificial platforms
made of emerald, and there were lotus beds the color of
sapphires and emeralds, crowded with birds. There they
saw great golden trees splendid as the rising sun surrounding
lotus ponds with clear waters, filled with turtles and large
fish made of pure gold. And they saw gold and silver palaces
covered with fretworks of pearl, with round windows of
pure gold, and with floors made of gold and silver set with
emeralds.

Everywhere the monkeys saw fine mansions and blos- 49.25
soming, fruit-bearing trees looking like coral set with gems.
And all about were golden bees and honey, and beds and
seats glittering with gems and gold. And on all sides they
saw costly chariots and piles of vessels made of gold, silver
and brass, as well as heaps of aloe wood and heavenly sandalwood. And they saw pure, edible roots and fruit, and
costly drinks, sweet and flavorful; and piles of heavenly,
costly garments, and of bright-colored wool blankets and
black antelope skins.

Searching here and there in that cavern, the splendid, 49.30
heroic monkeys saw a woman not far from them. They saw
that she was a fasting ascetic clothed in bark garments and
a black antelope skin, who seemed to blaze with power, and
they were greatly frightened. Then Hánuman, huge as a
mountain, greeted the old woman with his palms cupped
in reverence and asked her, "Tell us, who are you? And

papraccha, «kā tvaṃ? bhavanaṃ bilaṃ ca
ratnāni c' êmāni, vadasva, kasya?»

50.1 Ity uktvā Hanumāṃs tatra punaḥ kṛṣṇ'|âjin'|âmbarām
abravīt tāṃ mahā|bhāgāṃ tāpasīṃ dharma|cāriṇīm:
«idaṃ praviṣṭāḥ sahasā bilaṃ timira|saṃvṛtam
kṣut|pipāsā|pariśrāntāḥ parikhinnāś ca sarvaśaḥ.
mahad dharaṇyā vivaraṃ praviṣṭāḥ sma pipāsitāḥ
imāṃs tv evaṃ|vidhān bhāvān vividhān adbhut'|ôpamān
dṛṣṭvā vayaṃ pravyathitāḥ saṃbhrāntā naṣṭa|cetasaḥ.
kasy' ême kāñcanā vṛkṣās taruṇ'|āditya|saṃnibhāḥ
śucīny abhyavahāryāṇi mūlāni ca phalāni ca
50.5 kāñcanāni vimānāni rājatāni gṛhāṇi ca
tapanīya|gavākṣāṇi maṇi|jāl'|āvṛtāni ca?
puṣpitāḥ phalavantaś ca puṇyāḥ surabhi|gandhinaḥ
ime jāmbūnada|mayāḥ pādapāḥ kasya tejasā?
kāñcanāni ca padmāni jātāni vimale jale
kathaṃ matsyāś ca sauvarṇā caranti saha kacchapaiḥ?
ātmānam anubhāvaṃ ca kasya c' âitat tapo|balam
ajānatāṃ naḥ sarveṣāṃ sarvam ākhyātum arhasi!»
evam uktā Hanumatā tāpasī dharma|cāriṇī
pratyuvāca Hanūmantaṃ sarva|bhūta|hite ratā:
50.10 «Mayo nāma mahā|tejā māyāvī dānava'|rṣabhaḥ.
ten' êdaṃ nirmitaṃ sarvaṃ māyayā kāñcanaṃ vanam.
purā dānava|mukhyānāṃ Viśvakarmā babhūva ha
yen' êdaṃ kāñcanaṃ divyaṃ nirmitaṃ bhavan'|ôttamam.
sa tu varṣa|sahasrāṇi tapas taptvā mahā|vane

this dwelling, this cavern, these jewels—to whom do they belong?"

WHEN HE HAD spoken in this fashion, Hánuman once 50.1
more addressed that righteous, illustrious ascetic woman, clothed in black antelope skin:

"Exhausted by hunger and thirst, and thoroughly fatigued in every way, we rashly entered this cavern though it was shrouded in darkness. Since we were thirsty, we entered this great opening in the earth. But now that we have seen miraculous objects of such various kinds as these, we are frightened, bewildered and stupefied. Whose are these golden trees, bright as the newly risen sun, and these pure,
edible roots and fruit, and these palaces of gold and houses 50.5
of silver, with round windows of pure gold, and covered with fretworks of precious stones? Whose power created these sacred, sweet-smelling trees of gold, blossoming and bearing fruit, and these golden lotuses in clear water? And how is it that golden fish swim here along with turtles? Please tell us everything—about yourself and your greatness and whose ascetic power this reveals—for we are all ignorant."

Addressed in this way by Hánuman, the righteous ascetic woman, who was devoted to the welfare of all beings, replied:

"There was once a glorious bull among *dánava*s named 50.10
Maya, who possessed magical powers. It was he who fashioned this entire golden forest by magic. He who fashioned this excellent, heavenly, golden dwelling was once the chief architect for the *dánava* leaders. After performing austerities in a great forest for thousands of years, he obtained all

Pitā|mahād varaṃ lebhe sarvam Auśanasaṃ dhanam.
vidhāya sarvaṃ balavān sarva|kām'|ēśvaras tadā
uvāsa sukhitaḥ kālaṃ kaṃ cid asmin mahā|vane.
tam apsarasi Hemāyāṃ saktaṃ dānava|puṃgavam
vikramy' âiv' âśaniṃ gṛhya jaghān' ēśaḥ Puraṃdaraḥ.
50.15 idaṃ ca Brahmaṇā dattaṃ Hemāyai vanam uttamam
śāśvataḥ kāma|bhogaś ca gṛhaṃ c' êdaṃ hiraṇ|mayam.
duhitā Merusāvarṇer ahaṃ tasyāḥ Svayaṃprabhā
idaṃ rakṣāmi bhavanaṃ Hemāyā, vānar'|ôttama.
mama priya|sakhī Hemā nṛtta|gīta|viśāradā.
tayā datta|varā c' âsmi rakṣāmi bhavan'|ôttamam.
kiṃ kāryaṃ kasya vā hetoḥ kāntārāṇi prapadyatha?
kathaṃ c' êdaṃ vanaṃ durgaṃ yuṣmābhir upalakṣitam?
imāny abhyavahāryāṇi mūlāni ca phalāni ca
bhuktvā pītvā ca pānīyaṃ sarvaṃ me vaktum arhatha!»

51.1 Atha tān abravīt sarvān viśrāntān hari|yūthapān
idaṃ vacanam ek'|âgrā tāpasī dharma|cāriṇī:
«vānarā, yadi vaḥ khedaḥ pranaṣṭaḥ phala|bhakṣaṇāt
yadi c' âitan mayā śrāvyaṃ śrotum icchāmi, kathyatām!»
tasyās tad vacanaṃ śrutvā Hanumān Mārut'|ātmajaḥ
ārjavena yathā|tattvam ākhyātum upacakrame:
«rājā sarvasya lokasya Mahendra|Varuṇ'|ôpamaḥ
Rāmo Dāśarathiḥ śrīmān praviṣṭo Daṇḍakā|vanam
51.5 Lakṣmaṇena saha bhrātrā Vaidehyā c' âpi bhāryayā
tasya bhāryā Janasthānād Rāvaṇena hṛtā balāt.
vīras tasya sakhā rājñaḥ Sugrīvo nāma vānaraḥ

the wealth of Úshanas as a boon from Grandfather Brahma. Mighty master of every object of his desire, he created all of this and then lived happily in this great forest for some time. But the lord Indra, smasher of citadels, took his thunderbolt and attacked and killed that bull among *dánava*s, who was attached to the *ápsara*s Hema. And Brahma bestowed upon 50.15
Hema this wonderful forest, this golden mansion and the everlasting enjoyment of every object of her desire.

Best of monkeys, I am Svayam·prabha, daughter of Meru·savárni. I watch over this dwelling of Hema's. My dear friend Hema is skillful at dancing and singing. Granted a boon by her, I watch over this fine dwelling. But why and for what purpose have you come to such a wilderness? And how did you discover this inaccessible forest? After you have eaten these edible roots and fruit and drunk some water, you must tell me everything."

THEN, WHEN ALL the monkey-troop leaders had rested, 51.1
the ascetic woman, devoted to righteousness, her thoughts focused, said these words to them: "Monkeys, if your fatigue has been dispelled by eating fruit, and if your story is proper for me to hear, I wish to hear it. Please tell it." Hearing these words of hers, Hánuman, son of Máruta the wind god, began to tell his tale frankly and truthfully.

"Majestic Rama Dásharathi, king of all the world, the equal of great Indra or Váruna, entered the Dándaka forest
with his brother Lákshmana and his wife Vaidéhi. His wife 51.5
was forcibly abducted from Jana·sthana by Rávana. It was a friend of that king, the heroic monkey named Sugríva, king

rājā vānara|mukhyānāṃ yena prasthāpitā vayam
‹Agastya|caritām āśāṃ dakṣiṇāṃ Yama|rakṣitām
sah' âibhir vānarair mukhyair Aṅgada|pramukhair vayam.
Rāvaṇaṃ sahitāḥ sarve rākṣasaṃ kāma|rūpiṇam
Sītayā saha Vaidehyā mārgadhvam iti› coditāḥ.
vicitya tu vayaṃ sarve samagrāṃ dakṣiṇāṃ diśam
bubhukṣitāḥ pariśrāntā vṛkṣa|mūlam upāśritāḥ.
51.10 vivarṇa|vadanāḥ sarve sarve dhyāna|parāyaṇāḥ.
n' âdhigacchāmahe pāraṃ magnāś cintā|mah"|ârṇave.
cārayantas tataś cakṣur dṛṣṭavanto mahad bilam
latā|pādapa|saṃchannaṃ timireṇa samāvṛtam.
asmādd haṃsā jala|klinnāḥ pakṣaiḥ salila|reṇubhiḥ
kurarāḥ sārasāś c' âiva niṣpatanti patatriṇaḥ
‹sādhv atra praviśām' êti› mayā t' ûktāḥ plavaṃ|gamāḥ.
teṣām api hi sarveṣām anumānam upāgatam
‹gacchāmaḥ praviśām' êti› bhartṛ|kārya|tvar"|ânvitāḥ.
tato gāḍhaṃ nipatitā gṛhya hastau parasparam
idaṃ praviṣṭāḥ sahasā bilaṃ timira|saṃvṛtam.
51.15 etan naḥ kāryam etena kṛtyena vayam āgatāḥ.
tvāṃ c' âiv' ôpagatāḥ sarve paridyūnā bubhukṣitāḥ.
ātithya|dharma|dattāni mūlāni ca phalāni ca
asmābhir upabhuktāni bubhukṣā|paripīḍitaiḥ.
yat tvayā rakṣitāḥ sarve mriyamāṇā bubhukṣayā,
brūhi, pratyupakār'|ârthaṃ kiṃ te kurvantu vānarāḥ?»
evam uktā tu sarvajñā vānarais taiḥ Svayaṃprabhā
pratyuvāca tataḥ sarvān idaṃ vānara|yūthapān
«sarveṣāṃ parituṣṭ" âsmi vānarāṇāṃ tarasvinām
carantyā mama dharmeṇa na kāryam iha kena cit.»

of the monkey chiefs, who dispatched us with these prominent monkeys headed by Ángada to the southern region, which, guarded by Yama, is traversed by Agástya. We were all exhorted to hunt together for the *rákshasa* Rávana, who changes form at will, and for Sita Vaidéhi.

But when we all had searched the entire southern region, we rested at the foot of a tree, starving and completely
exhausted. All of us were pale-faced and lost in brooding 51.10
thought. Sunk in an ocean of care, we could not reach its far shore. Then, casting our gaze about, we spied an enormous cavern concealed by vines and trees and shrouded in darkness. Out of it flew birds—geese, ospreys and sarus cranes—dripping with water and with droplets of water on their wings. So I said to the monkeys, 'Very well, let's go in!' All of them agreed. In their haste to accomplish their master's purpose, they cried, 'Let's go! Let's go in!'

Then, tightly grasping each other's hands, we clambered down. And so we rashly entered this cavern shrouded in
darkness. This was our purpose. With this object we came. 51.15
And then all of us, emaciated and starving, came upon you. In keeping with the laws of hospitality, you gave us, tormented by hunger, roots and fruit, which we have eaten. Since you saved us when we were all dying of hunger, you must now say what the monkeys can do to repay your kindness."

When the monkeys had addressed Svayam·prabha in this way, the all-knowing woman replied to all the monkey-troop leaders: "I am well pleased with all of you swift monkeys, but since I am engaged in religious practices, I have no need of anything."

52.1 EVAM UKTAḤ śubhaṃ vākyaṃ tāpasyā dharma|saṃhitam
uvāca Hanumān vākyaṃ tām anindita|ceṣṭitām:
«śaraṇaṃ tvāṃ prapannāḥ smaḥ sarve vai, dharma|cāriṇi,
yaḥ kṛtaḥ samayo 'smākaṃ Sugrīveṇa mah"|ātmanā
sa tu kālo vyatikrānto bile ca parivartatām.
sā tvam asmād bilād ghorād uttārayitum arhasi!
tasmāt Sugrīva|vacanād atikrāntān gat'|āyuṣaḥ
trātum arhasi naḥ sarvān Sugrīva|bhaya|śaṅkitān.
52.5 mahac ca kāryam asmābhiḥ kartavyaṃ, dharma|cāriṇi,
tac c' âpi na kṛtaṃ kāryam asmābhir iha vāsibhiḥ.»
evam uktā Hanumatā tāpasī vākyam abravīt:
«jīvatā duṣkaraṃ manye praviṣṭena nivartitum.
tapasas tu prabhāvena niyam'|ôpārjitena ca
sarvān eva bilād asmād uddhariṣyāmi vānarān.
nimīlayata cakṣūṃṣi sarve, vānara|puṃgavāḥ,
na hi niṣkramituṃ śakyam a|nimīlita|locanaiḥ.»
tataḥ saṃmīlitāḥ sarve sukumār'|âṅgulaiḥ karaiḥ
sahasā pidadhur dṛṣṭiṃ hṛṣṭā gamana|kāṅkṣiṇaḥ.
52.10 vānarās tu mah"|ātmāno hasta|ruddha|mukhās tadā
nimeṣ'|ântara|mātreṇa bilād uttāritās tayā.
tatas tān vānarān sarvāṃs tāpasī dharma|cāriṇī
niḥsṛtān viṣamāt tasmāt samāśvāsy' êdam abravīt:
«eṣa Vindhyo giriḥ śrīmān nānā|druma|lat"|āyutaḥ.
eṣa Prasravaṇaḥ śailaḥ sāgaro 'yaṃ mah"|ôdadhiḥ.
svasti vo 'stu, gamiṣyāmi bhavanaṃ, vānara'|rṣabhāḥ.»
ity uktvā tad bilaṃ śrīmat praviveśa Svayaṃprabhā.

When the ascetic woman of blameless actions had spo- 52.1
ken those fine words consistent with righteousness, Hánuman made this reply:

"We have all come to you for refuge, righteous woman.
The time allotted to us by great Sugríva elapsed while we
have been wandering about in this cavern. Please deliver us
from this dreadful cavern. Since we have transgressed Sugríva's command, we are as good as dead. Please save us,
for we are all overwhelmed with our terror of Sugríva. We 52.5
have a great task to accomplish, righteous woman, but we
cannot accomplish that task if we stay here."

Addressed in this way by Hánuman, the ascetic woman
replied, "It is difficult, I believe, for anyone who has entered
here to get out alive. However, by the power of asceticism
that I have gained through my religious penances, I shall
rescue all of you monkeys from this cavern. Close your eyes,
all you bulls among monkeys, for those whose eyes are not
shut cannot get out."

Delighted and eager to escape, they all quickly closed
their eyes and covered them with their delicate-fingered
hands. And once they had covered their faces with their 52.10
hands, she delivered the great monkeys from the cavern in
the twinkling of an eye. Then the righteous ascetic woman
reassured all those monkeys who had emerged from that
difficult place and said this:

"This is the majestic Vindhya mountain, with all its different trees and vines. There is Mount Prasrávana. And the
great body of water over here is the sea. Farewell, bulls
among monkeys. I must return home." And with these
words, Svayam·prabha reentered that magnificent cavern.

tatas te dadṛśur ghoraṃ sāgaraṃ Varuṇ'|ālayam
apāram abhigarjantaṃ ghorair ūrmibhir ākulam.
52.15 Mayasya māyā|vihitaṃ giri|durgaṃ vicinvatām
teṣāṃ māso vyatikrānto yo rājñā samayaḥ kṛtaḥ.
Vindhyasya tu gireḥ pāde saṃprapuṣpita|pādape
upaviśya mahā|bhāgāś cintām āpedire tadā.
tataḥ puṣp'|âtibhār'|âgrāl latā|śata|samāvṛtān
drumān vāsantikān dṛṣṭvā babhūvur bhaya|śaṅkitāḥ.
te vasantam anuprāptaṃ prativedya parasparam
naṣṭa|saṃdeśa|kāl'|ârthā nipetur dharaṇī|tale.
sa tu siṃha'|ṛṣabha|skandhaḥ pīn'|āyata|bhujaḥ kapiḥ
yuva|rājo mahā|prājña Aṅgado vākyam abravīt:
52.20 «śāsanāt kapi|rājasya vayaṃ sarve vinirgatāḥ
māsaḥ pūrṇo bila|sthānāṃ, harayaḥ, kiṃ na budhyate?
tasminn atīte kāle tu Sugrīveṇa kṛte svayam
prāy'|ôpaveśanaṃ yuktaṃ sarveṣāṃ ca van'|âukasām.
tīkṣṇaḥ prakṛtyā Sugrīvaḥ svāmi|bhāve vyavasthitaḥ
na kṣamiṣyati naḥ sarvān aparādha|kṛto gatān.
apravṛttau ca Sītāyāḥ pāpam eva kariṣyati
tasmāt kṣamam ih' âdy' âiva prāy'|ôpaveśanaṃ hi naḥ
tyaktvā putrāṃś ca dārāṃś ca dhanāni ca gṛhāṇi ca
yāvan na ghātayed rājā sarvān pratigatān itaḥ:
vadhen' âpratirūpeṇa śreyān mṛtyur ih' âiva naḥ.
52.25 na c' âhaṃ yauvarājyena Sugrīveṇ' âbhiṣecitaḥ
nar'|êndreṇ' âbhiṣikto 'smi Rāmeṇ' âkliṣṭa|karmaṇā.

And so the monkeys beheld the terrible ocean, abode of Váruna, boundless, wildly roaring, agitated by terrible waves. Now, while they had been searching Maya's moun- 52.15
tain stronghold constructed by magic, the month fixed by the king as a time limit had elapsed. So as the illustrious monkeys sat on a foothill of the Vindhya mountain amid trees in full flower, they fell prey to anxiety. Seeing the trees with their tops laden with spring blossoms and covered over by hundreds of creepers, they became frightened. Telling each other that it was spring, they slumped to the ground because they had not achieved their object within the allotted time. Then Ángada, the heir apparent, a wise monkey with long, full arms and shoulders like a lion's or a bull's, said these words:

"We have all departed on account of the monkey-king's 52.20
instructions. Don't you realize, monkeys, that an entire month went by while we were in the cavern? Since the time allotted by Sugríva himself has passed, it would be proper for all of us forest-dwelling monkeys to fast to death.

Sugríva, who has been appointed as our master, is harsh by nature; because we have offended against him, he will not forgive any of us when we go back. If we have no news of Sita, he will do a great evil. Therefore it would be fitting for us to abandon our sons, wives, wealth and homes and fast to death this very day, rather than all be put to death by the king on our return. Better death right here than shameful execution. It was not Sugríva who had me consecrated as 52.25
heir apparent; rather, it was the lord of men, Rama, untiring in action, who consecrated me. So when the king, who is already hostile to me, discovers my transgression, he will

sa pūrvaṃ baddha|vairo māṃ rājā dṛṣṭvā vyatikramam
ghātayiṣyati daṇḍena tīkṣṇena kṛta|niścayaḥ.
kiṃ me suhṛdbhir vyasanaṃ paśyadbhir jīvit'|ântare?
ih' âiva prāyam āsiṣye puṇye sāgara|rodhasi.»
etac chrutvā kumāreṇa yuva|rājena bhāṣitam
sarve te vānara|śreṣṭhāḥ karuṇaṃ vākyam abruvan:
«tīkṣṇaḥ prakṛtyā Sugrīvaḥ priyā|saktaś ca Rāghavaḥ
adṛṣṭāyāṃ ca Vaidehyāṃ dṛṣṭv" âsmāṃś ca samāgatān
52.30 Rāghava|priya|kām'|ârthaṃ ghātayiṣyaty asaṃśayam
na kṣamaṃ c' âparāddhānāṃ gamanaṃ svāmi|pārśvataḥ.»
plavaṃ|gamānāṃ tu bhay'|ârditānāṃ
śrutvā vacas Tāra idaṃ babhāṣe:
«alaṃ viṣādena! bilaṃ praviśya
vasāma sarve yadi rocate vaḥ.
idaṃ hi māyā|vihitaṃ su|durgamaṃ
prabhūta|vṛkṣ'|ôdaka|bhojya|peyaṃ
ih' âsti no n' âiva bhayaṃ Puraṃdarān
na Rāghavād vānara|rājato 'pi vā.»
śrutv" Âṅgadasy' âpi vaco 'nukūlaṃ
ūcuś ca sarve harayaḥ pratītāḥ:
«yathā na hanyema tathā|vidhānam
asaktam ady' âiva vidhīyatāṃ naḥ!»

resolve upon a harsh punishment and have me killed. How would it be for my friends to witness such a calamity at my life's end? No, I shall sit right here fasting to death on the holy shore of the sea."

Now, when all those great monkeys heard what the prince and heir apparent said, they replied piteously:

"Sugríva is harsh by nature, and Rághava is devoted to his beloved. When Sugríva sees that we have come back without
finding Vaidéhi, he will undoubtedly have us killed out of a 52.30
desire to please Rághava. Besides, it is not proper for those who have offended their master to return to his side."

When he heard the words of the fearful monkeys, Tara said, "Enough of this despondency! If you like, we can all go back into the cavern and live there. Constructed by magic, it is quite inaccessible and has plentiful water, food, drink and trees. There we will be safe even from Indra, smasher of citadels, let alone from Rághava or the king of monkeys."

Pleased at hearing words agreeable also to Ángada, the monkeys all said, "Let us at once and without delay devise some means whereby we will not be killed."

53–54
DESPAIR OF DISCOVERY

53.1 Tathā bruvati Tāre tu tār"|âdhipati|varcasi
atha mene hṛtaṃ rājyaṃ Hanumān Aṅgadena tat.
buddhyā hy aṣṭ'|âṅgayā yuktaṃ catur|bala|samanvitam
caturdaśa|guṇaṃ mene Hanumān Vālinaḥ sutam
āpūryamāṇaṃ śaśvac ca tejo|bala|parākramaiḥ
śaśinaṃ śukla|pakṣ'|ādau vardhamānam iva śriyā
Bṛhaspati|samaṃ buddhyā vikrame sadṛśaṃ pituḥ
śuśrūṣamāṇaṃ Tārasya Śukrasy' êva Puraṃdaram.
53.5 bhartur arthe pariśrāntaṃ sarva|śāstra|viśāradam
abhisaṃdhātum ārebhe Hanumān Aṅgadaṃ tataḥ.
sa caturṇām upāyānāṃ tṛtīyam upavarṇayan
bhedayām āsa tān sarvān vānarān vākya|saṃpadā.
teṣu sarveṣu bhinneṣu tato 'bhīṣayad Aṅgadam
bhīṣaṇair bahubhir vākyaiḥ kop'|ôpāya|samanvitaiḥ:
«tvaṃ samarthataraḥ pitrā yuddhe, Tāreya, vai dhuram
dṛḍhaṃ dhārayituṃ śaktaḥ kapi|rājyaṃ yathā pitā.
nityam asthira|cittā hi kapayo, hari|puṃgava,
n' ājñāpyaṃ viṣahiṣyanti putra|dārān vinā tvayā.
53.10 tvāṃ n' âite hy anuyuñjeyuḥ, pratyakṣaṃ pravadāmi te.
yath" âyaṃ Jāmbavān Nīlaḥ Suhotraś ca mahā|kapiḥ
na hy ahaṃ ta ime sarve sāma|dān'|ādibhir guṇaiḥ
daṇḍena na tvayā śakyāḥ Sugrīvād apakarṣitum.
vigṛhy' āsanam apy āhur durbalena balīyasaḥ.
ātma rakṣā|karas tasmān na vigṛhṇīta durbalaḥ.
yāṃ c' êmāṃ manyase dhātrīm etad bilam iti śrutam

Now, as Tara, splendid as the lord of stars, was speak- 53.1
ing in this way, Hánuman thought that Ángada had taken over the kingship. Hánuman believed that Valin's son possessed the eight kinds of intelligence, the four strengths and the fourteen qualities; that he was constantly increasing in power, strength and prowess, like the moon growing in majesty at the start of the bright fortnight; and that he was like his father in valor, equal to Brihas·pati in intelligence, and as attentive to Tara as Indra, smasher of citadels, was to Shukra.

So Hánuman began to try to win over Ángada, who, 53.5
though skilled in every science, was weary of his master's purpose. Resorting to the third of the four expedients, he sowed dissension among all those monkeys by a wealth of arguments. Then, when they were all at odds with one another, he intimidated Ángada with many frightening arguments combining anger and expediency.

"Son of Tará, you are more capable than your father. And, like your father, you could take firm control of the vanguard in battle and of the kingdom of the monkeys. But monkeys are always fickle-minded, bull among monkeys. Without their sons and wives, they will not tolerate being ordered
about by you. I shall speak out clearly to you: They will not 53.10
enter your service. You will not be able to alienate Jámbavan, Nila, the great monkey Suhótra, me, and all these other monkeys from Sugríva with such expedients as conciliation and gifts, nor by punishment. They say that when a stronger person has waged war against a weaker one, he can then sit quietly, but not the reverse. Therefore, to save himself, a weak person should not wage war. And this cavern you have

etal Lakṣmaṇa bāṇānām īṣat|kāryam vidāraṇe.
svalpaṃ hi kṛtam Indreṇa kṣipatā hy aśaniṃ purā,
Lakṣmaṇo niśitair bāṇair bhindyāt patra|puṭaṃ yathā.
Lakṣmaṇasya ca nārācā bahavaḥ santi tad|vidhāḥ.
53.15 avasthāne yad" âiva tvam āsiṣyasi, paraṃ|tapa,
tad" âiva harayaḥ sarve tyakṣyanti kṛta|niścayāḥ.
smarantaḥ putra|dārāṇāṃ nity'|ôdvignā bubhukṣitāḥ
kheditā duḥkha|śayyābhis tvāṃ kariṣyanti pṛṣṭhataḥ.
sa tvaṃ hīnaḥ suhṛdbhiś ca hita|kāmaiś ca bandhubhiḥ
tṛṇād api bhṛś'|ôdvignaḥ spandamānād bhaviṣyasi.
na ca jātu na hiṃsyus tvāṃ ghorā Lakṣmaṇa|sāyakāḥ
apavṛttaṃ jighāṃsanto mahā|vegā durāsadāḥ.
asmābhis tu gataṃ sārdhaṃ vinītavad upasthitam
ānupūrvyāt tu Sugrīvo rājye tvāṃ sthāpayiṣyati.
53.20 dharma|kāmaḥ pitṛvyas te prīti|kāmo dṛḍha|vrataḥ
śuciḥ satya|pratijñaś ca nā tvāṃ jātu jighāṃsati.
priya|kāmaś ca te mātus tad|arthaṃ c' âsya jīvitam
tasy' âpatyaṃ ca n' âsty anyat tasmād, Aṅgada, gamyatām!»

54.1 ŚRUTVĀ HANUMATO vākyaṃ praśritaṃ dharma|saṃhitam
svāmi|satkāra|saṃyuktam Aṅgado vākyam abravīt:
«sthairyaṃ sarv'|ātmanā śaucam ānṛśaṃsyam ath' ārjavam
vikramaiś c' âiva dhairyaṃ ca Sugrīve n' ôpapadyate.
bhrātur jyeṣṭhasya yo bhāryāṃ jīvito mahiṣīṃ priyām
dharmeṇa mātaraṃ yas tu svīkaroti jugupsitaḥ

been hearing about, which you believe is your protection, would be easily split open by Lákshmana's arrows.

Very little damage was done long ago by Indra when he hurled his thunderbolt. But Lákshmana would tear it open with his sharp arrows as if it were a leaf-cup. And Lákshmana has many such iron arrows. No sooner would you take up 53.15
your position, scorcher of your foes, than all the monkeys will make up their minds to desert. Remembering their sons and wives, constantly anxious, hungry and distressed by the difficult conditions, they will turn their backs on you. Deprived of well-wishing friends and relations, you will be terrified even by a quivering blade of grass. Nor will Lákshmana's swift and terrible arrows, unbearable and deadly, fail to strike you once you swerve from your duty.

But if you go with us and approach Sugríva humbly, he will establish you in the kingship through regular succession. Your paternal uncle wishes to do right and desires your 53.20
affection. Firm in his vows, honest and true to his promise, he would never want to kill you. And he wishes to please your mother: that is the sole purpose of his life. Moreover, he has no other offspring. Therefore, Ángada, you should go back."

Upon hearing Hánuman's polite words, which were 54.1
consistent with righteousness and full of reverence for his master, Ángada replied:

"Steadfastness, absolute integrity, benevolence, uprightness, valor and firmness are not to be found in Sugríva. That disgusting person who appropriated his living elder brother's beloved wife and queen, who is by rights his mo-

kathaṃ sa dharmaṃ jānīte yena bhrātrā durātmanā
yuddhāy' âbhiniyuktena bilasya pihitaṃ mukham?
54.5 satyāt pāṇi|gṛhītaś ca kṛta|karmā mahā|yaśāḥ
vismṛto Rāghavo yena sa kasya sukṛtaṃ smaret?
Lakṣmaṇasya bhayād yena n' âdharma|bhaya|bhīruṇā
ādiṣṭā mārgituṃ Sītāṃ dharmam asmin kathaṃ bhavet?
tasmin pāpe kṛtaghne tu smṛti|hīne cal'|ātmani
āryaḥ ko viśvasej jātu tat|kulīno jijīviṣuḥ?
rājye putraṃ pratiṣṭhāpya sa|guṇo nirguṇo 'pi vā
kathaṃ śatru|kulīnaṃ māṃ Sugrīvo jīvayiṣyati?
bhinna|mantro 'parāddhaś ca hīna|śaktiḥ kathaṃ hy aham
Kiṣkindhāṃ prāpya jīveyam anātha iva durbalaḥ?
54.10 upāṃśu|daṇḍena hi māṃ bandhanen' ôpapādayet
śaṭhaḥ krūro nṛśaṃsaś ca Sugrīvo rājya|kāraṇāt.
bandhanāc c' âvasādān me śreyaḥ prāy'|ôpaveśanam.
anujānīta māṃ sarve gṛhān gacchantu, vānarāḥ!
ahaṃ vaḥ pratijānāmi na gamiṣyāmy ahaṃ purīm.
ih' âiva prāyam āsiṣye. śreyo maraṇam eva me.
abhivādana|pūrvaṃ tu rājā kuśalam eva ca
vācyas tato yavīyān me Sugrīvo vānar'|ēśvaraḥ.
ārogya|pūrvaṃ kuśalaṃ vācyā mātā Rumā ca me.
mātaraṃ c' âiva me Tārām āśvāsayitum arhatha.
54.15 prakṛtyā priya|putrā sā sānukrośā tapasvinī
vinaṣṭaṃ mām iha śrutvā vyaktaṃ hāsyati jīvitam.»

ther; the evil person who blocked the mouth of the cave when his brother had ordered him to fight—how would he know what is right? To whom would he ever be grateful, 54.5
when he gave his hand in a solemn vow of mutual assistance and then forgot all about illustrious Rághava once he had received his help? How could there be any righteousness in someone who ordered us to search for Sita only out of fear of Lákshmana, not out of fear of unrighteousness? What decent member of his family who wishes to stay alive would ever trust in that wicked, forgetful, fickle-minded ingrate? And whether he has good qualities or not, once Sugríva has installed his son as king how could he permit me, his enemy's son, to live?

Since my plan has been disclosed and I have offended against him, how could I, powerless and weak as an orphan, survive once I reach Kishkíndha? Or, for the sake of the 54.10
kingship, that deceitful, cruel and crafty Sugríva may inflict on me a secret punishment like imprisonment. It is better for me to fast to death than suffer imprisonment and despair. So bid me farewell, all you monkeys, and go home. I solemnly vow to you that I will not go back to the city. I will sit right here and fast to death. Death alone is best for me.

But you must respectfully salute my younger father, King Sugríva, lord of the monkeys, and wish him well. And you must wish my mother Ruma health and good fortune. Also, please console my mother Tará. By her very nature that poor 54.15
woman is fond of her son and full of compassion, so when she hears that I have died here, she will surely give up her life." This much he said, and then, respectfully saluting his

etāvad uktvā vacanaṃ vṛddhān apy abhivādya ca
saṃviveś' Âṅgado bhūmau rudan darbheṣu durmanāḥ.
tasya saṃviśatas tatra rudanto vānara'|rṣabhāḥ
nayanebhyaḥ pramumucur uṣṇaṃ vai vāri duḥkhitāḥ.
Sugrīvaṃ c' âiva nindantaḥ praśaṃsantaś ca Vālinam
parivāry' Âṅgadaṃ sarve vyavasyan prāyam āsitum.
mataṃ tad Vāli|putrasya vijñāya plavaga'|rṣabhāḥ
upaspṛśy' ôdakaṃ sarve prāṅ|mukhāḥ samupāviśan
dakṣiṇ'|âgreṣu darbheṣu udak|tīraṃ samāśritāḥ.
54.20 sa saṃviśadbhir bahubhir mahī|dharo
mah''|âdri|kūṭa|pramitaiḥ plavaṃ|gamaiḥ
babhūva saṃnādita|nirjhar'|ântaro
bhṛśaṃ nadadbhir jaladair iv' ôlbaṇaiḥ.

elders, Ángada, dispirited and weeping, sat down on sacred *darbha* grass spread on the ground.

And as he sat there, the bulls among monkeys were saddened and wept, shedding hot tears from their eyes. Blaming Sugríva and praising Valin, they all surrounded Ángada and resolved to fast to death also. And so, once they had learned the intention of Valin's son, all those bulls among monkeys sipped water and, assembling on the northern shore of the sea, sat down facing east on sacred *darbha* grass whose tips pointed to the south.

Huge as mountain peaks, the many monkeys sitting there 54.20
roared so loudly that the mountain with its streams and caverns seemed to fill with the thundering of mighty storm clouds.

55–62
SAMPĀTI'S STORY

55.1 UPAVIṢṬĀS TU te sarve yasmin prāyaṃ giri|sthale
harayo gṛdhra|rājaś ca taṃ deśam upacakrame.
Sampātir nāma nāṃnā tu cira|jīvī vihaṃ|gamaḥ,
bhrātā Jaṭāyuṣaḥ śrīmān prakhyāta|bala|pauruṣaḥ.
kandarād abhiniṣkramya sa Vindhyasya mahā|gireḥ
upaviṣṭān harīn dṛṣṭvā hṛṣṭ'|ātmā giram abravīt:
«vidhiḥ kila naraṃ loke vidhānen' ânuvartate.
yath" âyaṃ vihito bhakṣyaś cirān mahyam upāgataḥ.
55.5 param|parāṇāṃ bhakṣiṣye vānarāṇāṃ mṛtaṃ mṛtam.»
uvāc' âivaṃ vacaḥ pakṣī tān nirīkṣya plavaṃ|gamān.
tasya tad vacanaṃ śrutvā bhakṣa|lubdhasya pakṣiṇaḥ
Aṅgadaḥ param'|āyasto Hanūmantam ath' âbravīt:
«paśya Sīt"|âpadeśena sākṣād Vaivasvato Yamaḥ
imaṃ deśam anuprāpto vānarāṇāṃ vipattaye.
Rāmasya na kṛtaṃ kāryaṃ rājño na ca vacaḥ kṛtam
harīṇām iyam ajñātā vipattiḥ sahas" āgatā.
Vaidehyāḥ priya|kāmena kṛtaṃ karma Jaṭāyuṣā
gṛdhra|rājena yat tatra śrutaṃ vas tad aśeṣataḥ.
55.10 tathā sarvāṇi bhūtāni tiryag|yoni|gatāny api
priyaṃ kurvanti Rāmasya tyaktvā prāṇān yathā vayam.
Rāghav'|ârthe pariśrāntā vayaṃ saṃtyakta|jīvitāḥ
kāntārāṇi prapannāḥ sma na ca paśyāma Maithilīm.

Now, the king of the vultures happened to come to that very place on the mountain where all those monkeys sat fasting to death. Sampáti was his name; and he was a long-lived, majestic bird famous for his strength and valor. He was the brother of Jatáyus. Emerging from a cave in the great Vindhya mountain, he spied the monkeys sitting there, and in his delight he spoke these words: 55.1

"They say that in this world a man's destiny inevitably follows him. Accordingly this food ordained for me has
come to me at long last. I shall eat these monkeys one 55.5
after another as they die." So said the bird upon seeing the monkeys.

But when Ángada heard these words of that bird who was greedy for food, he was deeply distressed and said to Hánuman:

"Look! With Sita as a pretext, Yama Vaivásvata, the god of death, has come to this place in person to destroy the monkeys. Rama's purpose has not been accomplished nor has the king's command been carried out. And now this unexpected calamity has suddenly befallen the monkeys. You have heard in its entirety the deed accomplished by
the vulture-king Jatáyus in his desire to help Vaidéhi. So it 55.10
is that all creatures, even those born as mere animals, will give up their lives as we are doing to help Rama. Worn out for Rághava's sake, we have given up our lives. We have ventured into the wilderness but have not found Máithili.

sa sukhī gṛdhra|rājas tu Rāvaṇena hato raṇe.
muktaś ca Sugrīva|bhayād gataś ca paramāṃ gatim.
Jaṭāyuṣo vināśena rājño Daśarathasya ca
haraṇena ca Vaidehyāḥ saṃśayaṃ harayo gatāḥ.
Rāma|Lakṣmaṇayor vāsām araṇye saha Sītayā
Rāghavasya ca bāṇena Vālinaś ca tathā vadhaḥ
55.15 Rāma|kopād aśeṣāṇāṃ rākṣasānāṃ tathā vadhaḥ
Kaikeyyā vara|dānena idaṃ hi vikṛtaṃ kṛtam.»
tat tu śrutvā tadā vākyam Aṅgadasya mukh'|ôdgatam
abravīd vacanaṃ gṛdhras tīkṣṇa|tuṇḍo mahā|svanaḥ:
«ko 'yaṃ girā ghoṣayati prāṇaiḥ priyatarasya me
Jaṭāyuṣo vadhaṃ bhrātuḥ kampayann iva me manaḥ?
katham āsīj Janasthāne yuddhaṃ rākṣasa|gṛdhrayoḥ?
nāma|dheyam idaṃ bhrātuś cirasy' âdya mayā śrutam.
yavīyaso guṇajñasya ślāghanīyasya vikramaiḥ
tad iccheyam ahaṃ śrotuṃ vināśaṃ, vānara'|rṣabhāḥ!
55.20 bhrātur Jaṭāyuṣas tasya Janasthāna|nivāsinaḥ
tasy' âiva ca mama bhrātuḥ sakhā Daśarathaḥ katham
yasya Rāmaḥ priyaḥ putro jyeṣṭho guru|jana|priyaḥ?
sūry'|âṃśu|dagdha|pakṣa|tvān na śaknomi visarpitum
iccheyaṃ parvatād asmād avatartum, ariṃ|damāḥ!»

56.1 ŚOKĀD BHRAṢṬA|svaram api śrutvā te hari|yūthapāḥ
śrad|dadhur n' âiva tad|vākyaṃ karmaṇā tasya śaṅkitāḥ.
te prāyam upaviṣṭās tu dṛṣṭvā gṛdhraṃ plavaṃ|gamāḥ
cakrur buddhiṃ tadā raudrāṃ «sarvān no bhakṣayiṣyati.

That vulture-king was fortunate, for he was killed in battle by Rávana. Thus he was free of fear of Sugríva and has attained the highest state. Through the deaths of Jatáyus and King Dasha·ratha, and through the abduction of Vaidéhi, we monkeys have fallen into this danger. The sojourn of Rama and Lákshmana in the forest with Sita, the slaying of Valin with Rághava's arrow, the slaughter of all the *rák-* 55.15
shasas through the wrath of Rama—all this misfortune was caused by the granting of boons to Kaikéyi."

Now, when the sharp-beaked vulture heard these words that had come from Ángada's mouth, he spoke in a loud voice:

"Who is this who troubles my heart by announcing in such words the death of my brother Jatáyus, who is dearer to me than life itself? How did there come to be a battle in Jana·sthana between the *rákshasa* and the vulture? It has been a long time since I have heard my brother's name. Bulls among monkeys, I would like to hear about the death of my younger brother, who recognized virtue and was praiseworthy for
his valor. How was it that Dasha·ratha—whose beloved 55.20
eldest son is Rama, beloved by his elders—was a friend of my brother Jatáyus, who lived in Jana·sthana? I cannot fly because my wings were burned by the sun's rays, but I would like to come down from this mountain, tamers of your foes."

Now, ALTHOUGH the monkey-troop leaders heard his 56.1
voice breaking with grief, they still did not trust his words and were afraid of what he might do. But as they were fasting to death, those monkeys, seeing the vulture, made

sarvathā prāyam āsīnān yadi no bhakṣayiṣyati
kṛta|kṛtyā bhaviṣyāmaḥ kṣipraṃ siddhim ito gatāḥ.»
etāṃ buddhiṃ tataś cakruḥ sarve te vānara'|rṣabhāḥ.
avatārya gireḥ śṛṅgād gṛdhram āh' Âṅgadas tadā:

56.5 «babhūva' Rkṣarajo nāma vānar'|êndraḥ pratāpavān
mam' āryaḥ pārthivaḥ, pakṣin, dhārmikau tasya c' ātmajau.
Sugrīvaś c' âiva Vālī ca putrāv ogha|balāv ubhau
loke viśruta|karm" âbhūd rājā Vālī pitā mama.
rājā kṛtsnasya jagata Ikṣvākūṇāṃ mahā|rathaḥ
Rāmo Dāśarathiḥ śrīmān praviṣṭo Daṇḍakā|vanam
Lakṣmaṇena saha bhrātrā Vaidehyā c' âpi bhāryayā
pitur nideśa|nirato dharmyaṃ panthānam āśritaḥ.
tasya bhāryā Janasthānād Rāvaṇena hṛtā balāt.

Rāmasya ca pitur mitraṃ Jaṭāyur nāma gṛdhra|rāṭ
dadarśa Sītāṃ Vaidehīṃ hriyamāṇāṃ vihāyasā.
56.10 Rāvaṇaṃ virathaṃ kṛtvā sthāpayitvā ca Maithilīm
pariśrāntaś ca vṛddhaś ca Rāvaṇena hato raṇe.
evaṃ gṛdhro hatas tena Rāvaṇena balīyasā.
saṃskṛtaś c' âpi Rāmeṇa gataś ca gatim uttamām.
tato mama pitṛvyeṇa Sugrīveṇa mah"|ātmanā
cakāra Rāghavaḥ sakhyaṃ so 'vadhīt pitaraṃ mama.
mama pitrā viruddho hi Sugrīvaḥ sacivaiḥ saha
nihatya Vālinaṃ Rāmas tatas tam abhiṣecayat.
sa rājye sthāpitas tena Sugrīvo vānar'|ēśvaraḥ

the terrible decision that he should eat them all. "Since we are fasting to death in any case, if he eats us, we shall in every respect accomplish our purpose and therefore quickly achieve success." All those bulls among monkeys concurred in that decision. So Ángada brought the vulture down from the mountain peak and said to him:

"Winged one, there was a splendid lord of monkeys, a 56.5
prince named Riksha·rajas. He was my ancestor; and his two
righteous sons, begotten by him, were Sugríva and Valin,
each as strong as a whole army. King Valin, world famous for
his deeds, was my father. Majestic Rama Dásharathi, king
of the whole world and a great chariot warrior of the Ikshvákus, was devoted to his father's commands and followed
the path of righteousness. And so he entered the Dándaka
forest with his brother Lákshmana and with his wife Vaidéhi. But his wife was forcibly carried off from Jana·sthana
by Rávana.

Now, the king of the vultures, Jatáyus by name, who was
a friend of Rama's father, saw Sita, the daughter of Vidéha,
being carried away through the sky. He deprived Rávana 56.10
of his chariot and returned Máithili to the earth; but since
he was old and exhausted, he was slain in battle by Rávana. And so the vulture was killed by Rávana, who was
more powerful than he. He was ritually cremated by Rama
and attained the highest state. Then Rághava formed an
alliance with my paternal uncle, great Sugríva, and killed
my father. For Sugríva and his ministers were hostile to my
father. And when Rama had killed Valin, he had Sugríva
consecrated. He established Sugríva in the kingship as lord

rājā vānara|mukhyānāṃ yena prasthāpitā vayam.
56.15 evaṃ Rāma|prayuktās tu mārgamāṇās tatas tataḥ
Vaidehīṃ n' âdhigacchāmo rātrau sūrya|prabhām iva.
te vayaṃ Daṇḍak"|âraṇyaṃ vicitya susamāhitāḥ
ajñānāt tu praviṣṭāḥ sma dharaṇyā vivṛtaṃ bilam.
Mayasya māyā|vihitaṃ tad bilaṃ ca vicinvatām
vyatītas tatra no māso yo rājñā samayaḥ kṛtaḥ.
te vayaṃ kapi|rājasya sarve vacana|kāriṇaḥ
kṛtāṃ saṃsthām atikrāntā bhayāt prāyam upāsmahe.
kruddhe tasmiṃs tu Kākutsthe Sugrīve ca sa|Lakṣmaṇe
gatānām api sarveṣāṃ tatra no n' âsti jīvitam.»

57.1 Ity uktaḥ karuṇaṃ vākyaṃ vānarais tyakta|jīvitaiḥ
sa|bāṣpo vānarān gṛdhraḥ pratyuvāca mahā|svanaḥ:
«yavīyān mama sa bhrātā Jaṭāyur nāma, vānarāḥ,
yam ākhyāta hataṃ yuddhe Rāvaṇena balīyasā.
vṛddha|bhāvād apakṣatvāc chṛṇvaṃs tad api marṣaye.
na hi me śaktir ady' âsti bhrātur vaira|vimokṣaṇe.
purā Vṛtra|vadhe vṛtte sa c' âhaṃ ca jay'|âiṣiṇau
ādityam upayātau svo jvalantaṃ raśmi|mālinam.
57.5 āvṛty' ākāśa|mārgeṇa javena sma gatau bhṛśam.
madhyaṃ prāpte ca sūrye ca Jaṭāyur avasīdati.
tam ahaṃ bhrātaraṃ dṛṣṭvā sūrya|raśmibhir arditam
pakṣābhyāṃ chādayām āsa snehāt parama|vihvalam.
nirdagdha|pakṣaḥ patito Vindhye 'haṃ, vānar'|ôttamāḥ,

of the monkeys; and it was that king of the monkey-lords who sent us out.

So, at Rama's behest, we hunted here, there and every- 56.15
where; but we did not find Vaidéhi any more than one finds the sunlight at night. Then, after searching the Dándaka forest most attentively, we entered, in our ignorance, a large cavern in the ground. And while we were searching that cavern constructed by the magic power of Maya, the month set by the king as a time limit for us elapsed. So although we are all obedient to the monkey-king, we have nonetheless violated his decree. Now we are fasting to death out of fear. For if Kákutstha, Sugríva and Lákshmana are angry, we will not survive even if we all return."

ADDRESSED IN these piteous words by the monkeys, who 57.1
had given up hope of living, the tearful vulture replied to the monkeys in a loud voice:

"It is my younger brother Jatáyus, monkeys, whom you have reported as killed in battle by mighty Rávana. Because I am old and without wings, I must endure hearing even that. For I no longer have the power to avenge my brother. Seeking victory, he and I long ago, at the time of Vritra's death, flew toward the sun, which blazed with its garland of sunbeams. Returning through the sky, we both flew with 57.5
tremendous speed. But when the sun reached the meridian, Jatáyus began to grow faint. When I saw my brother tormented by the sun's rays and greatly afflicted, I covered him affectionately with my wings. But my wings were burned up, and so I fell on Mount Vindhya. And since I have been

aham asmin vasan bhrātuḥ pravṛttiṃ n' ôpalakṣaye.»

Jaṭāyuṣas tv evam ukto bhrātrā Sampātinā tadā
yuva|rājo mahā|prājñaḥ pratyuvāc' Âṅgadas tadā:

«Jaṭāyuṣo yadi bhrātā śrutaṃ te gaditaṃ mayā
ākhyāhi yadi jānāsi nilayaṃ tasya rakṣasaḥ.
57.10 a|dīrgha|darśinaṃ taṃ vā Rāvaṇaṃ rākṣas'|âdhipam
antike yadi vā dūre yadi jānāsi, śaṃsa naḥ!»
tato 'bravīn mahā|tejā jyeṣṭho bhrātā Jaṭāyuṣaḥ
ātm'|ânurūpaṃ vacanaṃ vānarān saṃpraharṣayan:

«nirdagdha|pakṣo gṛdhro 'haṃ gata|vīryaḥ, plavaṃ|gamāḥ,
vāṅ|mātreṇa tu Rāmasya kariṣye sāhyam uttamam.
jānāmi Vāruṇāl̃ lokān Viṣṇos traivikramān api
dev'|âsura|vimardāṃś ca amṛtasya ca manthanam.
Rāmasya yad idaṃ kāryaṃ kartavyaṃ prathamaṃ mayā
jarayā ca hṛtaṃ tejaḥ prāṇāś ca śithilā mama.
57.15 taruṇī rūpa|saṃpannā sarv'|ābharaṇa|bhūṣitā
hriyamāṇā mayā dṛṣṭā Rāvaṇena durātmanā.
krośantī ‹Rāma Rām' êti› ‹Lakṣmaṇ' êti› ca bhāminī
bhūṣaṇāny apavidhyantī gātrāṇi ca vidhunvatī.
sūrya|prabh" êva śail'|âgre tasyāḥ kauśeyam uttamam
asite rākṣase bhāti yathā vā taḍid ambude.

tāṃ tu Sītām ahaṃ manye Rāmasya parikīrtanāt.
śrūyatāṃ me kathayato nilayaṃ tasya rakṣasaḥ.
putro Viśravasaḥ sākṣād bhrātā Vaiśravaṇasya ca
adhyāste nagarīṃ Laṅkāṃ Rāvaṇo nāma rākasaḥ.
57.20 ito dvīpe samudrasya saṃpūrṇe śata|yojane

Sect 6

349-357

living here, best of monkeys, I have had no news of my brother."

When he was addressed in this fashion by Jatáyus's brother Sampáti, the very wise heir apparent Ángada then replied:

"If you are indeed Jatáyus's brother, and if you heard
what I just said, tell us if you know this *rákshasa*'s hiding
place. If you know whether short-sighted Rávana, king of 57.10
the *rákshasas*, lives near or far away, then tell us." Then, to
the delight of the monkeys, Jatáyus's glorious elder brother
spoke words that were becoming to him:

"Though I am only a vulture whose wings are burned
and whose strength is gone, by my words alone I shall provide great assistance to Rama. For I know all about Váruna's
worlds and Vishnu's three strides, as well as the wars of the
gods and demons and the churning of the nectar of immor-
tality. Though old age has robbed me of my strength and
my vital energies grow weak, my first duty is to accomplish
this task of Rama's. I myself saw evil Rávana carrying off 57.15
a beautiful young woman adorned with every ornament.
Crying, 'Rama! Rama! Lákshmana!' she was throwing off
her ornaments and was struggling in his grasp. Her fine silk
garment was shining against the dark *rákshasa* like the sun's
light on a mountain peak or lightning against a thunder
cloud.

I think it must have been Sita, for she was calling out Rama's name. Now listen as I describe that *rákshasa*'s dwelling.
This *rákshasa* is called Rávana. He is actually the son of Víshravas and brother of Kubéra, and he inhabits the city of
Lanka. That lovely city, Lanka, was built by Vishva·karman 57.20
on an island in the ocean a full one hundred leagues from

tasmil̃ Laṅkā purī ramyā nirmitā Viśvakarmaṇā.
tasyāṃ vasati Vaidehī dīnā kauśeya|vāsinī
Rāvaṇ'|ântaḥ|pure ruddhā rākṣasībhiḥ surakṣitā.
Janakasy' ātmajāṃ rājñas tasyāṃ drakṣyatha Maithilīm
Laṅkāyām atha guptāyāṃ sāgareṇa samantataḥ.

saṃprāpya sāgarasy' ântaṃ saṃpūrṇaṃ śata|yojanam
āsādya dakṣiṇaṃ kūlaṃ tato drakṣyatha Rāvaṇam.
tatr' âiva tvaritāḥ kṣipraṃ vikramadhvaṃ, plavaṃ|gamāḥ,
jñānena khalu paśyāmi dṛṣṭvā pratyāgamiṣyatha.
57.25 ādyaḥ panthāḥ kuliṅgānāṃ ye c' ânye dhānya|jīvinaḥ
dvitīyo bali|bhojānāṃ ye ca vṛkṣa|phal'|âśinaḥ.
bhāsās tṛtīyaṃ gacchanti krauñcāś ca kuraraiḥ saha
śyenāś caturthaṃ gacchanti gṛdhrā gacchanti pañcamam.
bala|vīry'|ôpapannānāṃ rūpa|yauvana|śālinām
ṣaṣṭhas tu panthā haṃsānāṃ Vainateya|gatiḥ parā
Vainateyāc ca no janma sarveṣāṃ, vānara'|rṣabhāḥ.

garhitaṃ tu kṛtaṃ karma yena sma piśit'|āśanāḥ
ihastho 'haṃ prapaśyāmi Rāvaṇaṃ Jānakīṃ tathā.

asmākam api Sauparṇaṃ divyaṃ cakṣur|balaṃ tathā.
tasmād āhāra|vīryeṇa nisargeṇa ca, vānarāḥ,
ā|yojana|śatāt sāgrād vayaṃ paśyāma nityaśaḥ.
57.30 asmākaṃ vihitā vṛttir nisargeṇa ca dūrataḥ
vihitā pāda|mūle tu vṛttiś caraṇa|yodhinām.
upāyo dṛśyatāṃ kaś cil laṅghane lavaṇ'|âmbhasaḥ

here. And it is there that sorrowful Vaidéhi lives clothed in silk, imprisoned in Rávana's women's quarters, and closely watched by *rákshasa* women. It is there in Lanka, protected on all sides by the sea, that you will find King Jánaka's daughter Máithili.

If you go down to the edge of the sea and then cross over to its southern shore a full one hundred leagues beyond, you will find Rávana there. You must swiftly proceed there at once, monkeys. I know by virtue of my special insight that
you will surely find Sita and return. The first path in the sky 57.25
is that of the sparrows and of others who live on grain. The second is that of the crows, who eat ritual offerings, and of those who eat the fruit of trees. White scavenger vultures and *krauñchas* travel on the third, together with ospreys. On the fourth go falcons, while vultures use the fifth. The sixth path is that of the strong, vigorous geese, young and beautiful. The highest is the path of the sons of Vinatá, and all of us are descended from Vinatá's son, bulls among monkeys.

We have become flesh-eaters by doing a forbidden deed. Standing right here, I can see the daughter of Jánaka and Rávana.

We also have Supárna's divine power of vision. Therefore, both by our nature and by the potency of our food, we can
always see further than one hundred leagues, monkeys. For 57.30
nature has ordained for our sustenance food seen from afar, just as the food right beneath their feet has been ordained for the sustenance of cocks, who fight with their feet. So you must find some means to cross the salt sea. Then, once you have recovered Vaidéhi, you will have accomplished your

abhigamya tu Vaidehīṃ samṛddh'|ârthā gamiṣyatha.
samudraṃ netum icchāmi bhavadbhir Varuṇ'|ālayam
pradāsyāmy udakaṃ bhrātuḥ svar|gatasya mah"|ātmanaḥ.»
tato nītvā tu taṃ deśaṃ tīre nada|nadī|pateḥ
nirdagdha|pakṣaṃ Sampātiṃ vānarāḥ sumah"|âujasaḥ.
punaḥ pratyānayitvā vai taṃ deśaṃ patag'|ēśvaram
babhūvur vānarā hṛṣṭāḥ pravṛttim upalabhya te.

58.1 Tatas tad amṛt'|āsvādaṃ gṛdhra|rājena bhāṣitam
niśamya vadato hṛṣṭās te vacaḥ plavaga'|rṣabhāḥ.
Jāmbavān vai hari|śreṣṭhaḥ saha sarvaiḥ plavaṃ|gamaiḥ
bhū|talāt sahas" ôtthāya gṛdhra|rājānam abravīt:
«kva Sītā, kena vā dṛṣṭā, ko vā harati Maithilīm?
tad ākhyātu bhavān sarvaṃ, gatir bhava van'|âukasām!
ko Dāśarathi|bāṇānāṃ vajra|vega|nipātinām
svayaṃ Lakṣmaṇa|muktānāṃ na cintayati vikramam?»
58.5 sa harīn prīti|saṃyuktān Sītā|śruti|samāhitān
punar āśvāsayan prīta idaṃ vacanam abravīt:
«śrūyatām iha Vaidehyā yathā me haraṇaṃ śrutam
yena c' âpi mam' ākhyātaṃ yatra c' āyata|locanā.
aham asmin girau durge bahu|yojanam āyate
cirān nipatito vṛddhaḥ kṣīṇa|prāṇa|parākramaḥ.
taṃ māṃ evaṃ|gataṃ putraḥ Supārśvo nāma nāmataḥ
āhāreṇa yathā|kālaṃ bibharti patatāṃ varaḥ.

object and can go home. But now I want you to lead me to the ocean, the abode of Váruna, for I would like to perform the water offering for my great brother who has gone to heaven."

And so the mighty monkeys led Sampáti, whose wings had been burned off, to a place on the shore of the ocean, lord of all rivers. Delighted to have obtained news, the monkeys carried the lord of the birds back to his own place.

WHEN THE BULLS among monkeys heard the words sweet 58.1
as nectar that the vulture-king had spoken, they repeated them and were delighted.

Then Jámbavan, best of tawny monkeys, sprang up from the ground with all the other monkeys and spoke to the king of vultures:

"Where is Sita? Who saw her? Who carried off Máithili? Please tell us everything and so become the salvation of us forest-dwellers. Who is it that takes no heed of the power of the arrows of Lákshmana, Dasha·ratha's son, which strike with the force of thunderbolts when he himself looses them?"

So, to reassure further the joyful monkeys who were eager 58.5
to hear about Sita, kindly Sampáti said these words:

"Hear now how I learned of Vaidéhi's abduction, by whom I was told, and where that large-eyed lady is now. Because I was old and my prowess and vital strength were failing, I fell long ago on this inaccessible mountain that stretches for many leagues. Since I am in such a condition, my son Supárshva, the best of creatures that fly, sustains me with food at the proper times. Intense desire is natural for

tīkṣṇa|kāmās tu gandharvās tīkṣṇa|kopā bhujaṃ|gamāḥ
mṛgāṇāṃ tu bhayaṃ tīkṣṇaṃ tatas tīkṣṇa|kṣudhā vayam.
58.10 sa kadācit kṣudh"|ārtasya mama c' āhāra|kāṅkṣiṇaḥ
gata|sūryo 'hani prāpto mama putro hy anāmiṣaḥ.
sa mayā vṛddha|bhāvāc ca kopāc ca paribhartsitaḥ
kṣut|pipāsā|parītena kumāraḥ patatāṃ varaḥ.
sa mam' āhāra|saṃrodhāt pīḍitaḥ prīti|vardhanaḥ
anumānya yathā|tattvam idaṃ vacanam abravīt:
‹ahaṃ, tāta, yathā|kālam āmiṣ'|ârthī kham āplutaḥ
Mahendrasya girer dvāram āvṛtya ca samāsthitaḥ.
tatra sattva|sahasrāṇāṃ sāgar'|ântara|cāriṇām
panthānam eko 'dhyavasaṃ saṃniroddhum avāṅ|mukhaḥ.
58.15 tatra kaś cin mayā dṛṣṭaḥ sūry'|ôdaya|sama|prabhām
striyam ādāya gacchan vai bhinn'|âñjana|cay'|ôpamaḥ.
so 'ham abhyavahār'|ârthī tau dṛṣṭvā kṛta|niścayaḥ
tena sāmnā vinītena panthānam abhiyācitaḥ.
na hi sām'|ôpapannānāṃ prahartā vidyate kva cit,
nīceṣv api janaḥ kaś cit kim aṅga bata mad|vidhaḥ?
sa yātas tejasā vyoma saṃkṣipann iva vegataḥ.
ath' âhaṃ khe|carair bhūtair abhigamya sabhājitaḥ.
«diṣṭyā jīvasi, tāt' êti» abruvan māṃ maha"|rṣayaḥ,
«kathaṃ cit sa|kalatro 'sau gatas, te svasty asaṃśayam.»

gandhárvas, intense anger for serpents, intense fear for deer and intense hunger for us birds.

Now, one day after dark when I was suffering from hunger 58.10
and longing for food, my son arrived without any meat. And so, because of my old age and my anger, and because I was overcome by hunger and thirst, I berated my son, the best of creatures that fly. Distressed because there was no food for me, the joy of my life begged my pardon and spoke these words truthfully: 'Seeking meat at the proper time, father, I flew up into the sky and hovered, obstructing the pass of Mount Mahéndra. There I stayed all alone looking down, to cut off the path of those thousands of creatures who live
in the sea. And there I saw someone as black as a mound 58.15
of collyrium moving along carrying a woman as radiant as a sunrise.

Since I wanted something to eat, I made up my mind when I saw those two. But in a conciliatory way he politely asked me to let him pass. Nobody anywhere, even among the most despicable, attacks those who are conciliatory, so how could someone such as I do so? So he went by with such power that he seemed to compress the sky with his speed. Then I was approached by beings who could travel through the sky, and they greeted me. Those great seers said to me, "You are lucky to be alive, dear child! Since he had a woman with him, he has somehow passed you by. Undoubtedly, fortune is with you."

58.20 evam uktas tato 'haṃ taiḥ siddhaiḥ parama|śobhanaiḥ
sa ca me Rāvaṇo rājā rakṣasāṃ praveditaḥ
haran Dāśarather bhāryāṃ Rāmasya Janak'|ātmajām
bhraṣṭ'|ābharaṇa|kauśeyāṃ śoka|vega|parājitām.
Rāma|Lakṣmaṇayor nāma krośantīṃ mukta|mūrdhajām
eṣa kāl'|âtyayas tāvad› iti vākyavidāṃ varaḥ
etam arthaṃ samagraṃ me Supārśvaḥ pratyavedayat.
tac chrutv" âpi hi me buddhir n' āsīt kā cit parākrame.
apakṣo hi kathaṃ pakṣī karma kiṃ cid upakramet?
yat tu śakyaṃ mayā kartuṃ vāg|buddhi|guṇa|vartinā,
58.25 śrūyatāṃ, tat pravakṣyāmi bhavatāṃ pauruṣ'|āśrayam.
vāṅ|matibhyāṃ hi sārveṣāṃ kariṣyāmi priyaṃ hi vaḥ
yadd hi Dāśaratheḥ kāryaṃ mama, tan n' âtra saṃśayaḥ.
te bhavanto mati|śreṣṭhā balavanto manasvinaḥ.
sahitāḥ kapi|rājena devair api durāsadāḥ.
Rāma|Lakṣmaṇa|bāṇāś ca niśitāḥ kaṅka|patriṇaḥ
trayāṇām api lokānāṃ paryāptās trāṇa|nigrahe.
kāmaṃ khalu Daśagrīvas tejo|bala|samanvitaḥ
bhavatāṃ tu samarthānāṃ na kiṃ cid api duṣkaram.
tad alaṃ kāla|saṃgena! kriyatāṃ buddhi|niścayaḥ.
na hi karmasu sajjante buddhimanto bhavad|vidhāḥ.»

59.1 Tataḥ kṛt'|ôdakaṃ snātaṃ taṃ gṛdhraṃ hari|yūthapāḥ
upaviṣṭā girau durge parivārya samantataḥ.
tam Aṅgadam upāsīnaṃ taiḥ sarvair haribhir vṛtam
janita|pratyayo harṣāt Sampātiḥ punar abravīt:

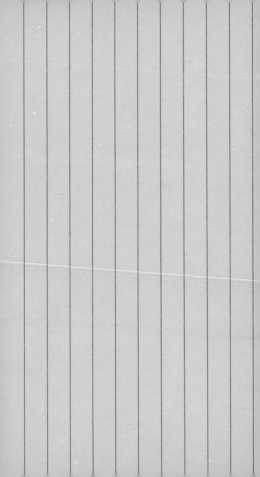

That is the way those most glorious *siddhas* addressed me. 58.20
And they told me that it was Rávana, king of the *rákshasas*, and that he was carrying off Rama Dásharathi's wife, the daughter of Jánaka. Her hair was flying loose and her jewels and silk garment had slipped off. She was overcome by intense grief and cried out the names of Rama and Lákshmana. And that is why I am late,' said Supárshva, foremost of the eloquent, as he informed me of this entire matter. Yet even when I heard that, I had no thought of taking any heroic action. For without wings, how can a bird undertake any action? Still, I can do something through my
faculties of speech and thought. Listen, and I shall tell you 58.25
what it is; but it depends on your valor. By speech and intellect I shall help you all, for Dásharathi's purpose is also mine. Of that there can be no doubt. You are very resolute, powerful and wise. When you join forces with the monkey-king, even the gods cannot assail you. Moreover, the sharp, heron-feathered arrows of Rama and Lákshmana are sufficient either to protect or to destroy even the three worlds. It is no doubt true that ten-necked Rávana is splendid and mighty; still, nothing is impossible for you powerful creatures. So enough of this delay! Let your minds be resolute. For wise creatures like you do not hesitate to act."

When the vulture had offered the funerary libation for 59.1
his brother and bathed, the leaders of the monkey troops sat all around him on that inaccessible mountain. Inspiring their confidence, Sampáti spoke again joyfully to Ángada, who sat near him, surrounded by all those monkeys:

«kṛtvā niḥśabdam ek'|âgrāḥ śṛṇvantu harayo mama
tattvaṃ saṃkīrtayiṣyāmi yathā jānāmi Maithilīm.
asya Vindhyasya śikhare patito 'smi purā vane
sūry'|ātapa|parīt'|âṅgo nirdagdhaḥ sūrya|raśmibhiḥ.
59.5 labdha|saṃjñas tu ṣaḍ|rātrād vivaśo vihvalann iva
vīkṣamāṇo diśaḥ sarvā n' âbhijānāmi kiṃ cana.
tatas tu sāgarāñ śailān nadīḥ sarvāḥ sarāṃsi ca
vanāny aṭavi|deśāṃś ca samīkṣya matir āgamat.
hṛṣṭa|pakṣi|gaṇ'|ākīrṇaḥ kandar'|ântara|kūṭa|vān
dakṣiṇasy' ôdadhes tīre Vindhyo 'yam iti niścitaḥ.

āsīc c' âtr' āśramaṃ puṇyaṃ surair api supūjitam.
ṛṣir Niśākaro nāma yasminn ugra|tap" âbhavat.
aṣṭau varṣa|sahasrāṇi ten' âsminn ṛṣiṇā vinā
vasato mama, dharmajñāḥ, svar|gate tu Niśākare.
59.10 avatīrya ca Vindhy'|âgrāt kṛcchreṇa viṣamāc chanaiḥ
tīkṣṇa|darbhāṃ vasumatīṃ duḥkhena punar āgataḥ.
tam ṛṣiṃ draṣṭu|kāmo 'smi duḥkhen' âbhyāgato bhṛśam
Jaṭāyuṣā mayā c' âiva bahuśo 'bhigato hi saḥ.

tasy' āśrama|pad'|âbhyāśe vavur vātāḥ sugandhinaḥ
vṛkṣo n' âpuṣpitaḥ kaś cid aphalo vā na dṛśyate.
upetya c' āśramaṃ puṇyaṃ vṛkṣa|mūlam upāśritaḥ
draṣṭu|kāmaḥ pratīkṣe ca bhagavantaṃ Niśākaram.
ath' âpaśyam a|dūra|stham ṛṣiṃ jvalita|tejasam
kṛt'|âbhiṣekaṃ durdharṣam upāvṛttam udaṅ|mukham.
59.15 tam ṛkṣāḥ sṛmarā vyāghrāḥ siṃhā nāgāḥ sarīsṛpāḥ

"Keep still and listen to me attentively, monkeys, and I
shall tell you truly how I know about Máithili. Long ago,
when I had been scorched by the sun's rays and my body
overcome by its heat, I fell in a forest on a peak of these
Vindhya mountains. When I regained consciousness after 59.5
six nights, helpless and unsteady, I looked around in all
directions but could recognize nothing. But as I beheld
all the seas, mountains, rivers and lakes, and forests and
wooded places, my wits returned. I concluded then that
these mountains on the shore of the southern sea with their
peaks and deep caves, and flocks of joyful birds, must be
the Vindhyas.

Now, there was a holy ashram there that even the gods
revered. In it dwelt a seer of terrifying asceticism, named
Nishákara. After Nishákara had gone to heaven, I lived
here without the seer for eight thousand years, knowers
of righteousness. Descending slowly and laboriously from a 59.10
rugged peak of the Vindhyas, I regained with difficulty the
level ground with its sharp *darbha* grass. For I wished to see
that seer, whom Jatáyus and I had visited many times, and
so very painfully I approached him.

In the vicinity of his ashram, fragrant winds were blowing
and there were blossoms or fruit on every tree. Approaching
that ashram, I rested against the roots of a tree and waited,
eager to see holy Nishákara. Then, close by, I saw the unassailable seer, blazing with ascetic power, who was returning,
his face to the north, after his ritual bath. Bears, deer, tigers, 59.15
lions, elephants and snakes were approaching him on every
side, as living creatures surround their benefactor. Then, realizing that the seer had reached his ashram, those creatures

parivāry' ôpagacchanti dātāraṃ prāṇino yathā.
tataḥ prāptam ṛṣiṃ jñātvā tāni sattvāni vai yayuḥ
praviṣṭe rājani yathā sarvaṃ s'|âmātyakaṃ balam.
ṛṣis tu dṛṣṭvā māṃ tuṣṭaḥ praviṣṭaś c' āśramaṃ punaḥ.
muhūrta|mātrān niṣkramya tataḥ kāryam apṛcchata.
‹saumya, vaikalyatāṃ dṛṣṭvā romṇāṃ te n' âvagamyate.
agni|dagdhāv imau pakṣau tvak c' âiva vraṇitā tava.
dvau gṛdhrau dṛṣṭa|pūrvau me Mātariśva|samau jave
gṛdhrāṇāṃ c' âiva rājānau bhrātarau kāma|rūpiṇau.
59.20 jyeṣṭhas tvaṃ tu ca Sampātir Jaṭāyur anujas tava.
mānuṣaṃ rūpam āsthāya gṛhṇītāṃ caraṇau mama.
kiṃ te vyādhi|samutthānaṃ pakṣayoḥ patanaṃ katham?
daṇḍo v" âyaṃ dhṛtaḥ kena? sarvam ākhyāhi pṛcchataḥ!›»

60.1 «Tatas tad dāruṇaṃ karma duṣkaraṃ sāhasāt kṛtam
ācacakṣe muneḥ sarvaṃ sūry'|ânugamanaṃ tathā.
‹bhagavan, vraṇa|yuktatvāl lajjayā c' ākul'|êndriyaḥ
pariśrānto na śaknomi vacanaṃ paribhāṣitum.
ahaṃ c' âiva Jaṭāyuś ca saṃgharṣād darpa|mohitau
ākāśaṃ patitau vīrau jijñāsantau parākramam.
Kailāsa|śikhare baddhvā munīnām agrataḥ paṇam
raviḥ syād anuyātavyo yāvad astaṃ mahā|girim.
60.5 ath' āvāṃ yugapat prāptāv apaśyāva mahī|tale
ratha|cakra|pramāṇāni nagarāṇi pṛthak pṛthak.
kva cid vāditra|ghoṣāṃś ca Brahma|ghoṣāṃś ca śuśruva
gāyantīś c' âṅganā bahvīḥ paśyāvo rakta|vāsasaḥ.

withdrew, as do the whole army and the ministers when the king has entered his private quarters.

Then the seer, who was delighted to see me, reentered his ashram. But after a very short while he emerged and asked my purpose in coming. 'Dear friend, seeing your lack of feathers, I did not recognize you. Your wings have been burned by fire and your skin has been scarred. In the past I used to see two vulture brothers, the equals of the wind in speed. They were both kings of vultures, who could change
form at will. You, Sampáti, were the elder and Jatáyus was 59.20
your younger brother. Taking on human form, you used to clasp my feet. Is this some sign of disease in you? Or is this a punishment inflicted by someone? How did your wings fall off? I ask you to tell me everything.'"

"THEN I TOLD the sage all about that terrible, impossible 60.1
deed of following the sun that we had so rashly undertaken.

'Holy one, it is hard for me to speak because I am exhausted, and my senses are disturbed both by my injuries and by my shame. Jatáyus and I, heroes deluded by our pride, flew into the sky, vying with each other to test our prowess. On Kailása's peak in the presence of sages, we made a wager that we would pursue the sun as far as the
great sunset mountain. We both reached the sky at the same 60.5
time and saw, one after the other on the earth below, cities that seemed no bigger than chariot wheels. In one place we heard Vedic recitations and the sound of musical instruments, while in another we saw many lovely young women dressed in red, singing.

tūrṇam utpatya c' ākāśam āditya|patham āsthitau
āvām ālokayāvas tad vanaṃ śādvala|saṃsthitam.
upalair iva saṃchannā dṛśyate bhūḥ śil'|ôccayaiḥ
āpagābhiś ca saṃvītā sūtrair iva vasuṃ|dharā.
Himavāṃś c' âiva Vindhyaś ca Meruś ca sumahān nagaḥ
bhū|tale saṃprakāśante nāgā iva jal'|āśaye.
60.10 tīvra svedaś ca khedaś ca bhayaṃ c' āsīt tad" āvayoḥ
samāviśata mohaś ca mohān mūrchā ca dāruṇā.
na dig vijñāyate Yāmyā n' Āgneyā na ca Vāruṇī
yug'|ânte niyato loko hato dagdha iv' âgninā.

yatnena mahatā bhūyo ravịḥ samavalokitaḥ
tulyaḥ pṛthvī pramāṇena bhāskaraḥ pratibhāti nau.
Jaṭāyur mām anāpṛcchya nipapāta mahīṃ tataḥ.
taṃ dṛṣṭvā tūrṇam ākāśād ātmānaṃ muktavān aham.
pakṣābhyāṃ ca mayā gupto Jaṭāyur na pradahyata.
pramādāt tatra nirdagdhaḥ patan vāyu|pathād aham.
60.15 āśaṅke taṃ nipatitaṃ Janasthāne Jaṭāyuṣam
ahaṃ tu patito Vindhye dagdha|pakṣo jaḍī|kṛtaḥ.
rājyena hīno bhrātrā ca pakṣābhyāṃ vikrameṇa ca
sarvathā martum ev' êcchan patiṣye śikharād gireḥ.»

61.1 «Evam uktvā muni|śreṣṭham arudaṃ duḥkhito bhṛśam
atha dhyātvā muhūrtaṃ tu bhagavān idam abravīt:

Flying swiftly up to the sky, we reached the path of the sun, and beheld a forest so far below that it looked like a plot of grass. The earth with its multitudes of mountains seemed strewn with mere stones, and the land with its rivers seemed overlaid with threads. On the round surface of the earth, Himálaya, Vindhya and vast Mount Meru looked
like elephants in a pond. But then we began to experience 60.10
intense sweating, fatigue and fear. And we were seized by confusion, which soon gave way to a dreadful stupor. We could no longer tell which way was south, southeast or west. The fixed world seemed to have been destroyed, as if consumed by fire at the end of the world.

With a great effort we gazed once again at the shining sun, which by then looked as large as the earth to us. Then, without taking leave of me, Jatáyus plummeted toward the ground. When I saw him, I swiftly hurled myself from the sky. Shielded by my wings, Jatáyus was not burned. But through my own carelessness, I was burned and fell from
the sky, the pathway of the wind. I suspect that Jatáyus fell in 60.15
Jana·sthana, while I, with my wings burned, fell senseless in the Vindhya mountains. Bereft of my kingdom, my brother, my wings and my strength, I wish only to die; and so I shall hurl myself from a mountain peak.'"

"WHEN I HAD spoken this way to that best of sages, I wept 61.1
in my great desolation. But after meditating for a moment, the holy one said this:

‹pakṣau ca te prapakṣau ca punar anyau bhaviṣyataḥ
cakṣuṣī c' âiva prāṇāś ca vikramaś ca balaṃ ca te.
Purāṇe sumahat kāryaṃ bhaviṣyaṃ hi mayā śrutam
dṛṣṭaṃ me tapasā c' âiva śrutvā ca viditaṃ mama.
rājā Daśaratho nāma kaś cid Ikṣvāku|nandanaḥ
tasya putro mahā|tejā Rāmo nāma bhaviṣyati.
61.5 araṇyaṃ ca saha bhrātrā Lakṣmaṇena gamiṣyati
tasminn arthe niyuktaḥ san pitrā satya|parākramaḥ.
nairṛto Rāvaṇo nāma tasyā bhāryāṃ hariṣyati
rākṣas'|êndro Janasthānād avadhyaḥ sura|dānavaiḥ.
sā ca kāmaiḥ pralobhyantī bhakṣyair bhojyaiś ca Maithilī
na bhokṣyati mahā|bhāgā duḥkha|magnā yaśasvinī.
param'|ânnaṃ tu Vaidehyā jñātvā dāsyati Vāsavaḥ
yad annam amṛta|prakhyaṃ surāṇām api durlabham.
tad annaṃ Maithilī prāpya vijñāy' Êndrād idaṃ tv iti
agram uddhṛtya Rāmāya bhū|tale nirvapiṣyati.
61.10 «yadi jīvati me bhartā Lakṣmaṇena saha prabhuḥ
devatvaṃ gatayor v" âpi tayor annam idaṃ tv iti.»
eṣyanty anveṣakās tasyā Rāma|dūtāḥ plavaṃ|gamāḥ
ākhyeyā Rāma|mahiṣī tvayā tebhyo, vihaṃ|gama.
sarvathā tu na gantavyam īdṛśaḥ kva gamiṣyasi?
deśa|kālau pratīkṣasva pakṣau tvaṃ pratipatsyase.
utsaheyam ahaṃ kartum ady' âiva tvāṃ sa|pakṣakam
iha|sthas tvaṃ tu lokānāṃ hitaṃ kāryaṃ kariṣyasi.
tvay" âpi khalu tat kāryaṃ tayoś ca nṛpa|putrayoḥ
brāhmaṇānāṃ surāṇāṃ ca munīnāṃ Vāsavasya ca.

'You shall have new wings again and flight feathers as well, and also new eyes, vitality, valor and strength. For in an ancient legend I heard about a very great matter that will come to pass. I know this both by hearing about it and by seeing it directly through the power of my asceticism. There will be a king, a descendant of the Ikshvákus, named Dasha·
ratha, and he will have a glorious son named Rama. Truly 61.5
valiant, he will go to the forest with his brother Lákshmana, directed to this end by his father.

The king of *rákshasa*s, a *rákshasa* named Rávana, whom neither gods nor *dánava*s can kill, will abduct his wife from Jana·sthana. Renowned and illustrious Máithili will be so plunged in sorrow that she will not eat, even though enticed with desirable foods. Realizing this, Indra Vásava will give Vaidéhi a most excellent food that resembles nectar and is unavailable even to the gods. Receiving this food and recognizing that it is from Indra, Máithili will remove a
portion and scatter it on the ground for Rama, saying, "This 61.10
food is for my master Rama, and Lákshmana, too, whether they are alive or have become gods." Then monkeys will come as messengers from Rama to search for his queen; and you, bird, must tell them where she is.

So by no means are you to leave here. In any case where could you go in your condition? Just await the proper time and place, and you will recover your wings. Of course, I could restore your wings right now; but if you stay here you will perform a service that will benefit the whole world. This you must surely do for those two princes and for the
brahmans, gods, sages and Indra Vásava. I, too, should like 61.15
to see the brothers Rama and Lákshmana. However, I do

61.15 icchāmy aham api draṣṭuṃ bhrātaru Rāma|Lakṣmaṇau
n' êcche ciraṃ dhārayituṃ prāṇāṃs, tyakṣye kalevaram.»

62.1 «Etair anyaiś ca bahubhir vākyair vākya|viśāradaḥ
māṃ praśasy' âbhyanujñāpya praviṣṭaḥ sa svam āśramam.
kandarāt tu visarpitvā parvatasya śanaiḥ śanaiḥ
ahaṃ Vindhyaṃ samāruhya bhavataḥ pratipālaye.
adya tv etasya kālasya s'|âgraṃ varṣa|śataṃ gatam
deśa|kāla|pratīkṣo 'smi hṛdi kṛtvā muner vacaḥ.
mahā|prasthānam āsādya svar|gate tu Niśākare
māṃ nirdahati saṃtāpo vitarkair bahubhir vṛtam.
62.5 utthitāṃ maraṇe buddhiṃ muni|vākyair nivartaye
buddhir yā tena me dattā prāṇa|saṃrakṣaṇāya tu
sā me 'panayate duḥkhaṃ dīpt" êv' âgni|śikhā tamaḥ.
budhyatā ca mayā vīryaṃ Rāvaṇasya durātmanaḥ
putraḥ saṃtarjito vāgbhir, ‹na trātā Maithilī katham?›
tasyā vilapitaṃ śrutvā tau ca Sītā|vinā|kṛtau
na me Daśaratha|snehāt putreṇ' ôtpāditaṃ priyam.»
tasya tv evaṃ bruvāṇasya Sampāter vānaraiḥ saha
utpetatus tadā pakṣau samakṣaṃ vana|cāriṇām.
sa dṛṣṭvā svāṃ tanuṃ pakṣair udgatair aruṇa|cchadaiḥ
praharṣam atulaṃ lebhe vānarāṃś c' êdam abravīt:
62.10 «Niśākarasya maha"|rṣeḥ prabhāvād amit'|ātmanaḥ
āditya|raśmi|nirdagdhau pakṣau me punar utthitau.
yauvane vartamānasya mam' āsīd yaḥ parākramaḥ
tam ev' âdy' âvagacchāmi balaṃ pauruṣam eva ca.

not wish to remain alive that long, and so I shall abandon my body.'"

"AND SO, PROPHESYING to me with these and many other 62.1
words, the eloquent seer took leave of me and entered his ashram. But, as for me, I crept very slowly from the mountain cave and climbed Mount Vindhya to wait for you. More than a hundred years have passed since then; but, taking the sage's words to heart, I kept waiting for the right time and place. But since Nishákara took the final journey and went to heaven, pain has tormented me, and I have been filled
with many doubts. Still, by remembering the sage's words, 62.5
I have driven away thoughts of death as they arose. And the resolution he gave me to preserve my life dispels my sorrow as does a blazing flame the darkness.

Since I knew the strength of evil Rávana, I scolded my son with these words: 'Why did you not rescue Máithili?' For although my son heard her wailing and knew the two princes had been robbed of Sita, he did not perform the service called for by my affection for Dasha·ratha."

And while Sampáti was speaking to the monkeys in this way, two wings sprouted on him before the very eyes of those forest-dwellers. And when he saw the rosy-feathered wings that had appeared on his body, he felt unequaled joy and said this to the monkeys:

"Through the power of the great seer Nishákara of bound- 62.10
less intellect, my wings, which were burned by the sun's rays, have grown again. Now I feel the very same prowess, strength and courage that I had in my youth. Make every

sarvathā kriyatāṃ yatnaḥ. Sītām adhigamiṣyatha.
pakṣa|lābho mam' âyaṃ vaḥ siddhi|pratyaya|kārakaḥ.»
ity uktvā tān harīn sarvān Sampātiḥ patatāṃ varaḥ
utpapāta gireḥ śṛṅgāj jijñāsuḥ kha|gamo gatim.
tasya tad vacanaṃ śrutvā prīti|saṃhṛṣṭa|mānasāḥ
babhūvur hari|śārdūlā vikram'|âbhyuday'|ônmukhāḥ.

62.15 atha pavana|samāna|vikramāḥ
plavaga|varāḥ pratilabdha|pauruṣāḥ
Abhijid|abhimukhāṃ diśaṃ yayur
Janaka|sutā|parimārgaṇ'|ônmukhāḥ.

effort. You will find Sita. The fact that I have regained my wings should make you confident of success."

Then, when Sampáti, best of creatures that fly, had spoken in this way to all those monkeys, he flew up from the mountain peak, a bird eager to test his flight. But those tigers among monkeys heard his words with joyful hearts,
anticipating the success their valor would bring. Then those 62.15
best of monkeys, who moved like the wind and who had regained their courage, went to the quarter facing Ábhijit, eager to search for Jánaka's daughter.

63–66
PREPARING FOR THE GREAT LEAP

63.1 ĀKHYĀTĀ GṚDHRA|rājena samutpatya plavaṃ|gamāḥ
saṃgatāḥ prīti|saṃyuktā vineduḥ siṃha|vikramāḥ.
Sampāter vacanaṃ śrutvā harayo Rāvaṇa|kṣayam
hṛṣṭāḥ sāgaram ājagmuḥ Sītā|darśana|kāṅkṣiṇaḥ.
abhikramya tu taṃ deśaṃ dadṛśur bhīma|vikramāḥ
kṛtsnaṃ lokasya mahataḥ pratibimbam iva sthitam.
dakṣiṇasya samudrasya samāsādy' ôttarāṃ diśam
saṃniveśaṃ tataś cakruḥ sahitā vānar'|ôttamāḥ.
63.5 sattvair mahadbhir vikṛtaiḥ krīḍadbhir vividhair jale
vyātt'|āsyaiḥ sumahā|kāyair ūrmibhiś ca samākulam
prasuptam iva c' ânyatra krīḍantam iva c' ânyataḥ
kva cit parvata|mātraiś ca jala|rāśibhir āvṛtam
saṃkulaṃ dānav'|êndraiś ca pātāla|tala|vāsibhiḥ
roma|harṣa|karaṃ dṛṣṭvā viṣeduḥ kapi|kuñjarāḥ.
ākāśam iva duṣpāraṃ sāgaraṃ prekṣya vānarāḥ
viṣeduḥ sahasā sarve, «kathaṃ kāryam iti» bruvan.
viṣaṇṇāṃ vāhinīṃ dṛṣṭvā sāgarasya nirīkṣaṇāt
āśvāsayām āsa harīn bhay'|ārtān hari|sattamaḥ:
63.10 «na viṣādena naḥ kāryaṃ. viṣādo doṣavattaraḥ,
viṣādo hanti puruṣaṃ bālaṃ kruddha iv' ôragaḥ.
viṣādo 'yaṃ prasahate vikrame paryupasthite.
tejasā tasya hīnasya puruṣ'|ârtho na sidhyati.»

FILLED WITH joy at what the king of vultures had told them, the monkeys, courageous as lions, leaped up all together and roared. Having heard Sampáti's words, the delighted monkeys, eager to see Sita, proceeded to the ocean, the abode of Rávana. Approaching it, the monkeys of terrifying valor gazed upon the ocean, which seemed like a whole reflection of the great world. Together those splendid monkeys reached the northern shore of the southern ocean and made camp there. 63.1

But those elephants among monkeys lost heart when they saw that hair-raising ocean churning with waves. Filled with *dánava* lords who dwelled in the underworld, and with all sorts of huge and grotesque creatures with enormous bodies and gaping mouths playing in its waters, in one place it seemed to sleep, in another it seemed to play, while in still another it was covered with billows the size of mountains. Gazing upon the sea, as impossible to cross as the sky, all the monkeys suddenly lost heart and said, "How can we possibly do it?" Noticing that the army had become despondent at the sight of the ocean, Ángada, best of monkeys, comforted the fear-stricken monkeys: 63.5

"There is no need for us to be despondent. Despondency is very pernicious. Despondency destroys a person just as an angry snake destroys a child. This despondency is overpowering you just when the time for valor is at hand. The efforts of a person who is without valor never succeed." 63.10

tasyāṃ rātryāṃ vyatītāyām Aṅgado vānaraiḥ saha
hari|vṛddhaiḥ samāgamya punar mantram amantrayat.
sā vānarāṇāṃ dhvajinī parivāry' Âṅgadaṃ babhau
Vāsavaṃ parivāry' êva marutāṃ vāhinī sthitā.
ko 'nyas tāṃ vānarīṃ senāṃ śaktaḥ stambhayituṃ bhavet
anyatra Vāli|tanayād anyatra ca Hanūmataḥ.
63.15 tatas tān hari|vṛddhāṃś ca tac ca sainyam ariṃ|damaḥ
anumāny' Âṅgadaḥ śrīmān vākyam arthavad abravīt:
«ka idānīṃ mahā|tejā laṅghayiṣyati sāgaram?
kaḥ kariṣyati Sugrīvaṃ satya|saṃdham ariṃ|damam?
ko vīro yojana|śataṃ laṅghayeta, plavaṃ|gamāḥ?
imāṃś ca yūthapān sarvān mocayet ko mahā|bhayāt?
kasya prasādād dārāṃś ca putrāṃś c' âiva gṛhāṇi ca
ito nivṛttāḥ paśyema siddh'|ârthāḥ sukhino vayam?
kasya prasādād Rāmaṃ ca Lakṣmaṇaṃ ca mahā|balam?
abhigacchema saṃhṛṣṭāḥ Sugrīvaṃ ca mahā|balam?
63.20 yadi kaś cit samartho vaḥ sāgara|plavane hariḥ,
sa dadātv iha naḥ śīghraṃ puṇyām abhaya|dakṣiṇām!»
Aṅgadasya vacaḥ śrutvā na kaś cit kiṃ cid abravīt.
stimit" êv' âbhavat sarvā sā tatra hari|vāhinī.
punar ev' Âṅgadaḥ prāha tān harīn hari|sattamaḥ:
«sarve balavatāṃ śreṣṭhā bhavanto dṛḍha|vikramāḥ
vyapadeśya|kule jātāḥ pūjitāś c' âpy abhīkṣṇaśaḥ.
na hi vo gamane saṃgaḥ kadā cid api kasya cit
bruvadhvaṃ yasya yā śaktir gamane, plavaga'|rṣabhāḥ!»

When the night had passed, Ángada and the monkeys met once again with the monkey elders and took counsel. Surrounding Ángada, the monkey army looked as splendid as the host of Maruts surrounding Vásava. For who else but Valin's son, or perhaps Hánuman, would be able to steady
the monkey army? First honoring the monkey elders and 63.15
the army, Ángada, majestic subduer of his foes, made this sensible speech:

"Which powerful monkey will now leap across the sea? Which of us will make foe-conquering Sugríva true to his promise? Which hero can leap a hundred leagues, monkeys? Which one will free all these troop leaders from their great fear? Through whose favor shall we return from here happy and successful, to see once more our wives, our sons and our homes? Through whose favor may we joyfully approach
Rama, mighty Lákshmana, and mighty Sugríva? If there is 63.20
among you any monkey capable of leaping over the sea, let him now quickly give us the sacred gift of protection from danger."

But when they heard Ángada's words, not one of them said a thing. Indeed, the entire monkey army was as if transfixed. So Ángada, best of monkeys, addressed the monkeys once again: "You are all outstanding among the mighty and unswerving in your valor. You were born in renowned families and have been honored repeatedly. Nothing has ever hindered any one of you in your movement. Let each of you, then, bulls among monkeys, declare how far he can leap."

64.1 TATO 'ṄGADA|vacaḥ śrutvā sarve te vānar'|ôttamāḥ
svaṃ svaṃ gatau samutsāham āhus tatra yathā|kramam
Gajo Gavākṣo Gavayaḥ Śarabho Gandhamādanaḥ
Maindaś ca Dvividaś c' âiva Suṣeṇo Jāmbavāṃs tathā.
ābabhāṣe Gajas tatra, «plaveyaṃ daśa|yojanam.»
Gavākṣo, «yojanāny āha gamiṣyām' îti viṃśatim.»
Gavayo vānaras tatra vānarāṃs tān uvāca ha,
«triṃśataṃ tu gamiṣyāmi yojanānāṃ, plavaṃ|gamāḥ.»
64.5 Śarabho vānaras tatra vānarāṃs tān uvāca ha,
«catvāriṃśad gamiṣyāmi yojanānāṃ na saṃśayaḥ.»
vānarāṃs tu mahā|tejā abravīd Gandhamādanaḥ,
«yojanānāṃ gamiṣyāmi pañcāśat tu na saṃśayaḥ.»
Maindas tu vānaras tatra vānarāṃs tān uvāca ha,
«yojanānāṃ paraṃ ṣaṣṭim ahaṃ plavitum utsahe.»
tatas tatra mahā|tejā Dvividaḥ pratyabhāṣata,
«gamiṣyāmi na saṃdehaḥ saptatiṃ yojanāny aham.»
Suṣeṇas tu hari|śreṣṭhaḥ proktavān kapi|sattamān,
«aśītiṃ yojanānāṃ tu plaveyaṃ, plavaga'|rṣabhāḥ.»
64.10 teṣāṃ kathayatāṃ tatra sarvāṃs tān anumānya ca
tato vṛddhatamas teṣāṃ Jāmbavān pratyabhāṣata:
«pūrvam asmākam apy āsīt kaś cid gati|parākramaḥ
te vayaṃ vayasaḥ pāram anuprāptāḥ sma sāmpratam.
kiṃ tu n' âivaṃ|gate śakyam idaṃ kāryam upekṣitum
yad arthaṃ kapi|rājaś ca Rāmaś ca kṛta|niścayau.
sāmprataṃ kāla|bhedena yā gatis tāṃ nibodhata
navatiṃ yojanānāṃ tu gamiṣyāmi, na saṃśayaḥ.»
tāṃś ca sarvān hari|śreṣṭhān Jāmbavān punar abravīt,
«na khalv etāvad ev' āsīd gamane me parākramaḥ.
64.15 mayā mahā|balaiś c' âiva yajñe Viṣṇuḥ sanātanaḥ
pradakṣiṇī|kṛtaḥ pūrvaṃ kramamāṇas trivikramaḥ.

THEN, WHEN THOSE extraordinary monkeys had heard 64.1
Ángada's words, each of them—Gaja, Gaváksha, Gávaya,
Shárabha, Gandha·mádana, Mainda, Dvívida, Sushéna and
Jámbavan—declared in turn his own prowess at leaping.

Gaja said, "I can jump ten leagues." And Gaváksha stated,
"I can jump twenty leagues." The monkey Gávaya then told
the monkeys, "I can leap thirty leagues, leaping monkeys."
The monkey Shárabha then said to the monkeys, "I can do 64.5
forty leagues, without any doubt." Then valorous Gandha·
mádana told the monkeys, "Without a doubt I can go fifty
leagues." And the monkey Mainda said to the monkeys,
"I can leap more than sixty leagues." Then glorious Dvívida responded, "There is no doubt that I can do seventy
leagues." The best of tawny monkeys Sushéna declared to
those outstanding apes, "I might do eighty leagues, bulls
among leaping monkeys."

As they were speaking, Jámbavan, the eldest among them, 64.10
honored them all and then responded: "Once I, too, had a
certain prowess in leaping, but now I have reached the end
of my prime. Even so, I cannot disregard this matter upon
which both the king of the monkeys and Rama are so firmly
resolved. Know then how well I can leap now after all this
time: I can leap ninety leagues without any doubt."

And Jámbavan spoke further to all those excellent monkeys: "But my prowess in leaping was by no means always
so limited. Long ago, at great Bali's sacrifice, I reverently cir- 64.15
cled eternal Vishnu of the three strides as he strode onward.
Now I am old and my prowess in jumping is diminished.

sa idānīm ahaṃ vṛddhaḥ plavane manda|vikramaḥ.
yauvane ca tad" āsīn me balam apratimaṃ paraiḥ.
saṃpraty etāvatīṃ śaktiṃ gamane tarkayāmy aham
n' âitāvatā ca saṃsiddhiḥ kāryasy' âsya bhaviṣyati.»

ath' ôttaram udār'|ârtham abravīd Aṅgadas tadā
anumānya mahā|prājño Jāmbavantaṃ mahā|kapim:
«aham etad gamiṣyāmi yojanānāṃ śataṃ mahat
nivartane tu me śaktiḥ syān na v" êti na niścitam.»

64.20 tam uvāca hari|śreṣṭho Jāmbavān vākya|kovidaḥ,
«jñāyate gamane śaktis tava hary|ṛkṣa|sattama.
kāmaṃ śata|sahasraṃ vā na hy eṣa vidhir ucyate
yojanānāṃ bhavāñ śakto gantuṃ pratinivartitum.
na hi preṣayitā, tāta, svāmī preṣyaḥ kathaṃ cana
bhavat' âyaṃ janaḥ sarvaḥ preṣyaḥ, plavaga|sattama.
bhavān kalatram asmākaṃ svāmi|bhāve vyavasthitaḥ.
svāmī kalatraṃ sainyasya. gatir eṣā, paraṃ|tapa.
tasmāt kalatravat, tāta, pratipālyaḥ sadā bhavān
api c' âitasya kāryasya bhavān mūlam, ariṃ|dama.
64.25 mūlam arthasya saṃrakṣyam, eṣa kāryavidāṃ nayaḥ
mūle hi sati sidhyanti guṇāḥ puṣpa|phal'|ādayaḥ.
tad bhavān asya kāryasya sādhane satya|vikramaḥ
buddhi|vikrama|saṃpanno hetur atra paraṃ|tapaḥ.
guruś ca guru|putraś ca tvaṃ hi naḥ, kapi|sattama.
bhavantam āśritya vayaṃ samarthā hy artha|sādhane.»

But in my youth no other could equal my strength. I suppose that at present I can go only so far; and that is not enough to bring about the success of this undertaking."

Now wise Ángada honored the great monkey Jámbavan and then made this noble response: "I can leap the great distance of a hundred leagues, but I am not sure whether or not I have the power to return."

But the best of monkeys, eloquent Jámbavan, said to him, 64.20
"Your power to leap is well known, foremost of apes and monkeys. Granted you are capable of leaping a hundred or even a thousand leagues and returning, still it would not be proper for you to do so. For a commander is one who dispatches others, my child, and must on no account be dispatched himself. It is for you, best of monkeys, to dispatch all of us. Since you have been established in the rank of commander, you are our wife. For the commander is the wife of the army, scorcher of your foes: That is the way of the world. Therefore like a wife you must always be protected, my child. Moreover, you are the root of this undertaking,
tamer of your foes. One must carefully guard the root of 64.25
an undertaking: This is the policy of those who understand how things are to be done. If the root is intact, good results like flowers and fruit will surely follow. Therefore you who are truly valiant and full of intelligence and valor are the only means for accomplishing this undertaking, scorcher of your foes. For you are our master and the son of our master, best of monkeys; only by relying on you will we be able to achieve our object."

ukta vākyaṃ mahā|prājñaṃ Jāmbavantaṃ mahā|kapiḥ
pratyuvāc' ôttaraṃ vākyaṃ Vāli|sūnur ath' Âṅgadaḥ:
«yadi n' âhaṃ gamiṣyāmi n' ânyo vānara|puṃgavaḥ
punaḥ khalv idam asmābhiḥ kāryaṃ prāy'|ôpaveśanam.
64.30 na hy akṛtvā hari|pateḥ saṃdeśaṃ tasya dhīmataḥ
tatr' âpi gatvā prāṇānāṃ paśyāmi parirakṣaṇam.
sa hi prasāde c' âtyarthaṃ kope ca harir īśvaraḥ
atītya tasya saṃdeśaṃ vināśo gamane bhavet.
tad yathā hy asya kāryasya na bhavaty anyathā gatiḥ
tad bhavān eva dṛṣṭ'|ârthaḥ saṃcintayitum arhati.»
so 'ṅgadena tadā vīraḥ pratyuktaḥ plavaga'|rṣabhaḥ
Jāmbavān uttaraṃ vākyaṃ provāc' êdaṃ tato 'ṅgadam:
«asya te, vīra, kāryasya na kiṃ cit parihīyate
eṣa saṃcodayāmy enaṃ yaḥ kāryaṃ sādhayiṣyati.»
64.35 tataḥ pratītaṃ plavatāṃ variṣṭhaṃ
ek'|ântam āśritya sukh'|ôpaviṣṭam
saṃcodayām āsa hari|pravīro
hari|pravīraṃ Hanumantam eva.

65.1 ANEKA|śata|sāhasrīṃ viṣaṇṇāṃ hari|vāhinīm
Jāmbavān samudīkṣy' âivaṃ Hanumantam ath' âbravīt:
«vīra vānara|lokasya sarva|śāstravidāṃ vara,
tūṣṇīm ek'|ântam āśritya, Hanuman, kiṃ na jalpasi?
Hanuman, hari|rājasya Sugrīvasya samo hy asi
Rāma|Lakṣmaṇayoś c' âpi tejasā ca balena ca.
Ariṣṭaneminaḥ putro Vainateyo mahā|balaḥ
Garutmān iva vikhyāta uttamaḥ sarva|pakṣiṇām.
65.5 bahuśo hi mayā dṛṣṭaḥ sāgare sa mahā|balaḥ

When wise Jámbavan finished speaking, the great monkey Ángada, son of Valin, made this reply: "But if neither I
nor any of these other bulls among monkeys is to go, then
surely we are again obliged to fast to death. For if we do not 64.30
carry out the orders of the wise lord of monkeys, I do not
see how we can save our lives even if we return to him. For
that monkey has the power of clemency and even more so
of punishment. If we went back without having carried out
his instructions, we would die. You alone understand this
matter. Therefore please consider it carefully so that this
undertaking does not fail."

Answered by Ángada, Jámbavan, that bull among leaping
monkeys, then replied to him: "There is nothing lacking for
this undertaking of yours, hero; and I shall now call upon the
one who will accomplish it." Then the foremost of monkeys, 64.35
Jámbavan, called upon that foremost of monkeys and best
of jumpers, renowned Hánuman, who was sitting at ease
off by himself.

Perceiving that the monkey army of hundreds of thou- 65.1
sands was despondent, Jámbavan spoke to Hánuman in
this way:

"Hero of the monkey folk, you are the best of those who
know every science. Why do you sit quietly by yourself
without speaking, Hánuman? For you, Hánuman, are equal
in valor and strength to the monkey-king Sugríva and even
to Rama and Lákshmana. You are as celebrated as Gáruda, Aríshta·nemi's mighty son, the child of Vinatá and the
greatest of all birds. Many times have I seen that illustrious, 65.5
swift and mighty bird snatching serpents from the ocean.

bhujagān uddharan pakṣī mahā|vego mahā|yaśāḥ.
pakṣayor yad balaṃ tasya tāvad bhuja|balaṃ tava
vikramaś c' âpi vegaś ca na te ten' âpahīyate
balaṃ buddhiś ca tejaś ca sattvaṃ ca, hari|sattama,
viśiṣṭaṃ sarva|bhūteṣu, kim ātmānaṃ na budhyase?

apsar" âpsarasāṃ śreṣṭhā vikhyātā Puñjikasthalā
Añjan" êti parikhyātā patnī Kesariṇo hareḥ.
abhiśāpād abhūt, tāta, vānarī kāma|rūpiṇī
duhitā vānar'|êndrasya Kuñjarasya mah"|ātmanaḥ.
65.10 kapitve cāru|sarv'|āṅgī kadācit kāma|rūpiṇī
mānuṣaṃ vigrahaṃ kṛtvā yauvan'|ôttama|śālinī.
acarat parvatasy' âgre prāvṛḍ|ambuda|saṃnibhe
vicitra|māly'|ābharaṇā mah"|ârha|kṣauma|vāsinī.
tasyā vastraṃ viśāl'|âkṣyāḥ pītaṃ rakta|daśaṃ śubham
sthitāyāḥ parvatasy' âgre Māruto 'paharac chanaiḥ.
sa dadarśa tatas tasyā vṛttāv ūrū susaṃhatau
stanau ca pīnau sahitau sujātaṃ cāru c' ānanam.

tāṃ viśāl'|āyata|śroṇīṃ tanu|madhyāṃ yaśasvinīm
dṛṣṭv" âiva śubha|sarv'|âgnīṃ Pavanaḥ kāma|mohitaḥ.
65.15 sa tāṃ bhujābhyāṃ pīnābhyāṃ paryaṣvajata Mārutaḥ
manmath'|āviṣṭa|sarv'|âṅgo gat'|ātmā tām aninditām.
sā tu tatr' âiva saṃbhrāntā suvṛttā vākyam abravīt:
‹eka|patnī|vratam idaṃ ko nāśayitum icchati?›
Añjanāyā vacaḥ śrutvā Mārutaḥ pratyabhāṣata:
‹na tvāṃ hiṃsāmi, suśroṇi, mā bhūt te, subhage, bhayam.
manas" âsmi gato yat tvāṃ pariṣvajya, yaśasvini,
vīryavān buddhi|saṃpannaḥ putras tava bhaviṣyati.›

The might of your arms equals that of his wings, and your valor, speed, strength, wisdom, power and courage are not less than his, best of monkeys. Do you not realize that you are superior to all beings?

The celebrated *ápsaras* Púñjika·sthala, foremost among *ápsaras*es, was known as Áñjaná, the wife of the monkey Késarin. Because of a curse, my child, she became a monkey who could change her form at will, a daughter of the great monkey-lord Kúñjara. Although she was a monkey, 65.10
she could change form at will and was lovely in every limb. Once, in the prime of her youth, she took human form and, wearing a costly silk garment and marvelous garlands and ornaments, she wandered about on the summit of a mountain that looked like a rain cloud. And as the large-eyed woman stood on the mountaintop, Máruta, the wind god, gently pulled away her lovely yellow garment with its border of red. Then he saw her firm, rounded thighs, and her full, close-set breasts, and her fine and lovely face.

When he saw this glorious woman with her large, wide hips, her slender waist and her beautiful limbs, the wind god Pávana was infatuated with desire. With his whole 65.15
body overpowered by love and his heart lost to her, Máruta embraced that blameless woman with his stout arms. But the virtuous woman became agitated and said these words, 'Who wishes me to break my vow as a faithful wife?' Hearing Áñjaná's words, Máruta replied, 'Woman of lovely hips, I shall not harm you. Do not be afraid, lovely one. Glorious woman, since by embracing you I have united with you through my mind, you shall bear a wise and mighty son.' Addressed in this way, great monkey, your mother was

abhyutthitaṃ tataḥ sūryaṃ bālo dṛṣṭvā mahā|vane
phalaṃ c' êti jighṛkṣus tvam utpluty' âbhyapato divam.
65.20 śatāni trīṇi gatv" âtha yojanānāṃ, mahā|kape,
tejasā tasya nirdhūto na viṣādaṃ tato gataḥ.
tāvad āpatatas tūrṇam antarikṣaṃ, mahā|kape,
kṣiptam Indreṇa te vajraṃ krodh'|āviṣṭena dhīmatā.
tataḥ śail'|âgra|śikhare vāmo hanur abhajyata
tato hi nāma|dheyaṃ te ‹Hanumān iti› kīrtyate.
tatas tvāṃ nihataṃ dṛṣṭvā Vāyur gandha|vahaḥ svayam.
trailokye bhṛśa|saṃkruddho na vavau vai prabhañjanaḥ.
saṃbhrāntāś ca surāḥ sarve trailokye kṣubhite sati
prasādayanti saṃkruddhaṃ Mārutaṃ bhuvan'|ēśvarāḥ.
65.25 prasādite ca Pavane Brahmā tubhyaṃ varaṃ dadau
a|śastra|vadhyatāṃ, tāta, samare, satya|vikrama.
vajrasya ca nipātena virujaṃ tvāṃ samīkṣya ca
Sahasranetraḥ prīt'|ātmā dadau te varam uttamam.
svacchandataś ca maraṇaṃ te bhūyād iti vai, prabho,
sa tvaṃ Kesariṇaḥ putraḥ kṣetrajo bhīma|vikramaḥ
Mārutasy' āurasaḥ putras tejasā c' âpi tat|samaḥ.
tvaṃ hi Vāyu|suto, vatsa, plavane c' âpi tat|samaḥ.

delighted. And so in a cave she bore you, great-armed one, a bull among monkeys.

As a child in the great forest you once saw the sun rising, and, thinking it was a fruit, you wished to seize it. So you leaped up and flew into the sky. You leaped upward for three 65.20
hundred leagues, great monkey, and though the sun's heat tormented you, you were not discouraged. But as you flew swiftly through the sky, great monkey, wise Indra was filled with rage and hurled his thunderbolt at you. Then, as you fell on a mountain peak, your jaw was broken on the left side. And that is why you are named Hánuman, that is, 'Big Jaw.'

Now, the bearer of fragrances, the wind god himself, seeing you stricken, became enraged at all three worlds. And so the tempestuous wind god ceased to blow. With the three worlds disturbed, all the gods became agitated, so those lords of the worlds propitiated angry Máruta. Once 65.25
Pávana was propitiated, Brahma gave you the boon that you could not be killed by any weapon in battle, dear child of true valor. Gratified at seeing you undamaged by the blow of his thunderbolt, thousand-eyed Indra also gave you an excellent boon, which is that your death should occur only when you wish it, lord. And so, dreadful in your valor, you are both Késarin's son, since his wife bore you, and the flesh-and-blood son of Máruta, whom you equal in power. You are indeed the son of the wind, dear boy, and his equal in flight.

vayam adya gata|prāṇā. bhavān asmāsu sāmpratam.
dākṣya|vikrama|saṃpannaḥ pakṣi|rāja iv' âparaḥ.
65.30 trivikrame mayā, tāta, sa|śaila|vana|kānanā
triḥ sapta|kṛtvaḥ pṛthivī parikrāntā pradakṣiṇam.
tadā c' âuṣadhayo 'smābhiḥ saṃcitā deva|śāsanāt
niṣpannam amṛtaṃ yābhis tad" āsīn no mahad balam.
sa idānīm ahaṃ vṛddhaḥ parihīna|parākramaḥ.
sāmpratam kālam asmākaṃ bhavān sarva|guṇ'|ânvitaḥ.
tad vijṛmbhasva vikrāntaḥ, plavatām uttamo hy asi
tvad|vīryaṃ draṣṭu|kām" êyaṃ sarvā vānara|vāhinī.
uttiṣṭha, hari|śārdūla, laṅghayasva mah"|ârṇavam!
parā hi sarva|bhūtānāṃ, Hanuman, yā gatis tava.
65.35 viṣaṇṇā harayaḥ sarve, Hanuman, kim upekṣase?
vikramasva mahā|vego Viṣṇus trīn vikramān iva!»
tatas tu vai Jāmbavat" âbhicoditaḥ
pratīta|vegaḥ Pavan'|ātmajaḥ kapiḥ
praharṣayaṃs tāṃ hari|vīra|vāhinīṃ
cakāra rūpaṃ mahad ātmanas tadā.

66.1 Saṃstūyamāno Hanumān vyavardhata mahā|balaḥ.
samāvidhya ca lāṅgūlaṃ harṣāc ca balam eyivān.
tasya saṃstūyamānasya sarvair vanara|puṃgavaiḥ
tejas" āpūryamāṇasya rūpam āsīd anuttamam.
yathā vijṛmbhate siṃho vivṛddho giri|gahvare
Mārutasy' āurasaḥ putras tathā saṃprati jṛmbhate.
aśobhata mukhaṃ tasya jṛmbhamāṇasya dhīmataḥ
ambarīṣ'|ôpamaṃ dīptaṃ vidhūma iva pāvakaḥ.

My vitality is gone now. Among us at present you alone are full of skill and valor, like a second king of the birds. At 65.30
the time of Vishnu's three strides, dear child, I reverently circled the world with its mountains, forests and woods twenty-one times. At that time I gathered, at the gods' command, the herbs by means of which the nectar of the immortals was produced. I had great strength in those days. But now I am old, bereft of all prowess. At the present time you alone among us are possessed of all virtues.

Therefore rouse yourself, for you are valiant and the greatest of jumpers. The whole monkey army is eager to witness your strength. Rise up, tiger among monkeys. Leap across the great ocean. For your ability to leap, Hánuman,
is beyond that of all other beings. All the monkeys are de- 65.35
spondent, Hánuman. Why do you not heed them? Show your prowess, as did mighty Vishnu when he took his three strides."

Urged on by Jámbavan, Pávana's monkey-son, whose speed was well known, then delighted the army of monkey heroes by making his body gigantic.

As HE WAS BEING praised, mighty Hánuman began to 66.1
grow. Growing mightier still, he waved his tail in delight. Praised by all those bulls among monkeys, he swelled with power, and his appearance was unsurpassed. The mighty jaws of the son of Máruta the wind god now gaped wide, like those of a huge lion in his mountain lair. And as wise Hánuman's jaws gaped open, his mouth, blazing like the
sun, shone like a smokeless fire. Rising up from the midst 66.5

66.5 harīṇām utthito madhyāt saṃprahṛṣṭa|tanū|ruhaḥ
abhivādya harīn vṛddhān Hanumān idam abravīt:
«arujan parvat'|âgrāṇi hut'|âśana sakho 'nilaḥ
balavān aprameyaś ca vāyur ākāśa|gocaraḥ.
tasy' âhaṃ śīghra|vegasya śīghragasya mah"|ātmanaḥ
Mārutasy' āurasaḥ putraḥ. plavane n' âsti me samaḥ.
utsaheyaṃ hi vistīrṇam ālikhantam iv' âmbaram
Meruṃ girim asaṃgena parigantuṃ sahasraśaḥ.
bāhu|vega praṇunnena sāgareṇ' âham utsahe
samāplāvayituṃ lokaṃ sa|parvata|nadī|hradam.
66.10 mam' ōru|jaṅghā|vegena bhaviṣyati samutthitaḥ
saṃmūrchita|mahā|grāhaḥ samudro Varuṇ'|ālayaḥ.
pannag'|âśanam ākāśe patantaṃ pakṣi|sevitam
Vainateyam ahaṃ śaktaḥ parigantuṃ sahasraśaḥ.
udayāt prasthitaṃ v" âpi jvalantaṃ raśmi|mālinam
an|astam|itam ādityam abhigantuṃ samutsahe.
tato bhūmim asaṃspṛśya punar āgantum utsahe
pravegen' âiva mahatā bhīmena, plavaga'|rṣabhāḥ.
utsaheyam atikrāntuṃ sarvān ākāśa|gocarān
sāgaraṃ kṣobhayiṣyāmi dārayiṣyāmi medinīm!
66.15 parvatān kampayiṣyāmi plavamānaḥ, plavaṃ|gamāḥ,
hariṣye c' ōru|vegena plavamāno mah"|ârṇavam!
latānāṃ vīrudhāṃ puṣpaṃ pādapānāṃ ca sarvaśaḥ
anuyāsyati mām adya plavamānaṃ vihāyasā
bhaviṣyati hi me panthāḥ Svāteḥ panthā iv' âmbare.
carantaṃ ghoram ākāśam utpatiṣyantam eva ca
drakṣyanti nipatantaṃ ca sarva|bhūtāni, vānarāḥ.

of the monkeys, his fur bristling, Hánuman respectfully greeted the elder monkeys and said this:

"Ánila, god of the wind, companion of fire the oblation-eater, is boundless and strong. Ranging the sky, he shatters the mountaintops. And I am the flesh-and-blood son of that impetuous, swift-moving god of the wind, great Máruta. No one is my equal in leaping. For without pause I can go a thousand times around vast Mount Meru, which seems to touch the sky. Driving the ocean before me with the force of my arms, I could flood the world together with
its mountains, rivers and lakes. The force of my thighs and 66.10
shanks will heave up the ocean, abode of Váruna, and stun its mighty sea creatures. I can fly circles around the snake-eater Vainatéya a thousand times as he flies through the sky attended by other birds.

Even after the blazing sun garlanded with rays has set forth from the sunrise mountain, I can overtake it before it sets. And then, through my great and awesome speed, I can return without once touching the ground, bulls among monkeys. I can outstrip all those who range the skies. I shall stir up the ocean! I shall tear up the earth!

In leaping I shall make the mountains tremble, leaping 66.15
monkeys. And as I leap the sea, the force of my thighs will carry along the blossoms of vines, shrubs and trees on every side. They will follow behind me as I leap through the sky this very day, so that my path will resemble the Milky Way in the heavens. All beings will see me leaping upward, flying through the terrible sky and alighting, monkeys. You shall see me, leaping monkeys, blocking out the sky like great Mount Meru, as I move along swallowing up the heavens, as

mahā|Meru pratīkāśaṃ māṃ drakṣyadhvaṃ, plavaṃ|gamāḥ,
divam āvṛtya gacchantaṃ grasamānam iv' âmbaram!
vidhamiṣyāmi jīmūtān kampayiṣyāmi parvatān
sāgaraṃ kṣobhayiṣyāmi plavamānaḥ samāhitaḥ!
66.20 Vainateyasya vā śaktir mama vā Mārutasya vā
ṛte Suparṇa|rājānaṃ Mārutaṃ vā mahā|balam
na hi bhūtaṃ prapaśyāmi yo māṃ plutam anuvrajet.
nimeṣ'|ântara|mātreṇa nirālaṃbhanam ambaram
sahasā nipatiṣyāmi ghanād vidyud iv' ôtthitā.
bhaviṣyati hi me rūpaṃ plavamānasya sāgaram
Viṣṇoḥ prakramamāṇasya tadā trīn vikramān iva.
buddhyā c' âhaṃ prapaśyāmi manaś|ceṣṭā ca me tathā
ahaṃ drakṣyāmi Vaidehīṃ, pramodadhvaṃ plavaṃ|gamāḥ!
Mārutasya samo vege Garuḍasya samo jave
ayutaṃ yojanānāṃ tu gamiṣyām' îti me matiḥ.
66.25 Vāsavasya sa|vajrasya Brahmaṇo vā Svayaṃbhuvaḥ
vikramya sahasā hastād amṛtaṃ tad ih' ānaye.
Laṅkāṃ v" âpi samutkṣipya gaccheyam iti me matiḥ.»
tam evaṃ vānara|śreṣṭhaṃ garjantam amit'|âujasam
uvāca parisaṃhṛṣṭo Jāmbavān hari|sattamaḥ:
«vīra Kesariṇaḥ putra vegavan Mārut'|ātmaja,
jñātīnāṃ vipulaṃ śokas tvayā, tāta, praṇāśitaḥ.
tava kalyāṇa|rucayaḥ kapi|mukhyāḥ samāgatāḥ
maṅgalaṃ kārya|siddhy|arthaṃ kariṣyanti samāhitāḥ.
ṛṣīṇāṃ ca prasādena kapi|vṛddha|matena ca
gurūṇāṃ ca prasādena plavasva tvaṃ mah"|ârṇavam!
66.30 sthāsyāmaś c' âika pādena yāvad āgamanaṃ tava
tvad|gatāni ca sarveṣāṃ jīvitāni van'|âukasām.»

it were. I shall scatter the clouds. I shall make the mountains tremble. Intent upon my leaping, I shall stir up the sea.

Only King Supárna Vainatéya, Máruta the wind god, and 66.20
I have such power. Indeed, except for those two, I know of
no being who could keep pace with me as I leap. In no more
than the time it takes to wink an eye, I shall rush swiftly
across the self-supporting sky, like lightning streaking from
a cloud. As I leap over the sea, my form will seem to be
that of Vishnu when he made his three strides. I know in
my mind that I shall find Vaidéhi, and the workings of my
heart tell me the same. So rejoice, monkeys! Equal to Máruta in force and to Gáruda in speed, I feel certain that I can
jump ten thousand leagues. Attacking Indra Vásava armed 66.25
with his thunderbolt or self-existent Brahma, I could take
the nectar of the immortals from their hands by force and
bring it here. And I feel certain that I could even uproot
Lanka and carry it away."

That finest of tawny monkeys, Jámbavan, was thoroughly delighted and said to that excellent and immeasurably powerful monkey who was boasting in this fashion:

"Heroic son of Késarin! Swift offspring of Máruta! Dear
child! You have dispelled the profound grief of your kinsmen. The assembled monkey chiefs, desiring your welfare,
will earnestly offer blessings for the success of your undertaking. By the grace of the seers, by the grace of your supe-
riors, and with the consent of the monkey elders, you must
leap over the ocean! And we shall stand on one foot until 66.30
your return, for the lives of all the forest-dwelling monkeys
depend on you."

tatas tu hari|śārdūlas tān uvāca van'|âukasaḥ:
«n' êyaṃ mama mahī vegaṃ plavane dhārayiṣyati.
etāni hi nagasy' âsya śilā saṃkaṭa|śālinaḥ
śikharāṇi Mahendrasya sthirāṇi ca mahānti ca.
etāni mama niṣpeṣaṃ pādayoḥ, patatāṃ varāḥ,
plavato dhārayiṣyanti yojanānām itaḥ śatam.»

tatas tu Māruta|prakhyaḥ sa harir Mārut'|ātmajaḥ
āruroha naga|śreṣṭhaṃ Mahendram ari|mardanaḥ
66.35 vṛtaṃ nānā|vidhair vṛkṣair mṛga|sevita|śādvalam
latā|kusuma|saṃbādhaṃ nitya|puṣpa|phala|drumam
siṃha|śārdūla|caritaṃ matta|mātaṅga|sevitam
matta|dvija|gaṇ'|ôdghuṣṭaṃ salil'|ôtpīḍa|saṃkulam.
mahadbhir ucchritaṃ śṛṅgair Mahendraṃ sa mahā|balaḥ
vicacāra hari|śreṣṭho Mahendra|sama|vikramaḥ.

pādābhyāṃ pīḍitas tena mahā|śailo mah"|ātmanā
rarāsa siṃh'|âbhihato mahān matta iva dvipaḥ.
mumoca salil'|ôtpīḍān viprakīrṇa|śil"|ôccayaḥ
vitrasta|mṛga|mātaṅgaḥ prakampita|mahā|drumaḥ.
66.40 nānā|gandharva|mithunaiḥ pāna|saṃsarga|karkaśaiḥ
utpatadbhir vihaṃgaiś ca vidyādhara|gaṇair api
tyajyamāna|mahā|sānuḥ saṃnilīna|mah"|ôragaḥ
śaila|śṛṅga|śil"|ôdghātas tad" âbhūt sa mahā|giriḥ.
niḥśvasadbhis tadā tais tu bhujagair ardha|niḥsṛtaiḥ
sa|patāka iv' ābhāti sa tadā dharaṇī|dharaḥ.
ṛṣibhis trāsa|saṃbhrāntais tyajyamānaḥ śil'|ôccayaḥ
sīdan mahati kāntāre sārtha|hīna iv' âdhvagaḥ.

Then that tiger among monkeys said to those forest-dwelling monkeys, "The earth will not withstand the force of my leap. But these peaks of Mount Mahéndra, which abounds in masses of stone, are big and firm. They will withstand the crushing force of my feet as I leap the hundred leagues from here, you foremost of those who leap."

Then that monkey, crusher of his foes, the son and very image of Máruta the wind god, climbed Mahéndra, greatest
of mountains. It was covered with all sorts of trees and full of 66.35
creepers and flowers, while its trees were always laden with fruit and flowers, and its grassy plots frequented by deer. Full of waterfalls, it was inhabited by lions and tigers, frequented by rutting elephants, and noisy with its flocks of mating birds. His valor equal to great Indra's, that mighty and excellent monkey strode across high-peaked, lofty Mount Mahéndra.

Crushed under the feet of that great monkey, the great mountain cried out like a mighty rutting elephant attacked by a lion. Out poured gushing streams of water, while masses of rock were scattered about, great trees were violently shaken, and the deer and elephants were terrified.
Hosts of *vidya·dharas*, *gandhárva* couples intent on drink- 66.40
ing and sexual pleasure, and birds flying up—all abandoned the ridges of the great mountain. Its mighty serpents hid themselves and its rocks and stony peaks clashed together. Then, with those hissing serpents half-protruding from it, the mountain looked as if it were decked with flagpoles. Abandoned by seers fleeing in terror, the rocky mountain sank lower, like the heart of a traveler left behind in some vast wilderness by his caravan. Endowed with speed, intent

sa vegavān vega|samāhit'|ātmā
    hari|pravīraḥ para|vīra|hantā
manaḥ samādhāya mah"|ânubhāvo
    jagāma Laṅkāṃ manasā manasvī.

on speed, that heroic slayer of enemy heroes, that wise and noble monkey, composed his mind and turned his thoughts to Lanka.

GLOSSARY

ÁDITI mother of the gods including the sun and Váruna

ADÍTYAS sons of Áditi

AGÁSTYA famous sage, son of Mitra·Váruna and Úrvashi, often associated with the south

AGNI god of fire

ANÁNTA the great snake associated with Vishnu and said to support the earth

ÁNGADA son of Valin and Tará

ANJANÁ mother of Hánuman

ANUHLÁDA son of the *daitya* Hiránya·káshipu

ÁPSARASES celestial maidens or nymphs, known for their beauty; frequently seen in the service of superior gods, especially Indra

ARÍSHTA·NEMI the sage Káshyapa, father of Gáruda and Áruna, husband of Vínata

ÁRUNA brother of Gáruda, father of the vultures Jatáyus and Sampáti, son of Káshyapa and Vínata

ÁSURAS a class of demons, the elder brothers of the gods

ASHVINS twin deities of the Vedic pantheon renowned for their beauty

AYÓDHYA capital city of the Ikshvákus

BALI the *daitya* who obtained sovereignty over the three worlds

BHÁRATA Dasha·ratha's second son, by Kaikéyi

BRAHMA the creator divinity of the Hindu "trinity," who is regarded as the "Grandfather" of all living creatures.

BRAHMA·LOKA the world or heaven of Brahma

BRIHAS·PATI preceptor of the gods

CHÁRANAS celestial singers

DAITYAS a class of demons descended from Diti

DÁNAVAS a class of demons descended from Danu

DASHA·GRIVA "ten·necked," epithet of Rávana

DASHA·RATHA Rama's father and king of Ayódhya

DÁSHARATHI any descendant of Dasha·ratha, used of Dasha·ratha's four sons, especially Rama

DÚNDUBHI *ásura* son of Maya

GÁNDHARVAS a class of semi-divine beings known for their musical abilities; the *gándharva* women are noted for their beauty

GÁRUDA king of birds; Vishnu's mount; brother of Súmati, Ságara's younger wife; son of Káshyapa and Vinatá

GHRITÁCHI an *ápsaras* who is the mother of Kusha·nabha's one hundred daughters

GÚHYAKAS demigods who attend Kubéra and guard his treasures

HÁNUMAN Rama's monkey companion who aids in the finding of Sita and the destruction of the demon king Rávana. Son of the wind god and counselor to Sugríva

HUTÁSHANA fire as "consumer of the sacrifice"

IKSHVÁKU family name of the royal house of Ayódhya

INDRA king of the gods who leads their hosts into battle against the *ásuras*; in the post-Vedic tradition, he is particularly noted for his adultery

INDRA·LOKA the world or heaven of Indra; paradise

JÁMBAVAN king of the *rikshas*

JÁNAKA lord of Míthila and the father of Sita

JÁNAKI patronymic of Sita

JANAS·THANA part of the Dándaka forest

JATÁYUS a vulture, friend of Dasha·ratha, who died trying to prevent Sita's abduction

KAIKÉYI junior wife of Dasha·ratha and mother of Bhárata

KAKÚTSTHA "descendant of Kakútstha," a common epithet of princes of the Ikshváku dynasty, especially Rama and his brothers

KARTIKÉYA god of war, the son born from Shiva's semen; his stepmothers were the Kríttikas, the Pleiades

KÉSARIN husband of Anjaná, Hánuman's mother

KÉSHAVA epithet of Vishnu

KIM·PÚRUSHAS here same as *kim·nara*

KIM·NARAS mythical creatures with the head of a horse and a human body; the *kim·nara* women are famed for their beauty

KISHKÍNDHA capital city of monkey-kings (sometimes a cave)

KUBÉRA god of wealth, son of Víshravas and half brother of Rávana. Kubéra is the king of the *yakshas* and the *kim·naras*

LÁKSHMANA son of Dasha·ratha by Sumítra, and Rama's constant companion

LANKA Rávana's capital city, location of Sita's confinement

MAHÉSHVARA "great lord," epithet of Shiva or Vishnu

MÁITHILI "woman of Míthila," epithet of Sita

MÁRUTA wind god, father of Hánuman

MARUTS storm gods, sons of Diti, companions of Indra

MAYA architect of the *ásuras*

NÁMUCHI *ásura* slain by Indra

PAKA·SHÁSANA "punisher of the *daitya* Paka," epithet of Indra

PULÓMAN father of Indra' s wife Shachi

PURAM·DARA "destroyer of strongholds," epithet of Indra

RÁGHAVA any descendant of Raghu, used especially of Rama and his brothers

RAGHU son of Kakútstha and ancestor of Rama

RAHU *ásura* who causes eclipses by swallowing the sun or the moon

RAJA·SUYA great sacrifice performed by a universal monarch as a sign of undisputed sovereignty

RÁKSHASAS a class of violent and bloodthirsty demons regarded as the implacable enemies of brahmanical culture and civilization. Their king is the ten-headed Rávana, who rules from the splendid island fortress of Lanka

RAMA eldest son of Dasha·ratha by Kausálya, and hero of the story

RÁVANA main antagonist of the "Ramáyana;" the *rákshasas'* ten-headed overlord who abducts Sita

RUDRAS sons or companions of the storm god

RUMA wife of Sugríva

SHACHI wife of Indra

SHAKRA a common epithet of Indra

SAMPÁTI vulture brother of Jatáyus, who aids the monkeys in their search for Sita

SHÁNKARA epithet of Shiva

SHATA·KRATU "having one hundred powers;" epithet of Indra

SAUMÍTRI son of Sumítra, matronymic of Lákshmana

SIDDHAS semi-divine beings of great purity, possessing magical powers

SITA daughter of Jánaka, wife of Rama

SHIVA one of the three main gods of the Hindu trinity, along with Brahma and Vishnu. He is famed for his asceticism and is the husband of Uma (Párvati)

SHRI goddess of royal dignity and of good fortune and prosperity

SUGRÍVA younger brother of Valin, king of the monkeys; friend and ally of Rama

SHUKRA preceptor of the *ásuras*

SUMÍTRA junior-most wife of Dasha·ratha, mother of Lákshmana and Shatru·ghna

SUPÁRNA epithet of Gáruda

TARA name of a monkey-general of Sugríva

TARÁ wife of Valin

TARÉYA matronymic of Ángada

ÚSHANAS preceptor of the *ásuras*, Shukra

VAIDÉHI epithet of Sita

VAINATÉYA matronymic of Gáruda and Áruna

VAISHRÁVANA "descendant of Víshravas;" Kubéra, god of wealth

VAIVÁSVATA patronymic of Yama

VALIN king of the monkeys, husband of Tará and son of Indra; he is the elder brother of Sugríva

VÁRUNA god of the ocean and regent of the west

VÁSAVA epithet of Indra

VASUS a class of gods, originally the principal gods themselves

VAYU god of the wind, father of Hánuman

VIDÉHA kingdom of Jánaka, Sita's father

VIDYA·DHARAS a class of semi-divine beings; the women are famed for their beauty

VINATÁ mother of Gáruda and Áruna

VISHNU one of the three main gods of the Hindu "trinity," along with Brahma and Shiva. He is said to be incarnated on earth in the form of Rama in order to kill the demon Rávana

VÍSHRAVAS brahman father of Kubéra and Rávana

VISHVA·KARMAN god of craft, architect of the gods

VRITRA a demon slain by Indra

YAKSHAS semi-divine beings associated with Kubéra; the women are known for their beauty

YAMA god of death and regent of the south

YAYÁTI ancient king, son of Náhusha

INDEX

Sanskrit words are given in the English alphabetical order, according to the accented CSL pronunciation aid. They are followed by the conventional diacritics in brackets.